THE NOVELS OF
ANTHONY TROLLOPE

JAMES R. KINCAID

The Novels of
Anthony Trollope

Oxford
at the Clarendon Press
1977

Oxford University Press, Walton Street, Oxford OX2 6DP

OXFORD LONDON GLASGOW NEW YORK
TORONTO MELBOURNE WELLINGTON CAPE TOWN
IBADAN NAIROBI DAR ES SALAAM LUSAKA ADDIS ABABA
KUALA LUMPUR SINGAPORE JAKARTA HONG KONG TOKYO
DELHI BOMBAY CALCUTTA MADRAS KARACHI

British Library Cataloguing in Publication Data

Kincaid, James Russell.
The novels of Anthony Trollope.
Bibl. – Index.
ISBN 0-19-812077-X
1. Title.
823'.8   PR5687
Trollope, Anthony – Criticism and interpretation.

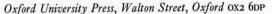

*Printed in Great Britain
at the University Press, Oxford
by Vivian Ridler
Printer to the University*

for
Anne and Elizabeth

PREFACE

ANTHONY TROLLOPE's subtlety and radiant good sense make preface-writing seem fully as preposterous and pompous as it is. Thanking here and pouring scorn there, a great pleasure in both cases, must be hurried along. I owe a special debt to several distinguished Trollope scholars: Hugh L. Hennedy read through the manuscript carefully, correcting misinterpretations, misstatements of fact, and misspellings liberally; Ruth apRoberts gave me the benefit of her extraordinary understanding of Trollope and her equally extraordinary good nature, reading even the paragraphs dealing with her own work without any specifiable acts of violence; George Butte generously allowed himself to be drawn into a fierce correspondence on Trollope and his art that has been extremely valuable to me. Joan Webber and Gerald Bruns both read various parts at various times with a generosity and perception I take for granted and probably always will. I am very grateful to my research assistants, Roberta Bavry, Ken Burrows, and especially John Lauritsen, for all sorts of precise and amiable help. I destroyed the only copy of *How the 'Mastiffs' Went to Iceland* to be had within hundreds of miles, thus keeping my wife, Suzanne, from being able to claim that she had read all of Trollope at a pace faster than my own and with a comprehension to match. As usual, she did none of the useful things Dorothea did for Casaubon, leaving me to my own devices as to pigeonhole systems and the like, but, also as usual, she is no distance at all from the thinking that went into all this. I would, finally, like to express my appreciation to the John Simon Guggenheim Memorial Foundation for supplying the time and money supporting most of the research and all of the writing of this book.

An earlier version of the reading of *Barchester Towers* was published in *ELH*, 37 (1970), 595–612, as '*Barchester Towers* and the Nature of Conservative Comedy' and is used here with the kind permission of The Johns Hopkins University Press. The section of Chapter 1 called 'The Forms of Victorian Fiction' first appeared in slightly altered form in *Victorian Newsletter* (Spring 1975) and is reprinted here by the permission of the editors.

What a pity it is that so powerful and idiomatic a writer should be so incorrect grammatically and scholastically speaking!

Elizabeth Barrett Browning

His work resists the kind of formal analysis to which we subject our better fiction.

Bradford Booth

Of all writers, he is the one least adapted for most kinds of academic approach.

C. P. Snow

But do not suppose that you have made an ass of yourself,—that is, in any special degree.

Mr. Monk to Phineas, *Phineas Finn*

He had found an unknown memoir respecting Bacon, written by a German in the Latin language, published at Leipzig. . . . He could translate that. It is always easiest for the mind to work, in such emergencies, on some matter as to which no creative struggles are demanded from it.

Ralph the Heir

He reads by steam, and he has two or three young men with him to take it all down and make other books out of it;—just as you see a lady take a lace shawl and turn it all about till she has trimmed a petticoat with it. It is the same lace all through,—and so I tell father it's the same knowledge. . . . He is going to write a very learned book. Only everybody will be dead before it can be half finished.

The Duke's Children

'Aunt Sophie forgets that they don't manage these things in England just as we [Americans] do.'

'I don't know why there should be a difference.'

'Nor do I;—only there is. You haven't read so many of their novels as I have.'

'Who would ever think of learning to live out of an English novel?'

He Knew He Was Right

CONTENTS

ABBREVIATIONS

AN&Q	American Notes and Queries
BNYPL	Bulletin of the New York Public Library
CE	College English
CJ	Cambridge Journal
CritQ	Critical Quarterly
ELH	Journal of English Literary History
HLQ	Huntington Library Quarterly
MLN	Modern Language Notes
MLQ	Modern Language Quarterly
MLR	Modern Language Review
MP	Modern Philology
MR	Massachusetts Review
N&Q	Notes and Queries
NCF	Nineteenth-Century Fiction
NYTBR	New York Times Book Review
PBSA	Papers of the Bibliographical Society of America
PQ	Philological Quarterly
PR	Partisan Review
REL	Review of English Literature
SAQ	South Atlantic Quarterly
SEL	Studies in English Literature, 1500–1900
SP	Studies in Philology
TSLL	Texas Studies in Literature and Language
VNL	Victorian Newsletter
VS	Victorian Studies
ZAA	Zeitschrift für Anglistik und Amerikanistik (East Berlin)

References made in the text to Trollope's writings are to chapter numbers, unless otherwise specified.

PART I

Trollope and the Traditions of Fiction

CHAPTER 1

INTRODUCTION

THE TROLLOPE problem has always been defined most forcefully by passages like this one:

> Now we have come to our last chapter, and it may be doubted whether any reader,—unless he be some one specially gifted with a genius for statistics,—will have perceived how very many people have been made happy by matrimony. If marriage be the proper ending for a novel,—the only ending, as this writer takes it to be, which is not discordant,—surely no tale was ever so properly ended, or with so full a concord, as this one. Infinite trouble has been taken not only in arranging these marriages but in joining like to like,—so that, if not happiness, at any rate sympathetic unhappiness, might be produced. (*Ayala's Angel*, 64)

or this one:

> But let the gentle-hearted reader be under no apprehension whatsoever. It is not destined that Eleanor shall marry Mr. Slope or Bertie Stanhope. And here perhaps it may be allowed to the novelist to explain his views on a very important point in the art of telling tales. (*Barchester Towers*, 15)

This narrative voice, interrupting, defining, applying, complicating, anticipating, parodying the action, playing with the conventions the novel is at the same time exploiting ruthlessly, has been to readers and critics both a joy and an embarrassment. Why does that voice so continually disrupt the illusion, reminding us that the novel is not history at all, but just art, mere make-believe? Why does it so deliberately attack not only the plot of that particular novel but all plots, as if Trollope were conducting a running battle with Aristotle?

The narrator is not, of course, the only source of worry in Trollope. There is the nondescript style, the absence of symbolism, the refusal to abandon certain low-mimetic and ironic views, and the consequent failure to reach the sublimity of tragedy, and, perhaps worst of all, the attachment to romantic comedy formulas, an attachment apparently so fixed that those formulas are shamelessly duplicated in novel after novel. 'The heroine', says the narrator of *Orley Farm*, 'must by a certain fixed law be young and marriageable' (2). But who so set the law? And if indeed one determines to obey this law, why call our attention to it and thus increase its unnaturalness and diminish its force? Why, finally, all this artificiality coupled with such apparently lifelike realism? If one accepts as accurate Hawthorne's famous argument that Trollope's art was 'just as real as if some giant had hewn a great lump out of the earth, and put it under a glass case, with all its inhabitants going about their daily business, and not suspecting that they were made a show of',[1] why is it we are so very much aware of the giant, the difficulties he has with the hewing, and the shape and form of the glass case?

Is Trollope the last of the old-fashioned novelists, working snugly within safe conventions and allowing to his readers a full indulgence in the nostalgic pleasure of recognition, or is he the first of the practitioners of 'open form', anticipating the freest experiments in fiction and holding a moral outlook so advanced it is best understood as 'situation ethics'? The first conclusion is the one given most commonly in Trollope's own century and ours—until the last decade, when the second suspicion has grown upon us. My own sense is that both answers are, in their way, correct. Trollope clearly does not abandon the assumptions of the comedy of manners tradition nor the aesthetics of closed form, but neither does he fully accept them. The result is an exposition of the traditional values of, say, Jane Austen, with a running counter-exposition which casts doubt on the validity or existence of these values; the secure formal pattern, correspondingly, is made fluid, pried open in various places and with various tools. Values are countered but not subverted; the shape of the whole is made elastic, but it is not destroyed. Though this mixed form is, in fact, characteristic of the Victorian novel in general, Trollope's use of it is perhaps both the subtlest and the most radical.

Also, one should add, the most slippery. Though the final effect is generally harmonious, the means to this complex harmony are often found through disruption. The rhetoric, like the apparent pattern, shifts direction quietly but with startling effects, and we come to recognize as typical passages like the following, where

---

[1] Trollope was so fond of this quotation that he used it twice with obvious approval, in 'The Genius of Nathaniel Hawthorne', *North American Review*, 129 (1879), 205, and, with minor variations, in *An Autobiography*, ed. Frederick Page and Michael Sadleir (London: Oxford Univ. Press, 1950), p. 145. Further references to *Autobiography* will be cited in the text.

comfort is being given to travellers ashamed of their ignorance and provinciality: 'Why be discomforted because you cannot learn the mysteries of Italian life, seeing that in all probability you know nothing of the inner life of the man who lives next door to you at home? There is a whole world close to you which you have not inspected. What do you know of the thoughts and feelings of those who inhabit your own kitchen?' (*Travelling Sketches*, p. 108). Is this passage satiric, a disguised call to action, introspection, and increased sympathy? Is it cynical, a rhetorical attack on the reader? Or is it genuinely chummy and sophisticated, taking the edge off the point by repeating it several times and thus really meaning to tell us, 'Be happy in your prejudice'? Or is it neutral, moving us away from the promised comfort ('Why be discomforted . . .') to a desolate reminder of our aloneness, and then removing the emotional force, asking simply that we recognize that though we do not now and never will join with other human life, we should not be too disappointed in this condition? While on the whole I prefer the last alternative, it is clearly neither fine nor comprehensive enough to catch the actual effect of the passage. And such a passage represents the difficulty and challenge of Trollope. His obvious modernity is combined with a resolute and equally obvious old-fashionedness, and we are as unlikely now to find secure and simple 'comfort' in the total effect of a Trollope novel as we are in the passage of presumed consolation just quoted.

THE AUGUSTAN TROLLOPE

But 'comfort' was precisely the one trivial sensation generally allowed to readers of Trollope by proponents of the new novel. According to Henry James, 'with Trollope we were always safe',[2] so safe that 'to become involved in one of his love stories is very like sinking into a gentle slumber'.[3] Virginia Woolf said that Trollope's world is so 'complete' that 'in whatever direction we reach out for assurance we receive it'.[4] Well, he gives comfort, clearly, not only to readers, but to critics who can place him this securely. He is, for nearly all of them,[5] the symbol of an end of a tradition. Arnold Bennett said,

---

[2] 'Anthony Trollope', *Partial Portraits* (London: Macmillan, 1888), p. 100.

[3] Rev. of *The Belton Estate*, *Nation*, 2 (4 Jan. 1866), 21.

[4] 'Phases of Fiction', *Collected Essays* (London: Chatto and Windus, 1966), ii. 58.

[5] A bizarre exception is Ford Madox Ford, who adopts the alternate device of claiming that Trollope is absolutely outside of tradition, that he stands, with Jane Austen, Shakespeare, and Richardson, 'so absolutely alone that nothing very profitable can be

'Trollope merely carried to its logical conclusion the principle of his mightier rivals.'[6] Because the tradition is presumably so distant and so moribund, writers can sometimes even be generous: Virginia Woolf was willing to allow perfection to Trollope and Jane Austen but argued that it was necessary 'to escape from the dominion of that perfection': 'if fiction had remained what it was to Jane Austen and Trollope, fiction would by this time be dead'.[7] We can recognize such an argument as an invention necessary to the proud fable of the transformation of the novel and its aesthetics. But the fable became very popular, and writers less open-hearted than Virginia Woolf were able to dismiss Trollope more contemptuously. To Gissing he was 'an admirable writer of the pedestrian school',[8] and to Edith Wharton 'Trollope might conceivably have been a lesser Jane Austen', had it not been for the 'reaction against truth'[9] undergone by the entire age.

The hero of the counter-reaction in favour of 'truth' was usually either James or, more commonly, Meredith, who, according to Virginia Woolf, 'has destroyed all the usual staircases by which we have learnt to climb'.[10] The construction of these new staircases out of the ruins of the old is very heady and satisfying work. The satisfactions were not unavailable even to Trollope's contemporaries, particularly after the publication of *The Prime Minister* (1876); by then, such periodicals as the *Saturday Review* were able to suggest confidently that with Trollope 'prose fiction has almost reached its limits'[11]—lower limits, they clearly meant. The legend has become so powerful that it troubles and sometimes controls even the best of modern critics. William Myers claims that, unlike Dickens, Trollope 'smoothly conforms' to convention; Raymond Williams makes the same point exactly, this time using George

said about them by a writer analysing British fiction in search of traces of main-currents of tradition'. As a result, Trollope is 'inimitable'; beyond that 'there is very little to be said' (*The English Novel: From the Earliest Days to the Death of Joseph Conrad*, Philadelphia and London: Lippincott, 1929, pp. 119–20). This is very high praise, but it has the same effect as dismissing Trollope.

6 *Books and Persons: Being Comments on a Past Epoch, 1908–1911* (New York: George H. Doran, 1917), p. 135.

7 'The Novels of George Meredith', *The Second Common Reader* (New York: Harcourt, Brace, 1932), p. 254.

8 *The Private Papers of Henry Ryecroft* (London: Constable, 1903), p. 213.

9 *The Writing of Fiction* (New York: Scribners, 1925), p. 63.

10 'The Novels of George Meredith', p. 247.

11 Rev. of *The Prime Minister*, *Saturday Review* 42 (14 Oct. 1876), 481.

Eliot instead of Dickens as the contrast to Trollope's smooth conventionality, his failure to respond to the climactic cultural disturbances of the time.[12] Trollope becomes not just a representative of a dead tradition but that tradition itself: 'His value as a factor in the historical and aesthetic development of the English novel is that he walks solidly (one can hear his footfall) down the middle of the road of tradition.'[13]

This puts very bluntly what James had said so subtly; for it was primarily James who created this symbol of Trollope and then identified it with a tradition that he wished to reject. This image of Trollope and of the tradition has the sort of truth that art has; it convinces without making necessary or even proper a reference to mundane fact. Hunting for the original of James's version of Trollope is about as rewarding as hunting for the original of Mr. Pickwick. James's terribly effective propaganda is thus his worst criticism, if one makes the mistake of regarding it as criticism. It is myth-making. In arguing for and explaining his own methodology and his own aesthetics, it suits James to sharpen his distinctions by inventing some opposition, some fixed symbol for alternate methods and assumptions. He called this symbol Trollope. One can observe the slow creation of that symbol, beginning with the unrestrained and angry attacks by the young partisan, where he sneers at Trollope for creating 'stupid' books 'written for children',[14] with stories about characters little better than 'a company of imbeciles'.[15] Nothing in these early reviews is more surprising than their rage, marked especially by a repetitiousness very unusual for James and a cheap sarcasm worthy of Quintus Slide. These sorts of attacks, clearly, would convince no one, but James soon hit upon the secret of his propagandistic symbol, a cool and apparently judicious freezing of Trollope into the absolutely uniform, safe, photographic realist we know so well from the myth, though not at all from the novels. With his more characteristic ponderousness, James announces, 'It became long ago apparent that Mr. Trollope had only one manner.'[16] Once

[12] Myers, 'George Eliot: Politics and Personality', *Literature and Politics in the Nineteenth Century*, ed. John Lucas (London: Methuen, 1971), p. 105; Williams, *The English Novel: From Dickens to Lawrence* (New York: Oxford Univ. Press, 1970), pp. 84–6.
[13] Richard Church, *The Growth of the English Novel* (London: Methuen, 1951), p. 171.
[14] Rev. of *The Belton Estate*, *Nation*, p. 22.
[15] Rev. of *Miss Mackenzie*, *Nation*, 1 (13 July 1865), 51.
[16] Rev. of *Can You Forgive Her?*, *Nation*, 1 (28 Sept. 1865), 409.

that point is established, once the image is fixed so firmly, James can proceed to equate it with the outmoded tradition.

He does so most brilliantly in the deceptively warm essay on Trollope published in *Partial Portraits*. Here Trollope is praised as 'one of the most trustworthy, though not one of the most eloquent, of the writers who have helped the heart of man to know itself' (p. 133). The great beauty of the last phrase draws our attention away from the qualification about eloquence and the oddly diminished term 'trustworthy'. 'His great, his inestimable merit was a complete appreciation of the usual' (pp. 100–1). Again, the repetitions at the beginning, almost eulogistic in piling 'inestimable' on top of 'great' counterbalance and perhaps obscure the fact that Trollope is really being identified with craft, seen in a subtly belittling way. He is 'trustworthy'; he appreciates 'the usual'; he satisfies 'the taste for emotions of recognition' (p. 133). Trollope is thus the unaware artist, in fact the great unconscious beast of tradition itself. James's serious criticism of Trollope's use of the narrator is very artfully inserted as a minor qualification, even jocularly stated, but we can recognize the artist at work. Most of the work of defining and defending James's own rules is done by implied contrast. Only rarely do the counter-assumptions show through. But when they do, they reveal to us what really is happening, as when James protests that the *only possible* analogy for a novel is history. As argument, the exclusiveness of this is sheer nonsense, but it is disguised argument, of course, and, as such, was enormously persuasive, lending its hand to the formation of disciplineships and the subsequent canonization of dramatic methods, 'showing and telling' textbooks, and the range of very rigid general assumptions so effectively demolished by *The Rhetoric of Fiction*. The image James creates of Trollope played a very crucial part in this amazingly effective propaganda. Whether James indeed regarded his aesthetic as the one thing needful or even the one thing possible and whether he actually believed in the literal truth of his symbol are not, to me, interesting questions, but the power of that symbol is undeniable, controlling as it has virtually all commentary on Trollope, both from friend and foe, until the last decade.

Early defenders had a difficult time finding firm ground on which to stand. Leslie Stephen said that to enjoy Trollope 'we must cease to bother ourselves about art'.[17] Most were content to sink him into

---

[17] 'Anthony Trollope', *National Review*, 38 (1901–2), 78.

the tradition, exactly as James had done. Saintsbury felt that a Trollope novel was the best possible representative 'of the *average* novel of the third quarter of the century',[18] a point sadly repeated almost to parody by avowed Trollopians: 'His novels . . . give the normal man's reactions to his age. . . . They arise from a feeling of tolerant contentment with the things that be.'[19] Michael Sadleir's critical biography must be respected in many ways, but for the most part it adds cement to the statue, labelling Trollope as 'The Voice of an Epoch',[20] as if he were now not just any old novelist, but any old Victorian middle-class fellow. Bradford Booth, caught in the centre of the sterner critical practices of the New Criticism, is even more apologetic, offering Trollope as 'one of ours', 'a writer who seems to represent the apotheosis of normality'.[21] The image of Trollope as a uniform figure, symbolizing an entire tradition, often appears in suggestions that Trollope's novels are somehow in-distinguishable, even in quality—'so many novels on an equally fine level'![22]—and in the appalling reason usually given for the popular revival of Trollope during World War II: 'We reread the novels of Trollope, and relive the warmth and comfort of the mid-Victorians',[23] says Harry Levin. Maybe so. It is possible that the myth became so strong that even reading the novels could not break its spell.

The objections to Trollope pronounced over the years have taken surprisingly few turns. He is non-dramatic, non-symbolic, non-tragic. His method and subject-matter are one, and they are both bad. Especially bad is his satisfaction with low-mimetic materials and comic or ironic tones. Carlyle said he was 'irredeemably imbedded in commonplace, and grown fat upon it',[24] and critics less censorious have just as seriously underestimated the displacement from reality in his novels: according to Virginia Woolf, he gives us 'the same sort of refreshment and delight that we get from seeing

---

[18] *A History of Nineteenth-Century Literature (1780–1900)* (London: Macmillan, 1919), p. 339.

[19] John H. Wildman, *Anthony Trollope's England*, Brown Univ. Studies, vol. v (Providence: Brown Univ. Press, 1940), p. 8.

[20] The title of the first chapter of *Trollope: A Commentary*, 3rd edn. (London: Oxford Univ. Press, 1961).

[21] *Anthony Trollope: Aspects of His Life and Art* (Bloomington, Ind.: Indiana Univ. Press, 1958), p. 5.

[22] Hugh Walpole, *Anthony Trollope* (New York: Macmillan, 1928), p. 67.

[23] Harry Levin, *Refractions: Essays in Comparative Literature* (New York: Oxford Univ. Press, 1966), p. 318.

[24] *Thomas Carlyle: Letters to His Wife*, ed. Trudy Bliss (London: Gollancz, 1953), p. 381 (27 July 1865).

something actually happen in the street below'.[25] Because of the subject-matter, he seems to exercise no particular art; most of all, he is unable to reach to the high level of tragedy. The contemporary critics complained about this,[26] as have a good many since that time. Trollope himself had a wonderful answer to such complaints: 'Who would not sooner be Prometheus than a yesterday's tipsy man with this morning's sick-headache?'[27] Just as in Aldous Huxley's 'Tragedy and the Whole Truth', a strong low-mimetic bias is expressed, a singular suspicion that tragedy is all bombast and rhetorical flattery. It's all a matter of which genre one chooses to cheer for, clearly, and we can recognize in these arguments the fallacy that James so skilfully propagated, a fallacy of arbitrary generic rankings. Robert Scholes protests against James's dogmatisms as 'failures in generic logic',[28] and *The Rhetoric of Fiction* is a studious exposure of this fallacy. Even before Wayne Booth, Paul Elmer More, in one of the finest essays on Trollope, pointed out that while it is true that Trollope did not do what Balzac and Dostoevsky did, neither did they write the chronicles of Barsetshire.[29] He implies, I think rightly, that this is all a sane and fully responsive person would say. Genres or, in Northrop Frye's terms, mythoi are of neutral quality. Each makes different demands, has different conventions, addresses different responses, but to blame Trollope for not writing tragedy is to commit the most absurd of critical blunders. This failure in 'generic logic' has, however, controlled the aesthetics of the novel and certainly the criticism of Trollope until recently.

THE MODERN TROLLOPE

With the work of recent critics, most notably A. O. J. Cockshut, Robert Polhemus, J. Hillis Miller, and Ruth apRoberts, a new

---

[25] 'Phases of Fiction', *Collected Essays*, ii. 57.

[26] David Skilton illustrates how pervasive this complaint was among Trollope's reviewers and discusses some of its symptoms and causes (*Anthony Trollope and His Contemporaries: A Study in the Theory and Conventions of Mid-Victorian Fiction*, London: Longman, 1972, pp. 40–5, 79–99). This fallacy is expressed with particularly nonsensical solemnity by Julian Hawthorne, 'The Maker of Many Books', *Confessions and Criticisms* (Boston: Ticknor, 1887), p. 152. See also Mario Praz, 'Anthony Trollope', *The Hero in Eclipse in Victorian Fiction*, trans. Angus Davidson (London: Oxford Univ. Press, 1956), pp. 278–80.   [27] 'The Genius of Nathaniel Hawthorne', p. 213.

[28] 'Towards a Poetics of Fiction: An Approach through Genre', *Novel*, 2 (1968–9), 104.

[29] 'My Debt to Trollope', *Demon of the Absolute*, New Shelburne Essays, vol. i (Princeton: Princeton Univ. Press, 1928), p. 90.

image of Trollope's novels has begun to emerge, one that is certainly more strikingly modern, tougher, more ironic and complex. Cockshut sees Trollope on a 'Progress to Pessimism',[30] a course that clearly appears to him, and possibly to us, a very satisfying one. Polhemus similarly argues for Trollope's modernity in thematic terms, investigating his treatment of change and arguing that his pessimistic general conclusion is 'that mutability somehow always wins'.[31] Certainly this image of an embittered novelist viewing man as a helpless object in the clutches of history is strikingly different from the notion of the trustworthy dummy who looked down into the street below and copied what he saw. Most of us will see it also as an improved, if equally lop-sided, version. The view of Trollope as the creator of 'a world without God', 'a purely human world of intersubjective relations',[32] may give us pause, but it has surely led to some recent criticism that has been both revitalizing and illuminating.

The best of this recent work is represented by Ruth apRoberts's bold attempts to define the heart of Trollope's method and concern.[33] She argues that while Trollope is essentially moral, he consistently regards a set moral system as a sign of intellectual *naïveté*. In place of such consistencies, he insists on a flexible morality, based on a relativity that can find its only test and certainty in empiricism. 'His stance is that of what we now call Situation Ethics' (p. 52);[34] judgements must refer to people and particular circumstances and not to fixed principles. Trollope projects this new situational relativism through his use of 'the multiple ironic perspective' (p. 125), more particularly by 'casuistry', by acting as 'advocate for each one of his

---

[30] *Anthony Trollope: A Critical Study* (Collins, 1955, rpt. New York: New York Univ. Press, 1968). The phrase is used as a title for Part II of the work.

[31] *The Changing World of Anthony Trollope* (Berkeley: Univ. of Cal. Press, 1968), p. 21.

[32] J. Hillis Miller, *The Disappearance of God: Five Nineteenth-Century Writers* (Cambridge, Mass.: Harvard Univ. Press, 1963), p. 13.

[33] *The Moral Trollope* (Athens, Ohio: Ohio Univ. Press, 1971).

[34] This argument is also supported in various ways by Robert Polhemus, who, in *The Changing World of Anthony Trollope*, discusses the 'relativism' of Trollope's late novels (pp. 215-49). A similar claim for the late novels is made by Alice Green Fredman, *Anthony Trollope*, Columbia Essays on Modern Writers, No. 56 (New York: Columbia Univ. Press, 1971), p. 44. See also Clement Greenberg, *Art and Culture: Critical Essays* (Boston: Beacon Press, 1961), p. 247; Frank O'Connor, 'Trollope the Realist', *The Mirror in the Roadway: A Study of the Modern Novel* (New York: Knopf, 1956), p. 167; and especially James Gindin, 'Trollope', *Harvest of a Quiet Eye: The Novel of Compassion* (Bloomington, Ind.: Indiana Univ. Press, 1971), pp. 28-56.

characters' and refusing to mediate among these conflicting advocacies.

apRoberts is clearly aware of the formal implications of these arguments on method and states that Trollope 'has a corresponding Situation Aesthetics' (p. 52), but she has enough on her hands without developing this point. In *The Form of Victorian Fiction*, however, J. Hillis Miller has modernized not only Trollope but all other Victorian novelists by arguing that they are moving in the world of 'open form'. This argument provides a tie between Victorian and modern novels and could release us from all those claims for a miraculous transformation, some 'mutation in the form of the novel'[35] that came about on the happy day when the modern novel was born. Still, one wonders in this case if we have really been freed from the mutation legend or if the date of the miracle has not simply been moved back. Surely we do not want to celebrate now the emancipation of the nineteenth-century novel from the smug conventionality and securely closed form of the century before. The modernization of Trollope and of the Victorian novel generally seems to be a necessary development, but it is unlikely that all the 'old-fashioned' elements can be explained away completely by this means.

Is Trollope really a 'tolerant casuist', an exponent of 'situation ethics'? Are conventional patterns of morality, even conventional absolutes, really disrupted (rather than merely diversified)? Is there finally no standard in a Trollope novel but 'empiricism'? The answers, naturally, are not easy, but I think one can more accurately say 'no' than 'yes'. It is true that the novels consistently attack all forms of purism and absolutism, but not generally to establish simple relativism in their place. The standards are all there; they are made more difficult to apply and far more difficult to define; most of all, there is less communal agreement on what they are. But they are dependent on codes which are not to be defined by situations. The test is whether one has the proper instincts and sensitivity to behave, say, with honesty in an extremely difficult situation, but the definition of honesty is referred to the instincts and sensitivity and to the action, not to the situation. The situation tests; it is not determinant.

The most common standard for moral behaviour in Trollope is the code centred on the word 'gentleman'. Though the maddening vagueness of the term and Trollope's equally maddening coy

---

[35] For one of many examples, see Alan Friedman, *The Turn of the Novel* (New York: Oxford Univ. Press, 1966), p. xiii.

assertions of his inability to define it, may tempt us to reject the whole notion, it is his central absolutism. It is also a code that exists outside situations. Situations of great complexity may require a gentleman to behave in ways that appear odd, but we, as readers, are made to see the consistency of the moral logic. The climax of *The Last Chronicle of Barset* and of the entire Barsetshire series is the joining of the worldly, sociable archdeacon and the introspective, tragic Mr. Crawley on the basis of that code. They may recognize nothing else in common, but this term 'gentleman' speaks directly to Crawley and in an important way brings him to life by revealing his connection with humanity and, indeed, the connection of all humanity with the absolute. Crawley's case seems to be one demanding a special judgement, the application of situation ethics. But when characters in the novel try to use these criteria they are always shown to be open-hearted but morally limited. When John Eames, for instance, claims that 'You must not judge him as you do other men' (40), the judicious Walker argues that such special pleading carries grave dangers with it—dangers especially for Mr. Crawley: 'What do we mean when we say that one man isn't to be trusted as another? We simply imply that he is not what we call responsible' (40). Similarly, Mark Robarts tells Dr. Tempest, 'You must look to the circumstances' (54), and is met with another judicious rebuke, allowing poor Robarts no defence but the grumbling 'I don't know the meaning of the word "delicate".' In the end, situation ethics are just not delicate or complex enough.

Very much the same point is made in Dr. Wortle's apparently bizarre behaviour in defending the bigamous Peacockes. Again, this is not an example of situation ethics but an unconventional assertion of a solid code. ' "To me,"—said the Doctor,—"to me she is as pure as the most unsullied matron in the country." Upon this Mr. Peacocke, jumping from his chair, seized the Doctor's hand, but could not speak for his tears' (*Dr. Wortle's School*, iv. 10). These men meet, just as did Crawley and the archdeacon, over a declaration of a rigorous gentleman who speaks in defiance of a situation. In this late novel, the Doctor actually is the most conventionally moral person around. He violates morality that is 'common' not conventional, appealing to the traditional romantic code of gentlemanly behaviour. Trollope's refusal to define that code is a recognition, as apRoberts would justly point out, of its necessary flexibility, but while the code must recognize situations, it cannot be controlled by them. In the end, the code rests on a belief in truth and the reflection of truth in behaviour, honesty. Let us 'make ourselves an honest people' (1), wails the starkly didactic narrator of *The New Zealander*, a work which asserts as its central principle that 'harm cannot come of truth' (4). While it cannot be denied that the novels act to make such assertions more complex, the absolute standard never disappears, and Trollope is forced over and over to define his villains as those who might appear to be gentlemen but who lack the first and most basic requirement: an instinctive aversion to a lie.

This is not to deny that empirical standards are present in Trollope, but they seldom if ever stand in a normative position. Ordinarily, empiricism is one extreme pole of the novel's value system, a position seductive but dangerous. It is usually played off against an opposite moral purism. While many novels follow a course wherein the hero is educated away from his initial naïve absolutism, these heroes almost never move to the opposite extreme but instead find some intermediate position in which the two opposites are perilously balanced. They must learn to account for situations without being controlled by them. The most prominent example of this education to balance is provided by the life of Phineas Finn. He must attempt to find in political life some mean between the principled abstractions of Turnbull and the unprincipled cynicism of Erle or Fitzgibbon. The abstractions are highly suspect because they provide the self-indulgent, unproductive, and finally anti-social pleasures of 'opposition', but the pure empiricism that never tests measures, that has contempt for convictions, and that gives its soul to that purely relativistic agency, the party, is equally suspect. While the Barsetshire chronicle had clearly moved toward a successful union of these two poles, the public and private selves, the political novels really argue for their final irreconcilability, carrying on this argument, particularly in *The Prime Minister*, by a subtle examination of the deficiencies in and the small satisfactions available to, the empirical life as defined by Erle, St. Bungay, and the office of Prime Minister.

On method, apRoberts's arguments seem to me quite persuasive but not fully comprehensive. Trollope's advocacy, I think, is never an end but a means to complicate the traditional norms without abolishing them. He defends the indefensible and satirizes heroes, of course, but in order to support a difficult but not relativistic morality. The neutrality of pure advocacy is itself an issue in many novels and is, without exception, subject to withering contempt. The sneering portrait in *The Eustace Diamonds* of the lawyer/ politician is to the point here: 'As a large-minded man of the world, peculiarly conversant with the fact that every question has two sides, and that as much may often be said on one side as on the other, he has probably not become violent in his feelings as a political partisan. Thus he sees that there is an opening here or an opening there, and the offence in either case is not great to him' (4). The problem is that this is apRoberts's portrait of Trollope—without the sneer. But the sneer makes all the difference. Neutral advocacy always made Trollope uneasy at least, even when, as with Cicero, he is engaged in his most ingenious special pleading: 'To me it is marvellous and interesting rather than beautiful, to see how completely Cicero can put off his own identity and assume another's, in any cause, whatever it be, of which he has taken the charge' (*The Life of Cicero*, i. 1). apRoberts argues that Cicero is a model for Trollope's own artistic methods, and that his portrait of Cicero's devices is thus a form of self-portrait. Compelling as this argument is, it does seem to me that however much Cicero may himself have been an empiricist, neither Trollope's judgement nor his portrait of Cicero is empirical. The essential defence Trollope makes is that Cicero was 'almost a Christian, even before the coming of Christ' (ii. 14), and the standards are made as clear and consistent as Trollope can make them. He admits imperfections in Cicero, largely those connected with his advocacy and such shifting positions that apRoberts might attribute to 'situation ethics', but he is anxious to show Cicero's basic consistency, his never-changing 'political idea' (i. 3) and his generally constant ethics. Where he can, he asserts Cicero's elevation *over* situations—while others, 'I may almost say all', were stealing, 'he kept his hands clean' (i. 4)— arguing that Cicero lived and died for a principle. The work clearly *is*, as apRoberts says, a most ingenious apology, but the terms of the apology are, I think, much more conventional than she allows. In the end, he tries his best to turn Cicero into 'a modern gentleman' (ii. 10), the most solid traditional ethical standard in Trollope. He is embarrassed by Cicero's genuine relativism and searches hard in his life for something more like flexible consistency.

Trollope's method and his morality, then, appear to me very much tied to situations, but only because situations test and make solid an ethical code that would otherwise remain abstract and superficial.

The situations can diversify, even break, codes, but the codes derive always from a civilized base independent of the situations. Even the passages of circumstantial pleading always move away from the special case to the general principle, not in the other direction. Trollope is one of the most rigorous testers of accepted moral codes; he can even be cynical about them. But honour and truth, chivalric attitudes toward women, responsibilities to class, and a host of other principles, though never easy and certainly never safely divorced from the rough requirements of human life, are there in the end, just as they were, say, for Don Quixote, one of Trollope's favourite models. Trollope's method and morality are no less but no more modern than are Cervantes'.

There are other things about a Trollope novel just as obstinately old-fashioned: the use of the interpretive narrator, of course, but also his display of fondness for the forms of romantic comedy. 'In the centre of almost every tale [by Trollope], we are taken to the heart of a spotless, loving, refined, brave English girl',[36] said an early reviewer, and Mrs. Oliphant similarly located Trollope's principal claim to attention in his 'uncanny' and detailed knowledge of 'the thoughts that go through a girl's mind when she is in the full tide of her individual romance'.[37] While it is quite true that Trollope did not adopt the values of romantic comedy uncritically,[38] neither did he altogether reject them. His oft-repeated assertion that 'there must be love in a novel' (*Autobiography*, p. 142) is playful, but it is not cynical. More important even than the accurate exploration of the heart of an English girl in love is Trollope's repeated use of the forms of comedy. We do sense in Trollope, for all his self-conscious and reflexive manœuvring of comic convention, a general confirmation of that convention. His comic novels move as surely toward union as do Shakespeare's comic plays; they are as suspicious of outsiders and as relentlessly communal in their emphases.[39] Even

[36] Frederic Harrison, 'Anthony Trollope's Place in Literature', *Forum*, 19 (May 1895), 332.

[37] Rev. of *The Claverings* and *The Last Chronicle of Barset*, *Blackwood's*, 102 (Sept. 1867), 277.

[38] It is sometimes felt that he did: 'the tragedy of Trollope's career is his capitulation to the stereotype of romantic love' (Bradford Booth, *Anthony Trollope*, p. 164).

[39] For discussions of the sense of community in Trollope see Paul Elmer More, 'My Debt to Trollope'; J. Hillis Miller, *The Form of Victorian Fiction: Thackeray, Dickens, Trollope, George Eliot, Meredith, and Hardy* (Notre Dame, Ind.: Univ. of Notre Dame Press, 1968), pp. 117, 123; and Rebecca West, 'A Nineteenth-Century Bureaucrat', *The Court and the Castle: Some Treatments of a Recurrent Theme* (New Haven: Yale Univ. Press, 1957), pp. 133, 148.

those psychological forces in Trollope's novels that have attracted much recent attention finally yield in most cases to a more general, social view. Mr. Crawley himself is initiated not into selfhood but into Barsetshirehood; his search is not so much for an integrated being as for a proper relation to other men. Admittedly, in some other instances the isolation remains, but even there the rhetorical power of that isolation comes from its resistance to the urgent unifying force of the comic form. Lily Dale, Louis Trevelyan, even the widowed Duke of Omnium, all exist in worlds (and novels) which are potentially comic.

There is, then, a firm sense of comic form in Trollope to contribute to his old-fashionedness along with the very talkative and not at all 'unreliable' narrator. But they do not work together, and that, in a sense, is the Trollope problem. Far from controlling the comic pattern, strengthening and defining our response to it, the narrator functions almost always to disrupt the smooth operation of the pattern, often by calling our attention to its artificiality. We sense, therefore, a form that both is and is not confirmed, a basic duality between the conventional comedy and the conventional narrator who is employed in highly unconventional ways.

The same tension marks our fullest reaction to Trollope, from whatever angle. No one has ever been able to decide whether, even in the broadest sense, his views are liberal or conservative; Trollope's statement to the effect that he was both at the same time typically confuses the matter: 'I consider myself to be an advanced, but still a conservative Liberal' (*Autobiography*, p. 291). A similar and more important dualism lies in the conflict between the 'self-effacing' and 'transparent'[40] narrative style and the self-conscious sophistication of the commenting narrator. Finally, on the highest level of generalization, we find J. Hillis Miller claiming for Trollope a form that is dynamic, open, and temporal;[41] Jerome Thale asserts just as confidently that the form is 'static', closed, and spatial.[42] John Hagan becomes so impatient with all these apparent contradictions that he drops the work of choosing one set or the other or of balancing them

---

[40] David Skilton, *Anthony Trollope and His Contemporaries*, p. 138, is among the few critics to recognize this dualism and to remark that it causes 'one of the contradictions' in much criticism of Trollope.

[41] A fuller treatment of the argument of *The Form of Victorian Fiction* is given in the next section.

[42] 'The Problem of Structure in Trollope', *NCF* (*Nineteenth-Century Fiction*), 15 1960–1), 149, 156.

and lashes out at Trollope for failing to reconcile 'these two opposing forces' and thus leaving 'in vital areas of his fiction uncertainty and ambiguity to a very high degree'.[43] To Hagan, at least, Trollope is clearly neither the eighteenth-century and Aristotelian, nor the modern, artist. Perhaps Trollope is being attacked here for being what he most certainly was, a Victorian novelist, one who naturally shared with his contemporaries a *mixed* form, neither fully opened nor closed. What appear to be contradictions in Trollope are very similar to contradictions in the works of his colleagues, and they are not so much the damnable results of 'uncertainty' as they are the natural results of the typical form of the Victorian novel.

THE FORMS OF VICTORIAN FICTION

Mr. Micawber, determined to see for himself what his country intends to do for him, steps round the corner in Canterbury and sees his former London lodger. He confuses David by treating him as an old and dear friend, an equal in age and experience: 'Still in the wine trade?' (17). He insists on addressing him always with terms like 'the friend of my youth, the companion of earlier days!' (27).[44] These words carry a great deal of warmth and delight, at least to the reader, but David is made oddly uncomfortable both by this address and this man. He is not only embarrassed; he is disoriented: the steady, logical world in which he is living has been disrupted. And we too sense a fundamental disjunction of some sort. In a parallel scene Micawber himself is embarrassed when he later admits to David that he is working for Uriah Heep. Micawber speaks in such a stammering and shambling way that even his eyeglass droops, and we are again aware of some queer dislocation, some discomfort that far exceeds the apparent cause.

Micawber's embarrassment is perhaps more easily explained than is David's. G. K. Chesterton, for instance, pointed out that Micawber was upset not so much at being caught up in villainy as being caught up in the plot.[45] The man who has spent his life outside the

---

[43] 'The Divided Mind of Anthony Trollope', *NCF*, 14 (1959–60), 2.

[44] References are to the Oxford Illustrated Dickens edition of *David Copperfield* (London: Oxford Univ. Press, 1948).

[45] I find now either that Chesterton did not in fact say this or that I cannot locate the point where he did. The sentence seems to me in so many ways Chestertonian, however, that I feel sure he *would* have said it had he found his syntax galloping in that direction. Whatever support such an argument can gather might come from Chesterton's *Appreciations and Criticisms of the Works of Charles Dickens* (1913; rpt. New

confines of time and space is, it seems, now trapped by them. He has no real place in the plot, that is, in the regularized pattern wherein David disciplines his heart and learns to live comfortably, successfully, and, most of all, regularly. Naturally Micawber is embarrassed at being seen in such company. By the same token, perhaps one can explain the earlier scene by saying that David, playing his part in the plot, is both annoyed and threatened by meeting a man who, so he thinks, is far beyond such things. David inhabits, or is trying to inhabit, the world of steady and linear progress. It is a distinctly Aristotelian world, with clearly defined and morally intelligible connections and a pleasing, regular shape. It is principally a world of space, and we, as readers, react to it as we would to art that exists in space, not in time, as we would to architecture, not to music. We are aware at any point in our reading of the vital relationship of that particular point to the whole and of the anticipated satisfaction at seeing that whole completed. Taken by itself, David's life traces a pattern whose meaning is completely and fully contained. Taken by itself, this form is just that of most eighteenth-century novels.

But David's closed world is not, of course, the total world of the novel in which he exists. The spatial form is combated by an alien structure that is clearly temporal. Against the closed pattern which David tries to maintain, a radically open pattern is pressed. Micawber's wild rearrangement of their ages is an assertion of his ability to live outside linear controls, outside reason itself. And it is reason that provides support for such things as plots. The predictably recurrent rhythms that David finds are repeatedly thrown against the defiantly irregular rhythms of Micawber's world. Even such recurrence as there is with the Micawbers—Mrs. Micawber's eloquent vows never to desert her husband, for instance—is so totally without cause that it makes us think not of rational rhythms but of the rhythms of a marionette or a jack-in-the-box. And these figures are, we know, in part parodies of human beings. Just so, Mr. Micawber parodies the basic assumptions of David's world. We notice this conflict between two rhythms not only when Micawber is on the scene but in such things as Murdstone's bizarre arithmetical puzzles, Aunt Betsey's war with donkeys, Barkis's elephantine wooing, more prominently in Dora and her implicit comment on a life of regularity, account books, and the disciplining of the heart,

York: Haskell House, 1966), pp. 129–39 and *Charles Dickens* (rpt. New York: Schocken Books, 1965), pp. 199, 266–7.

but most clearly in David's memory, which refuses to be either rational or linear and which continually calls up scenes of irrational nightmare—fears of a vengeful and risen father, for instance—or irrational comfort and love through memories of his mother.

The conjunction of two basic forms, then, is fundamental to this novel; it is the basis on which it is built. The gap created when the Aristotelian, linear, rational David meets the existential, jagged, irrational Micawber is paradigmatic of this novel and stands, I think, as an adequate symbol for the form of most Victorian fiction. Perhaps the subtlest example of this mixed form is worked out in *Middlemarch*, where all the characters imagine they are occupying a magical, existential world but are in fact caught in one that is all too inexorably plot-ridden. One thinks also of the disjunction between temporal demands and a linear plot that occurs in those scenes between Becky Sharp and Amelia, Madeline Neroni and Eleanor Bold, Quilp and Little Nell, Mr. Pecksniff and old Martin Chuzzlewit. How many Victorian novels carry on a major action that is simultaneously parodied on another level!

The principle of parody is only the most obvious development of the conflict I have mentioned between the closed form the nineteenth-century novel inherited from the century before and the open form that has become common in our century.[46] The perception of some conflict is, of course, not new. Earlier critics often spoke of a split between plot and character when talking about Becky Sharp or Micawber or Melmotte, arguing that the authors became so fond of their created people that the primary demands of plot were more or less forgotten. We all remember the argument and the conclusion consequent on it to the effect that the Victorian novel was nearly altogether formless, one great 'loose, baggy monster'. All this doubtless came from regarding the nineteenth-century novel as if it were written in the eighteenth century. Those modern critics who work from Aristotelian bases, notably members of the Chicago school, seem to me nearly as helpless when faced with the junction of

---

[46] Open form is variously defined. Robert M. Adams (*Strains of Discord: Studies in Literary Openness*, Ithaca: Cornell Univ. Press, 1958) sees openness as a deliberate thematic ambiguity: 'The open form . . . includes a major unresolved conflict with the intent of displaying its unresolvedness' (p. 13). Miller uses the term, however, more in the formal sense defined by Alan Friedman (*The Turn of the Novel*). Friedman refers openness 'to an ending which does not contain or "close off" the rising pressure of conscience in a novel' (p. xvi). For Friedman, openness is not a matter of meaning but 'a process of ethical experience which does not close' (p. xvi).

forms in the nineteenth-century novel. Sheldon Sacks's *Fiction and the Shape of Belief* is forced to offer the term 'serious action' to provide a category that will somehow contain novels that are neither clearly comic nor tragic. But something more radical in the way of assumptions is needed.

And most of us do make more radical assumptions, in one way or another, most commonly by assuming that Victorian novels were written not in the eighteenth century but in our own. We very likely talk to students and to each other about these novels as if the major action, what I have called the closed form, were not there. Who spends class time or space in scholarly journals on Agnes Wickfield, or the second Cathy, or Hetta Carbury, or even Will Ladislaw? With novels less well known we can go further. In discussing *Barnaby Rudge*, for instance, critics have sometimes said, more than a little boastfully, that they have forgotten the lines of the major action and that they were going on undisturbed to talk about the riot scenes, or the treatment of madness, or the anti-pastoral, or virtually anything other than the narrative lines.

While perhaps avoiding this excess, we all tend to reverse the Aristotelian tendency and to simplify these novels in another direction, regarding them wishfully as if they were all prefigurations of *The Trial* or *Absalom, Absalom!* The result is not so much a distortion as an illumination that is only partial; the most serious practical result of this mistaken assumption is that it is untrue to the richness and complexity of the nineteenth-century novel, substituting a relatively certain and unified pattern for one that is tentative and mixed. From this point of view, *The Trial* and other modern examples of open form are much simpler than *The Trial*'s model, *Bleak House*, and the other nineteenth-century examples of mixed form. Barbara Hardy says that Victorian novelists 'seem to be caught between the assured conventionality of an earlier age of fiction and the assured brave dislocations of the next',[47] but if there is a trap, it is one that offers rich compensations to those caught in it.

The best analogy outside literature for this mixed form is provided by J. Hillis Miller's comments on *The Disappearance of God*. Miller's central image is a God who is not dead but beyond reach; He still lingers in memory and perhaps in fact. This tantalizing symbol provided for the Victorians a structure and at least a hint of

[47] 'Towards a Poetics of Fiction: An Approach through Narrative', *Novel*, 2 (1968–9), 8.

coherence, but that coherence could not be confidently maintained against the new sense of emptiness and causelessness. So, by extension, a closed form was no longer satisfactory. Still, neither was an open form, for such a form rests on assumptions of incoherence and irrationality which are too certain and too final. The only possible form, then, is one which mirrors that suspended, hesitant state the Victorians talked about as 'doubt'. The form, like the state of mind, refuses to rest in either of the alternate comforts of security or denial.

But the comforts of denial and the relative certainty we ourselves feel about open form are not easy to give up. Miller himself has later, in *The Form of Victorian Fiction*, for some reason denied to the novel the complexity resulting from the disappearance of God he had so brilliantly described. The novelists, he says, were somehow sure that God was dead and were thus exempt from the particular tensions felt by the poets; consequently, 'the form taken by Victorian fiction implies a new notion of structure, and this new structure derives from the new metaphysical situation. Because there no longer seems to be any supernatural foundation for society or for the self, Victorian novels are likely to take the form of an incomplete self-generating structure, a structure in which the temporal dimension is constitutive in a new way' (pp. 33-4). The Victorian novel, he says, is a version of the dramatic monologue (p. 3), another new nineteenth-century form.

What Miller draws our attention to is certainly there, but he has perhaps done his work too well and made us see the temporal structure, the open form, too exclusively. In some terms, for instance, the Victorian novel certainly is much like the dramatic monologue, but these similarities in any case are purely those of technique. What the novel has that the dramatic monologue does not, in fact what the novel clings to that the dramatic monologue deliberately rejects, is a sense of context, more broadly a traditional narrative pattern. It is easy to see formal resemblances between *Wuthering Heights* and *Antony and Cleopatra*, but to what does 'Porphyria's Lover' connect? One cannot be sure, precisely because the narrative patterns in the dramatic monologue are artificially curtailed, made ambiguous in context, or in some other way totally suspended and thus made incomplete. In the novel the formal pattern is given context and a total shape; the opposition is more subtle. The resultant form is itself tentative, recognizing the incoherence fully but refusing to acknowledge that the incoherence is necessarily final and unchanging.

This mixed form, I believe, dominates the Victorian novel in its full range, from those which seem most open, say the late novels of Dickens, to those of Trollope, apparently the most closed. *Our Mutual Friend*, for instance, among the most apocalyptic and modern of Victorian novels, takes as its main action a plot that is drawn straight from tradition, in this case the tradition of romantic comedy, with all its customary paraphernalia of mysterious wills, class barriers and reluctant parents overcome, a rush of marriages at the close, and clear didactic themes of moral education. Set against this —well, we all know from recent criticism what is set against this: the nervous disjointed language of the novel, the violent and expansive symbolism of the river and the dust, the removal of the social world altogether out of the sphere of humanity. Both patterns are present. When we see Bradley Headstone beating his head in desperation we are aware simultaneously of two broad purposes: one serving the closed form, whereby he is the wrong and merely troublesome suitor clearly on the road to eventual punishment, and the other serving the open form, whereby his anguish and sexual frustration reach outward as expressions of both social and cosmological injustice not to be explained by or contained within a comic plot. Even the most distinctly existential, temporal characters in the novel—the cripple Jenny Wren, say, or Mr. Venus, the man who has reached a kind of commercial stardom by the ingenious articulation of human bones—are still brought into the closed pattern: they both perform in romantic plots and are finally married. It is true that when the humorous villain Silas Wegg is thrown out of the window into the cart of night soil, the image penetrates the closed pattern and suggests a horrible connection between commerce, filth, civilization, and humanity; but this same scene also confirms the closed pattern by suggesting just as clearly a thousand traditional comic episodes in which the villain is exposed.

CHAPTER 2

FORM AND CONVENTION IN TROLLOPE

BY THE same token, those quiet and apparently backward-looking novels by Trollope find a variety of means to disengage us from the forward movement of the narrative action, to cast doubts on its conclusiveness or even authority, and to create in the reader the same recognition of these dual forms, the open pattern at war with the closed one. I take it that the closed pattern here is even more obvious than it is in Dickens; surely no one adhered more closely to conventional narrative designs than Trollope. Correspondingly, the means for dislocating the total form of the novel from this closed pattern are much quieter and more subtle in Trollope than they are in Dickens, but they are probably more radical. At any rate, the weapons are different. Whereas Dickens generally creates this disjunction by means of the characters and images, Trollope finds his means for opening the closed form primarily outside the main action, in the dramatized narrator and in disruptive minor actions or subplots. In Trollope, the major action is usually itself undisturbed; the complications come from the rhetorical directions given by the narrator and the often subversive or at least critical subplots. Far less frequently, Trollope establishes moral and thematic ambiguity directly, usually, as in *Cousin Henry*, through the use of a bizarre point of view. In a few places the major action itself becomes subversive of its tradition. The use of chronicles and recurring characters also acts to open the form by attacking the absolute completeness of the individual novel. But generally Trollope depends on the narrator and the minor plots to establish a rhythm that counters, without denying, the rhythm of the primary action. In order to establish the integrity of the counter-movement, the work done by the narrator and the subplots must be done very slowly, by an accumulation of hints, so that it really sets up a growing shadow to the main pattern and its values and assumptions. Early critics were quick to realize what Walter Allen called

Trollope's 'art of the cumulative';[1] *The Spectator*, for instance, said, 'Mr. Trollope's genius demands space'; his 'imagination paints not by intension, but by extension'.[2] Trollope himself often inserted complaints or apologies in his short stories to the effect that 'Our story must be necessarily too short to permit us to see how the affair grew in all its soft and delicate growth' ('The Last Austrian Who Left Venice'). Just so, and that delicacy, that careful establishment of counter-tensions is what we miss here. This thinness explains why Trollope's short stories and short novels are, without exception, of little interest to us, to Trollope's contemporaries, or to Trollope himself.

TROLLOPE AND PLOT

Another reason for Trollope's failure in short fiction is that it generally must depend heavily on plot; there he has little chance to develop the usual counter-pattern. Trollope has no opportunity to manipulate those 'hundred and twenty little incidents [which] must be dribbled into the reader's intelligence . . . in such manner that he shall himself be insensible to the process' (*Is He Popenjoy?* (1)) and thus was left with nothing but the major action, the 'plot', a part of fiction for which he expressed the most profound contempt. In the longer fiction Trollope found a wonderful variety of means for carrying on this battle against the dominance of plots and the whole world that was implied by plots, particularly the notion that a coherent action could suggest by itself a morality that was anything more than merely coherent. The complexity of Trollope's novels arises mainly from the fact that this coherence is both attacked and supported. Trollope writes a plot with one hand, while with the other he knifes at it.

'Plot there is none' claimed the Longman's reader in his report on *Barchester Towers*,[3] and, however overstated that may be, we know that he is indeed on to something. Trollope later confirmed the reader's suspicion to some extent, acknowledging that he spent very little time indeed on plots. He could pretend that the construction of a plot was 'a labour of Hercules' 'altogether beyond my power of accomplishment', and could even parody his own

[1] *The English Novel: A Short Critical History* (London: Phoenix House, 1954), p. 192.
[2] Rev. of *Sir Harry Hotspur of Humblethwaite*, 43 (26 Nov. 1870), 1415.
[3] Quoted in Sadleir, *Trollope: A Commentary*, p. 170.

carelessness about plot.[4] Still, his genuine attitude is clear enough: plot is 'the most insignificant part of a tale', which, if overemphasized, can turn the whole art into a mere 'wooden show'.[5] Nothing in Trollope's art is more important or more startling than his attempts to draw his readers away from primary concern with the plot. That such devices were more than mere crotchets and that they were consistent with his total form was certainly apparent to Trollope, at least in his attacks on the causal connections that we wrongly imagine tie together human life: 'Men and women when they are written about are always supposed to have fixed resolutions, though in life they are so seldom found to be thus armed' (*Castle Richmond*, 16). The sort of causality implied by plots seems to Trollope simply untrue to life as he sees it, a point grasped to some extent by at least one early reviewer: 'But the realist in fiction is careless about plot. His sole object is to describe men's lives as they really are; and real life is fragmentary and unmethodical.'[6]

Beyond this, there is a clear sense in Trollope that the Aristotelian assumptions about coherence and order, particularly a coherence between will and act, no longer hold. Trollope insisted over and over that 'character' was supreme in his art, not plot,[7] a judgement that might seem a simple-minded misunderstanding of Aristotle,

[4] 'A Walk in a Wood', *Good Words*, 20 (Sept. 1879), 595; see also *An Autobiography*, pp. 256–7, 320.

[5] *An Autobiography*, p. 126. The *Saturday Review* notice of *An Autobiography* commented sarcastically, 'Many . . . will fulminate against his theory that a good plot is "the most insignificant part of a tale"—though Mr. Howells will, of course, be enchanted' (56, 20 Oct. 1883, 506).

[6] *North British Review*, 40 (June 1864), 372. Though this sort of analysis is rare indeed, it was common for reviewers at least to notice Trollope's unusual treatment of plot. The *Athenaeum* reviewer of *Ayala's Angel* marvelled at a plot constructed with such a very 'slender thread' (No. 2795, 21 May 1881, 686); the *Saturday Review* says it was ready to call *Phineas Redux* 'an excellent novel' but for the doubt 'whether it can be called a novel at all. . . . Can that be a novel where there is no plot?' (37, 7 Feb. 1874, 186). Somewhat more direct was the comment on *Can You Forgive Her?*: 'There is, as usual, no plot' (*Saturday Review*, 20, 19 Aug. 1865, 242).

[7] W. J. Harvey provides the most sophisticated support for Trollope's argument: 'The plots of novels, abstractly considered, do not have the disturbing quality of myth; the deeper and wider significance of these works—their "symbolic" values—depend upon our primary sense of character' (*Character and the Novel*, Ithaca: Cornell Univ. Press, 1965, p. 23, n. 1). James Gindin's definition of the 'novel of compassion' includes mention of this rejection of plot: it 'is also generally anti-Aristotelian in ignoring Aristotle's injunction that the plot or the action should embody all the issues in the work of art' (*Harvest of a Quiet Eye*, p. 4). David Goldknopf's arguments that plot is not 'indigenous to the novel *genre*' (487) are relevant here too ('What Plot Means in the Novel', *Antioch Review*, 29 [1969–70], 483–96).

unless we take Trollope to mean that action and meaning have now been divorced. Aristotle's essential notion that the fable should contain in itself all the rhetorical power, independent of the telling, asks us to agree that a pattern of meaning can be inferred from a pattern of action. But Trollope, and of course other Victorians, are not at all confident on that point. The sense of being is more and more separate from action, and if one is not necessarily what one does, then it finally does make sense to talk about placing character above plot. Trollope suggests that, most often, complexity of being is hidden or denied by simplicity of action. That the split is not absolute means that the plot is not abandoned, but a thousand cautions are necessary. We must read the plot properly, make it far more complex than it may appear, place the emphases exactly, and, finally and most importantly, not regard it with too much seriousness.

There are other, more particular, explanations for Trollope's attack on plots. Any completed action, any fulfilled pattern is always protested against on account of its falseness to life, its dangerous simplifying quality, and its terrible ability to minister to our desire to 'want it all to be over', Joyce Carol Oates's wonderful description of fulfilment. Trollope very often ends a romantic comedy with a strong cautionary joke to the effect that marriages are very sad completions to the joy of the engagement, that all pleasure is at an end as one turns from the altar, and the like. Partly this is his way of disrupting the symmetry of the plot and 'opening' the form, but such jokes also express his temperamental distrust of futuristic thought, of Utopias, and even of generalized goals of any kind, heaven included. His novels set themselves squarely against the same linear and progressive views which dominate nineteenth-century thought. Thus there is a kind of backward-looking melancholy we sense even in many of the most conventional comedies, a resistance to any pattern that implies an ending. This resistance surely is Trollope's conservatism in its most profound form.

But other temperamental factors and artistic choices are important in Trollope's attitudes toward plot as well. His tie to the tradition of the comedy of manners is very real, and, in accord with that tradition, he often projects the sense that plot or action is simply too gross to account for the really important aspects of life: the tiny daily acts of kindness or sensitivity that make up the moral life. These are the issues that translate into 'the minute ramifications of tale-telling'[8] Trollope says he thought about in place of plot. The nineteenth-century sense of history as a record neither of great events nor of great men but of the almost unobserved lives of trivial people is strong in Trollope. He accepted as fully as Jane Austen and Thackeray the assumption that events of great moral consequence occur at Box Hill, not at Waterloo. Trollope's bias in favour of ironic realism makes him despise the pernicious effects of that 'school of art, which delighted to paint the human face as perfect in beauty' (*The Eustace Diamonds*, 35), and he sees in the world just as few heroes as did Thackeray. Unlike Thackeray, however, Trollope can view the absence of heroism with great flexibility. That there is no heroic action is sometimes seen with dismay but more often with mild satisfaction, as a cause for a celebration of the joys of non-heroic conversation, non-heroic dinner parties, and, especially, non-heroic love: 'What would the world come to if none but absolute true heroes were to be thought worthy of women's love? What would the men do? and what— oh! what would become of the women?' (*Framley Parsonage*, 21).

The dissolution of the world that sustained Aristotle's assumptions, then, is accepted only tentatively by Trollope, but even when the old order and unity seem most distant there is no necessary cause for despair. The loss is also a victory. The absence of fulfilment can suggest the absence of endings. Equivocal heroism and equivocal balance of plot and anti-plot, of gain and loss, of irony and comedy, make up the world of the Trollope novel. The central equivocation is formal, as I have argued, involving the opening of the closed form, a delicate operation for which Trollope had many instruments at hand: the action itself, the narrator, and the chronicle device.

TROLLOPE'S USE OF ACTION: MAIN PLOTS AND SUBPLOTS

Opening the form through a manipulation of the elements in the main plot is so rare in Trollope (however common it may be in other Victorian novelists) that it could safely be ignored but for one fact: he shows a marked tendency to resist one of the major traditional requirements of romantic comedy, namely the full-hearted satisfaction women feel in anticipating marriage. The victory is also seen as a trap, and Trollope's sensitivity to this dilemma and to the 'woman question' at large is so intense in the novels that even the

[8] 'A Walk in a Wood', p. 595.

major action is often rendered ambiguous. When he was safely
away from the intricacy of his fiction and into the simplicity of
ideas, Trollope could announce with almost desperate confidence
that 'the necessity of the supremacy of man [over woman] is as
certain to me as the eternity of the soul'.[9] Nor is Trollope's lecture
on the higher education of women any more suggestive of interesting
notions on the subject. But within the novels themselves, the
platitudes disappear completely, and the easy answers of both male
supremacists and feminists[10] alike are seen to be irrelevant entirely
to the dilemma of the woman faced with no satisfying alternatives.
For many of Trollope's heroines, life offers only the challenge of
making a brilliant marriage. Failure means absolute emptiness, but
so may success. Success in any case may mean a loss of freedom or
selfhood, a very limited victory indeed. To Pamela Hansford Johnson, Trollope is of all nineteenth-century novelists the most sensitive to women.[11] However that may be, the counterplay to romantic
comedy is often remarkably strong. Even as early as *The Noble Jilt*
(1850) the heroine resists a perfect marriage with the argument,
'Love's not enough to fill a woman's heart' (I. i). And that, surely, is
an attack on the major premiss of all romantic comedy.

Trollope often traces with great insight the common paths
women follow through courtship, where their attempt to preserve
their independent being leads them finally to feeling isolated,
perverse, and consequently guilty. This course results so often in a
desire for punishment that the narrator can sarcastically comment,
'With many women I doubt whether there be any more effectual
way of touching their hearts than ill-using them and then confessing

---

[9] To Adrian H. Joline, 2 Apr. 1879, *The Letters of Anthony Trollope*, ed. Bradford
A. Booth (London: Oxford Univ. Press, 1951), p. 418—hereafter cited as *Letters*.

[10] Patricia Thompson, in *The Victorian Heroine: A Changing Ideal, 1837-1873*
(London: Oxford Univ. Press, 1956), has great fun with Trollope, calling him the
'high priest of marriage', who allowed Victorians to feel that 'their ideal of wifely submission was in its finest hour' (p. 111). The fact that his women are high-spirited *and*
anxious for marriage, she says, makes Trollope the perfect spokesman for anti-feminism
(pp. 110-12). There is a similar argument in A. O. J. Cockshut's *Anthony Trollope*:
'He is so confident of male supremacy that he can look benevolently on "women's
rights" ' (p. 178), an echo of Michael Sadleir's thin jokes on Trollope as the last of the
'masculine' novelists and Q. D. Leavis's attack on his 'smoking-room sentimentality'
(*Fiction and the Reading Public*, London: Chatto and Windus, 1932, p. 252).

[11] 'Trollope's Young Women', in *On the Novel*, ed. B. S. Benedikz (London: J. M.
Dent, 1971), p. 33. See also Beatrice Curtis Brown, *Anthony Trollope*, 2nd edn. (London:
Arthur Barker, 1967), p. 68. J. A. Banks places Trollope's treatment of women in the
historical context of the feminist movement ('The Way They Lived Then: Anthony
Trollope and the 1870's', *VS*, 12, 1968-9, 190-5).

it. If you wish to get the sweetest fragrance from the herb at your feet, tread on it and bruise it' (*Miss Mackenzie*, 10). The punishment and the granting of an illusory sense of power almost always do the trick. The desire for freedom becomes by its very strength the source for an equally strong desire for neurotic submission. Alice Vavasor is Trollope's fullest treatment of this twisted psychological progress, but many of his marriages are haunted by the notion that women can exist as real beings only in sacrifice: 'To sacrifice herself is the special heroism which a woman can achieve. . . . A woman can soar only by suffering' ('The Lady of Launay'). By withholding the full satisfactions of the traditional comic form, such an argument thus suspends the completion of the form itself.

With married women Trollope's treatment is often even harsher, more sarcastic in reference to the easy notions of comic tradition. Though it may be an overstatement to suggest that his views on marriage have 'a certain affinity to those of James Thurber',[12] marriage is certainly not often a very romantic affair in a Trollope novel. When a character in *Brown, Jones, and Robinson* accuses a friend of wanting a wife simply to be a 'household drudge', the answer tells us a great deal not only about the falseness of the tradition but also about the potential desolation implied by Trollope's counterplots: 'So I would,—only drudge don't sound well. Call her a ministering angel instead, and it comes to the same thing' (13). Women who have been successful in marriage often find that they have triumphantly made their way into nothing at all. The most moving image of this state in Trollope is that of Lady Glencora, whose whole life as heiress, wife, and Duchess of Omnium may be seen as a fight to escape being nothing. And she, the strongest and wittiest of women, fails. This important exception aside, however, Trollope does keep his central action free from subversion.

But not those subsidiary actions that work around and impinge on the main plot. Trollope's wide and very careful reading in Elizabethan and Jacobean drama is very suggestive in this regard, for he used the co-ordinated double and triple plot in ways similarly rich. As in the early drama, Trollope's plots comment one upon the other, most commonly by offering in the minor plots an action that runs counter to, or even burlesques, the main plot, thus disrupting its easy symmetry and complicating our responses. The various plots in Trollope are very often co-ordinated principally through

---

[12] James Pope Hennessy, *Anthony Trollope* (Boston: Little, Brown, 1971), p. 97.

mirrored themes and motifs rather than through the actual narrative. We often have the sense that the plots are more properly seen as parallel rather than interwoven, and that such actual contact as is made among them in the action itself is perfunctory or accidental. But this is what we would expect of Trollope, who desires above all to embody the means of his fable at least partly *outside* the action. We should not, then, expect a great deal of narrative glue to be expended on making the plots stick together on the literal level. In Trollope's art we must infer meanings that go beyond or run counter to plot, a demanding business, of course, and one that requires precise rhetorical control lest readers run wild in the critical woods of appearance and reality, on one hand, or, on the other, see the novels as careless botches. Trollope himself insisted that 'every sentence, every word, through all those pages, should tend to the telling of the story' (*Autobiography*, p. 237), and, with unusual sententiousness, that 'though the novel which you have to write must be long, let it be all one' (*Autobiography*, p. 238). But many critics, Victorian and modern, bring the charge of disunity against him, not all, however, with such disarming candour as the *Saturday Review* on *Phineas Finn*: 'The last thing in the world apparently that is aimed at is the working out of a simple and harmonious whole. The multiplication of figures is the chief thing, and the system of continuing the story indefinitely . . . baffles criticism. You can never say that the whole displeases you, because you can never be sure that you have got the whole.'[13]

It is never easy to 'get the whole' in these novels, largely because these subplots are almost always used not to reinforce but to counter the main action and thus open the form. Our initial sense of disharmony, therefore, is quite appropriate. Very often, as in *He Knew He Was Right*, the various plots give different answers to the same question. Even more often the subplots carry on a burlesque of the wish-fulfilment romance that is controlling the main plot,[14] or, with the humorous subplots, solve with ridiculous ease the agonizing

---

[13] *Saturday Review*, 27 (27 Mar. 1869), 432.

[14] Trollope's parody of romance extends beyond the novels. His burlesque, 'The Gentle Euphemia, or "Love Shall Still be Lord of All"', *Fortnightly Review*, 4 (1 May 1866), 692–9, is vigorous indeed, as are his various sarcastic comments on the classic romances; for example, 'A student of English imaginary literature should know the Arcadia, but even a student will hardly read it. I tried very hard but could not reach the end' (quoted in Gladys Green, 'Trollope on Sidney's "Arcadia" and Lytton's "The Wanderer"', *Trollopian*, 1, No. 3, Sept. 1946, 46).

problems occupying the main characters and thus both highlight and trivialize that agony. The actions involving such figures as Mr. Moulder, Amelia Roper, the widow Greenow, Madalina Demolines, Miss Jemima Stanbury, and Ruby Ruggles are generally not much admired, but they actually form one of Trollope's most flexible and useful agencies for creating his mixed form.

TROLLOPE'S NARRATOR

At one point in Trollope's last, unfinished novel, *The Landleaguers*, the narrator breaks into the action to give his views on a political policy, 'cordially' agreeing here and violently disagreeing there. 'Of my disagreement', he says, 'no one will take notice;—but my story cannot be written without expressing it' (39). Why not? The story itself does not in any sense depend on his expression of disagreement, and it appears that he means to tell us only that he cannot go on with the story until he gets this argument out of his system. The point of view becomes dislocated and the use of the narrator self-indulgent, out of control, illegitimate. The instance seems to deserve all the witty attacks ever made on Trollope's intrusive narrators, but, by itself, it hardly seems to justify them fully. In fact, such passages are almost as rare as examples of blasphemy or indecency. Trollope's most serious and pressing claim to be recognized as a major artist rests principally with his subtle and organic use of the dramatized narrator. Still, the attacks have been so effective that early admirers of Trollope were sometimes forced to defend him, somewhat comically it now appears, by hailing him as the first of the disappearing authors.[15]

Even though it is no longer so necessary to mount a general defence of Trollope's practice, there is still little agreement as to the actual effect of these narrators. The four most important modern Trollope critics line up two against two on the question of whether the narrator is used to achieve 'aesthetic distancing' or to pull us directly into the work. Cadbury and apRoberts are on the distancing side; Hillis Miller and Polhemus argue for immersion.[16] The

---

[15] Wilbur L. Cross, *The Development of the English Novel* (New York: Macmillan, 1924), praises Trollope's 'withdrawal, so to speak, behind the scenes' (p. 216); Richard Burton, *Masters of the English Novel: A Study of Principles and Personalities* (New York: Holt, 1909) goes further: 'First among modern novelists, Trollope stands invisible behind his characters' (p. 253).

[16] William Cadbury, 'Character and the Mock Heroic in *Barchester Towers*', *TSLL*, 5 (1963–4), 509–19; Ruth apRoberts, *The Moral Trollope*, p. 55; J. Hillis

suggestion that they both are right, depending on which passage one examines, and that Trollope's narrator in fact draws us into the fiction or distances us from it according to the demands of the moment is embarrassingly obvious, but, I think, accurate. It should be noted, however, that the argument for distancing is especially valuable, since Trollope's deceptively gregarious narrator has so often deluded commentators.

Many critics who disliked Trollope's narrator intruding at all disliked even more his intruding in such a vulgar way and assuming such an unwarranted chumminess. The assumption made most often is that the narrator is there to make things easy, to give assurances, to comfort, even to flatter.[17] James, naturally, capitalized on this misreading of Trollope's effects, claiming with his characteristic waspish sarcasm that Trollope's realism allowed him to catch an 'exact and on the whole becoming image'.[18] James's remarks on the flattering narrator seem to me less clever, however, than the narrator's own: the typical novel reader, he says, desires amusement, disdains education, and wants a story in which 'elevated sentiment prevails'; he must be made to feel, of course, 'that the elevated sentiments described are exactly his own' (*Ralph the Heir*, 56). The chummy narrator, it appears, can be deceptively nasty. The 'good-humoured geniality' of Thackeray seemed to Trollope to be a defect, causing 'the reader to be almost too much at home with his author' (*Thackeray*, 9). Trollope's own narrators are neither so matey nor so consistent.

It is true that the narrator is often charged with the responsibility of making whatever connections there are. Characters tend to wheel about in space, each imagining that he is the isolated centre of some tragedy or wild romance. The narrator characteristically corrects that tendency and provides some sense of community. But it is often an ironic community of the exact sort being resisted by the main plot, which is most often comic. Neither formally nor thematically nor rhetorically do the narrator and the major action

---

Miller, *The Form of Victorian Fiction*, p. 85; Robert Polhemus, *The Changing World*, p. 5. The best and most flexible practical criticism on this point is in Arthur Mizener's 'Anthony Trollope: The Palliser Novels', *From Jane Austen to Joseph Conrad*, ed. Robert C. Rathburn and Martin Steinmann, Jr. (Minneapolis: Univ. of Minn. Press, 1958), pp. 160–76.

[17] See, for example, Geoffrey Tillotson, 'Trollope's Style', *Mid-Victorian Studies*, by Geoffrey and Kathleen Tillotson (London: Athlone Press, 1965), pp. 56–61.

[18] *Partial Portraits*, p. 101.

co-ordinate. The chief function of the narrator, on all levels, is to disrupt. The easy geniality, the flattering warmth is largely of the surface. Frank O'Connor brilliantly points out that Trollope's narrator's 'favorite device is to lead his reader very gently up the garden path of his own conventions and prejudices and then to point out that the reader is wrong'.[19] Though this is naturally not the single narrative strategy, one observes how very often Trollope's objective descriptions, particularly of bizarre persons or unsavoury motives, imperceptibly alter, drop the objectivity gradually, and move us inward. We suddenly realize that it is not 'it' being discussed but 'we'. Trollope does literally shift the pronouns, adopting a technique of the sermon, a standard device of application. He so disguises the technique, however, that we are led not to contemplation, the end desired by the sermon, but to radical identification— with Ferdinand Lopez, for instance, one of the most repellent of his characters: 'And so he taught himself to regard the old man as a robber and himself as a victim. Who among us is there that does not teach himself the same lesson?' (*The Prime Minister*, 45). We come to recognize as symptomatic Trollope's repeated use of 'And so he taught himself', suggestive as it is of the irrational way people form their beliefs and the foundations for their behaviour. It is suggestive as well of the quiet and artful way in which the narrator is seeking to educate the reader by establishing control over his imagination.

Controlling the imagination, he can thus educate it, make it grow. The strategy is typically Romantic, as are the pedagogical principles: educate the imagination by stretching it, pushing it away from customary positions and values, and making it live with wild old mariners, idiot boys, and mad mothers, 'rendering it the receptacle of a thousand unapprehended combinations of thoughts'. On the face of it, Trollope's novels and works like 'Alastor' or 'Christabel' are poles apart. But the serenity and ordinariness of Trollope's world often cover perverse identifications he expects us to make or highly unusual values we are forced to accept. One important use of the narrator is to nudge us, against our conscious knowledge and probably against our will, into accepting a most extraordinary value system. Perhaps the clearest example is found in *Barchester Towers*, where the exceptionally friendly and chatty narrator is used with great subtlety, and we are forced to relax into

<hr>

[19] 'Trollope the Realist', pp. 167–8.

heightened insight. The narrator works from the beginning to establish a surface rhetoric of intimacy and relaxation. 'Our doctrine', he says, 'is, that the author and the reader should move along together in full confidence with each other' (15). The point of this comment and, to a large extent, of the novel itself is that we are all of us men, whether bishops, archdeacons, authors, or readers. He denies explicitly the author's special claim to knowledge and authority, and also appears to deny his fiction the prerogative to surprise, lecture, and edify. On the first level, the rhetoric works by direct flattery, giving the sense that we—the author and the reader— are undeluded, tolerant, realistic, and not bamboozled, as are the characters, by power or position. Since this comfortable rhetorical assumption appears to demand so little, the reader can easily enough accept it. The point of view thus establishes not only a sense of clear and typical realism but a relaxation of the reader's cautions and an easy identification with the novel's most important point: that the joy of life comes in renouncing power and its corollary notions of progress and in accepting the common, the kindly, and the established. Unlike most moral comedies, where the dominant rhetorical mode is attack and where the reader is asked to sharpen his critical faculties, here we are especially asked not to be so eager to judge. The tactful comedy involving Mr. Quiverful and the wardenship, for instance, makes just this point. Trollope brilliantly establishes the entirely understandable impatience of Mrs. Quiverful with her husband's apparent 'sentimental pride' and over-scrupulousness. At the same time, he shows the equally understandable judgement of 'the outer world' that Mr. Quiverful was rapacious and dishonourable. The narrator concludes, 'It is astonishing how much difference the point of view makes in the aspect of all that we look at!' (24). The rhetorical insistence is on moderation and acceptance.

At the same time, however, this basic relaxation is used to promote a clear and startling set of values. For example, the narrator early injects some facetious and good-natured complaints about sermons: 'There is, perhaps, no greater hardship at present inflicted on mankind in civilised and free countries, than the necessity of listening to sermons. No one but a preaching clergyman has, in these realms, the power of compelling an audience to sit silent, and be tormented' (6). He goes on through a rather long paragraph on this 'bore of the age', working exactly for the expansive, unbuttoned attitude in the reader that can recognize the experience as a common one and respond to that recognition with laughter. The next paragraph begins clearly in the same vein, and the reader is encouraged to lean back and companionably agree some more. But the tone and direction are quietly changed. The 'preaching clergyman' becomes the 'young parson', 'my too self-confident juvenile friend', 'my insufficient young lecturer', and the attack is shifted from the general target of boring preachers to the quite specific one of ignorant youth presuming to lecture age. Young clergymen are advised to 'read to me some portion of those time-honoured discourses which our great divines have elaborated in the full maturity of their powers'. Otherwise, 'it all means nothing'. The true harshness and severity of the last comment and of the pervasive assault on youth are masked not only by the light tone but by the introductory rhetoric, which leads us so very gently into the subject. The initial chummy platitudes do disappear, but the tone remains the same and the reader is encouraged to slide into the narrator's position and recognize a 'secret' set of values altogether different from those in the romantic comedy being carried out in the plot. Later in the novel, then, the issue can be brought up without the elaborate introduction. When Mr. Arabin is preparing to read himself in at St. Ewold's, the narrator reflects with deceptively genial irony on the fact that 'it often surprises us that very young men can muster courage to preach for the first time to a strange congregation' (23). He again goes on and on in mock wonder at how those 'who have never yet passed ten thoughtful days' 'are not stricken dumb by the new and awful solemnity of their position'. After a few paragraphs the irony becomes much sharper, though, as the reader is led to the very ungenial reflection that perhaps the process of ordination 'banishes the natural modesty of youth'. We are thus urged to relax into positions which are finally very aggressive and specialized.

As the major action of the novel becomes more idealized, the tone of the narrator becomes sharper and more cynical, so as to insist on his opposition. *The Small House at Allington*, for instance, locates the major action in the highly principled loyalty and constancy of Lily Dale, a romantic image so exalted that it might be incredible, were it not for the very crusty narrator: 'But men are cowards before women until they become tyrants; and are easy dupes, till of a sudden they recognise the fact that it is pleasanter to be the victimiser than the victim—and as easy' (14). It is this

narrator who allows us to see the major action of the novel as a
record both of romantic loyalty and of neurotic perversity.

The values are not always this aggressive, of course; particularly
in the very late, 'dark' novels the narrator sometimes adopts a
distinct mildness. His apologies to the reader no longer carry
the mock humility of *Barchester Towers*, but a genuine courtesy,
as if seeking to re-establish through the reader a league of gentlemen in order to confront a novelistic world where gentlemen no
longer exist. Such a narrative tone is especially apparent in *Mr.
Scarborough's Family* and *The Landleaguers*. Instead of forcing the
reader to act with Mr. Harding, in other words, the narrator seeks
to create Mr. Harding in his narrator and in his reader.

But many narrative comments have no apparent relation to
values. They seem to have no thematic function at all and act only
to remind us that we are reading a novel. Passages of this sort are
very common: 'As the personages of a chronicle such as this should
all be made to operate backwards and forwards on each other from
the beginning to the end, it would have been desirable that the
chronicler should have been able to report that the ceremony was
celebrated by Mr. Emilius. But as the wedding did not take place
till the end of the summer, and as Mr. Emilius at that time never
remained in town, after the season was over, this was impossible'
(*The Eustace Diamonds*, 77). Mr. Emilius is clearly an excuse for a
joke on the structure of the novel itself, a joke that is used deliberately
to make us think of fabricated plots, crude artistic manipulations.
Sometimes the narrator will offer some burlesque critical commentary, as in *The Three Clerks*, where he compares at some length his
'devil', Undy Scott, to Varney and Bill Sykes [*sic*], suggesting that
he would have hanged the villain, 'had I drunk deeper from that
Castalian rill whose dark waters are tinged with the gall of poetic
indignation' (44). Just as James said, Trollope took delight 'in
reminding the reader that the story he was telling was only, after all,
a make-believe'. Those 'suicidal' 'little slaps at credulity'[20] are basic
to Trollope's art and to the aesthetic assumptions we must grant
if we are to appreciate that art.

'It is impossible to imagine what a novelist takes himself to be
unless he regard himself as an historian and his narrative as a
history.'[21] The venerable analogy that James here ignores and tries
to dismiss to the realm of impossibility is provided by the image of

[20] *Partial Portraits*, p. 116.   [21] *Partial Portraits*, p. 116.

the artist as maker.[22] The shoemaker gave Trollope his favourite sarcastic reference, but the assumption that art is not something observed but something made is a serious one. Such art is what Albert Cook calls 'reflexive'; 'it *considers itself*'.[23] Many characters think of themselves as actors in stories, and at one remarkable point in *Lady Anna* a group of lawyers are urged to remember that they are characters in a comedy and that 'generosity and valour always prevailed over wealth and rank with ladies in story' (30). All this has the slightly dizzying effect of holding one mirror up not to life but to another mirror. Art reflects art. The major role in constructing this reflexive mirror is borne not by the characters, however, but by the narrator. He reminds us over and over that what we are engaged with in reading this novel is art, not life, and that art, unlike life, is an affair of convention, tradition, pure artifice.[24]

In *Doctor Thorne*, for example, we are promised right off that the 'hero' (lots of discussion given on that point, of course) will avoid an unhappy end, since the narrator is 'too old now to be a hard-hearted author' (1). Similarly, he says of Mary, 'she is my heroine, and, as such, must necessarily be very beautiful' (3). The artifice is deliberate and dramatic; there is no possibility *at these moments* of imagining that the action has an autonomous life, of confusing art and life. Again and again, the reader is reminded of the very large gap separating the two. In *Doctor Thorne* the narrator interrupts a vital courtship scene to remind us of the difference between narrative and real time. It takes him a long time to tell about some hand-squeezing, he says, but in life it would take only a moment. Failing 'a quick spasmodic style' where 'five words and half-a-dozen dashes and inverted commas' (8) could simulate a correspondence, his art must, sadly, differ greatly from life. Not

---

[22] Robert Scholes and Robert Kellogg, *The Nature of Narrative* (New York: Oxford Univ. Press, 1966), examine the tradition of the novelist as maker as an alternative to the bard and *histor*. They also give a tightly reasoned attack on the narrow dogmatism of 'disappearance-of-the-author' aesthetics (pp. 265–79).

[23] *The Meaning of Fiction* (Detroit: Wayne State Univ. Press, 1960), p. 25; see pp. 24–37.

[24] It has been argued, by an early reviewer (rev. of *The Small House at Allington*, *Saturday Review*, 17, 14 May 1864, 595–6) and more recently by both Robert Polhemus (*The Changing World*, p. 6) and Wayne C. Booth (*The Rhetoric of Fiction*, Chicago: Univ. of Chicago Press, 1961, p. 206), that such commentary has the opposite effect, demonstrating that the characters and action are so real that the narrator cannot manipulate them if he would. Obviously as long as the argument is carried on at this level of generality, the coin can be turned over and over. Conviction in this case must depend on concrete demonstration.

only is no attempt made to simulate action, but he very pointedly
wants us to recognize the divorce here of art and life, as he does also
in a famous passage in *Phineas Finn*, where he admits that his
recounting of a cabinet assembly probably does not bear much
relation to actuality. 'But then, again,' he adds, 'there is this safety':
no one in the general public will ever know whether he was accurate
or not (29).

Lest we become too involved in the action, the narrator is always
round the corner with the signs reminding us that such a response
would be far too simple. At moments of most intense emotion, when
the action threatens to become what we might call 'tough' or
'honest', that is, when we forget most completely that this is art,
the narrator finds some way to slide between us and our absorption.
In the very touching scene where the pathetic and courageous
Marie Melmotte is beaten by her father, for instance, the narrator
offers us a discussion of the propriety of depending on 'spectacle',
a quotation from Horace to support his argument, then a translation
of it—'Let not Medea with unnatural rage/Slaughter her mangled
infants on the stage'—and finally an assurance that he will not
'harrow' us with such details. The playful language and the grotesque inappropriateness of Medea's tragic exaltation to Marie's
pointless struggle for tiny, grubby rewards make it appear almost as
if the narrator were making fun of the action. Well, he almost is.
As the action pulls us in more strongly, the narrator pushes back
on us all the harder.

The effect of this technique is to create a balance in our response,
complicating greatly our participation in the action without simply
overturning and thus inverting our position. The narrator never
gives a sense that he can quite manipulate at will; it is always clear
that, even if he is subject to no laws, he will good-naturedly agree
to abide by certain conventions. Why? Because we, as readers, are
more comfortable that way. 'Since you demand it, I'll provide it',
he says. But he says it, in effect, openly, thus calling our attention
to the artificiality not only of the convention but of our demands as
well. He will give us happy endings, plenty of marriages, punishments for villains, and the like, but not without letting us see that
one source of these patterns is the simple egoism inside ourselves.
The effect is the exact opposite of reassurance. We are urged, on
one hand, to find full meaning in pattern suggested by the action,
but there is a concurrent sense of the artificiality, even falseness of

that pattern, a sense that genuine life is to be found only outside all pattern. The narrator counters the notion that life or its true reflection in fiction can be explained by easily perceived form: 'The editor specially insists on a Nemesis' (19), according to the literary parody in *The Three Clerks*. At the same time, life is not certainly altogether without form either. The attack really is upon simple and regular patterns, upon certainty itself, either of a controlled or uncontrolled life. The hypnotic plain narrative, the beautifully transparent style, and all the power of the traditional narrative myths are balanced against this playful narrator and his cunning reminders of the irrational and the unformed. He not only reminds us of these frightening qualities but locates them within ourselves. There is, thus, on the most general level, a formal opposition between the demands and promises of the action and the corrosive remarks of the narrator. The battle is never won, and the disruption is never conclusive. We are engaged in reading a Trollope novel not in the simple and final subversion of the main action but in the richer and more demanding *process* whereby the conflict between art and life is carried out.

The process is made most evident to us as the plot is worked out alongside a running commentary on the mere artificiality of that plot. For instance, the narrator reminds us in novel after novel that he despises all secrets and that he will therefore, 'for the comfort of my readers', tell us all right away (*Miss Mackenzie*, 17). Those who like plots should close the book; those more adventurous should 'look for your interest' elsewhere in the story (*Dr. Wortle's School*, i. 3). The reason for all this, presumably, is the author's disdain for artificiality: 'I abhor a mystery. I would fain, were it possible, have my tale run through, from its little prologue to the customary marriage in its last chapter, with all the smoothness incidental to ordinary life' (*The Bertrams*, 13). He deliberately refuses to withhold information, he says, because such selection and ordering is unnatural. But of course by calling our attention to that presumed naturalness and congratulating himself on it, he is exposing the fact that even apparent naturalness is the artificial semblance of nature. Thus he is merely emphasizing a different sort of control, a different artifice.

For it is the total form of the novel that the narrator is finally interested in disrupting. In order to open the closed form, its symmetry must be attacked, and we therefore expect and indeed find the narrator going to work vigorously on all the essential parts of the form, particularly those places where we are, in any case, most conscious of form: the beginning and the end. Trollope's novels customarily begin with a beginning that includes some discussion of the nature of beginnings. Though often moderate in comparison with the attacks on endings, opening commentary always at least notes that the beginnings *are* beginnings, and more elaborate essays are sometimes included, as in *Doctor Thorne*, *The Eustace Diamonds*, and *Mr. Scarborough's Family*, three novels which, because they are unusual in being highly 'plotted', therefore require special attention from the artificer. The opening of *Is He Popenjoy?* contains an amusing passage discussing the relative advantages of various opening strategies, an idea expanded to considerable length in *The Duke's Children*, where an entire chapter, entitled 'In Medias Res', is devoted to a discussion of the problem and a jocular demonstration of its difficulties. It even contains a sample opening for analysis: 'Certainly, when I threw her from the garret window to the stony pavement below, I did not anticipate that she would fall so far without injury to life or limb' (9).

But the endings draw much more attention, suggesting as they do the notion of completion, the confirmation of pattern. Here Trollope's narrator brings forth the critical machinery with great display in almost every novel. 'The last details' of romance, he says in *The Last Chronicle of Barset*, 'if drawn out to their natural conclusions, are apt to be uncomfortable, if not dull' (51), and he good-naturedly protects us from the discomfort and the dullness. By doing so, of course, even greater discomfort is added—but never dullness. In many endings the narrator calls attention to artificiality by suggesting that such conclusions are simply unnecessary (*The Bertrams*, for instance); in *John Caldigate* he says he will add the ending just so readers will not think him indolent or cold-hearted. More pointed is the ending of *The Three Clerks*: 'It need hardly be told in so many words to an habitual novel-reader that Charley did get his bride at last.' The narrator in *The Warden* plainly says that he would leave out the ending altogether 'were it not for the custom of the thing'. Occasionally he suggests that he allows things to happen simply because of the artificial convention: 'And of whom else must we say a word? Patience, also, of course, got a husband— or will do so' (*Doctor Thorne*). *Barchester Towers* similarly ends with some facetious remarks on giving rose-coloured endings, false as they are, because that colour is in fashion. The light jokes on marriage that obtrude at the end of *Ayala's Angel* subtly disrupt the integrity of the comic solution; the dark jokes on the same subject at the end of *Framley Parsonage* have the same effect but are far less subtle: 'when the husband walks back from the altar, he has already swallowed the choicest dainties of his banquet. The beef and pudding of married life are then in store for him;—or perhaps only the bread and cheese. Let him take care lest hardly a crust remain— or perhaps not a crust.' The disruption is, however, just that; it is never destruction. The form is opened, but not parodied. At the conclusion of *Dr. Wortle's School*, for instance, the narrator says, 'I cannot pretend that the reader shall know, as he ought to be made to know, the future fate and fortunes of our personages. They must be left still struggling.' He goes on refusing to tell the future of this person, guessing at what might happen to another. In one sense this is rather a fake openness, since we have a very good idea what will happen, and all the commentary about the continued 'struggling' of these people is not totally discordant with the dynamic quality usually striven for in a comic ending. If struggling, they are still living, even if not quite happily ever after. Even this most extreme form of the narrator's call to artificiality, therefore, functions to provide a balance; full parody is never allowed.

This formal result is supported by a very strong and very unusual rhetoric. Trollope almost surely found this mixed form, in fact, not through thinking about form at all but through a concentration on the effect of his work on the reader. His comments on form are occasional and perfunctory, but he was most interested in rhetoric and spoke on it often and with intensity. He emphasized over and over that the reader's sympathy is the crucial matter, without which 'no novel is anything'.[25] For Trollope as for many other Victorians, art now had to shoulder responsibilities once taken by religion; novels, Trollope said, 'have in great measure taken the place of sermons'.[26] He exposes his own religious method most openly in *The Eustace Diamonds*, where he addresses 'my reader, whose sympathies are in truth the great and only aim of my work' (35), explaining that by identifying with the very imperfect (very imperfect indeed in *The Eustace Diamonds*) characters in these novels we

[25] 'On English Prose Fiction as a Rational Amusement', *Anthony Trollope: Four Lectures*, ed. Morris L. Parrish (London: Constable, 1938), p. 124.
[26] 'Novel-Reading', *The Nineteenth Century*, 5 (Jan. 1879), 27.

learn instinctively and gradually a greater tolerance and charity for the very imperfect people around us and for our very imperfect selves. Even when our imaginations are quite weak we benefit, very much as does Mrs. Wortle who, bewildered by her husband's charity towards the erring Mrs. Peacocke, tries to put herself in that poor woman's place: she finds it 'extremely difficult to imagine herself to be in such a position'. But she does as well as she can: 'It was terrible to think of,—so terrible that she could not quite think of it; but in struggling to think of it her heart was softened towards this other woman' (*Dr. Wortle's School*, iv. 7). This is the paradigm for Trollope's rhetorical strategy: just as James said, an artist creates his readers just as he creates his characters.

The moral heart-softening is a task undertaken jointly by the narrative itself and the commenting narrator. The end in view is to make us active, not contemplative, and it is principally up to the narrator to get us in motion, to force us into final collaboration[27] with the artist. He must make us willing to undergo the terrible difficulty of imagining and forging the work. To force us into this most taxing and dangerous endeavour, the narrator must be as sly and as devious as possible. James's notion that Trollope 'never played with a subject, never juggled with the sympathies or the credulity of his reader'[28] could not be more wrong; in fact many of the early objections to Trollope's use of point of view seem to stem from some vague sense that the narrator is far too devious, asking the reader for far too much. Such deviousness is 'extra-professional'; it violates 'the contract of the writer with the reader'.[29] It does indeed, and we are often so battered by this rhetoric and its great demands that we might feel like joining in the protest. Sometimes a single passage is so vigorously sentimentalized and then so joltingly desentimentalized, it all seems unfair. The lonely and supersensitive Duke of Omnium, for instance, forms a warm friendship with the impoverished Lady Rosina De Courcy, even though she has nothing at all to give: 'But nevertheless he liked Lady Rosina, and was never bored by her. She was natural, and she

[27] R. G. Collingwood has a famous discussion of this strategy in art generally: *Principles of Art* (Oxford: Clarendon Press, 1938), pp. 311–15.

[28] *Partial Portraits*, p. 103.

[29] The first complaint was in 'Mr. Trollope's Novels', *The National Review* (Oct. 1858), reprinted in *Trollope: The Critical Heritage*, ed. Donald Smalley (London: Routledge and Kegan Paul, 1969), p. 83; the second in the *Saturday Review*'s notice of *Doctor Thorne*, 5 (12 June 1858), 618.

wanted nothing from him. When she talked about cork soles she meant cork soles. And then she did not tread on any of his numerous corns' (*The Prime Minister*, 27). A cartoon caption that could measure a reader's response might read, 'Sigh—Ahh—Biff—Oof—Grunt'. The attack on convention is made in order finally to support it in a renewed, revitalized form; and the attack on the reader is conducted in order to make him finally into the artist. So it is all worth it.

THE CHRONICLE FORM

There are the two official chronicles, of course, but in a sense all of Trollope's writing is together a chronicle. Any particular novel may, we feel, suddenly invade the territory of another, and we are therefore not surprised when Lord Rufford, Larry Twentyman, and other friends from *The American Senator* turn up in the hunting field in *Ayala's Angel* four years later; Bishop Proudie seems the natural candidate for the new Commissioner in *He Knew He Was Right*. We sometimes do get the feeling that each novel is just a different slice of the same world. Extend the boundaries and, sure enough, there will be the Duke of Omnium or Quintus Slide or Mr. Gresham or Mrs. Quiverful. All this tends to establish an illusion of continuance, whereby the limits of the individual novel are no longer absolute. J. Hillis Miller cites this illusion as the main source of the 'open-endedness' of Trollope's novels; those recurrent characters suggest 'that the life of the individual and of the community is a continuing process'.[30] True enough, certainly, but my own feeling is that, even here, the suggestion of recurrence and continuation acts only to suspend the full completion of the spatial pattern. The novels are not so much open as opened—caught, really, in the process of being opened.

Even the characters who recur both are and are not the same. They are called by the same names, but they also serve the special and unique demands of the novel in which they appear. They bring with them some prior associations, but these associations may be modified or even transformed. There is, then, both a continuity and a discontinuity in recurring characters, just as the novels in which they appear manifest both an open and closed form. The most prominent illustration is Lady Glencora. In *Can You Forgive Her?* she is seen very largely as a victim, whose wit is sharpened principally as a weapon, as an external sign of her inward resolution never to

---

[30] *The Form of Victorian Fiction*, p. 138.

give way entirely, to preserve something of the dignity of her being. Though she feels herself humiliated by this marriage, a victim of brute, unfeeling force, she finds a partial adjustment in a pattern of witty attack, which allows her a measure of vengeance and self-assurance. In the next novel, *Phineas Finn*, however, she is not only far less central but has a very different part to play, a part, more-over, which demands a different character. She is now praised for her capacity to change, to find ease in her position; 'she adapts herself', the old Duke says fondly (57). She is now the fidgety, class-conscious aristocrat. She wants to exercise all the power she can muster to persuade either Marie or the Duke not to marry the other one and upset the smooth running of things: 'Nobody had felt the injustice of such coercion when applied to herself more sharply than had Lady Glencora. But she had lived to acknowledge that such coercion might be proper, and was now prepared to use it in any shape in which it might be made available' (62). The narrator is aware of the irony here, of course, but the explanation for Lady Glencora's change—her 'education' and her selfishness—is very lame. The fact is that she is now asked not only to do different things but really to *be* someone slightly different. The Glencora of *Can You Forgive Her?* would never have calculated the costs so closely; she would have felt sympathetic to the recklessness of a marriage between Marie and the Duke and would have seen in it a chance to punish both her husband and, in a deeper way, herself for her own submission. Such psychology, central in the opening novel of the chronicle, is not continued in *Phineas Finn*, however, so Glencora no longer manifests all the same traits. The character both is and is not the same. As the series goes on, we can trace further shifts. In the seamy world of *The Eustace Diamonds*, Lady Glencora becomes seamy herself, acting as a shadow character to Lizzie Eustace, some of whose features she adopts. In the last novels, Lady Glencora, now Duchess of Omnium, becomes more central, duplicating in *The Prime Minister* her husband's search for an escape from nothing. In *The Duke's Children*, the Duchess, though now dead, figures again in the Duke's memory as the rebel lover of Burgo Fitzgerald. Lady Glencora, like all the other chronicle characters, is made to conform both to the demands made by the previous novels and to the more particular demands of the novel at hand. As these demands conflict, we are made aware of the fact that the novel both does and does not have its individual integrity. Its form is both dependent on the other novels and also independent of them—both opened and closed.

When asking, then, just how old-fashioned or how modern Trollope is, one must attend fully to both fields of assumptions and methods that come together in his novels. But this does not mean that the only answer we can justly give to important questions about Trollope and his tradition are of the infuriating 'yes-and-no' sort. His affinities are clear enough: his ties are to Jane Austen and Thackeray, not to Charlotte Brontë and Dickens; and there clearly are traditions to which he can either be connected or disconnected. He is, broadly speaking, a realist, and he generally writes comic novels. So much has been commonly agreed upon, and one can proceed from there.

TROLLOPE AND THE TRADITION OF REALISM

Trollope's adoption of the standards of formal realism appears to be wholehearted. Not only did he openly reject all the conventional patterns of idealization and wish-fulfilment, but he even made repeated and very pointed jokes in his novels about the artificiality of any 'literary' convention. He proclaims his devotion to 'real life' with an insistent sincerity that is hard to ignore. Early reviewers generally took him at his word, certainly; the *Nation* called him 'the last of the realists'.[31] William Dean Howells apparently recognized in Trollope a close approximation of his own practices and therefore gave very high praise: 'In all time the most artistic, that is to say the most truthful English novelist was Anthony Trollope.'[32] Trollope himself, like virtually every other artist since time began, claimed that his model was life itself: 'It has always been my object to draw my little pictures as like to life as possible.'[33] There was nothing he hated so much as 'exaggeration'; that was the fault of Dickens, of the 'abominable' novels of Mrs. Stowe, of Rhoda Broughton—even his own mother 'was unable to avoid the pitfalls of exaggeration'.[34]

---

[31] 'Mr. Trollope's Last Novel', *Nation*, 31 (19 Aug. 1880), 139.

[32] 'Novel-Writing and Novel-Reading: An Impersonal Explanation', ed. William M. Gibson, *BNYPL*, 62 (1958), 21. The praise is repeated in Howells' *My Literary Passions: Criticism and Fiction* (New York: Harper and Brothers, 1895), where Trollope is called 'one of the finest of artists' (p. 247).

[33] 'The Genius of Nathaniel Hawthorne', p. 204.

[34] On Dickens, see *Autobiography*, p. 248; on Mrs. Stowe, letter to Lady Pollock, n.d., *Letters*, p. 500; on Rhoda Broughton, in a letter to her, 28 June 1868, *Letters*, p. 222 ('The fault here is of exaggeration'); on his mother, *Autobiography*, p. 33.

Without underrating Trollope's reluctance to depend much on plot and sensational incident or his reliance on the quiet subtlety of revealing dialogue, one should still not be taken in too completely by his claims. Trollope was not taken in himself. In a famous passage in the *Autobiography*, he protests against the crudity of the distinction between realist and sensationalist, arguing that every good novel should not just mix the two but *be* both realistic and sensational, 'and both in the highest degree' (pp. 226–7). He saw very clearly that 'realism' was itself a convention, referring to 'life' no more or no less than stories about giants and dragons: 'And yet in very truth the realistic must not be true—but just so far removed from truth as to suit the erroneous idea of truth which the reader may be supposed to entertain.' Realism is defined as 'that which shall seem to be real' (*Thackeray*, 9). This *seeming*, of course, will be governed by the expectations of the reader, expectations which, in turn, are controlled by the tradition and the rhetorical ability of the novelist.

This 'seeming-to-be-real' realism was to be obtained, Trollope argued, primarily through a careful use of language. One must not, as Scott so often did, 'leave on the mind of the most unpractised reader a sensation of made up words'.[35] The style must achieve simulation of truth, no easy task certainly: the novelist must 'steer between absolute accuracy of language—which would give to his conversation an air of pedantry, and the slovenly inaccuracy of ordinary talkers,—which if closely followed would offend by an appearance of grimace, as to produce upon the ear of his readers a sense of reality' (*Autobiography*, p. 240). Trollope is speaking here of dialogue, but we can recognize the basic formula for his plain, nondescript style: a language so carefully constructed around the reader's idea of reality that the language itself will seem to become transparent.[36] At its best, the style will be so artfully developed that not only the evidence of art but the style itself will disappear, creating the illusion of a direct participation with reality, not with 'made up words' but with actual 'talk'. The idea of clarity is

[35] Quoted in Bradford A. Booth, 'Trollope on Scott: Some Unpublished Notes', *NCF*, 5 (1950–1), 226.

[36] The great lucidity of Trollope's style is discussed by Ruth apRoberts, 'Anthony Trollope, or the Man with No Style at All,' *VNL*, No. 35 (1969), pp. 10–13, and by P. D. Edwards, *Anthony Trollope*, Profiles in Lit. Series (London: Routledge and Kegan Paul, 1969), p. 5. Trollope recognized the effect his style had: 'No doubt many a literary artist so conceals his art that readers do not know that there is much art. But they like the books and read them,—not knowing why' (letter to Henry Merivale Trollope, 19 Nov. 1877, *Letters*, p. 386).

inseparable, then, from ideas of rhetoric: when Bell, in *The Small House at Allington*, tells her mother, 'I like a book to be clear as running water, so that the whole meaning may be seen at once', Mrs. Dale answers, 'The quick seeing of the meaning must depend a little on the reader, must it not?' (44). One man's clarity may be another's murkiness, but the reader is the final judge. He must be convinced of the reality of the art, whatever reality in fact may be. In this sense, Trollope's style works effectively in the service of pure realism.

When we think of how often artists like Dickens asked their language to do what it could not, it is astonishing how seldom Trollope's style fails to provide for him just the transparency he wants. There are times in *La Vendée*—'female beauty and female worth will be made to suffer ten thousand deaths from the ruthless atrocities of republican foes' (14)—and in *Nina Balatka*—'She is to me my cup of water when I am hot and athirst' (6)—when Trollope depends on style to give a certain foreign flavour, and the results are ludicrous enough. Trollope mastered a disappearing style and generally knew better than to ask it to appear and to work for him. He achieves his effects very largely through a uniform and plain style, a liberal use, for instance, of 'imprecise, multi-purpose words' like 'pretty'[37] that appear to make no special demands on the reader and thus claim no special attention. The style is so unmetaphoric that the very rare bursts—'the air was as soft as a mother's kiss to her sleeping child' (*The Vicar of Bullhampton*, 2)—are very startling. Even passages of analysis tend to mask their art by leading us, at their climax, to the styleless comfort of a proverbial saying about touching pitch and being defiled, the wind being tempered to the shorn lamb, and the like. Very often the simple, unpretentious diction allows for and hides a syntax that is repetitious and thus obviously arranged, artificial: '"Because you have been bad," say they who are not bad to those who are bad . . .' (*The Vicar of Bullhampton*, 52). The bald repetitions alert us to the simple-mindedness of what is to come. This deceptively plain language can be used to make the most intricate artistic manœuvrings unobtrusive—psychological probing and analysis, for instance:

[37] This point is made by David Aitken, whose analyses of Trollope's style, ' "A Kind of Felicity": Some Notes about Trollope's Style', *NCF*, 20 (1965–6), 337–53, are very useful, as are those by Hugh Sykes Davies, 'Trollope and His Style', *REL*, 1, No. 4 (Oct. 1960), 73–85, and *Trollope*, Writers and Their Work, No. 118 (London: Longmans, 1960), 29–32, and by Geoffrey Tillotson, 'Trollope's Style'.

'And though, after a fashion, [Lizzie] knew herself to be false and bad, she was thoroughly convinced that she was ill-used by everybody about her' (*The Eustace Diamonds*, 21). The easy-going 'after a fashion' tells us, without seeming to, how Lizzie can hold contradictory notions in her mind; it indicates levels of consciousness with quiet delicacy. In a similar way, the Duke's anger at his wife's vulgar transformation of Gatherum is analysed: 'It angered him to think that there was so little of simplicity left in the world that a man could not entertain his friends without such a fuss as this. His mind applied itself frequently to the consideration of the money, not that he grudged the loss of it, but the spending of it in such a cause. And then perhaps there occurred to him an idea that all this should not have been done without a word of consent from himself' (*The Prime Minister*, 19). As the Duke's thoughts proceed from the blandly general to the intensely personal, the sentences become more roundabout, circumlocutionary. The first motive stated is easy, flattering, and directly available to his mind: 'It angered him'. The second is more difficult, brings up troubled associations (since some of the money was originally Glencora's): 'His mind applied itself frequently to the consideration'. The last issue, the inner circle, is at the heart of his dilemma and the secret power struggle he is having with his wife: 'And then perhaps there occurred to him an idea'. The layers of the Duke's mind, from the outer shell of public morality to the inner doubts of his own position, are exposed with great suggestiveness. And with fine indirectness: the 'perhaps' in the last sentence does an enormous amount of work. A writer more self-consciously 'psychological' would have required a few sentences at least to do what Trollope's 'perhaps' does.

Style is seen by Trollope, then, as a means for creating an illusion, particularly the illusion that there is no style.[38] Language does not so much create as serve; in *The Duke's Children* style is spoken of as a mere 'vehicle' for the important wares (26). The wares in this case are the details of the pure story: 'Now among us plain English', Trollope said, 'a plain narrative, whether in verse or prose, is everything.'[39] The idea is that the style should clear the way for the

---

[38] An illusion accepted with naïve enthusiasm by George Meredith (see letter to John Morely, 31 Mar. 1877, *The Letters of George Meredith*, ed. C. L. Cline, Oxford: Clarendon Press, 1970, i. 593) and by Lord David Cecil, *Victorian Novelists: Essays in Revaluation* (London: Constable, 1934; rpt. Chicago: Univ. of Chicago Press, 1958), p. 262.

[39] Rev. of Henry Taylor's Poems, *Fortnightly Review*, 1 (1 June 1865), 130.

narrative, providing maximum power to the hypnotic spell of the story, to the force of the traditional narrative pattern. Style, thus, serves the closed form and is, on the whole, a means by which Trollope makes the ancient patterns of comedy seem modern and real. This 'old-fashioned' style stands against such opening devices as those employed by the dramatized narrator and the subplots, thus ensuring one part of the tension. To this extent the style does tie Trollope to the tradition of realism.

But the typically realistic world is one which is very sharply *seen*. It is a crowded, materialistic world which convinces us of its total reality generally by convincing us of the reality of the objects in it. It is a world of things, a visual world. Trollope's world, however, is much more aural than visual. There is often a sense of a crowd but very seldom a sense of a scene. A less cinematic art would be difficult to imagine. There is rarely much sense of setting—'I myself cannot describe places',[40] Trollope lamented—and even less of physical objects. People are there, of course, but they are defined by their talk. Talk becomes about the only objective correlative in Trollope. That is why the narrator, the best talker of all, is such an important character.

Trollope does seem materialistic in a certain sense, as in his war on abstractions and his hilarious means for refuting Ruskin's attack on English taste by citing 'the market value of a Titian in England at the present day'.[41] Trollope's admiration for money is really an admiration for getting money, for ambition, that is, and for the power and comfort it can secure. His materialism, in other words, is really non-objective. With important objects like Gatherum Castle, the symbolism is made to work psychologically and not physically. The Castle is the cluster of associations it calls forth: fear, worship, awe, envy, hatred, discomfort. None of these has any compelling reference to its physical being.

Trollope's frequent joke about the necessity for providing descriptions for his characters is to the point here. Even more than the usual reminders of artifice inserted throughout, these comments direct us away from an illusion of real life to a sense of artificiality so extreme it finally has no visual shape. The implication is that reality is entirely divorced from our usual modes of perception; it exists only in pure art, outside of nature altogether. In *An Old*

---

[40] 'Henry Wadsworth Longfellow', *North American Review*, 132 (1881), 390.
[41] Rev. of *Sesames and Lilies*, *Fortnightly Review*, 1 (15 July 1865), 634.

Man's Love he admits to having misgivings about providing descriptions at all but agrees finally to give one of his heroine: 'But the attempt must be made, if only for fashion sake' (3). He tries to proceed but soon interrupts the attempt: 'But yet I am not describing her after the accepted fashion.' At the end of the description he is dissatisfied and annoyed, particularly annoyed with the stupid reader who has forced him to such useless labour: 'All the power of language which the writer possesses has been used in thus reproducing [her features]. But now, when this portion of his work is done, he feels sure that no reader of his novel will have the slightest idea of what Mary Lawrie was like.' What Mary Lawrie 'was like' has nothing at all to do with how she appeared. So we may as well close our eyes entirely.

Trollope is, then, both tied to and separated from the realist tradition. He admired Jane Austen and Thackeray, had problems liking the work of his friend George Eliot, was equivocal about Scott and quite unequivocal about Dickens. He had little in common with his great contemporaries: the real ties are backwards to Jane Austen and forwards to the late James and Virginia Woolf. Trollope felt totally estranged from Dickens, whose views and methods could not be more distant. Granting a certain power to Dickens, Trollope still felt that there was something monstrous about that power, something brutal and coarse about the method: 'ignorant, and thick-skinned' was the way he described him to George Eliot.[42] With Eliot herself he had scarcely more in common. Though sharing many of the same ironic perceptions and the same biases toward realism, George Eliot's intellectualized fiction and her rhetoric of contemplation were alien to Trollope. Try as he might, he could not believe fully in her method: *Daniel Deronda* is 'all wrong in art': 'She lacks ease'; 'She is sometimes heavy—sometimes abstruse, sometimes almost dull,—but always like an egg, full of meat.'[43] Both Trollope and George Eliot believed in the novel as an effective moral agency, both were realists, both used a narrator as a strong rhetorical weapon. The fact that Trollope felt so distant from

[42] Letter to George Eliot and George Henry Lewes, 27 Feb. 1872, *Letters*, p. 291. There is an interesting contrast worked out between Trollope and Dickens by James Gindin, *Harvest of a Quiet Eye*, pp. 54–5. The only strong parallel I can find is in the use of Americans, where Trollope seems sometimes to borrow from Dickens.

[43] See letter to Mary Holmes, 27 May 1876, *Letters*, p. 354; *Autobiography*, p. 246; and letter to Mary Holmes, 18 Sept. 1874, *Letters*, p. 323.

her art suggests how central to him was his own particular rhetoric of deceptive ease and relaxation. This brilliant rhetorical narrator is doubtless a legacy from Trollope's acknowledged master, Thackeray, and there is a strong critical tradition linking the two. Actually, though, the correspondence is easily exaggerated. The melancholy tone, a conservative sense of loss and bitterness, and the rhetorical tricks available to the narrator are sometimes similar. These are important ties, but the dissimilarities are very great. Despite his veneration for *Henry Esmond*, Trollope looked on Thackeray mostly as a satirist, an occupation for which he felt very little respect.[44] He thought that satire was an easy oversimplification and that Thackeray's 'zeal was at last greater than his discrimination' (*Thackeray*, 2). Thackeray's rhetoric, correspondingly, urges the reader to judge just where Trollope wants to suspend or to complicate judgement. Thackeray, finally, is a moralist whose ties to the eighteenth century are far stronger than Trollope could understand or sympathize with. As a result, Trollope's book on Thackeray is so grumbling and so often harsh that, as with George Eliot, the good will seems a little forced. It should not surprise us that Thackeray's family was upset by Trollope's efforts.

The strongest and most revealing connection, in any event, is not with Thackeray but with Jane Austen. Kathleen Tillotson points out that of the great novelists of the period only Trollope speaks of reading her in his youth.[45] The other major novelists seem to have been far more influenced by Scott, about whom Trollope spoke with very restrained enthusiasm.[46] Jane Austen was 'my chief favourite among novelists',[47] and she provided Trollope with a method and an aesthetic. Not that their novels are identical, of course. R. H. Hutton, in one of those rare and quite brilliant flashes of nineteenth-century criticism, says about all there is to say on the essential differences between Jane Austen's pastoral world, where one has a sense of 'perfect seclusion, ample opportunity, plenty of space, and plenty of time' and the *invaded* world of Trollope, where everyone 'is more or less under pressure' and where

---

[44] 'And satyre runs ever into exaggeration, leaving the conviction that not justice but revenge, is desired' (letter to Alfred Austin, 2 May 1870, *Letters*, p. 266).

[45] *Novels of the Eighteen-Forties* (Oxford: Clarendon Press, 1954), p. 144.

[46] He says he marvels 'at the power of story-telling, at the infinite imagination, and 20-horse-power of vivacity—But there is an infinity of padding, and a great amount of very lax work' (letter to Mary Holmes, 8 July 1875, *Letters*, p. 342).

[47] To Richard Bentley, 20 Nov. 1869, *Letters*, p. 250.

'everywhere time is short'. There is, he says, a 'sense of the aggres-
siveness of the outer world' in Trollope that Jane Austen's world is
without. Because of this, while Austen's characters are purely and
always themselves, 'Trollope's people are themselves so far as the
circumstances of the day will allow them to be themselves'; 'very
often', however, they 'are much distorted from their most natural
selves'.[48] But despite these differences, despite the fact that in
Trollope Jane Austen's methods and assumptions are being tested
under new conditions, Trollope received from Austen what he most
needed: a confirmation of the wonderful potential in the comedy of
manners tradition for exploring human life with delicacy and
profundity.

TROLLOPE AND THE COMEDY OF MANNERS TRADITION

Bradford Booth lamented that 'Trollope rarely attempts more than
the comedy of manners'.[49] That is true enough, though it hardly
carries with it the penalties Booth imagined. Trollope's attachment
to the tradition of the comedy of manners is, however, as deceptive
as his realism. While he accepts many of the values and assumptions
dear to the comedy of manners, he does not accept fully the comedy
of manners form. The morality and the grounds for behaviour are
traditional, but there is a sense that the world at large no longer
gives support to these assumptions and that they are, therefore,
detached, sometimes even absurd. They seem no longer to provide
the source for community, and the establishment of community,
after all, is the basis of comedy. Unlike the novels of Jane Austen,
a Trollope novel cannot merely test and confirm these values. In
each novel they must be redefined, remade, and reinstituted. As
with the tradition of realism, then, Trollope works in the comedy of
manners tradition without having any of the comforts of a tradition.
There is a complex of values, positions, and beliefs there ready-
made, but where is that sort of life now manifest? Who will accept
these values to the point of being guided by them? Who, even, will
understand? There is an implicit sense of opposition to the comedy
of manners values, then, that is made clear in the disruption of
form. All the old confidence is gone and with it the patterned
symmetry.

---

[48] 'From Miss Austen to Mr. Trollope', *Spectator*, 55 (16 Dec. 1882), 1609–11.

[49] *Anthony Trollope*, p. 24. Booth says that this is the reason his novels 'do not
move us profoundly' (p. 43).

But the values themselves are there as they always were. The standards of enlightened and sophisticated civilization are central. The stability provided allows for understanding, for the expression of warmth and kindness through wit. The central discovery of the comedy of manners is perhaps that the confidence that allows for indirection also allows for far more radiance than simple, blunt openness. Trollope writes to his brother, for instance, on hearing that they expect a child: 'The pleasures of paternity have been considerably abridged, since the good old Roman privilege of slaying their offspring at pleasure, has been taken from fathers. But the delights of flagellation, though less keen, are more enduring. One can kill but once; but one may flog daily.'[50] Often the civilized standards are supported by attacks on the *naïveté* of alternate modes, particularly on modes of simplicity like the romance or pastoral: 'Robinson Crusoe could hardly have been particular about his bed; and though in fiction many comforts have been attributed to him, the thoughtful reader, reading between the lines, will have recognised his many deficiencies' (*How the 'Mastiffs' went to Iceland*, p. 7). This tone, though prissier than usual in Trollope, does suggest the judicious coolness of the undeluded, the sense that one's own being and one's civilization are so firmly rooted and secure that they can do very well without excitement. Excessive zeal is seen as immature, potentially dangerous, since it exhibits a distrust of the basic security and thus threatens it: 'I am no Puritan myself, and fancy that had I lived in the day of the Puritans, I should have been anti-Puritan to the full extent of my capabilities' (*North America*, 3).[51]

One naturally strives, therefore, for command and understanding of the self, not for radical transformations.[52] Thus the great importance of the motif of education. Despite Trollope's distrust of rationalism—Robespierre, he says, 'seems almost to have been sent into the world to prove the inefficacy of human reason to effect human happiness' (*La Vendée*, 22)—the emphasis on education does tie him to certain rational notions of progressive development and logical training. Trollope's novels manage, however, to

---

[50] To Thomas Adolphus Trollope, 5 Oct. 1852, *Letters*, p. 17.

[51] Similar to this are his comments on patriotism; for example, 'One is patriotic only because one is too small & too weak to be cosmopolitan' (letter to Kate Field, 23 Aug. 1862, *Letters*, p. 118).

[52] Trollope wrote in the margin of his copy of Bacon's essay 'Of Nature in Men': 'A Man should surely train his nature and not strive to alter it' (see Michael Sadleir, 'Trollope and Bacon's Essays', *Trollopian*, 1, No. 1 (Summer 1945), 28.

accept the belief in education and the trust in maturity while rejecting the rationalistic premises. He was consistently strong on the superiority of age to youth, claiming that youth had no advantage whatever for any real work; in fact age 'is so much better [than youth] that it may be doubted whether youth is justified in making public its work by any other consideration than that of the doubt whether maturity may come'.[53] The means for reaching this maturity, however, were to Trollope much more simple than they were to rationalists. In the place of deliberate, careful training, Trollope put his trust in time and experience. The absolute opposite of James Mill, Trollope would have regarded a child of five who knew Greek and Latin as a freak, probably less mature, in his sense, than one who had banged about, in a miscellaneous, unplanned way, in the nursery and in schools. Over and over, his novels define education in terms of the training of the imagination[54] through a complex and gradual battle with experience, not as a development of the intellect through a planned immersion in recognized fields of knowledge. Arithmetic may perhaps be taught in this way but nothing important: 'The simple teaching of religion has never brought large numbers of Natives to live in European habits; but I have no doubt that European habits will bring about religion' (*South Africa*, ii. 188). The subtle 'habits' of a civilization are equivalent to its spiritual life, and one must develop the sensitivity to recognize that.

Trollope's works are neither sentimental nor naïve about civilization. His considerations on the spread of the glories of Western civilization through colonization contain many sarcastic references to the improvement of other cultures by extinguishing them, the great difficulty of making 'a wretched savage understand that you intend to do good to him, when he clearly does perceive that you intend to take away from him everything that he calls his own'.[55] There is very often present a Hobbesian view of man and of the uses of civilization: 'Mankind in general take pleasure in cruelty, though those who are civilized abstain from it on principle' (*The Three Clerks*, 40). Despite all this, Trollope's tough view of civilization is never cynical. His basic myth is one of wholeness, of home

---

[53] To Alfred Austin, 2 May 1870, *Letters*, p. 266.

[54] A point discussed also by Polhemus, *The Changing World*, p. 240.

[55] *The Tireless Traveller: Twenty Letters to the Liverpool Mercury by Anthony Trollope, 1875*, ed. Bradford A. Booth (Berkeley and Los Angeles: Univ. of Cal. Press, 1941), p. 133.

and family; he had a 'feeling for the vast integrity of civilization'.[56] Despite the defects of that civilization, then, he understands that the stability of the myth requires continuity and that those who would 'improve' the civilization are therefore those who do not understand it, who have never been educated to full citizenship. Idealists and Utopian reformers in Trollope are usually, like Mr. Turnbull in the political novels, men with no private being, hollowed-out people with no imagination, unfortunate outcasts from the very civilization they seek to transform. Like Dickens, Trollope often uses America as a symbol for the rubbish heap where all the uncivilized reformers are piled; the capital, Washington, 'raised up with all imaginable perfections and in accordance with high-flown theories',[57] is unfit for comfortable life. The theoretical man is, finally, dead, divorced from life.

But the theoretical man, more exactly the unconscious man, seems in most Trollope novels to be everywhere. He can no longer be symbolically contained in America. As a result there is in Trollope no less than in Matthew Arnold a characteristic tone of lost-cause melancholy. The values are there, as always, clear and firm, but they seem to have no currency. As a result we often get the sense that the narrator is defining values that nowhere really exist, that he is using the world of the narrative to plead hopelessly for another world. 'What is there which damaging time does not diminish?' Trollope quotes from Horace (*The New Zealander*, 4), and we recognize in this tone his essential conservatism.[58] Trollope does not sentimentalize the past, and in fact often pokes fun at that sort of sentimentality, that feeling for 'the sweet mediaeval flavour of old English corruption' (*Clergymen of the Church of England*, p. 28). His conservatism is rather a feeling for a greater wholeness that could be found in values more purely instinctual and traditional than modern man can recognize. The pressures modern man feels and creates for himself in Trollope's world build up layers of defences, a cover of insensitivity that makes impossible the delicate,

[56] Paul Elmer More, 'My Debt to Trollope', p. 124.
[57] 'The Present Condition of the Northern States of the American Union', *Four Lectures*, ed. Morris L. Parrish, p. 52.
[58] Many of Trollope's contemporaries recognized 'the essential and deep-rooted conservatism of his mind' (T. H. S. Escott, *Anthony Trollope: His Work, Associates and Literary Originals*, London: John Lane, 1913, p. 105) that existed at a level where his 'instincts and feelings' dominated his presumably liberal theories; see [Lucas Collins], 'Autobiography of Anthony Trollope', *Blackwood's*, 134 (Nov. 1883), 592.

imaginative behaviour that is at the heart of the moral life of the comedy of manners. Men are so hidden from themselves and from one another that mere blindness has replaced a confident, if equally thoughtless, instinct. Hence, the appeal for openness, the recurrence of the expressed desire for simple honesty. The feeling is exactly the same as that in Tennyson's *Idylls of the King*, where an equally desperate appeal is made for honesty. Tennyson's Arthur is not at all unlike such Trollope characters as Roger Carbury,[59] equally displaced and absurd.

One must finally accept things as they are: 'Things are very far from being perfect. Things are always very far from being perfect.'[60] But the acceptance of an untransformed world is a brave act in Trollope's novels. Though absolutely central to the comedy of manners form, the rejection of illusion is far more dangerous in Trollope than in Jane Austen. It is an act necessary for maturity and the full moral life, but it is both triumphant and desolating: 'It is sad to say it, and sad to think of it, but failure is the ordinary lot of man' (*Clergymen of the Church of England*, p. 74). The liberation found when delusions are cast away is often matched by a strong sense that the real world's freedom may not amount to much. An imaginative and fully mature physician in *He Knew He Was Right* says, 'The truth is, Mr. Burgess . . . a doctor doesn't know so very much more about these things than other people' (51). This is a fine and moral statement, reassuring in its affirmation of a union of all men. But it doesn't give us much hope against disease. On one hand, the joys of the small things to be realized *now* are exalted, but there is a price to pay. As Lady Chiltern says, 'We all profess to believe when we're told that this world should be used merely as a preparation for the next; and yet there is something so cold and comfortless in the theory that we do not relish the prospect even for our children' (*Phineas Redux*, 2). This is heady and exhilarating; it allows us to escape from futurism and to live fully now. But it removes our prop against death. And Trollope is resolute in rejecting the myths of sacrifice and redemption.

Aware as Trollope is of the price one pays for this bleak awareness, he protects us against the full desolation of this view by

---

[59] Trollope seemed to think of this character as some absolute alternative to deviousness. In his notes for the novel, reprinted in Sadleir's *Trollope: A Commentary*, p. 426, the entire character of Carbury is thus set by his openness: 'ROGER CARBURY of Carbury Hall in Norfolk. 38. Straightforward.'

[60] 'Higher Education of Women', *Four Lectures*, ed. Morris L. Parrish, p. 77.

insisting over and over again on a distinction between men and the abstractions they seem to need: 'In my days I have written something about clergymen but never a word about religion' (*South Africa*, i. 258). The distinction becomes even finer: man as a social being is sharply separated from man as a private person; the former might be guilty of all sorts of stupidity and cruelty, but the individual as he really is is generally seen as well-meaning, if not quite innocent.[61] People in Trollope do not become objectified as they do in Dickens; they never quite become their occupations. This protection of the essential private self makes for a dislocated world, but it can also make for comedy. Collective vices are intolerable, but any individual frailty can not only be tolerated but welcomed: 'Readers will also find that by devoting an hour or two on Saturday to the criticisms of the week, they will enable themselves to have an opinion about the books of the day. The knowledge so acquired will not be great, nor will that little be lasting; but it adds something to the pleasure of life to be able to talk on subjects of which others are speaking' (*Autobiography*, p. 269).

This essential division explains many contradictions. It explains, for instance, why Trollope could, on the one hand, express approval for making money—'we know that the more a man earns the more useful he is to his fellow-men' (*Autobiography*, p. 106); he became furious with Ruskin's attack on the Goddess of Getting on,[62] who, to Trollope, was a goddess to be respected. On the other hand, he attacks rigorously the corrosive effects of a system which is based on the very drive he praises. The vile effects of capitalism on fox hunts, on club life, on the customs of courtship, on married life, on the spiritual being of the age are pitilessly scourged. Properly seen, though, there is no contradiction. Because the social fabric has been nearly dissolved by the shifty and incoherent power of money, people in Trollope are far more free to move, but they are faced with far greater dangers than in the old stratified world. Because women are invested with a great symbolic stability, their position in a fluid society is even more tenuous. There is, then, one genuine ambiguity in Trollope, taken as a whole: approval is given both to those who strive, who make money, who *do*, who achieve power,

---

[61] [Lucas Collins], 'Autobiography of Anthony Trollope', p. 593, emphasizes this point, and Sadleir remarks that Trollope 'regarded private persons with a friendly optimism but society with cynical distrust' (*Trollope: A Commentary*, p. 153).

[62] See his review of Ruskin's *Crown of Wild Olives*, *Fortnightly Review*, 5 (15 June 1866), 381–4.

and to those who are humble, passive, and retiring. The two irre-
concilables are finally combined in the brilliantly ironic position of
the Duke of Omnium as Prime Minister. He advances to the very
heart of power and finds there nothing at all.

All these points really represent a cluster of values, of course,
a rich and integrated network of assumptions modified from the
original convention but modified as a whole and not sporadically.
As such, they represent an artistic source far deeper than an 'idea'.
I suppose it is true that Trollope had no real ideas as such, a fact
that has disturbed many.[63] In areas where ideas are necessary, he
was weak: his journalism is tiresome; his travel books are very thin;
and his literary criticism is surely among the poorest ever written.
In place of ideas he has only a few crotchets. But ideas seem so
unnecessary to literature, at least to the tradition of the comedy of
manners, that Trollope's defect in this regard seems a positive
virtue. His crotchets are transformed by his engulfing imagination
out of the bare, pitiful world of thought into his fictional world as
rich symbols. Even the opinions he held most firmly, say on fox-
hunting, civil service examinations, and politics, have no chance to
make it as ideas in his fiction. We know from Trollope's letters, his
journalism, and his *Autobiography* that he was a passionate, almost
manic, defender of fox-hunting, that he hated competitive examinations deeply, and that he had very strong views on the importance
of being in the House of Commons, even if he strikes us as cynical
on the subject of what one does when one gets there.

Though Trollope doubted whether he had not dragged fox-
hunting into too many novels (*Autobiography*, p. 64), he need not have
worried. Fox-hunting may be used for a million fictional purposes,
but it usually stands as a very effective symbol for community and
for joy, whose ends—well, never mind the ends, since the means
are so satisfying. It is the process of hunting that is crucial, let the
results be as asinine, even as cruel, as they may be. It gets people
together, and 'a man in a hunting county who opposes the county
hunt must be a misanthrope, willing to live in seclusion, fond of
being in Coventry, and in love with the enmity of his fellow-
creatures' (*Castle Richmond*, 24). It also provides some joy in the

---

[63] James, ironically, complained often in his early reviews of the absence of ideas in
Trollope. For modern continuations, see Arthur Mizener, 'Anthony Trollope: The
Palliser Novels', p. 161, and Clara C. Park, 'Trollope and the Modern Reader', *MR*, 3
(1961–2), 577–91. T. S. Eliot's classic attack on this general fallacy is extended by
W. J. Harvey, *Character and the Novel*, pp. 25–6.

doing, and the experiencing of joy is something 'in which we Englishmen most signally fail'; 'there are so many of us who have nothing
that we like' (*The New Zealander*, 10). The hunt is justified in terms
of what it does, not in terms of what it is, and what it does must be
understood psychologically, in the complex experience, not abstractly
in the sterile area of generalized morality or 'ideas'. Thus Trollope's
idea is shaped by the fiction into something like an anti-idea.

The same thing happens with competitive examinations. Though
the commentary here is admittedly somewhat sharper, again the
protest leaves the realm of ideas and enters the fabric of the novel.
Competitive exams are dangerous not only because the abstract
theories of equality they imply are abstractly bad but also because
they demonstrate a disregard for the traditional values being promoted by the novel. Exams are crude just where delicacy is needed.
They are, further, enemies of community and, thus, of the comic
form being promoted: 'The world . . . will soon be like a fishpond,
very full of fish, but with very little food for them. Every one is
scrambling for the others' prey, and they will end at last by eating
one another' (*The Three Clerks*, 11). Finally, such exams are
completely heartless: 'With us, let the race be ever to the swift, the
victory always to the strong. And let us always be racing, so that the
swift and strong shall ever be known among us. But what, then, for
those who are not swift, not strong?' (*The Bertrams*, 1). None of
these values is imported into the novels for the purpose really of
condemning the operation of the civil service; they are intrinsic to
these novels and thus are welcome as compact and clear symbols for
a cluster of values which is forward-looking, self-centred, contemptuous of tradition, and thus, finally, anti-comic. Because the
examination system is based on the judgement of results, its utility
as a symbol for the simple-minded belief in ordered, patterned life
is obvious. Trollope loves to attack the platitude, 'Whatever is
worth doing is worth doing well', since the whole point in his comic
novels is in the *doing*, not in displaying the final product. Thus he
hates excellence and promotes the simple value of 'competence'.
His one absolutism is the pure value of work. Thus in his book on
Thackeray he is obsessed with his subject's 'idleness' and, despite
his best intentions, cannot pay much attention to the fine novels.
Thus, too, he could not stop for a moment to contemplate a finished
novel before starting to write the next. Contemplation is to Trollope
the erecting of a tombstone; endings are a kind of death.

Politics, therefore, is exactly like fox-hunting, or the civil service (without exams), or whist, or writing novels. It is the greatest work of man in process, and an Englishman's greatest ambition should be to serve in Parliament. But he should never mistake the life-giving greatness of politics with getting things done. And so it is with all life. Marrying is wonderfully joyous, but marriage itself can easily turn empty. And love, the heart of Trollope's world, is finally defined in this way: 'The beauty of it all was not so much in the thing loved, as in the loving' (*He Knew He Was Right*, 25).

We can see, then, why Trollope is so little interested in ideas, in reforms, in alternatives or changes. In part, he is the traditionalist, holding to the values of the past; in part he is, as Rebecca West says, akin to the modern existentialist in seeing life as absurd, alternatives as ludicrous.[64]

THE SHAPE OF TROLLOPE'S CAREER

So Trollope is both tied to the comedy of manners and the realist traditions and liberated from them. He is both the most conventional and most modern of writers, and his formal patterns both adhere to convention with great and sensitive determination and at the same time force convention to abandon all its old reliances. It is no wonder, then, that it is not easy to perceive the form of one novel, let along to describe a clear and symmetrical shape in the career of an artist who made war on symmetry. There are so many difficult questions: why did Trollope begin his career with a novel which calls into question the very values he was later to propound? What does one do with the late novels, which often are dark but which also can be mellow or even very light, as is *Ayala's Angel*? What about novels that are ambiguous—*The American Senator* or *Cousin Henry*? And how does one handle bizarre things like *The Fixed Period* or *An Old Man's Love*? Perhaps it would be most reasonable to abandon a search for pattern and discuss the novels, say, alphabetically by title.

Patterns have, of course, been perceived, most notably by Cockshut in his strong polemic on behalf of Trollope's late novels. They are, he says, darker, more 'satiric', more profound. Some support has been given to this position both by Robert Polhemus, who says that after *Doctor Thorne* Trollope's 'vision of life grows darker' and

[64] *The Court and the Castle*, p. 157.

that 'after *Phineas Redux* Trollope gave up on his society',[65] and by James Pope Hennessy, who finds in 'his later novels a tone of murky pessimism'.[66] At least Pope Hennessy seems not to equate pessimism with the sublime, a problem, surely, with many such views of a writer's progress. And most readers will probably grant that, on the whole, the late novels do seem to reflect a world with fewer possibilities. Still, an insistence on a regular pattern that leads downhill is likely to result, as it does in Cockshut, in some highly arbitrary rearrangements of the novels' emphases: this section is declared to be perfunctory, that one profound; some plots and indeed some novels are disregarded altogether. Strange value judgements must be smuggled in, and dismal novels like *Kept in the Dark* elevated over brilliant ones like *Ayala's Angel*. Psychological emphases must be played up and social ones played down, in direct defiance of the novels, which generally see even the most bizarre psychological phenomena in social terms. Here, for instance, is the narrator of *He Knew He Was Right* on insanity: 'There is perhaps no great social question so imperfectly understood among us at the present day as that which refers to the line which divides sanity from insanity' (38).

Most important, rigid views of pattern are usually based on some fallacious connections between art and 'belief', whereby the tone of novels can be traced to changes in the author's opinions or general outlook. But everywhere we look in Trollope we find 'opinions' being altered to suit the demands of the novel. In *The Last Chronicle*, *The Way We Live Now*, or *The Eustace Diamonds*, art and artistry are equated generally with falseness and lies; in *Ayala's Angel* with life itself. The prominent conflict between youth and age in *The Prime Minister* is equally prominent in the next chronicle novel, *The Duke's Children*, but the terms are exactly reversed. Examining the novels to find Trollope's view of America, to take an obvious instance, one is met with dizzying inconsistency. In *He Knew He Was Right* (1869) there are the conventional portraits of the bombastic bore and the feminist poet, but the Spalding girls are all one could hope for and the treatment on the whole is good-natured and positive. In *The Way We Live Now* (1875) America is seen through

---

[65] *The Changing World*, pp. 59, 186. To be fair, one should note that Polhemus traces a pattern more inclusive, more complex, and surely more accurate than Cockshut's, noting, for instance, the mellowing of the very last novels (see ibid., p. 215).

[66] *Anthony Trollope*, p. 145.

both Mrs. Hurtle and Hamilton K. Fisker as a violent and terribly frightening place. In *The American Senator* (1877) it is not frightening at all but childishly rationalistic, not a jungle but one large, earnest cramming establishment. There is a harsh use of American feminists in *Is He Popenjoy?* (1878), but the view in *The Duke's Children* (1880) is so warmly positive it has led some to speak of Trollope's recantation or apology. What, then, do we make of *Dr. Wortle's School* (1881), which simply reiterates the America of *Martin Chuzzlewit*, or of the bitter anti-Americanism of *The Land-leaguers* (1883)?

The answer surely is that the form of great novels has little, if anything, to do with 'opinions'. 'Like most novelists, Trollope had a repertoire of shapes and themes to meet his fictional aims', says William Cadbury.[67] Exactly, and the narrative patterns chosen for novels work together with themes to form a whole. The integrity of any novel or any group of novels cannot, then, be referred outside the system to anything as simple as the writer's views. Trollope used to joke about the writing of novels being related to the efficiency of digestion, which may have more truth in it than the views-and-opinions notion. All this is not to deny the existence of pattern or that the later novels are often different from the early ones. But different is not better,[68] and all change is not a change of mind.

What consistency there is in Trollope is most apparent to me in terms of his tendency to work with the narrative myth of comedy[69]

[67] 'Shape and Theme: Determinants of Trollope's Forms', *PMLA*, 78 (1963), 332. Cadbury's articles constitute some of the most important modern criticism on Trollope. He defends the early comic novels ('profundity is not a chicken from the egg of gloom', p. 331) and develops a comprehensive and suggestive system for grouping Trollope's novels formally. In addition to this *PMLA* article, Cadbury's work includes 'Character and the Mock Heroic in *Barchester Towers*', *TSLL*, 5 (1963–4), 509–19 and 'The Uses of the Village: Form and Theme in Trollope's *The Vicar of Bullhampton*', *NCF*, 18 (1963–4), 151–63.

[68] Most who do see the difference also, unlike Cadbury, see an improvement, even when they quarrel with Cockshut. John C. Kleis, for instance, says that the late novels are not more pessimistic, but more mature and comprehensive ('Passion vs. Prudence: Theme and Technique in Trollope's Palliser Novels', *TSLL*, 11, 1969–70, 1414). The recent publication of *The New Zealander* (Oxford: Clarendon Press, 1972), written in 1855 but unpublished until now, has done something to shake the Progress-to-Pessimism notions. The editor, N. John Hall, remarks that Trollope's career is nothing if not consistent: 'Trollope was [in later novels] not so much gloomy and pessimistic as serious and critical, and never more so than in 1855' (p. xv).

[69] The best examination of Trollope and the forms and traditions of comedy is by William A. West, '*The Last Chronicle of Barset*: Trollope's Comic Techniques', *The*

in its full range, from understated romantic comedy to highly ironic comedy of accommodation. The basic goal here is fulfilment through integration. The most important variation comes about when the myth of integration is parodied. The result is a pattern whereby comic educations are conducted but without comic knowledge being gained or comic rewards being bestowed—what Northrop Frye terms the mythos of winter, irony,[70] where the central images are of isolation, motion without purpose, meaningless frustration. The rhetoric is made to deceive us, to make us expect a resolution which, when it comes, is turned on its head.

Within these broad ranges of comedy and irony one can see a pattern, I suppose, but only if one squints hard enough to blur all the irregularities. It seems to me more useful for my purposes to place the novels according to rough groupings tied loosely to their dominant narrative patterns and to their chronology. I propose the following as a convenient grouping of this sort: The Early Comedies (1847–67), The Barsetshire Series, Variations in Irony (1867–75), The Palliser Series, The Late Experimental Novels. The last category is admittedly particularly lame, but it expresses a sense that Trollope's late novels, from *The American Senator* to *An Old Man's Love*, have about nothing in common other than the fact that each seems to challenge in very different ways the bases of the forms it operates in. The 'experiments' have about them a similar confidence and a sense of freedom in their expansion of this or that element of comedy or irony, their challenge to the limits of those patterns. This order may reveal little about Trollope's progress toward anything at all, but it will allow for an examination of novels both in terms of their individual forms and in relation to other novels which adopt similar strategies. The chronicle novels are isolated both in order to emphasize their uniqueness and to show their collective tie to the novels which were interspersed with them.

Classic British Novel, ed. Howard M. Harper, Jr., and Charles Edge (Athens: Univ. of Georgia Press, 1972), pp. 121–42.

[70] There is a good treatment of Trollope's ironic *technique* in *The Moral Trollope*, pp. 55–71, 190–97, but apRoberts does not deal very fully with the narrative pattern of irony I am discussing here. E. S. Dallas has the finest description of one of the effects of this irony, a sort of delayed backlash effect: he says that, after we finish reading, 'we begin to think to ourselves,—"But, after all, how very stupid the people are to act in that way; they acted like idiots; they were to all appearance continually doing the very opposite of what they ought to have done, and with full knowledge running their heads against walls" ' ('Anthony Trollope', *The Times*, 23 May 1859, p. 12).

The hope is to demonstrate relationships, but more important to illustrate Trollope's formal sophistication and variety, the astonishing dexterity he showed in both confirming and radically modifying tradition, opening the same form he was shaping, looking backward and forward at once.

PART II

The Novels

CHAPTER 3

THE EARLY COMEDIES
(*1847-1867*)

THE BARSETSHIRE chronicle consists of a series of variations on the comic myth of renewal and preservation. Viewed as a sequence, the novels exhibit quite a wide variety, testing the comic proposition by probing it in different directions and with different means in each novel. Viewed against the background of the novels surrounding it, those whose publication was interspersed with the series, the chronicle's unity and basic stability become clear. Whereas the Barsetshire series moves carefully in different areas of comedy, the other early novels career wildly about and sometimes knock down the fences. The early novels outside the chronicle explore the limits of comedy with more abandon and often with the singleness of direction we associate with experiments. Though they are clearly more than just sketches preliminary to the chronicle novels, they define a wide range of themes and techniques which could be tested and refined for use within that chronicle. These early comic novels are less assured and less accomplished than the Barsetshire novels, but not for that reason always less interesting.

The pattern of experimentation seems clear enough once the Barsetshire series is extracted from Trollope's early career. After the apprenticeship novels—*The Macdermots of Ballycloran* (1847), *The Kellys and the O'Kellys* (1848), and *La Vendée* (1850)—and the eccentric *The Three Clerks* (1858), the next three novels—*The Bertrams* (1859), *Castle Richmond* (1860), and *Orley Farm* (1862)— explore in ever-increasing complexity the dark, ironic corners of comedy, and the following three[1]—*Rachel Ray* (1863), *Miss Mackenzie* (1865), and *The Belton Estate* (1866)—suddenly switch position and develop the possibilities of romantic comedy.

Trollope's first three novels—*The Macdermots*, *The Kellys*, and *La Vendée*—have had their defenders, at least the first two novels

---

[1] One of the many difficulties is that the second chronicle begins at this point with *Can You Forgive Her?* (1864). I can only repeat weakly that I am trying for convenient groupings, not rigorous categories.

have,[2] but they do seem to be the sorts of novels which are better in contemplation than in actual reading. Trollope himself appears to have sensed this, claiming a host of virtues for *The Macdermots*, but adding that 'the execution was *very bad*'[3] [his italics]. It is true that, as with most neglected Trollope novels, one is quite surprised to see how good they actually are, but the fact that each of these three novels seeks to exploit such radically different modes—first tragedy, then comedy, then historical romance—suggests that Trollope was searching very hard for his genre. He found it only with the publication of *The Warden*, five years after *La Vendée* failed so badly.

The Macdermots illustrates one problem Trollope always had with the novels set in Ireland. It establishes a norm for judging human activities that is so elemental and stark as to render utterly superfluous the delicate values the novel is otherwise trying to establish. It could be argued that, in fact, the Irish setting comes closer to working in this novel than in any other, since this is a tragedy which traces the decay of the old gentlemanly code in the new and chaotic world. Thady Macdermot is finally executed for trying to defend his sister's honour, a motive very few are impressed by or even understand. With him goes the whole great system of values Trollope spent nearly the rest of his career examining and, most often, trying to revivify and thus preserve. This first novel, then, uncharacteristically casts aside the values that will later be central. It examines the desperation wrought by the break-up of the chivalric code and allows physical violence to occupy the centre of the novel. One Hyacinth Keegan's foot is hacked off in five dull chops: 'the second cut the flesh, and grated against the bone' (25). It is, as the *North British Review* said, a novel of 'unmixed pain',[4] not without power, but clearly a false start for Trollope.

---

[2] Hugh Walpole is most enthusiastic, calling the neglect of the early Irish novels 'absolutely astounding' (*Anthony Trollope*, p. 25); James Pope Hennessy gives a milder defence (*Anthony Trollope*, pp. 109–10); and Robert A. Donovan carefully examines the ties between these first novels and the later work in 'Trollope's Prentice Work', *MP*, 53 (1955–6), 179–86. Comments on *La Vendée* are often quite entertaining: to Sadleir the novel is 'a work of unexampled dreariness' (*Trollope: A Commentary*, p. 146); Pope Hennessy says it is neither 'well-written [nor] competent' (*Anthony Trollope*, p. 137); Avrom Fleishman allows that it has all the subtlety of Cooper's division between frontiersmen and injuns (*The English Historical Novel: Walter Scott to Virginia Woolf*, Baltimore: Johns Hopkins, 1971, p. 177); Trollope couldn't restrain himself from joking about it too, offering an apologetic comment of a sentence or two and then saying, 'As far as I can remember, this morsel of criticism is the only one that was ever written on the book' (*Autobiography*, pp. 80–1).   [3] To Mary Holmes, 1 May 1874, *Letters*, p. 317.
[4] *North British Review*, 40 (June 1864), 394.

The Kellys and the O'Kellys is closer to Trollope's usual manner, but here the multiple plot he was later to master flies totally out of control,[5] and one plot of madness and violence exists alongside the romantic comedy without any real integration. *La Vendée* is one of those historical novels that are 'not worth a damn'.[6] The demands of exalted language, the idealistic bias, the absolutist ethics, are all so clearly alien to Trollope's nature that the novel seems simply a mistake, an educational one, though, since he never again tried anything like it.

The Three Clerks, published after the first two novels in the Barsetshire series, is as anomalous as *La Vendée*, but it is not a failure. It is as if Trollope had tried his hand at becoming a disciple of Dickens and then withdrew, not because the results were uninspiring but because he was attracted to other, far less inhabited territory. Trollope himself viewed *The Three Clerks* as 'certainly the best novel I had as yet written' (*Autobiography*, p. 111); and though we may find it difficult to see how the novel could be rated higher than *The Warden* or *Barchester Towers*, it has its own virtues. Unlike any other Trollope novel, it is 'a really brilliant tale'.[7] This comment catches exactly the right note here and explains to us also how the novel differs from others in the Trollope canon. No other Trollope novel, with the possible exception of *Brown, Jones, and Robinson*, gives the impression of having the slightest desire to be thought 'brilliant'. But *The Three Clerks* does and is, and it is thus an anomaly.

It is very witty indeed, remarkably autobiographical, ethically and morally puristic; it is centred in London, reaches toward very drastic action and extreme solutions; it employs parody as a basic principle; it is didactic. In all these ways it is uncharacteristic. Perhaps it represents an experiment whose success was too easy, too 'brilliant' to be of further use. Or perhaps it is a novel written principally to test the methods and values of *Barchester Towers*, the major novel written just before this one. *The Three Clerks* extends some of the methods of *Barchester Towers* almost to the point of

---

[5] A similar criticism of the integration of the plots is given by Donovan, 'Trollope's Prentice Work', pp. 180–2.

[6] These were the words of advice given to Trollope by the foreman of the house at Messrs. Hunt and Blackett. Trollope, then peddling *The Three Clerks*, was told, 'Whatever you do, don't be historical; your historical novel is not worth a damn' (*Autobiography*, pp. 110–11).

[7] E. S. Dallas, 'Anthony Trollope', *The Times*, p. 12.

burlesque and seems thereby to establish the limits of the utility of broad satiric comedy, a method in which Trollope fast loses interest after this novel. *The Three Clerks* also inverts the values and many of the basic assumptions of *Barchester Towers*, thus testing their validity and power.

As in *Barchester Towers* the opposition between a serenely moral country and a rapacious city is maintained. But here the focus is on the city, which is only indirectly present in *Barchester Towers*. As in Dickens, the country is something 'out there', existing without defences and almost asking to be violated: 'It was quite clear that the wolf in sheep's clothing must be admitted into the pastoral family' (14). Trollope's terms are explicit, as is the sarcastic use of 'pastoral'. The world of *Barchester Towers* is only superficially sophisticated; its values are basically those of open and gentle undefended kindness. But here such openness is distrusted. The three clerks of the title roam out from London to invade a happy and unsuspecting country home. Although the mother of the three daughters who are swept down upon is the narrator's 'own chief favourite in the tale' (3), she is repeatedly criticized for not guarding her daughters closely enough. *Barchester Towers* makes sly fun of extreme idealizations of the natural state, but by comparison this novel is a bitter attack on Rousseau. Although London itself is a bleak and terrible place, the country is treated almost with contempt for its *naïveté*. As a result of these dark premises, the approved values are much more extreme and uncomplicated than is usual in Trollope. There is also a need felt by the narrator to make these values quite emphatic. Moralisms are very common, particularly moralisms that strive to clarify absolute standards: 'There are two kinds of honesty . . . that which the world sees and that which it does not see . . . nothing that is wrong can become right because other people do it' (26). The urgency here is quite apparent, as is the simplicity of the ethical standard. Trollope's usual strategy is to complicate quietly and gradually; here he tries the opposite device of simplifying startlingly and dramatically. In *Barchester Towers* the morality is so subtle and so calm that it can be centred in the withdrawn, inactive Mr. Harding. But here, though there is a character, Harry Norman, whose firm morality also seems central and who is similarly disqualified by that morality from action, the simplifying rhetoric and the drive to uncomplicate the moral position put the Harding character in a no-man's-land. Without a complex morality to support him, Norman appears merely an oddity. He spends most of the novel sulking, until everyone, including the narrator, loses patience with him, despite his firm honour, truth, and so forth. The impatience is hardly fair, though, since he could now hardly sit and play the cello. Playing the cello is not in *The Three Clerks* a moral act—as it clearly is in *Barchester Towers*.

The attempt to import Mr. Harding into this world was a clear mistake, and the centre of the novel is really taken over by Charley Tudor, whose closest relative in *Barchester Towers* is Bertie Stanhope. Tudor is an extreme but much more successful translation of the values of Mr. Harding into an ironic and dark world. He is the first in a long line of Trollope heroes who are, like Mr. Harding, quiet and imaginative, but who are, unlike him, weak, lacking in self-knowledge, and morally culpable. Charley Tudor is also, of course, a touchingly sentimentalized version of Trollope himself, which suggests one of the many reasons why, from Charley through Johnny Eames, Phineas Finn, and Lord Silverbridge, this figure seems to be invested with the most promise, with the best chance of dealing with a world that offers very little and demands much. Charley Tudor is more exactly like Trollope than the others are, of course, echoing many of his experiences and practising the same trades. But with Charley's authorship, biographical explanations probably should give way to generic ones: Charley's stories and his descriptions of the demands of his editor and readers are used not only to parody one sort of literature but to define by contrast another, specifically the novel Trollope is writing. Charley parodies plot-ridden works—we need 'an incident for every other paragraph'—episodic sensationalism—'The editor says that the unities are altogether thrown over now, and that they are regular bosh'—moral and topical didacticism—'The editor says that we must always have a slap at some of the iniquities of the times'—and tragedy—'there must be a Nemesis. The editor specially insists on a Nemesis' (19). These comments serve the cause of artifice, providing a running critical commentary on the narrative, its form and rhetorical requirements. The burlesque, in other words, is asked to take on the task usually handled by Trollope's narrators and the subplots. The method seems to work, but in its suddenness, its dramatic intensity, and most of all its necessary sacrifice of complexity to urgency it fails to serve the ends Trollope wanted most deeply for his art. *The Three Clerks*, good as it is, is only another false start.

With *The Bertrams*, Trollope's novels begin more serious and doubtless more useful tests of the implications of the Barsetshire series. The variations on comedy developed in the chronicle are kept within a range defined by the broader excursions of these other novels. The chronicle, for all its variety, stays pretty much to the centre of the comic spectrum. The edges are explored, first in one direction and then in the other, by the six surrounding novels. *The Bertrams*, *Castle Richmond*, and *Orley Farm* all deal with dark, ironic comedy. All seem interested in testing the seriousness of opposition that can be erected and still overcome in comedy; they search for the deepest wounds that may still be healed, the grimmest effects that can be counterbalanced or smoothed over. Only the last of these, *Orley Farm*, really succeeds.

The Bertrams is perhaps the least controlled of Trollope's dark comedies. What appears at the beginning to be the main plot is submerged so deeply and for so long that it has to be hauled to the surface with much unpleasant straining at the end; the startling religious theme seems to be connected only loosely to the love stories; the sort of padding critics complain about, usually mysteriously, is for once really there, in the long descriptions of exotic cities of the east, whirling dervishes, and suchlike strangeness. Most serious, the comic form is never made sufficiently flexible to contain the great suffering and the pervasive sense of the arbitrary that abounds in the novel. The comedy thus seems superficial or even superadded. People are rescued from extremity but for no apparent reason. The rewards come to those who suffer, but why? Comedy is not usually logical, of course, but here Trollope moves us so far out of the comic environment that we certainly are not expecting comic miracles. We had thought we were in a different world.

It is a world marked by the decay of private sensitivity and public coherence. A representative citizen remarks, 'Poetry is all very well; but you can't create a taste for it if it doesn't exist. Nobody that I know cares a d—— for Iphigenia' (1). And if no one cares a damn for such fully dramatized sufferings as Iphigenia's, what sort of response can we hope for to the small, muffled sufferings of ordinary people? We soon see. When Arthur Wilkinson fails to take a first at Oxford, the intensity of his pain is stressed very sharply. In Trollope's world, this complex and impure suffering is an exact equivalent to Iphigenia's. Now, however, Arthur finds almost no response at all. His friends are made a bit uncomfortable by his bad temper, and his family feels some chagrin—for themselves. His father is angry, 'but he felt no sympathy with his son' (3). 'His mother was all affection, and kindly suggested that perhaps what had happened was for the best: she kindly suggested this more than once, but her imagination carried her no farther' (3). Even Arthur is so pre-occupied licking his own wounds that he completely misreads the tone of his sweetheart's words and thus misses her declaration of love, 'understanding perhaps accurately the wants of his own heart, but . . . quite in the dark as to the wants of that other heart' (4). Suffering is as important in this novel as it is in George Eliot, but it has even less tragic resonance and seems, therefore, both more ineffectual and less redemptive. Everyone is 'quite in the dark as to the wants of that other heart'. The public at large is treated as a huge monster of insensitivity, with neither stability nor reason. The attack on 'vox populi, vox Dei' is as bitter and as explicit as it is in D. H. Lawrence. When a conscientious public ass asserts 'with intense reliance on the civilization of his own era', 'Public opinion is the best safeguard for a great man's great name', he is met with the following appropriate sarcasm: 'Quite true, sir, quite true . . . for the space of twenty-four hours' (33). With such a view of community, it is no wonder that the novel has to struggle desperately at the end to try and tuck in the loose corners which are wildly astray. It tries finally to look like a standard novel of vocation, but we have more likely responded to it as a novel of missed opportunities, whose standard is not comic fulfilment but the agonizing shortness of life and its pointlessness.

At the centre is the story of how two of the last sensitive people alive miss connections and torture one another for no good reason. Searching for some life finer than what he sees about him, George Bertram travels to Jerusalem full of pumped-up transcendental enthusiasm. This zeal hardly stands the test of the physical dis-comfort and revolting filth he encounters everywhere. He instinctive-ly disbelieves in the authenticity of everything except for the site of the Mount of Olives, which he believes in entirely on instinct, an in-stinct so strong that even his father's indifference—'Mount of Olives, eh? . . . What is there to see there?' (8)—cannot shake it. But it is, we see, the instinct of an Englishman for tidiness—the Mount of Olives is unique in being unsmelly—not the response of an exalted Christian to miraculous truth. A good deal of fun is made of this naïve enthusiasm, and the religious attack seems to be the same one conducted within the Barsetshire series on pious nonsense. But here the securities of Barsetshire are gone entirely, and the attack on religion, once begun, has no place to end, certainly not in the evidence of enlightened gentlemanly civility on which *The Warden* or *Barchester Towers* rested. George's loss of faith comes, in fact, when he realizes that religion is not a stay against chaos but merely a part of it. The religious life is neither more coherent nor more sensitive than any other, and his belief fails precisely when that point is made: Caroline Waddington tells him to look around him at the clergy and ask himself, 'Are they generally men of wide views and enlightened principles?' (10). His faith is gone in a flash, and there is nothing left for him but the Higher Criticism and this same Caroline Waddington.

Her love could, indeed, act as some replacement for religion; together they might make some stand against the ignorant armies clashing by night. But they are separated by a series of absurdly trivial misunderstandings. With Caroline, Trollope begins to develop the figure of the rebellious woman; she resists growing 'into a piece of domestic furniture, contented to adapt itself to such use as a marital tyrant might think fit to require of it' (9). The tone is slightly humorous and satiric, actually uncertain, marking an uneasiness Trollope feels at launching into the feminist issue. But such uneasiness is only the conscious and superficial reaction to a very deep and troubling sensitivity. Caroline refuses to marry George immediately because she wants to avoid, she says, the disagreeableness of semi-poverty. But the overt theme of prudence against 'love in a cottage'[8] is soon lost in an intricate exploration of the struggle between the two, a struggle which finally has no source other than the mere desire for power. George appeals to Caroline to relent, painting a picture of himself expiring in hopelessness and unrelieved hard work. She is subtly flattered as well as moved by an appeal that seems to recognize her power and is ready to agree, asking for a week to answer merely because of her fear of seeming too easy a conquest. George senses victory, though, and his breezy answer—take all the time you want—so obviously reasserts his own power that 'the fancied tone of triumph hardened her heart once more' (17). This terrible interplay continues without relief and without fault on either side, even without much cause. They both

---

[8] The *Saturday Review* said '*The Bertrams* is intended to advocate the expediency of "love in a cottage"' (rev. of *The Bertrams*, 7, 26 Mar. 1859, 368).

come soon to a desire for revenge; they both consequently feel guilt and are finally led to something even worse, a desire for punishment. George tries pouting, and she badly wants to feel herself unworthy: 'I confess his superiority; but these very merits, this great superiority, make it impossible that I should suit him as a wife' (23). This masochistic trap catches many Trollope women, Lily Dale most notably. But it has many configurations. Here, Caroline marries another man in order to punish herself, and she is rewarded by getting a much greater villain than she had bargained for.

It is true that the narrator sometimes becomes visibly uncomfortable with what is going on and tries to distance us from Caroline through weak jokes, calling her 'Juno', for instance, as if she were Mrs. Proudie. But she is not, and the incongruity we notice in such jokes marks the great difference between this novel and the Barsetshire series and also between the heart of the novel and the comic form it tries to maintain. At the end, the villain happily kills himself, and Caroline is able to marry George, not, however, with much gaiety: his proposal is 'a cold, sad, dreary matter'; her 'acquiescence' is 'melancholy'; and 'they now live together very quietly. . . . Their house is childless, and very, very quiet; but they are not unhappy' (47). The narrator, who has tried throughout in characteristically subversive fashion to force the reader to identify with the villain and with the agonies of George, ends the novel by forcing us to acknowledge the very weak consolation provided: 'Reader, can you call to mind what was the plan of life which Caroline Waddington had formed in the boldness of her young heart? Can you remember the aspirations of George Bertram as he sat upon the Mount of Olives, watching the stones of the temple over against him?' (47). The final sense, if not quite one of loss, is one of diminishment and damage so extensive that it counteracts any comic satisfaction we might otherwise receive.

Castle Richmond, the next novel in the group, is another of Trollope's recurrent geographical mistakes. The movement away from southern England again introduces materials that cannot be contained within the frame. Here it is the background of the Irish famine that works very oddly with the conventional love stories. The *Saturday Review* noted at once the incompatibility of the action and the setting of the novel: 'the milk and the water really should be in separate pails. Pastry and roast-beef should not be served on the same plate.'[9] The details of the relief plans, the road work that accomplishes nothing, and the starvation are so starkly impressive that Trollope is forced to heighten the major plot to the point of ludicrous sensationalism in order to avoid making it appear trivial. But it still does. At one point in the action a character wanders out of the rain and out of the love story into a hovel which has been hit by the famine. When he sees the cringing mother there and the corpse of her small daughter, his own troubles strike him as remarkably small. When some Countess or other, then, worried about the financial and social prospects of her child, wails ,'O my daughter', he thinks only of the woman in the cottage. Marriage, class, money become almost as nothing to him; he never forgets this measurement, nor do we. Trollope has tried to incorporate a *memento mori* symbol far too dramatic and insistent for the context. As in *The Bertrams*, the comedy here is uncomfortably subverted.

Orley Farm goes beyond the ironic edge of comedy altogether,[10] entering unmistakably the territory of 'the mythos of winter'. All appearances are wrong, and the best instincts are mistaken; the scoundrels have all the truth on their side. *Orley Farm* is concerned with mistakes and deceptions, heroic plans that go nowhere, the exercise of chivalric virtues that are now pointless. Lady Mason risks everything, committing forgery to save the land for a son who does not want it and who is humiliated by his mother's act of love; the land is restored to its rightful owner finally, but he does not want it either—he wants revenge, which he does not get. The chivalrous Sir Peregrine Orme decides to protect the harassed and innocent Lady Mason, offers to marry her, and then is forced to withdraw ignominiously when it turns out that she is not so very innocent; the trial 'clears' her only to expose her deeply to those she cares about; the same trial climaxes the image of purposeless torture, turning on the innocent and twisting truth into lies, and all to no end.

One of the subplots, the one involving the Staveley family, does follow a comic course, but this plot is so minor that Trollope almost forgot to complete it, and it is so overwhelmed by the ironic force of the other three plots that the good luck experienced there is made to

---

[9] Rev. of *Castle Richmond*, 9 (19 May 1860), 643. Trollope himself said he disliked all the characters but admired the plot and the narration of incidents (*Autobiography*, pp. 156–7). Given his own aesthetics, this is a very telling distinction.

[10] There are good discussions of *Orley Farm* by Robert Polhemus, *The Changing World*, pp. 76–88, and by Robert M. Adams, ' "Orley Farm" and Real Fiction', *NCF*, 8 (1953–4), 27–41.

seem just that: mere good luck. There is no essential comic rhythm, and the slight comic counterplot actually highlights this fact by forcing us to recognize the central patterns of denial. In this way the novel marks a great advance in Trollope's use of the commenting and defining subplot. Four plots are here interwoven with full success. Trollope's novels from this point on use this technique repeatedly and with great assurance. The next two chronicle novels after *Orley Farm*, *The Small House at Allington* and *Can You Forgive Her?*, owe a great deal to this experimental novel.

Trollope unites the plots of *Orley Farm* through their shared concerns with commerce and with law. Commerce is used to define the condition of the world, law the means for dealing with that condition. Commerce suggests an invasion of barbarous chaos; the legal mind is our own mind desperately and unsuccessfully trying to deal with this new state of affairs. The novel is really about Mr. Kantwise's modern furniture and what we do when the common materials of modern life are 'got up for cheatery' (42), as Mrs. Dockwrath says. But her husband, Samuel Dockwrath, is unable to see any defect in the furniture. He is without aesthetic or moral taste; he really fails to see that there is such a thing as 'cheatery'. And it is this man who ties together the plots, who initiates the action. In a crucial scene, Dockwrath forces himself into the commercial room of an inn at Leeds, hoping thereby to find more comfort for less money. When challenged about his credentials as a commercial man, he insists, 'In this enterprising country all men are more or less commercial' (6).[11] No one (including the reader) can challenge this, and we are moved as a result into the company of the essential commercial man, Mr. Moulder. Moulder's view of life is consistent with his occupation. Like Dockwrath, who cannot understand that he owes anything to Lady Mason except the rent, Moulder sees life as a series of bargains, even, or especially, his marriage: 'It ain't much', he tells his wife, 'I ask of you in return for your keep' (24). He is, by his terms, neither thoughtless nor unjust: 'When I took to the old girl there, I insured my life, so that she shouldn't want her wittles and drink' (24). Any belief in closer ties than this in the novel is seen as more or less sentimental. Mr. Moulder's Christmas, like Mr.

---

[11] Adams also cites this comment as a central and reverberating passage (' "Orley Farm" and Real Fiction'). His treatment of the commercial theme is excellent: 'behind the polite social façades are everywhere found the grotesque, obscene appetites of Mr. Moulder, the acquisitive personality *par excellence*' (p. 33).

Dockwrath at the cosy inn, seems to be a grim parody of *The Pickwick Papers*, as are the recurrent scenes of domestic disharmony and disruption: Mrs. Furnival's decision to live apart from her husband, Mrs. Joseph Mason's vicious inhospitality, Mrs. Dockwrath's secret communications to Lady Mason, Lady Mason's own futile love for her son, descending finally to the scene at the commercial room in Leeds.

But commerce is *just*, of course, as is the law. Mr. Moulder mounts an eloquent defence of the law: lawyers have a duty to their clients, just as he has one to the manufacturer, and 'It's not for me to say the sugar's bad, or the samples not equal to the last. My duty is to sell, and I sell;—and it's their duty to get a verdict' (61). The legal system, Moulder goes on, is 'the bulwark of the British Constitution' (61). It is, thus, the symbol for the national conscience and therefore for the national derailment. The defences of the law are seen as the defences of the mind against chaos. And such defences are not only paltry and ineffectual but dangerous. The novel's treatment of the law is very important but not very widely understood. At least two counterattacks have been issued by eminent legal professionals,[12] but both choose an unfortunate blustering tone and an attitude of superiority, and both, unhappily, miss the point. According to *Orley Farm* the law has two equally ineffective stances against the decay of a civilized community: a reliance on abstract principle—'the law' in theory—or a simple relativistic empiricism where all faith is placed in 'the practice of law'. As the communal values disintegrate, these tendencies in law both become stronger and draw further apart: principles become quixotic abstractions, practice mere vicious opportunism, the attempt to deny truth.

The abstractions of law violate the very basis of life by treating what is complex, dynamic, and intuitive as if it were simple, fixed, and rational. Comedy has always attacked law on these grounds, but the attack here is not from comedy. The living coherence of communal life has dissolved, and rigid principles, therefore, are not, as they are in comedy, held to be in violation of a greater reality but are now seen to be absurd, floating rules. Reason is not measured against comic instinct but against grim absurdity. The central man of

---

[12] Sir Francis Newbolt, *Out of Court* (London: Philip Allan, 1925), pp. 1–73, and Henry S. Drinker, 'The Lawyers of Anthony Trollope', in Willard Thorp and Henry S. Drinker, *Two Addresses Delivered to Members of the Grolier Club* (New York: The Grolier Club, 1950), pp. 25–47.

principle, Lucius, Lady Mason's son, seems almost to be a new Mr. Slope, now serious and very dangerous. He is a man of the times, educated, advanced, and quite just in the abstract: when his mother counsels waiting for next year's crops, he says, 'Wait! Yes, and what has come of waiting? We don't wait at all in doubling our population every thirty-three years; but when we come to the feeding of them we are always for waiting. . . . No more waiting for me, mother, if I can help it' (2). In another context, this hurry-up idealism could be seen comically, as a step on the road to the College of Spiritual Pathology, but here it is destructive. Lucius is a good man; he wants to serve his mother and the cause of right, but 'he knew but little as yet of the ordinary life of gentlemen in England' (20). And he never gets a chance to learn. The expected comic education, like all patterns, is thwarted, and harmless idealism is not so harmless.

In *Orley Farm*, it is obvious to men of experience that principles are dead and Utopias absurd, so they turn to empiricism. And the more complete the empiricism, the greater the degree of legal success. But it is just these highly successful men, Aram and Chaffanbrass, that 'make so many in these days feel the need of some Utopia' (65). No circle could be more vicious. The principles of law are disconnected from life, but the practice of law which is connected to life is compared to the profession of a dutiful hired killer or bravo (75).

But the law is obviously not responsible for this condition of things, nor can it be expected to deal with it. In a fine scene Sir Peregrine Orme and the lawyer, old Mr. Round, meet to discuss Lady Mason's case, but they find that, though they are decent and honourable men, they can do nothing. In fact *because* they are decent and honourable, they cannot even talk about the case; they can only testify to a melancholy respect for one another's character and withdraw in silence. Sir Peregrine's way, argues the great lawyer Mr. Furnival, shows generosity and 'poetic chivalry', but it is not 'the way of the world' (26). Old Orme's ways are now seen as naïve, simple-minded: ' "What is the purport of these courts of law", he asks, "if it be not to discover the truth, and make it plain to the light of day?" Poor Sir Peregrine! His innocence in this respect was perhaps beautiful, but it was very simple' (56). He is one of the last —'the number is becoming very few' (56)—of those who believe in decency. He dramatizes the passing away of the old and coherent world and its dependence on the final justice of communal instinct.

In such a world the law could work well, but it can no more deal with its absence than it can create such a world anew.

Sir Peregrine's grandson, young Perry, inherits his grandfather's virtues and his beliefs, but he is simply cast away by the new world. When he tries to act for Lady Mason by accusing Dockwrath of 'villainy', he seems to be the man from Mars or, more common in Trollope, the American visitor commenting on primogeniture or fox-hunting. Dockwrath says, 'Highty-tighty! What are you talking about, young man? The fact is, you do not know what you are talking about' (20). At the end, Perry's career is denied any satisfactory outcome. When he is unsuccessful in love, he reacts with great bitterness. But the bitterness is allowed no climax in any sort of tragic action, nor is it allowed to be drained off, as in comedy. He is not broken by his bitterness, and he realizes that he will have to deal with it: 'Oh, I dare say I shall marry some day. I feel now as though I should like to break my neck, but I don't suppose I shall' (80). Such a statement is tantamount to a recognition of how empty and unclimactic life is. It is the same emptiness we sense at the ending of this novel, the same deliberate refusal to provide resolutions. It is an 'unsatisfactory' ending, certainly, but, then, dissatisfaction is the basis of the rhetoric of irony.[13]

With the next three non-chronicle novels, *Rachel Ray* (1863), *Miss Mackenzie* (1865), and *The Belton Estate* (1866), Trolope explores the possibilities of the art of full and simple satisfaction. These novels represent the alternate pole of comedy; just as the three novels already discussed are much darker than any of the Barsetshire novels, so are these three much lighter, less disturbed. They are all comedies of nature, positing a serene confidence in natural impulses and the natural working of things. The problems that arise, therefore, are principally confined to removing the obstacles that stand in the way of natural forces, love most especially or, to say the same thing, sex. These are all comedies of generation and renewal, only slightly disguised celebrations of the instincts for survival or procreation. The blocking figures, such as they are, are Malvolio-types, enemies of youth, mirth, and pleasure; generally they are cast either as religious fanatics or class snobs. People are treated very gently; there are few outcasts and there is very little need for punishment. The world is harmonious and, for the most part, benign, and

---

[13] The only thing marring Robert M. Adams's fine essay, ' "Orley Farm" and Real Fiction', is the attack on the ending as indecisive, patched-up, a compromise (pp. 37-8).

Trollope's traditional instruments of disruption—the narrator and the subplots—are here used not to upset, but to support, a basic unity of design and effect. Though the three comedies become progressively more complex and admit difficulties more ominous, the change is slight, not enough to disguise the fact that these novels represent the base from which Trollope worked, a world realized in art which offers opportunities for fulfilment and unified being which the other novels deny, seeing them as remote and dreamlike.

Rachel Ray takes a strong stand in favour of youth, sex, and good beer. It is an extremely simple story of how the young man, Luke Rowan, got the girl, Rachel Ray, and the brewery. Virtually everything is on his side, even the hostile brewer's own family and the rector—certainly the girl. Such opposition as there is comes from Rachel's evangelical, widowed sister, Mrs. Dorothea Prime, Mrs. Prime's low-church lover, the Revd. Samuel Prong, Luke's snobbish mother, and a few petty misunderstandings. It is a novel about how to find 'the good times', an American phrase Trollope picked up and loved. In the process, society itself is cured of its slight neurosis, an uneasiness about sex, and is thus revitalized. Like the other two romantic comedies in this series, *Rachel Ray* is specifically a nationalistic novel, a pastoral that exalts not only nature but English nature, a celebration of that particular 'air of homeliness which made the sweetness of her womanhood almost more attractive than the loveliness of her personal charms' (7). Unlike the beauty of Italy or America, which is 'of the flesh' or 'of the mind', English beauty is 'of the heart', specially 'intended for domestic use' and thus 'the happiest of the three' (7).

England's natural beauty and natural sources of joy are clouded only slightly in this novel, and that cloud blows away by the end. It appears in the first place only because some people have grown distrustful of this world, have begun worrying about controls and future punishments, and have set up a false distinction between the wicked and the righteous. This morality is so stupidly self-destructive that it creates a division between marriage, which it wholly approves, and courtship, which it would ban entirely. The worthy vicar, appropriately named Mr. Comfort, asks the key question: 'And how are young people to get married if they are not allowed to see each other?' (5). But it is Mr. Comfort who is unconsciously responsible for part of the problem. He speaks a world-hating formula from the pulpit that is very dangerous. He doesn't really believe these slogans himself, of course: 'When he told the little children that this world should be as nothing to them, he did not remember that he himself enjoyed keenly the good things of this world' (5). He is not a hypocrite at all; it is just that he unconsciously assumes a sophistication in his audience which will apply with great moderation such lessons as he teaches. But the children of the congregation and those adult children like Rachel's mother may take the grim doctrine he preaches to heart. Mrs. Ray, in fact, 'believed too much' (1) of what he said and thus could not exercise her capacity to enjoy the world. The novel is as much the story of her liberation as it is of her daughter's love and marriage. And she is liberated from religion. On the surface, of course, the novel approves of no such radical position on religion, taking care to separate an approved, worldly religion from the low-church fears of those like Mr. Prong, who believed 'no sheep could nibble his grass in wholesome content, unless some shepherd were at work at him constantly with his crook' (6). The confidence in the basic rightness of the natural tendencies of life is felt so intensely that there is surely a sense that as one can get along without Mr. Prong and his crook, so one can get along without future rewards. Heaven is as irrelevant as hell. Mrs. Ray, then, is initiated into the religion of Comfort; she acquires the sophistication whereby she can experience the full delight of life.

In this serene world the usual dilemmas in Trollope's novels are diminished, drained of their potential to cause suffering. The recurrent figure of a woman trapped in horrible masochism is here reduced to the comic Mrs. Prime, who has found sackcloth 'grateful to the skin' (5). But she escapes from Mr. Prong and is clearly on her way to a rejuvenation in worldliness at the novel's close. More remarkable is Trollope's treatment of the hero, who is a gentle version of the usual wild absolutist. Luke's cause, the making of better beer, is comic in itself and is rendered doubly so by the fact that the few people in the area not addicted to cider don't mind the bad beer anyhow, rather respecting it as an institution. Luke loves to talk of brewing as providing 'opportunity for chemical experiments, and room for philosophical inquiry' (10), but this is all talk, we see. Underneath he is impulsive, romantic—quite unexperimental and unphilosophical. His rebellion amounts finally to asking Mrs. Ray formally for permission to court her daughter. His 'genuine radical-

ism' is only a version of Trollope's own belief in 'gradual progress'; he disdains 'equality' (26). Even those who disrupt the
sleepy world in order to bring new life to it are the mildest and least
threatening of invaders.

This quiet and sheltered world is protected by a very skilful
narrator, who begins, much as Dickens does in *Martin Chuzzlewit*,
by encouraging our cynicism and giving it full rein. The novel opens
by making fun of the very things it will finally hold dear—love,
marriage, and Mrs. Ray. Love is seen as some sort of biological joke,
marriage as a form of mutual support for neurotics, Mrs. Ray as a
weak fool. The rhetoric deliberately defuses the sentimentality only
to encourage it, tires our sarcasm by exercising it so vigorously.
The sentimentality in this novel is not only effective but is so disguised that it does not seem like sentimentality at all. The narrator
also helps protect us in the opposite direction, carefully distinguish-
ing the absolute freedom he countenances from licentiousness or
lust. Luke 'dabbled in romance, and probably wrote poetry in his
bedroom' (4), which is, in this world, just about all that Byronism
amounts to. There are no real dangers. More centrally, the narrator
suggests that Byronism is inverted Puritanism; Luke's harmless
'Byronic' courtship brings forth from poor Rachel's conscience the
whole battery of low-church condemnation: 'sin', 'iniquity',
'wickedness'. Byronism and Puritanism, it is suggested, are both
fearful, ingrown, and distrustful. The narrator in this way moves us
to the safe heart of the warm romantic comedy.

It is a comedy so undisturbed that Luke, after he has won everything, cannot help thinking that the obstacles have been rather petty:
'he could not but wish that there had been some castles for him to
storm in his career. Tapitt had made but poor pretence of fighting
before he surrendered; and as to Rachel, it had not been in Rachel's
nature to make any pretence' (28). The world has been waiting for
them all along. It is this easy confidence in the world and the corresponding full control of his art that made so many of Trollope's
contemporaries become sunny over the warmth that was in the
novel. George Eliot loved the 'subtleties' of its art,[14] and John
Addington Symonds wrote with an even fuller response to the
comedy: 'I would give everything I possess . . . for that hour at the
Churchyard style, for the difficulties surmounted, the strong nerves,

[14] See her letter to Trollope, 23 Oct. 1863, *The George Eliot Letters*, ed. Gordon S.
Haight (New Haven: Yale Univ. Press, 1955), iv. 110.

the true love, the simple life, the real work of those visions in Mr. Trollope's brain.'[15]

Miss Mackenzie is also a celebration of natural forces, and it admits also the opposition of social snobbery and low-church Puritanism. But there are new and darker problems here, too, namely, loneliness, age, and death. *Miss Mackenzie* enacts a fable of rejuvenation and rebirth, not of natural growth. Its models are works like *The Pickwick Papers* or *Persuasion*, and it narrates a similar magical story of the regaining of youth. Miss Mackenzie is nearly forty, 'neither beautiful nor clever', without particular softness or grace. She has spent all of her life around death and now struggles to find life before it is too late. This is a comedy which moves to a level of complexity and disturbance one step beyond *Rachel Ray*, where finally appearances were in full accord with reality and surfaces were depths. Miss Mackenzie's youth, however, is like her secret poetry, essential but hidden, and the novel is really a test of society and of this life to see if they can find that hidden self.

The basic position of the novel is announced with absolute directness by a former servant, Mrs. Buggins, who is now liberated from service and about to begin on life:

'To be sure, I'm an old woman . . . Who has said that I ain't? Not I; nor yet Buggins. We is both of us old. But I don't know why we is to be desolate and lonely all our days, because we ain't young. It seems to me that the young folks is to have it all to themselves, and I'm sure I don't know why.' Then she went, clearly resolved, that as far as she was concerned, the young people shouldn't have it all to themselves; and as Buggins was of the same way of thinking, they were married at St. Mary-le-Strand that very morning. (23)

Miss Mackenzie reaches the same resolution and finds the same happy end, but without such ease. She begins at once with a resolution 'that she would not content herself with a lifeless life, such as those few who knew anything of her evidently expected from her' (2), and strives to fight against loneliness, the opinion of the world, and, most important, her opinion of herself: 'She despised herself. Why, she knew not; and probably did not know that she did so. But, in truth, she despised herself, thinking herself to be too mean for a man's love' (11). Because of her self-hatred, she nearly settles for

---

[15] Letter to A. O. Rutson, 27 Mar. 1864, *The Letters of John Addington Symonds, 1844–1868*, ed. Herbert M. Schueller and Robert L. Peters (Detroit: Wayne State Univ. Press, 1967), i. 451.

several miserable substitutes for genuine life: the pathetic vulture existence of the single ladies of Littlebath who surround Mr. Stumfold and feed on his weak jokes cast out to satisfy the 'appetite for feminine rakishness' (4), or the proposals of some terribly undesirable suitors. Still, there is an inner-spirit; she can assure herself of her own sexuality by kissing herself in the mirror, thus keeping alive the growth of 'romance' which 'had only just been born' (9). She resists the many attempts to dominate her, as well as the bleak advice of her friend, Miss Todd: 'We single women have to be solitary sometimes—and sometimes sad.' After all, Miss Todd asserts, 'one can't go about as one did when one was young' (13). But when Miss Mackenzie answers, 'I had none of that when I was young,' Miss Todd relents: 'Hadn't you? Then I won't say but what you may be right to try and begin now' (13).

And so she does. It appears for a time as if she will lose in the attempt. She sees herself as torn between two lovers she does not love, 'like the ass who starved between two bundles of hay' (15). But this irony yields to romance; as she loses her money, she is rewarded with a suitor, John Ball, who is equally old (older really), equally worn, but also equally tough, rebellious, and finally equally prepared for rebirth. Miss Mackenzie, by refusing to give in, brings life to another, invoking that 'romance left within his bosom' despite the tedium of his life (7).

The pattern of resurrection is thus strengthened, echoed too in a few minor characters and made applicable to us by a busy narrator. This is perhaps Trollope's most focused novel; it never takes its eyes off the central figure for a moment. The narrator, therefore, spends most of his time nudging us into identification with Miss Mackenzie, by mock apologies—'Where she has been weak, who among us is not, in that, weak also?' (5)—and by consistent generalization of her actions and motives: 'She was doing what we all do' (6). He also artfully prepares the way for a comic resolution by parodying various idealized models of loneliness and patience, particularly Griselda and Mariana: 'I will not say that she was always waiting for some one that came not, or that she declared herself to be a-weary, or that she wished that she were dead' (1). The Mariana image also suggests a simplicity that is now gone. Miss Mackenzie's initial desolation at Littlebath is compared with Mariana's (13), but it is, in a way, worse. After all, Mariana could not have expected much society in a moated grange, but Miss Mackenzie had gone to Littlebath for company.

Miss Mackenzie's solitude is broken, of course, and the Mariana reference directs us both to the solution and to the comic argument that genuine problems and their answers are social, not metaphysical.

On the way to its solution, *The Belton Estate* raises problems that are no more metaphysical, but they are more serious. Despite its complexity, the novel has always seemed to be among Trollope's most forgettable. Among reviewers it inspired perhaps the least enthusiasm of any of his novels. It was the source of James's joke about 'sinking into a gentle slumber'; even Trollope seems to have regarded the book as a blank: 'I have not looked at it since it was published; and now turning back to it in my memory, I seem to remember almost less of it than of any book I have written.'[16] The comedy is very warm and very controlled, certainly, but it seems on the whole to exclude far less and to work with more difficult issues than either *Rachel Ray* or *Miss Mackenzie*.

The main line of the narrative is quite simple. Clara Amedroz, after finding her way out of a mistaken engagement with Captain Aylmer, marries Will Belton, who becomes Belton of Belton, restores the estate, and rejuvenates the family and the land. Clara exclaims at Will's first visit that 'he is going to build sheds, and buy cattle; and I don't know what he doesn't mean to do; so that we shall be alive again' (5). Clara's father had himself been so idle, had done such 'terrible evil' through neglect that his son, the natural heir, has committed suicide, leaving the estate to dissolve. Will restores the substance that is lost and restores meaning to the notion of gentleman. His slightly progressive views are blended with a strong and corrective family feeling so that his triumph merges all antitheses. It is a highly romantic comedy—'After all, what did the feeling of the world signify to them, who were going to be all the world to each other?' (32)—and one of great charity. Even Captain Aylmer and his bride are welcomed at the end.

But within these simple lines there are very strong obstacles to such easy comic fulfilment, presented not so much by the narrative complication of the Aylmer engagement as by Clara's urgent need to preserve her own freedom. The very energy and power with which Will can rejuvenate the land are a threat to Clara and her

---

[16] David Skilton (*Anthony Trollope and His Contemporaries*, p. 23) is the authority for the lack of enthusiasm among the reviews of *The Belton Estate*; James's comment is in his review of the novel in *Nation*, 2 (4 Jan. 1866), 21; Trollope's statement is in *An Autobiography*, p. 196.

desire to preserve that 'strong will of her own' (1). The novel deals within its comic framework with the same feminism that was so disruptive in *Can You Forgive Her?* The treatment here is no less subtle. Will's energy and also his kindness are to Clara an assumption of power that must be resisted. She tries to hold herself distant from his authoritarian assumptions by insisting on his cousinly or brotherly relationship to herself. She resists also the dominance of romance, which seems to her an admission of emptiness: 'It makes me feel ashamed of my sex', she says, 'when I find that I cannot talk of myself to another woman without being supposed to be either in love or thinking of love,—either looking for it or avoiding it' (5). But she is unable to carry on with Aylmer, sensing his great weakness and inferiority and instinctively forecasting the shipwreck ahead were she to marry him. The narrator sarcastically remarks, 'The theory of man and wife—that special theory in accordance with which the wife is to bend herself in loving submission before her husband—is very beautiful; and would be good altogether if it could only be arranged that the husband should be the stronger and the greater of the two' (11). Her rebellion against Aylmer, however, seems to throw her into the hands of another tyrant. But Will treats her release and her acceptance of him as a movement into freedom. She finds herself for a time in the usual masochism common to Trollope's strong women—'It was necessary [she thought] to her self-respect that she should be punished because of that mistake' (30). But she is freed by the jokes of her friends, Will's gentleness, and the example of Will's sister, who calls him a 'despot', but who shows how very complete her own selfhood and her own powers are. Clara yields, then, with lots of comments about submission and victimization. Partly these are jokes, but the resolution is not at all easy; it is won with delicacy and tact.

But the novel is not, despite this art, very memorable, primarily because the method it employs is so un-Trollopian. Trollope experiments here with a stylized and scenic novel, seeking to define issues and to create moods largely through symbolic images and through fixed pictorial attitudes. For once Trollope wants us to see, and the picture is simply not very sharp. It is an interesting experiment, but it is not a technique Trollope had refined, and the result is diffuse and unemphatic. The scenic pattern involves the joining of the lovely but unproductive Belton Castle in Somersetshire with the ugly but profitable Plaistow Hall in Norfolk. Belton lands are purely picturesque; the hills 'are broken into ravines and deep watercourses and rugged dells hither and thither; where old oaks are standing, in which life seems to have dwindled down to the last spark; but the last spark is still there, and the old oaks give forth their scanty leaves from year to year' (1). This country ministers directly to the eye. Plaistow is set in a county Trollope traditionally associates with a wasteland, but here, though ugly and almost uninhabitable, the flat lands are also productive. Plaistow Hall itself is a fine old Tudor building unfortunately ruined by a clumsy conversion into a farm. Belton has lost all utility and energy, Plaistow all beauty. They seem to exemplify the gloomy division Trollope announced elsewhere: 'In seeking for the useful, we are compelled to abandon the picturesque' (*Clergymen of the Church of England*, p. 28). But Will is able at the end to effect the unification of the two in a new junction of use and beauty; he employs these very terms and promises an end to the division between aristocratic lassitude and lower-class energy, between civilized life and the land that supports it.

The scenic method works in details as well. Such images as the rocks, 'the prettiest spot in England' (5), are used as psychological referents throughout. Clara thinks of this place where Will first proposed to her as 'that scene among the rocks'. This sort of association is quite unusual in Trollope, and it puts immense importance on the fixed scene rather than on the shifting momentum of dialogue and action. And that is one problem. Another is that there is a fairly conventional and heavily stressed use of seasonal imagery: Will comes in the summer, he is rejected in the winter, he persuades Clara to relent as the snows melt, and he is accepted just as the summer begins. The seasonal references are not in themselves objectionable, but they are highly sentimentalized and indistinct: for example, 'It was a lovely summer evening, at that period of the year in which our summer evenings just begin, when the air is sweeter and the flowers more fragrant, and the forms of the foliage more lovely than at any other time' (31).

The scenic method works well as long as Trollope is dealing with houses or with satiric references to the Aylmers—with the Aylmers because it suggests a particular fixed quality. But it does not work well with the dynamic implications of romantic comedy. Time and again we are offered attitudes in place of action, and psychological states are defined in reference to externals:

Immediately before the house door, between that and the old tower, there stood one of Farmer Stovey's haycarts, now empty, with an old horse between the shafts looking as though he were asleep in the sun. Immediately beyond the tower the men were loading another cart, and the women and children were chattering as they raked the scattered remnants up to the rows. Under the shadow of the old tower, but in sight of Clara as she sat in the porch, there lay the small beer-barrels of the hay-makers, and three or four rakes were standing erect against the old grey wall. (2)

This passage might be called 'directions for composing a mental genre study'. It recalls the Pre-Raphaelites and Tennyson's 'idyls of the hearth'. It is surprising that Trollope should attempt this mode, but it is characteristic that he should decide to have a try at almost anything and equally characteristic that he should recognize very clearly what was successful and what was not.

CHAPTER 4

THE BARSETSHIRE CHRONICLE

THE DIVERSE and often only partly successful experiments carried on during this period allow for the great control and assurance manifested in the Barsetshire chronicle. At least after the opening novel, the chronicle explores the possibilities of comedy within a range that is clearly defined. Ironic moments and ironic themes are present, but they never range out of control; nor is the comedy ever so easy and undisturbed as to approach the sleepiness of *The Belton Estate*. The Barsetshire series works without any ponderous epic machinery, but it deals with an epic theme: the establishment and preservation of a civilization. The civilization is first erected and defended from outsiders, flourishes, decays, and is then revived. Trollope duplicates the cycle Tennyson was to trace in *Idylls of the King*, with this difference: Tennyson's cycle moves from chaos back to chaos again, whereas Trollope's goes from victory back to victory.

It would, perhaps, be a mistake to claim for Trollope's chronicle a much tighter narrative organization than this. There are a few motifs that are repeated throughout, but they are not developed consistently or emphatically. The chronicle derives its unity not from a single narrative pattern or repeated themes[1] but from the most obvious connections through geography and character. For the most part these novels hang together because they are set in the same general area and concern many of the same people. There is a sense that the novels are really just different perspectives on the same action, different lighting effects tried on the same subject. Correspondingly, the basic pattern and basic coherence are more clearly formal than thematic. More exactly, the novels conduct an exploration of the range of comedy.

But the explorations are, as I have said, conducted within safe grounds. The basic assumptions of that world and its values are established by tradition, the tradition of the pastoral. It is a very delicate and fragile world, certainly, subject to threats from within

---

[1] The most extended discussion of the series does provide an argument for a unity that is essentially thematic: Hugh L. Hennedy, *Unity in Barsetshire* (The Hague: Mouton, 1971). Hennedy's fine discussion, which parallels my own at several points, also provides a strong structural argument.

and without, but it is pastoral all the same, with Mr. Harding as chief shepherd.[2] The conservative bias we note in these chronicles, so strong that it led Ronald Knox to call the whole series 'an epic of reaction',[3] is not really different from the defensive quality exhibited by the traditional pastoral in its need to protect itself from the great force of cosmopolitan, sophisticated values. The extraordinary thing about Trollope's pastoral is that it moves away from this reactionary tone after the first two novels, giving us a feeling in *Doctor Thorne* and *Framley Parsonage* that the values have been won and are in little need of protection. This solidity can be misleading, as the last two novels show, but running through the series is an unchanged belief that, at bottom, people's characters are firmly rooted in well-tried values and solid virtues. The traditional pastoral emphasis on natural values, natural virtue, the good heart, is preserved throughout. Nature takes quite a beating, it is true; for no sooner are the values defined and expressed than they tend to go into hiding. But since trouble, no matter how serious, never invades the centre of natural goodness, the values can, at last, be rediscovered and reasserted.

Despite this natural current of right feeling and basic goodness coursing through it, the series also exhibits variations and dramatic change. The image of mock war is present in most of the novels, for instance, but the nature and seriousness of the conflict change greatly. At first the enemy appears to be the forward-looking excesses of rationality, the stupid demands for order and regularity in a disorderly and comfortable world. But by the end there is such a fear of general irrationality that it is necessary to construct an order, not to fend off the builders. Pleasant irregularity becomes chaos by *The Last Chronicle*, and the hearty faith in what naturally is changes to a much less secure hope that natural goodness can avert what might very well be.

'Clergymen are only men', runs a dominant motif throughout. But what is in the first novels a comforting doctrine of unification becomes by the final novel a frightening one. 'All clergymen are men' in *Barchester Towers* means to the reader 'all men are clergymen', possessing in their common humility the source of all

---

[2] Hennedy also notes pastoral ties, particularly in *The Warden*, in which he finds echoes of 'Lycidas' (pp. 21–36).

[3] See his 'Introduction to the Barsetshire Novels' in his edition of *The Warden* (London: Oxford Univ. Press, 1952), p. xviii.

spirituality; in *The Last Chronicle*, 'all men are clergymen' seems to translate into 'all men are thieves'.

We notice a corresponding change in the position of women. Initially subject to a good deal of banter for not really understanding the full delicacies of moral behaviour, they are protected by the more refined sensitivities of men. By the end, the deep, if fairly murky, instincts of women hold together the society and give it a foundation from which to rebuild. As the genial surface falls apart, men tend to lose a sense of connection with the code, but women, though never grasping the intricacies of the code at its best moments of practice, are less likely to be led astray. The whole series moves inward, then, learning to distrust things as they are and formulating its comic base more and more on instincts that lie far below the surface.

The danger of this inward movement, as far as comedy is concerned, is that instincts tend to be incommunicable. A comedy established psychologically is less surely communal than one which collects its energies around the expulsion of an external threat, like Mr. Slope. In the early novels the tendency is to defend the sanctity of the private life against public invasion. There is such a confident sense of community that no need is felt to stress communal ties. One needs only to get away from the pesky nuisances of London, the *Jupiter*, and low-church liberals. But in the last two novels the emphasis shifts in the opposite direction, and it is necessary to attempt to bring back the private self into public life. *The Warden* ends with Mr. Harding withdrawing from society, *The Last Chronicle* with Mr. Crawley entering it. These actions paradoxically suggest the shift from a great confidence in social virtue to a distrust of it.

The shift is most apparent in the changing moral focus of these novels. Mr. Harding is established by the first two novels as the perfect man. In *Doctor Thorne* and *Framley Parsonage* the Doctor and Lady Lufton hold values almost identical to his. They are given greater power to act and they are less perfect, both facts reflecting the far greater serenity of the middle novels. There is no longer a need to separate virtue and action, nor is there a need to clarify the values by personifying them in a saint. But in *The Small House at Allington* the values are located only in characters like Lord De Guest, who try very hard to act but who are totally unable to arrange the comic resolution. In *The Last Chronicle* there simply is no longer a conventional moral centre.

These broad changes suggest the outlines of a three-part pattern, consisting of the definition of pastoral values, their fulfilment, and their collapse and reconstruction. *The Warden* and *Barchester Towers* clear the way for the series by defining its central values. They ward off the threats from London and thus lay claim to the pastoral world. Both novels are concerned with telling us who Mr. Harding is and establishing his moral position as central, but they do this principally by indirection, by declaring with great clamour that all other moral systems are either invalid or incomplete. This loud, indelicate quality sets *The Warden* and *Barchester Towers* apart from all of Trollope's other novels.[4] Trollope would have called them 'satyric', a term he used to express his dissatisfaction with *The Warden*, *The Way We Live Now*, much of Thackeray, all of Swift, and a great deal of other literature he did not like. These beginning novels in the chronicle are among Trollope's funniest novels, but it is an uncharacteristically simple (and for that reason highly successful) humour of expulsion that is employed. The villains are very clearly marked out, and Trollope only pretends to make them complex. Bertie Stanhope sending a couch rolling over Mrs. Proudie's dress, tearing it partly away, suggests the technique and vision of a Marx Brothers film. The scene works wonderfully within the novel, only because the novel's morality is very insistent indeed. It is not simple, but there is a sense, as in the Marx Brothers, that no one really understands and that ingenious excess is required. A lot of noise, therefore, is made to get us to side with the quiet Mr. Harding.

Doctor Thorne was welcomed by *Harper's* as a release 'from the audacious sarcasm of "Barchester Towers" ',[5] and it is likely to seem to us in many ways the first genuine Trollope novel. With this novel and *Framley Parsonage* there is a contented atmosphere provided by settled values. These values are not unchallenged, of course, and not everyone in the novels can live by them, but the reader now *is* assumed to understand and can therefore be urged quietly to participate in the action. The action in both novels involves recruitment, bolstering the ranks of the good. In both there is a sense of an expanding moral centre, and the confidence is very great. *Framley*

[4] William Cadbury points out that evaluation of *Barchester Towers* has always been difficult 'precisely because its excellences are of so different a kind from those of his other novels' ('Character and the Mock Heroic in *Barchester Towers*', p. 509). The same is true of *The Warden* and for the same reasons.

[5] Rev. of *Doctor Thorne*, 17 (Sept. 1858), 693.

Parsonage particularly carries an aura of luxuriance, fully deserving its characteristic tag, 'beautiful'. Its action is desultory, so much so that it is difficult to locate a central plot. But this very quality adds to its serenity, a serenity that is never dull because it is made so convincingly happy.

But in *The Small House at Allington* and *The Last Chronicle of Barset* a new invasion is mounted against the pastoral world, an invasion that so far succeeds that the full and easy confidence can never again be regained. Crosbie is different from Slope in that he fools everyone, not just women but even the Dales, staunch old conservative country gentry. As a result, virtue is twisted and turned inward. It is made perverse. In *The Small House*, the darkest novel in the series, confident and open love and the constancy of great honour are turned into a dangerous and rigid masochism. Natural values have little chance in an unnatural world, and Lily's rigidity ironically is made to appear the chief enemy of comedy. Everything yearns for her rebirth, but her virtue forbids her. Similarly, Mr. Crawley's great courage and heroism not only appear to be but are unnatural. Like Lily, he is forced into terrible psychological compensations, isolating himself and doing great damage. But Mr. Crawley is finally rescued—from poverty and from himself. As he comes back to life, so does society, and so does the code of the gentleman, of which he is the most extreme exemplification. The comic world is rebuilt with all its old values. The old supports are gone, of course, and the good heart has a much more difficult time of it. It is almost as if the pastoral itself is forced into the world of experience. By reforming the pastoral values in this new world, a new pastoral is, in effect, created, one less protected and permanent but more mature and more capable of dealing with the fallen world.

The cycles of a civilization based on the generous and complex code of gentlemanly instincts is thus established. The series moves from an ironic comedy of withdrawal to full-hearted romantic comedy, and then, in the final stages, to a dark comedy of experience whose principal model is *Paradise Regained* or, in the nineteenth century, Tennyson's *In Memoriam*. Clergymen are central to Trollope's chronicle because it is, like his model, a spiritual guide and a definition of the Church's proper religious mission. The essential doctrine is stated in *Barchester Towers*: 'Till we can become divine, we must be content to be human, lest in our hurry for a change we sink to something lower' (43). The dangers of slipping are there, but if we can put off the hurry for divinity, we can discover the grand contentment in being human. And that, Trollope's comedy insists, if not more wonderful than divinity, is great indeed—and a lot more certain.

The Warden *and* Barchester Towers: *The Pastoral Defined*

These novels are about Mr. Harding and his enemies. They seek to tell us all about the two sides and the conduct of the battle, and they seek to convince us that Mr. Harding wins by losing. But really all that is finally necessary is to give us, as James said, 'simply the history of an old man's conscience'.[6] Both novels are didactic portraits of Mr. Harding, complex in their means but quite single-minded in their ends. The ostensible issues matter very little in either novel, precisely because the morality advocated is aesthetic and intuitive rather than argumentative and rationalistic. *The Athenaeum* reviewer complained that *The Warden* showed 'too much indifference as to the rights of the case',[7] but 'the rights of the case' are never a serious issue. In both novels the resemblance to the novel of ideas is very slight; they are both much closer to being modern saints' lives. Neither relies much on action to define that saint but rather depicts him by way of contrast and comparison with a series of more or less static portraits. Very near to Mr. Harding at the centre is the old Bishop, but he is dead as *Barchester Towers* gets under way, and there is no one but the Thornes to take his place. In the next circle is his daughter Eleanor, whose closeness to him is limited by her moral dullness; next is his other daughter Mrs. Grantly and, separated further, her husband the archdeacon. The archdeacon clearly moves closer to the centre in the second novel, but he is never really very far away. Beyond this there is a great gulf to the 'new men', the reformers: Slope, Mrs. Proudie, and John Bold. On the far edge is the voice of the *Jupiter*, most powerful and most destructive of all. Though it would appear from this that Mr. Harding is quite alone and though the novels do isolate him from other characters, the effect is less gloomy than it might be since, after all, he has the very close company of the reader.

In my view, it is a mistake, and a common one, to ignore the primary rhetorical purpose of these two novels and to read them in terms of some 'reconciliation-of-opposites' theme. I do not believe

---

[6] *Partial Portraits*, p. 113.
[7] Rev. of *The Warden*, No. 1422 (27 Jan. 1855), p. 107.

that *The Warden* balances the views of Bold and the archdeacon or that *Barchester Towers* steers a course between past and future, conservative and liberal. Instead of the movement toward balance common to many other Trollope novels, *The Warden* and *Barchester Towers* describe patterns of disruption and consequent expulsion. Bold does not really have a 'case', nor does Slope. It is not that their positions are bad but that they are irrelevant. Their assumptions about life and morality are so askew that they must be admitted only to be expelled. Both novels are subtle but quite unequivocal attempts to establish a positive and enduring moral centre. And they do so by running the reforming rascals out of town.

The Warden appears to have been begun with some spirit of reforming zeal. Trollope may well have initially thought of the novel in terms of the sort of satiric method he used in *The New Zealander*, written immediately after *The Warden*, and it may even be true that 'for a moment, when he sketched out the plot of *The Warden*, Trollope half believed that he was on the side of the reformers'.[8] Trollope did speak of the novel later as if the satiric intention had got in the way of the moral intention, thinking that he was 'altogether wrong' in supposing that he could attack the evil and also those who did the attacking (*Autobiography*, pp. 94–5).[9] As far as the issues are involved, the novel does tend to do battle with both Bold and Grantly, but issues become trivial as the novel advances. It is almost as if Trollope discovered a new moral system on the way to writing a light topical satire. As this new intention takes over, the balance is upset completely, and the archdeacon is shifted as close to the centre as he well can be. The original intention makes the switch awkward, though, and the narrator is forced at the end to apologize for the picture of the archdeacon, saying that he is a much better man than he has been shown to be.

    [8] Knox, 'Introduction to the Barsetshire Novels', p. xviii.
    [9] Sadleir agreed absolutely with Trollope, calling the novel 'self-contradictory' (*Trollope: A Commentary*, p. 165). Though *The Warden* has attracted some excellent criticism, even the best of it sees the novel in terms of some sort of dualism, a balanced opposition. Ruth apRoberts devotes an important portion of *The Moral Trollope* (pp. 34–42) to this novel, which she regards as quintessential Trollope. The essays by William H. Marshall (in *The World of the Victorian Novel*, South Brunswick, N.J.: A. S. Barnes, 1967, pp. 322–36) and Sherman Hawkins ('Mr. Harding's Church Music', *ELH*. 29, 1962, 202–23) devoted to this novel are among the best work done on Trollope. Hawkins sees Mr. Harding as the antithesis of both Bold and Grantly; Marshall sees the central conflict as between Mr. Harding and Grantly's pre-Enlightenment consciousness. Both view the archdeacon more darkly and concentrate much more on the issues of the novel than I do.

He is that, of course, according to the terms in which the novel ends. In fact, the only thing holding him from the centre is a certain coarseness that blinds him to the futility and danger of fighting for mere issues. But in its inception the novel imagined itself also to be interested in issues, and thus there are touches of materialism and hypocrisy added to the character: the copy of Rabelais, the narrative commentary which insists that he is 'hard-hearted' (9), and a marital arrangement that anticipates the one later used with the Proudies. All this is a mistake, as the narrator is forced to admit. But it really does not matter a great deal in the end, since both Bold and Grantly are not so much opposing forces as flanking impotents who together teach Mr. Harding the proper moral position in respect to issues and conflict.

In terms of values, however, it is Bold's position, not the arch-deacon's, that is dangerous. The archdeacon, however feeble his support, is on the side of the angels, and Bold, however well in-tentioned, serves the other side. Much of the apparent complexity of the novel comes from the narrator's charitable disengagement of Bold as a man from his position and the corresponding satiric dis-engagement of the archdeacon as a man from his office. As men, they are all good, if vain and fairly stupid. But this charity, which might be mistaken for equivocation, is certainly not applied to the moral issues. All men are to be treated gently but not all moral attitudes. Such an argument is, however, in itself a moral position. It is the position held by Mr. Harding but certainly not by John Bold and the *Jupiter*, who forget that there are individuals, who fail utterly to see interconnections between public and private life, and who treat morality as if it were a set of abstractions altogether divorced from human beings. There is no equivocation in the novel's point here; the humanistic and complex morality of Mr. Harding is attacked by an inhuman, simple, and abstract code. There is no question which side we are forced to join.

John Bold's decent position is decent only in the abstract, and when decency is thus abstracted it becomes nearly indecent. Failing to recognize for a long time the complex ties between men and morality, he becomes almost totally a public man, a terribly self-conscious reformer who teaches himself to live in the soft glow of clichés. He is able 'to comfort himself in the warmth of his own virtue' (6), and he believes in the idiotic public response to him as the 'upholder of the rights of the poor of Barchester' (2). The narrator comments sarcastically, 'I fear that he is too much imbued with the idea that he has a special mission for reforming. It would be well if one so young had a little more diffidence himself, and more trust in the honest purposes of others—if he could be brought to believe that old customs need not necessarily be evil, and that changes may possibly be dangerous' (2). The comparison to a 'French Jacobin' (2) is pretty strong, as is Mr. Harding's 'disgust' (3) at his ungentlemanly conduct. When Bold tells Eleanor that he has nothing against her father 'personally', she asks, 'Then why should he be persecuted?' Bold can only respond to this central question with 'platitudes about public duty, which it is by no means worth while to repeat' (11). Bold's inability to understand the difference between Eleanor's feelings for her father and the hollow rhetoric of his own clichés is basic to the position he adopts. It does occur to him that the old men at Hiram's Hospital will only be hurt by his reforms—'to them it can only be an unmixed evil' (4)—'but he quiets the suggestion within his breast with the high-sounding name of justice' (4). The great point made against his position is that it disrupts a happy situation and makes everyone unhappy. And for what? For the sake of platitudes. At the end, Bold does understand his error: 'What is any public question but a conglomeration of private interests?' (15). He sees that a morality that separates public and private virtue is mad.

John Bold is not a bad man. He has, in fact, had the proper instincts all along. But he has been taught to 'quiet them within his breast' by the great organ of the new insanity, the *Jupiter*. The *Jupiter* symbolizes this abstract morality with its frightening power: 'What the Czar is in Russia, or the mob in America, that the *Jupiter* is in England' (7), says the archdeacon. The archdeacon allows the paper to stand for the alternate species of anarchy and dictatorship here, representing on one level his not very intelligent rage. There is, however, a point in the jumble, in that the *Jupiter* advocates with the single-minded simplicity of a tyrant the furious amorality of the mob. For public morality, the morality of abstractions and slogans, is no morality at all. It has no contact with people, just as Tom Towers, anonymous and out of reach, cannot be bothered to test his principles against human beings. His only morality, exactly like that of Slope, is a confident reliance on the virtue of his own elevation: 'How could a successful man be in the wrong!' (15).

In a world like this, the only positive moral act is the act of withdrawal. Mr. Harding, 'not so anxious to prove himself right, as to be so' (3), turns his back entirely on the doctrine of success. He sees that the law will not serve him—quite the contrary. Sir Abraham, his legal adviser, 'conquered his enemies by their weakness rather than by his own strength' (8). Mr. Harding's resignation, therefore, is a radical affirmation, a refusal to live by a morality which crudely equates virtue with success and therefore disregards the private life altogether. He rejects proof of being in favour of being itself and thus affirms the primacy of conscience. The rejection of public morality does not imply a final isolation. It merely suggests that the abstract simplicities of public morality are threatening to overwhelm the intricate realities of personal conscience. Mr. Harding instinctively recognizes this and therefore declares war on the *Jupiter* by refusing to fight. His act is a moral one and asserts a connection between will and act, between the public and private life, that Tom Towers will never see. It is gloomy in the sense that it gives up external and obvious power altogether. It temporarily sacrifices appearances to the *Jupiter* in order to define and defend the integrity of the complete moral being. But then, appearances never counted for much anyhow.

In *Barchester Towers* appearances count for just as little. In fact, this novel really just fleshes out the shorthand sketch given in *The Warden*, largely by means of a much fuller description of the enemies and a wonderfully indirect defence of Mr. Harding. In a sense, it is *The Warden* turned into art. Having discovered a moral and aesthetic position, Trollope seeks in *Barchester Towers* to sanctify Mr. Harding by far more crafty means. The novel is surely a comedy, for instance, but it establishes itself as such while quietly subverting many of the major tenets of traditional comedy. It inverts the usual pattern of struggle between parents and children basic to all comedy and cheers very strongly for the parents, celebrating their escape from the young. Basic to the novel is its rejection of the values and assumptions of youth, as shown by the open sneers at babies and the often cynical impatience with the principal lovers. All this, of course, paves the way for us to travel to the moral crux of the novel, the sixty-four-year-old Mr. Harding.

Other comic principles are just as certainly and purposefully overturned. For example, comedy traditionally rests on an apprehension of man as a member of a social group and works to re-establish the harmony of society by eliminating or converting the individualists. *Barchester Towers*, however, directly reverses this assumption, seeing men as decent individually but dangerous, silly, or contemptible in so far as they define themselves as parts of a social organization. Similarly, comedy normally—the tradition is so firm that one almost says 'naturally'—gives power to those who are approved: the good king is restored, the hero marries the girl, the money from the old will is accepted. In *Barchester Towers*, however, moral approval is directly proportionate to the decrease of power. More generally, comedy looks to the future and envisions a society cleansed and transformed by self-knowledge and joy. Most comedies deal principally with education and the resultant transcendence of the ordinary limitations of life; they are essentially progressive. Trollope's comedy, however, hates nothing so much as the callous notions of progress and sees forward movement as destruction. *Barchester Towers* looks to the past for its solidity and sees comic hope not in transformation but in preservation. Instead of seeking a transcendence of the ordinary, it revels in it. The most optimistic suggestion made by the novel is that the ordinary comforts of life are delicious, if only we perceive them fully and stop spoiling them by the continual anticipation of something better to come.

To establish this upside-down comedy, some extremely sly manœuvring is necessary. I have already indicated (pp. 34–36) how the narrator's deceptive warmth urges us to adopt values which are gradually more and more specialized and which finally are contemptuous of the young. Many of Trollope's famous comments on novel-writing really have much the same thematic function. The narrator reflects at one point that if Eleanor had given way to her rising tears, Arabin would have declared his love, and the whole mystery would have been cleared up. 'But then,' he asks with mock ingenuousness, 'where would have been my novel?' (30). Behind the companionable and easy rhetoric established by such an invitingly artless statement is a more quiet but more important attack on these almost-young lovers. Their actions are treated as mechanical, manipulable, and therefore trivial. The narrator takes them about as seriously as he expects the reader to, and the rhetoric here contributes to the irony which attends Mrs. Bold and Arabin throughout and which helps direct our moral concern to the elderly.

Though these passages do open the form of the novel, of course, they have a more particular thematic function. By attacking the very nature of form or pattern, particularly the whole notion of finality, they manifest a distrust for all neat patterns which point to the future. The narrator's position is that we must apprehend life as a continuous and organic movement, not as a fixed, forward-looking principle. His rhetoric brilliantly supports that very point and subtly directs our attention away from the conventional symbol of the time-bound Eleanor and Arabin, marrying, having children, and living happily ever after in power, and fixes it on the unconventional focus of the novel, the weak and retiring Mr. Harding.

Even more unconventional than the rhetoric, however, is the conservative comedy which is supported by the action and themes of the narrative itself. The organizing thematic principle in the novel is the notion of the fight.[10] On all levels—clerical, academic, journalistic, and personal—the central issues involve a struggle for power. The book asks such questions as who shall be warden?—who shall be dean?—who will replace Mr. Bold with Eleanor? These and equivalent questions involving values are given one answer: he who does not try. The real winners are those who do not fight. At the heart of the book is a profound protest against the competitive mode of life, and *Barchester Towers* thus establishes its comedy in direct hostility to the major progressive movements of the period: democracy and capitalism. But the issue goes deeper than this; the whole notion of power is relentlessly attacked. It is power that unites the issues of religion and love in the novel and establishes the most basic irony in the plot, when the arch-enemies Grantly and Slope end up on the same side in the war over the wardenship. All the values of the conservative comedy here arrange themselves around the belief in passivity and its accompanying antagonism to ambition.

The novel begins, in fact, with a bleak view of power and a repetition of the distinctions developed in *The Warden* between man as a human being, personally defined and decent, and man

---

[10] This point is developed most clearly by Robert W. Daniel in his Afterword to the Signet edition (New York, 1963), pp. 527-8, but it is implicit in many analyses of the novel. Most of the interpretations, however, read the comedy as developing from a coalition between the two factions. Bradford Booth's brief treatment (*Anthony Trollope*, p. 43), for instance, suggests that the proper balance in the novel involves a compromise of the forces of reform and of tradition. The more rigorous analyses of Robert Polhemus (*The Changing World*, pp. 35-50), W. David Shaw ('Moral Drama in *Barchester Towers*', *NCF*, 19, 1964-5, 45-54), and U. C. Knoepflmacher (*Laughter and Despair: Readings in Ten Novels of the Victorian Era*, Berkeley and Los Angeles: Univ. of Cal. Press, 1971, pp. 3-49) still accept this basic position.

as publicly defined, mad for power and dishonourable. Archdeacon Grantly's vigil at his father's death-bed brings into conflict the two sides of him, and though the question of 'whether he really longed for his father's death' is finally answered with a clear negative, the archdeacon is not able to keep his desire for power completely under control. When his father finally dies, he itches to send his father-in-law to telegraph the ministry and is, appropriately, too late. The narrator ends the chapter by discussing the archdeacon's disappointment and his desire for power and position. As usual, he removes all personal censure and attacks only the system itself. Clergymen, he says, are, like all of us, only men, and 'if we look to our clergymen to be more than men, we shall probably teach ourselves to think that they are less'. Thus the first chapter effectively begins to assert the need both for tolerance toward individuals and hostility toward corrupting systems of power.[11] Though as a worldly high-churchman the archdeacon is more obviously in accord with the principles valued by this novel, Trollope has an enormous amount of fun with this sputtering organization man, so eager for power and, in the end, so impotent: all his lectures go astray, all his plots come to nothing.

The attack on the alternate camp of churchmen is, however, the one that counts; for Mrs. Proudie and Mr. Slope are not only as much caught up in the lust of the fight as is the archdeacon but, in addition, are fighting for all the wrong values. Though the narrator introduces Mr. Slope (4) with an elaborate list of his similarities to Dr. Grantly, the implied differences are far more important. Where Dr. Grantly and the worldly high-church group assuage guilt, the Slopes and Proudies capitalize on it; Grantly is expansive and tolerant, while his enemies are restrictive and mean; Grantly is masculine, Slope, the most basic joke runs, is far less manly even than his comrade-in-arms, Mrs. Proudie. But no comparative listing can get close to the functional use made of the Proudies and Slope as negative illustrations to establish by contrast the novel's key position.

The Proudies are a symbol of local warfare and perverted ambition, and Trollope uses our laughter to attack both of them. Dr. Proudie, the epitome of the hen-pecked male, is still ludicrously ambitious and, sure enough, successful, all of which tells us something about the nature of success. He is known as a 'useful' clergy-

---

[11] U. C. Knoepflmacher's interesting and extended analysis of this opening scene argues for a basic ambiguity (*Laughter and Despair*, pp. 18–24).

man, a pawn of those who do indeed have power, particularly his wife. Mrs. Proudie is subject to some basic sexual humour and is a prototype of the big-bosomed, jewel-bedecked, pompous, and castrating females who are eternally attacked in literature. She reflects the novel's quiet but distinct anti-feminism.[12] By turning her into a kind of sexual amazon who, if all else fails, can still win her battles in the bedroom, Trollope appeals to sources of humour he so often claimed to have avoided. Slope, he says, might have had some chance in his fight with Mrs. Proudie had he been able to occupy her place at night. Since he cannot do this, Mrs. Proudie has, as we say, the ultimate weapon. These sorts of jokes transform both our tittering inhibitions and our sense of the grotesque into hostile laughter. Mrs. Proudie is besieged by other means too; she is not only rude but narrow, and no image is so firmly associated with her as that of the 'Sabbath-day schools' and their suggestion of dreary, crushing repression. Mrs. Proudie is indeed the enemy of comedy as well as the perfect comic butt. The dominant joke against her is that she is simply a man; she is ranked with men rather than women, the narrator says with a nudge and a wink, because of 'her great strength of mind' (33). There is more than a touch of the desperate in this sort of humorous attack, but by exaggerating the threat of conflict, it can call up laughter to eliminate that conflict and thereby suggest the positive values more clearly.

Compared with her chaplain, Mrs. Proudie is treated gently. It is the ambitious, progressive, and unctuous Slope who is the truly dangerous enemy and who is introduced so that the tendencies he represents may be expelled. In the process, he reveals a good deal about the moral premisses of this comedy. The very fact that his eloquence is 'not likely indeed to be persuasive with men, but [is] powerful with the softer sex' (4), for instance, suggests that he is as feminine as Mrs. Proudie is masculine and uses a similar sexual humour to assault him. But more important, his specialized success suggests the fatal lack of discrimination of women in general and Eleanor in particular.[13] Women, it turns out, are unable to see that

[12] George Meredith was especially struck by this quality in the novel, contrasting it with the works of the 'altogether feminine' Mrs. Oliphant and recommending it particularly to men as 'one of the most masculine delineations of modern life in a special class of society that we have seen for many a day' (rev. of *Barchester Towers*, *Westminster Review*, 68, Oct. 1857, 595).

[13] Hugh Walpole said Eleanor is 'Trollope's most tiresome heroine, and that is saying much' (*Anthony Trollope*, p. 46). True, but the effect, I think, is deliberate.

he is 'no gentleman', which, in terms of the code of *Barchester Towers*, means that they are morally cross-eyed. Slope's friends thus tell us nearly as much about him as his enemies. Eleanor is simply unable to understand her father when he gives the fundamental argument against Slope and, by implication, the central belief of the novel: 'It can hardly be the duty of a young man rudely to assail the religious convictions of his elders in the church. Courtesy should have kept him silent, even if neither charity nor modesty could do so' (8). When Eleanor objects that he may simply have been forced by his inner convictions to speak, Mr. Harding replies, 'Believe me, my child, that Christian ministers are never called on by God's word to insult the convictions, or even the prejudices of their brethren, and that religion is at any rate not less susceptible of urbane and courteous conduct among men than any other study which men may take up.' The fact that courtesy and urbanity, rather than truth or righteousness, are the supreme moral touchstones gets us right to the heart of this novel. Eleanor's inability to comprehend this doctrine immediately distances her a little from the novel's centre.

But Slope's contributions are not often so indirect. He is the most vocal apostle of the new world, the oily symbol of progress, and the 'new man' of the country: 'It is not only in Barchester', he says, 'that a new man is carrying out new measures and casting away the useless rubbish of past centuries. The same thing is going on throughout the country' (12). The 'useless rubbish' in this case is Mr. Harding. The attack on Slope, then, is an attack on the *Jupiter* and all the rude voices of discourtesy. Once the chaplain leaves Barchester, the society can function comfortably enough with the Proudies, who, at any rate, have no such horrid convictions about useless rubbish. Slope has, all along, been the chief threat to comic equilibrium, and he has been granted no virtues. It is true, of course, that Trollope makes an elaborate show of treating Slope with a consistent and fair moderation, insisting on his great courage and self-sufficiency. But Slope's courage is of the brand more aptly described by the vulgar term, 'guts', and is thus completely out of place in a world of English decency. He has, in fact, exactly the characteristics of the ruthless and cunning animals who inhabit the America of *Martin Chuzzlewit*, and in many ways Trollope echoes Dickens's vituperative rejection of the new doctrine of 'smartness' and the cult of success. Slope is a transplanted Colonel Scadder. The last reference to him makes his uncouth American newness even more explicit: 'It is well known that the family of the Slopes never starve: they always fall on their feet, like cats' (51). What had been matter of congratulation for Emerson in his strong celebration of the character of American youth, the 'sturdy lad from New Hampshire or Vermont', who '*teams it, farms it, peddles*' and 'always like a cat falls on his feet',[14] becomes a matter of repulsion for Trollope in his equally strong rejection of it.

One of the major instruments of this rejection is the Stanhope family, fresh, lively, and not very scrupulous negative comic agents. Essentially foreigners, they not only have the clear insight of outsiders but the proper rootlessness and can act without final consequences to themselves. They do a job which the morally approved and passive cannot really handle. In their cynical and good-natured power, then, they add both the necessary purgative force and the rebellious parody to the valued innocence. As in most comedies, once their job is done, these negative agents must be dismissed; for their real work involves disruption, not stability. They also suggest an amusing but also dangerous lack of commitment. In combating the self-deluded Proudies and Slopes, their flexibility and manœuvrability are admirable, but, as Trollope insists, their very good nature hides an essential indifference, even heartlessness, and they must therefore be shipped back to Italy at the end. If we look at them too long, we might recognize their worldliness and laziness as parodies of the approved courtesy and passiveness. 'I don't see why clergymen's sons should pay their debts more than other young men', says Charlotte (19). The cynicism is welcome and sounds very much like an echo of the narrator's insistence that we are all men, but the narrator really has a secret qualification, ignored by the Stanhopes. He suggests that we all are really gentlemen, pushing us upwards; the Stanhopes' cynicism levels downwards.

But Trollope handles these explosive agents with great tact. Their potential for danger is never realized, and their heartlessness is kept so well masked that they seem kindly, gentle, and, in the person of Bertie, essentially sweet. Bertie 'was above, or rather below, all prejudices' (9) and is always absolutely comfortable in his friendly indolence. He functions partly to attack work, prudence, and rigid convention and is, therefore, something of a reverse surrogate for the author and is given a kind of sneaky admiration and

[14] The famous passage occurs in 'Self-Reliance'.

approval. Absolutely without self-consciousness, Bertie is the
natural man and, as such, a perfect comic leveller. He enters Mrs.
Proudie's reception and immediately deflates the pompous bishop,
attacking him just where he is most vulnerable—in his notion of the
power bestowed by rank:

> 'I once had thoughts of being a bishop, myself.'
> 'Had thoughts of being a bishop!' said Dr. Proudie, much amazed.
> 'That is, a parson—a parson first, you know, and a bishop afterwards.
> If I had once begun, I'd have stuck to it. But, on the whole, I like the
> Church of Rome the best.'
> The bishop could not discuss the point, so he remained silent.
> 'Now, there's my father,' continued Bertie; 'he hasn't stuck to it. I
> fancy he didn't like saying the same thing over so often.' (11)

Bertie continually pursues the bishop with his conversation, and
his very amiability and openness—'I was a Jew once myself'—
expose the pompous churchman. Significantly, though most of the
clergy stare at Bertie 'as though he were some unearthly apparition',
'the archdeacon laughed'. And that laugh carries with it the signal
of moral approval for this fine comic executor. His climactic proposal (or anti-proposal) scene, then, is carefully arranged to support
the warm, uncommercial values. The narrator first makes it clear
that Bertie is revolted by the 'cold, calculating, cautious cunning'
(42) of the affair, not so much because it is iniquitous as because
it is '*prudent*'. He is the antithesis of the American-like Slope, instinctively repulsed by the game of power. In his gentle but firm
rejection of the 'new profession called matrimony' (42) he is rejecting
all scheming, forward-looking arrangements. He is, in this sense,
a heightened but not distorted symbol of the conservative tendency
of the novel.

His sister Madeline plays a more complex role and brings with her
a touch of a much blacker world and a more embittered spirit. However, she utilizes a kind of Freudian humour to transform her pain
into clever parody and continual witty victories. Her calling card—
'La Signora Madeline/ Vesey Neroni./—Nata Stanhope'—is itself
a fine parody of social forms, and she uses her daughter, 'the last
of the Neros', much as Becky Sharp uses little Rawdon, as an effective stage prop. Like her sister Charlotte, Madeline also sounds
like the narrator: 'Parsons, I suppose, are much the same as other
men, if you strip them of their black coats' (10). Madeline's distance
from that narrator is, however, clearly indicated by the violence of

the verb 'strip'. Signora Neroni's function is potentially harsh, and she can, clearly, be vicious. She plays Sam Weller to Mr. Harding's Pickwick and supplies all the force and aggression he lacks.

She also provides a bitter realism, which adds force and depth to the final solution: 'Marriage means tyranny on one side and deceit on the other. I say that a man is a fool to sacrifice his interests for such a bargain. A woman, too generally, has no other way of living' (15). Her cynicism is not explicitly supported, but since she does so much to ensure the solidity of the final approved society, the weight of her considerable experience and courage is assimilated into it. It is this crippled woman who is the most powerful. She manages not only to expose the hypocrisy and unprincipled ambition of Mr. Slope and to force Arabin to recognize that the 'good things of the world' are consonant with his religion (38) but actually hands him over to Eleanor, thereby arranging almost single-handedly the final disposition of the novel. The Signora Neroni has an absolutely sure moral instinct.[15] Though she traps the virtuous Mr. Thorne and exposes the gentle old man and his 'antediluvian grimaces and compliments which he had picked up from Sir Charles Grandison' (46) to some ridicule, she recognizes her error. And when Mr. Slope rudely laughs at him, she springs to the old man's defence, revealing the chaplain's failures with Mrs. Bold so ruthlessly that he dashes blindly from the room, while the avenged Mr. Thorne sits 'laughing silently'. She turns the tables on the powerful in this small scene as in the novel as a whole, adjusting the proper values and correcting our perspective. Because she is powerful, she cannot be made permanent in Barchester, but one suspects that she will be willing to come back from Italy should another Slope arrive. At any rate, she makes the cathedral town safe for the fragile values out of which the conservative comedy is built.

And all of the novel points toward the symbolic heart of this comic world and the structural centre of the novel in Miss Thorne's *fête-champêtre* at Ullathorne.[16] The party, at first seen as a monstrous

---

[15] Both Shaw, 'Moral Drama', p. 49, and Polhemus, *The Changing World*, pp. 41–3, have excellent remarks on this character. Her tendency to subvert polite society was apparently recognized even by the publisher's reader for Longman's, who was very upset about her effect on the clergymen in the novel and concluded that she was 'a great blot on the work' (quoted in Sadleir, *Trollope: A Commentary*, p. 170).

[16] These chapters are generally treated by critics as extraneous. They are, further, often read as straightforward satire. Shaw goes so far as to say, in reference to Miss Thorne's quintain, that her 'dangerous Celtic fantasies almost cost the life of young Henry Greenacres' [*sic*] ('Moral Drama', p. 51).

ritual of dedication to illusion and the dead, becomes the scene for clarity and rejuvenation, and the Thornes, viewed initially as hilariously superannuated, move closer to the approved position. The technique of diminishing perspective that Trollope uses here brings us closer to the Thornes and their values. Mr. Thorne is introduced in a tone of facetious detachment as a silly bore and a snob, supported by 'an inward feeling of mystic superiority to those with whom he shared the common breath of outer life' (22). His sister, 'a pure Druidess', simply exaggerates the fatuousness and obsolescence of her brother. The narrator's distance from these characters at first is so marked as sometimes to approach contempt: 'Miss Thorne was very anxious to revert to the dogs' (22). We are encouraged to laugh at these unreal and mechanistic anachronisms. The only tonal variation in this introductory chapter involves a kind of nostalgic tolerance which is blatantly patronizing: 'Who would deny her the luxury of her sighs, or the sweetness of her soft regrets!' The reader is led to view these people much as would Mr. Slope. But Trollope, even in this chapter, slyly exposes his method: 'All her follies have, we believe, been told. Her virtues were too numerous to describe and not sufficiently interesting to deserve description.' Her virtues are uninteresting only to the Slopes, and Trollope begins to reverse our position by forcing us much closer to the Thornes, quietly insisting in the next chapter on Miss Thorne's 'soft heart' and essential good nature and on Mr. Thorne's honesty and generous hospitality.

By the time of the party, some ten chapters later, the Thornes' dedication to the past is taken much more seriously. They are rather like the Tudor windows at Ullathorne, not pleasing to utilitarian and modern progressive minds but capable of giving immense 'happiness to mankind'. Instead of measurable candle-power, the Thornes give comfort and joy. Exactly unlike Bold who, with laudable motives, made everyone miserable, the Thornes proceed with murky ideas to make everyone happy. Our earlier laughter is directly rebuked, as the Thornes' mechanistic unself-consciousness is taken away and they are exposed as vulnerable and precious. In a fine scene just before the gathering, Miss Thorne tries to persuade her brother to ride at the quintain she has erected. Finally exasperated by the pressure she puts on him, he calls it a 'rattletrap' (35). Miss Thorne says nothing, but sips her tea and thinks of the past. As she does so, 'some dim faint idea of the impracticability of her own views flitted across her brain', and it occurs to her that 'perhaps, after all, her neighbours were wiser than herself'. The sadness of this moment of self-doubt brings a single tear to her eye, and Trollope uses that tear to establish the pervasive image of gentleness and kindness. 'When Mr. Thorne saw the tear in her eye, he repented himself of his contemptuous expression.' Miss Thorne, 'accepting the apology in her heart', tells her steward to be very lenient in admitting guests: 'If they live anywhere near, let them in.' As it happens, they entertain nearly the entire district, and we see that the Thornes' deviation from the common standard, which had once seemed so funny, really amounts to their attempt to be truly kind and generous: 'Miss Thorne . . . boldly attempted to leave the modern, beaten track and made a positive effort to entertain her guests' (36). Though she has only 'moderate success', this reflects sadly on the times—not on the hostess. After Trollope has cemented our attachment to the Thornes by this rhetoric of reversal, we are easily led, later in the novel, to accept what would ordinarily appear perverse—the functional shift of love (and sexual power) from those who are young to the old Mr. Thorne: 'But for real true love—love at first sight, love to devotion, love that robs a man of his sleep . . . we believe the best age is from forty-five to seventy; up to that, men are generally given to mere flirting' (37).

By this point the reader is also prepared to give full authority to Mr. Harding as the moral norm. The novel does include a pair of lovers, it is true, and does give them some prominence, but it seems to me an important critical error and a distortion of the crucial themes not to recognize the ironies which attend Eleanor and Mr. Arabin and the rhetorical instructions which move the reader away from them. It is particularly difficult to see how Eleanor can be accepted as a heroine. Not only is there a general distrust of women in the novel and a subtle but distinct anti-feminine tone, but there are explicit attacks on the young widow. Eleanor, very simply, is morally stupid,[17] and the dominant image connected with her is that of the parasite—clinging but deadly: 'Hers was one of those feminine hearts which cling to a husband . . . with the perfect tenacity of ivy. As the parasite plant will follow even the defects of the trunk which it embraces, so did Eleanor cling to and love the very faults of her husband' (2). Again, when Arabin finally proposes, the

---

[17] She seems to be stupid generally by the time of *The Last Chronicle of Barset*, as her handling of the check shows.

narrator insists on Eleanor's prospective happiness in the same terms: 'When the ivy has found its tower, when the delicate creeper has found its strong wall, we know how the parasite plants grow and prosper' (49). Even more subversive is the attack on Eleanor's selfish and sentimental use of her child: 'It was so sweet to press the living toy to her breast and feel that a human being existed who did owe, and was to owe, everything to her' (2). Her essential lack of self-knowledge is exactly like that of Thackeray's Amelia Sedley and is mirrored in the same image of child-worship as a form of self-worship. Because of this ignorance Eleanor eagerly enters into the fighting, defending Slope often not from a sense of fairness but simply from instincts of 'sheer opposition and determination not to succumb' (29). In the hilarious proposal scene with Mr. Slope, while we are expected fully to support the comic slap she gives him, we are also expected to delight in her embarrassment, the fruits of her ignorance. Both Eleanor's selfish reflections and Slope's champagne-induced 'tender-pious' (40) looks are finally ridiculed; the scene really makes fun of the triviality of the young. After this buffeting at Ullathorne Trollope makes the criticism of Eleanor explicit. She rushes home to cuddle her boy and assert that she would die without 'her own Johnny Bold to give her comfort' (44). The narrator cannot resist the appropriate sneer: 'This kind of consolation from the world's deceit is very common. Mothers obtain it from their children, and men from their dogs. Some men even do so from their walking-sticks, which is just as rational.'

While her eventual partner, Mr. Arabin, is not treated roughly, he is treated as more or less insignificant. Although not young, at forty he is not yet old enough to qualify for a favoured position in this novel. As a high-churchman most of his values can be approved, but he has dangerous ascetic tendencies and defends conflict for its own sake in terms which run exactly counter to the belief of the novel: 'But are we not here to fight? Is not ours a church militant?' (21). Further, his adolescent stammerings and gapings in the presence of women are subject to a good many jokes (30). He is not a bad man, just an unimportant one. The narrator even laughs about having to mention the details of his engagement at all (48). In the end Mr. Arabin becomes a kind of Mr. Harding-in-training, committed to the old-fashioned and accepting from his father-in-law the deanship. Even at the last, however, Trollope throws out one final barb at this nearly irrelevant couple. Instead of promising eternal love and a proliferation of young Arabins, the narrator lets them repeat the marriage vows and cynically adds, 'We have no doubt that they will keep their promises, the more especially as the Signora Neroni had left Barchester before the ceremony was performed' (53). This Dobbin and Amelia are certainly not allowed to dominate the novel.

But *Barchester Towers* is assuredly not 'A Novel Without a Hero'; after virtually eliminating the standard interest in young love, the final focus rests on the true hero, Mr. Harding. While Mr. Harding's values are largely defined by negation, he does display, here as in *The Warden*, an immense strength of resistance, the true power of the pacifist. He demonstrates exactly those beatitudes which the narrator blames Mr. Slope's religion for slighting: 'Blessed are the meek, for they shall inherit the earth—Blessed are the merciful, for they shall obtain mercy' (4). Mr. Harding 'had nothing to seek and nothing to fear' (5), the narrator says, implying clearly that he can be unafraid *because* he has renounced the ludicrous power struggle. His withdrawing from conflict allows him a unique clarity and an important capacity for self-doubt ('not . . . the usual fault of his order' (7), the narrator sarcastically adds). His particular strength lies in his 'nice appreciation of the feelings of others' (52). He alone has such clarity and generosity. While tolerant enough to allow 'the Pope the loan of his pulpit' (7), as Dr. Grantly says in exasperation, Mr. Harding is neither soft nor naïve. He immediately dislikes Slope for all the right reasons, and he firmly resists all the pressures put on him by his friends. His final triumph, then, reverses the general terms of comedy: his satisfaction, more complete than anyone else's (52), comes from declining power. In the world of fighting, Trollope argues, the man in the wrong is the one who is defensive, carefully storing up weapons, while the man in the right is confident and unarmed. 'The one is never prepared for combat, the other is always ready. Therefore it is that in this world the man that is in the wrong almost invariably conquers the man that is in the right' (37). Hence, one does not fight. But in not fighting one preserves the moral life, a life which can be expanded again—once Slope leaves and the *Jupiter* quiets down.

Doctor Thorne *and* Framley Parsonage: *The Pastoral Thriving*

In *Doctor Thorne* Mr. Harding's values are brought out of retirement. Here one must fight very hard, and in that sense the novel is much darker than *Barchester Towers*. Delicacy of conscience is no longer enough; even women must do battle: 'Honour, honesty, and truth, out-spoken truth . . . are worth more than maiden delicacy' (36). Many of the old comedy-of-manners premisses are here over-turned. Truth is hidden and no longer organic; it must therefore be sought and vigorously cultivated. Those who withdraw into con-science are simply swept aside by a world which has become nearly chaotic. The definitive social occasion is the Duke of Omnium's dinner, at which there is no civility, no politeness, only the loud feeding of 'hogs' (19). The only man of solid virtue, the Doctor, is outcast, and the Gresham estate and the whole world of settled value seem fast dissolving.

But out of this Trollope constructs one of his warmest comedies. The opening of the novel marks the apparent beginning of the end, but in the end we see the true beginning. The secret time sequence of the novel circles backward to before the time of the opening, remaking a past world and its values. The form of the novel thus attacks linear time and progressive logic. It formulates that attack and its deeply conservative consequences around an examination of a class fluidity that threatens to make the whole world into hogs. Behind all this is the railway, the new world of money, and thus an invasion of the pastoral far more serious than that posed by Mr. Slope with his low-church reforms. The essential problem is how to preserve Greshamsbury and its values from this invasion.

As the solution is worked out, however, a strong and moving complication is admitted. Unlike Slope, this invader, Sir Roger Scatcherd, is treated very largely as a victim, a man who is pulled into a vacuum of power created by the withdrawal of an effete and exhausted aristocracy. Once he begins to create, however, he is swallowed whole by that aristocracy. Inside the enemy territory, he has no chance. The whole problem begins, in fact, with an invasion from the upper class, Henry Thorne's rape of Scatcherd's sister. Incited by this act to revenge, Scatcherd finds the energy the aristocracy lacks, an energy that, in the end, feeds that same aristo-cracy and revitalizes it.[18] The informing myth is one of blood restoration, almost blood-sucking. The pagans with clubs who sym-bolically guard Greshamsbury, then, should be noted carefully, as

[18] Robert Polhemus also points out that Barsetshire needs Scatcherd, both 'his for-tune and some of his raw vitality'. He suggests that the theme of the novel is society's 'capacity to absorb change and to profit from it' (*The Changing World*, pp. 54, 58).

should the family motto, 'Gardez Gresham'. The narrator has great fun with the apparent ambiguity of this phrase, commenting that some believe it addresses the savages, asking them to guard and preserve the Greshams; others, with whom the narrator hesitantly sides, think it calls to those who seek to arrogate aristocratic power to 'beware the Gresham' (1). The ambiguity is mostly only apparent, not real. The Greshams are preserved by the energy (and money) they absorb from the lower class. The message is finally clear—and grim—enough.

Still, the aristocracy not only takes; it has much to give: a morality and a stability. Despite the Duke's party, the De Courcys, despite even Augusta and Mr. Moffat, the basic values have not been lost. Poorly represented they are, but that can be corrected. And corrected it is, by Doctor Thorne, who directs the action and creates a new world. The moral centre is not yet quite with the young, who are either silly or romantically weak, but Doctor Thorne is arranging things for them. Though presenting a far darker world than that of *Barchester Towers*, then, *Doctor Thorne* moves toward a beginning in an ending that is far more optimistic. It is a protected world still, but it is now protected not by withdrawal but by strong action. *Doctor Thorne* admits as much gloom as it can, as many anti-comic arguments, in order to move finally toward the conventional comic nucleus: the power of young love.

That the novel seems far warmer and less disturbed than all this suggests is due to the wonderful rhetorical control Trollope establishes over us and never loses for more than a moment throughout. He disguises the violence of the primitive myth of blood transfusion and reintegration and the very dark implications of class conflict by a variety of means, among which are a style more than ordinarily relaxed and a narrator of supreme serenity. Even the tedious opening with the extended and tedious apology for tediousness gives the impression of mere narrative. Throughout the book we often have the feeling that nothing is happening, that surely no novel so long has ever had so little going on. For great stretches of time the only apparent complication is provided by Sir Louis Phillipe, and the only thing holding up the resolution is his death, which we know will come before long. By thus suspending action and making the comic resolution so certain and so clear in all its details very early on, Trollope provides a cover that allows the comic form to contain much real darkness. The sense of confidence in the narrator is so strong and so generally unbroken that we are able to accept even the myth of sacrifice as if it were comic. The only real lapse in this control comes in the scene where Frank whips Mr. Moffat. Sending a scourge from the pastoral world to punish London seems a fine idea, but the tone both the narrator and other characters adopt toward the incident is unpleasantly vindictive, betraying a good deal of desperation and secret fear. But such revelations are never otherwise made in the main plot.

By keeping that plot apparently free of all substance, including action, Trollope can go to work with his narrator and subplots to make plain to us the terrible seriousness of the issues involved. It is almost as if the main plot were an ordinary bag into which very unusual materials were stuffed. That, at any rate, is part of the effect. The narrator, protected by the warmth of the main plot, can attack most of the standard comic conventions—the nature of the young hero, the beauty of the heroine, the nature of endings—not exactly with impunity but without destroying the comic form. He can urge on us a startling reality, as in the long description of Lady Arabella's hypochondria, which winds through some very leisurely jokes only to end with, 'Now the complaint of which Lady Arabella was afraid, was cancer' (14). The world so idealized and protected at the core is at the same time unsentimentalized and attacked around the edges. Even the ordinary practice of inserting a 'we' where we expect 'they' is used here with an unusual intent to shock. At one point, for instance, a lame old ostler laments the decay of the town of Courcy. The narrator points out how meaningless the new, bustling commerce is to those made desolate, and then rapidly removes the sentimentalized melancholy: 'There is nothing left for thee but to be carted away as rubbish—for thee and for many of us in these now prosperous days' (15). The threat made ludicrous in *Barchester Towers* is momentarily upon us with great immediacy. All this works against the undisturbed centre, forcing us to acknowledge both the depth of the problems and the capacity of the great old system to handle them calmly.

So it is with the minor actions surrounding the idyllic love-story of Mary and Frank. As we look away from that story we find almost unrelieved pain and barbarism: the destruction of the proud and courageous Scatcherd and the demolition of his wife and son, the horrible mercantile conscience of Mr. Moffat in love, Augusta's desperate quest for Mr. Gazebee and her betrayal, the Parliamentary election that comes to nothing, the reaction of society to Miss Dunstable and her Oil of Lebanon fortune, and Lady Arabella's fear of cancer. Only at the end, as the moment of resolution nears, does Trollope allow a minor action to echo the main plot. The story of the engagement of Beatrice and Mr. Oriel is a tactful reinforcement of comedy. He is a man who holds all the right values, 'thoroughly a gentleman' (32), and thus a shadow to Doctor Thorne or Frank, but he has developed a fanaticism about celibacy for the clergy. Such a belief parodies the real dissociation of Doctor Thorne and, before him, of Mr. Harding. The curing of Mr. Oriel's doctrinal lunacy quietly suggests the healing of the world and the expansion of its power. Good people can come out of hiding now.

But it is only at the end that the romantic comedy is allowed to dominate. Up until then it is really powerless and must wait upon the completion of another, more serious action. The real battle is not that of romance: lovers against the world, the true heart against prudence, that sort of thing. Such battles are waged, but they amount to nothing in comparison to the all-out class war, the fight between the worlds of Scatcherd and Gresham. The young lovers are not here, as they were in *Barchester Towers*, treated superciliously, but they must wait in reserve until the real war is over. Frank is made of the 'stuff . . . nature generally uses' (47) and so is Mary, but 'nature' cannot advance until the way has been made safe. The warm passivity valued in *Barchester Towers* can be regained only by some contact with the threatening world. The paradox is that the outside world must in a limited way be incorporated in order to avoid contamination. The principle is that of vaccination, and Mary is the perfect vaccine.

The maker and healer of the new pastoral is, of course, Doctor Thorne. The narrator introduces him by saying that Frank 'would have been the hero of our tale had not that place been pre-occupied by the village doctor' (1). The doctor must, like Prospero, create a world the young may inhabit, in which they may even pretend to be heroic. He alone believes that the symbolic union of love and money, self and society, may still be possible. Trollope's most extraordinary hero, Thorne achieves social power and the ability to act freely precisely because his own class and station are so ambiguous as to remove him from the class war. He can thus mediate between Scatcherd and Gresham and actually control both of them. Out of these two self-destructive and hostile classes he can form a new stability with the energy of the new world and the values of the old. Because he is removed from class anxieties, he can escape the terrors of aggressive social mobility and the collapse of values and stable personality such disintegration has brought about. In another sense, the doctor is not so much outside class as he is divided between two classes. He lives vigorously in one world but holds by the values of another. He protects himself in the midst of an unformed environment by an intense 'inner, stubborn, self-admiring pride' (2). Unlike Mr. Harding, he is essentially a fighter. He loves the values of aristocracy and is 'at heart . . . a thorough Conservative' (3), but 'he naturally hated a lord' (3). There is no contradiction here; the doctor simply forms an inner society in the absence of external ones; loving aristocratic values, he is bound to despise those who have betrayed them. Magically, this nearly schizophrenic man is also an artist, and he brings his inner world into being for others. He imposes what we would call his neurosis on to the world. Stubbornly refusing to let go of values that are dying, he saves them. There is a cost, of course, and the whole process of healing is a rough and damaging one. In this world, unlike that of most comedies, death is always present. The doctor, in fact, derives a great deal of his power because of this fact; even Lady Arabella must finally submit to him because she fears death. Doctor Thorne is a Mr. Harding, then, more elemental, more radically dissociated, but finally able to make bright a world even darker than Mr. Harding's.

He saves the world for Frank and Mary, for the nit-witty but lovely assumptions Frank makes—'I don't care a straw for the world' (39); 'I hate money' (29). Mary is much tougher, but it is the doctor who makes the world simple and conventional again. He does this by preserving Greshamsbury, appropriating Sir Roger's money—as loans while Sir Roger lives, absolutely when he dies—to keep the estate intact. The estate here stands, as it does in Jane Austen,[19] for the continuity of family and thus the continuity of values. Though the squire, his wife, and his connections may hardly seem worth saving, the estate itself has an importance that goes far beyond the present occupants. The narrator comments on this

---

[19] Much of Alistair M. Duckworth's fine explanation of the use of this symbol in Jane Austen is also applicable, with some modifications, to Trollope. See *The Improvement of the Estate: A Study of Jane Austen's Novels* (Baltimore: Johns Hopkins Press, 1971).

point with quiet understatement, saying that such estates as Greshamsbury are valuable because they remind us of what we once were and, now that he thinks of it, what we still more or less are: 'England is not yet a commercial country in the sense in which that epithet is used for her; and let us hope that she will not soon become so. She might surely as well be called feudal England, or chivalrous England' (1). As he thinks of it some more, the world of 'buying and selling' seems more repugnant, this chivalrous world more attractive.

But it is everywhere in decay. The ceremony of Frank's coming of age which opens the novel seems the beginning of the end. The aristocracy has almost entirely lost its sense of what it is, choosing like the De Courcys to withdraw or to pretend withdrawal in mock indignation from those who were 'diluting the best blood of the country, and paving the way for revolutions' (6). The squire does not even have the resources of this shabby pose; he has lost touch with himself and with his class: 'long as he had known him, the squire did not understand the doctor' (4). His failure to understand the doctor is his failure to understand the principles he presumably represents. He stupidly resists the energy of the new commercial class but fails to ward off their values, thus making the absolute worst of the situation. His daughter even takes her one commercial attribute, 'blood', and makes it into property, thus essentially materializing it: 'That which she had of her own was blood; having that, she would in all ways do what in her lay to enhance its value. Had she not possessed it, it would to her mind have been the vainest of pretences' (4). Poor Augusta is one of the sacrifices made on the way to preserving Greshamsbury.

The other great sacrifice is Scatcherd. Though like Slope 'a newspaper hero', 'the man for the time' (9), he wants to do no harm, has even a confused, hesitant respect for the values he is unconsciously threatening. Victimized by the failure of communal values, he is the individualist against his will. It is not that, like Slope, he loves the resources of his own being but that he has nothing else: 'For him there was no sympathy; no tenderness of love; no retreat, save into himself, from the loud brass band of the outer world' (22). He understands perfectly by the end that he has been lured by his great abilities into a terrifying emptiness: 'I'll tell you what, Thorne, when a man has made three hundred thousand pounds, there's nothing left for him but to die. It's all he's good for then' (10).

His son, Louis Phillipe, is, as his name indicates, his father's pathetic attempt to make contact with social values. But Louis Phillipe is a pure contrast to Frank. He grasps nothing but the surface rules and cannot follow even them. He is a decadent, living off cherry bounce and curaçao. He is also frightening. At the squire's dinner party we see that, though he is humiliated in one way, in another way he wins; as he sprays his rudeness about, the room gradually empties until only the doctor remains. Against the new barbarism the old values can only retreat in silence. Louis Phillipe is like Linton Heathcliff in that he is a freak biological accident, and much of the peculiar and uncomfortable delight we receive is in the accomplishment of our desire for these characters' deaths. Sir Louis and Linton drain off the bad blood. But neither is unaware of his function; Sir Louis senses his helplessness, the fact that he has been cast into a world that he can neither understand nor endure: 'I do wish to do what's right—I do, indeed; only, you see, I'm so lonely. As to those fellows up in London, I don't think that one of them cares a straw about me' (37). Like his father, he is left alone to be sacrificed.

But this potentially tragic ritual of sacrifice and renewal is handled so tactfully that, while deeply aware of it, we are satisfied that it is incorporated into the rhythms of comedy. Trollope uses all his art to be certain that we will recognize at the same time the perilous state of affairs generally, the great price paid by the innocent for a class victory, and also the wonderful joy of that victory. The pastoral is established now and nearly everyone can be included —even the Oil of Lebanon heiress, even Lady Arabella and the Duke of Omnium. The Scatcherds do not die for nothing.

There are no sacrificial deaths in *Framley Parsonage*, no deaths of any kind. Mrs. Crawley becomes ill, but she is ministered to by Lucy, and Lady Lufton sends marmalade. Together, they are more efficacious even than Doctor Thorne. That is because the pastoral world is not very seriously threatened; it even has the power now to go out and make war itself—and win. There are a few rebellious murmurs from Lord Lufton, and attempts are made on Mark Robarts by the degenerate liberals of West Barsetshire and on Miss Dunstable by the London world. But in the end all the stray particles snap back to the magnetic Lady Lufton and the powerful values she represents. She is forgiving and charitable, finally flexible, submitting to being educated herself, but never for a moment changing her values. The Duke is still there, but he has no chance against her. In their climactic meeting he has only the feeble weapon of sarcasm, but she has the enormous power of confident, silent dignity. She so stabilizes the pastoral world that not only are the Lufton estates secured, but the crumbling estate of Chaldicotes can be snatched away from the Duke and the London bureaucracy and added to the pastoral government. The pastoral almost seems to be undertaking colonization, with Lady Lufton as Empress.

The same patterns that dominated *Doctor Thorne*, the rebellion and consequent restoration symbolized in rebuilding the estate, are present here too. But now the problems are so greatly softened that there never seems to be any danger at all. *Framley Parsonage* represents the high point of the chronicle's celebration of the natural world. People are educated here, but their education causes them to return home, not to leave it. They grow into innocence, not experience. Even Lady Lufton is educated only to become more herself, the omnipotent and tolerant mother to all. In such a world all change seems trivial, even illusory; the threats to established power amount to so little, and the confirmation of that power seems so certain. Correspondingly, there is very little need for any action. Events, such as they are, follow no inexorable logic, but curl lazily back to where they began. Mrs. Gaskell exclaimed, 'I wish Mr Trollope would go on writing Framley Parsonage for ever. I don't see any reason why it should ever come to an end.'[20] Just as there is no real cause for alarm over any threats to Lady Lufton from rebellious sons or Dukes or time itself, so there is no reason for anticipating a particular course of action, certainly not an ending. Unlike the picaresque,[21] which the novel resembles slightly, the events themselves scarcely matter. Trollope himself spoke happily and with some sense of wonder at the enormous success of this 'hodge-podge' of a novel (*Autobiography*, p. 142). But in fact he had created a perfect English idyl, of the sort Tennyson tried for so very often and with less success.[22] *Framley Parsonage* is Trollope's improvement on 'The Miller's Daughter'.

[20] Letter to George Smith, 1 Mar. 1860, *The Letters of Mrs. Gaskell*, ed. J. A. V. Chapple and Arthur Pollard (Cambridge, Mass.: Harvard Univ. Press, 1967), p. 602.

[21] Cadbury, discussing this same sense of the unimportance of events, does link the novel to that tradition: 'The book is essentially picaresque' ('Shape and Theme', p. 328).

[22] The connections between Tennyson's English idyls and the Barsetshire series is discussed by Escott (*Anthony Trollope*, pp. 186–7). He suggests that Tennyson's poems paved the way for Trollope's pastoral.

Even more than in *Doctor Thorne*, Mr. Harding's values are given power, so much so that Lady Lufton completely dominates the novel, not only its conscience, as did Mr. Harding in the first part of the series, but its action as well. In fact, she is allowed to play here the parts of both Doctor Thorne and Lady Arabella. In a remarkable and successful experiment, Trollope makes her both the pivot of the value system and the major blocking figure. There is now no need for a detached intermediary like Doctor Thorne. The aristocracy itself—or at least a part of it—is in very good shape. Lady Lufton stretches herself and then relaxes into her normal attitude, and others break free of her only to return. It is a novel of charity and grace, not of protection but of expansion. There are no Scatcherds now, no really ominous forces, only a little corruption within.

Though there is perhaps no single major action, all the competing plots seem to have the same effect of releasing tension. Lady Lufton's values are themselves not at all demanding: 'She liked cheerful, quiet, well-to-do people, who loved their Church, their country, and their Queen, and who were not too anxious to make a noise in the world' (2). The only qualification that seems restrictive is the 'well-to-do' part, and, even here, Lady Lufton is not severe: she is quite willing to aid in repairing that defect if one qualifies on other grounds. Almost no one opposes her, and she is so confident in her power that she has free use of the great corollary of confidence, grace: 'Fanny . . . I have come to beg your pardon', she says with characteristic simplicity in a crucial and moving scene (5). The only comic tension is provided by Lady Lufton's stubborn resistance to Lucy, who really holds all her own values, and her equally stubborn campaign for Griselda Grantly, who holds none. This preference is explicable on many grounds. Lady Lufton is partly taken in by appearances, not fully realizing the degeneracy of the West Barsetshire which Griselda represents. But in fact she does see that Griselda is some sort of freak production of the *Jupiter*; her beauty is entirely public, a pure matter of reputation. Secretly, Lady Lufton is repulsed all along by Griselda's frozen quality. Her ladyship's aberration in taste here is caused most clearly by a lack of confidence that makes her rigid, unwilling to take chances. Shaken a little by her son's radical mutterings, Lady Lufton is momentarily attracted to one like Griselda who 'wanted the ease and *abandon* of youth' (11) and therefore seemed safe. In fact, Lady Lufton need not fear; she can absorb all of Lucy's naturalness and *abandon.* Lucy's appeal, unlike Griselda's, is private, idiosyncratic, but the absence of a loud public reputation is an asset. She enters the Lufton world without damaging it. She even brings new life to it—and to Lady Lufton—without at all disturbing the balance of power.

Lord Lufton's preferences have been right all along, primarily because he has never really left his mother. He is at first called a 'backslider' from old Tory principles, one who 'jeers and sneers at the old county doings' (2), and he makes some noises about how good a thing it is 'to have land in the market sometimes, so that the millionaires may know what to do with their money' (13). Still, we recognize that he is no threat, either to the estate or to what it symbolizes, his mother's values: 'The more we can get out of old-fashioned grooves the better I am pleased. I should be a Radical tomorrow—a regular man of the people—only I should break my mother's heart' (16). Lucy, who sees their future even more clearly, says that 'my grandmother's old tramway will be the safest and best after all. I have not left it very far, and I certainly mean to go back to it' (16). In the end, Lady Lufton decides to give way to the new generation, but the renunciation of power is nominal indeed. The last words of the novel assure us that she 'still reigns paramount in the parish'.

So much for rebellion. The story of Mark Robarts traces the same pattern but here with somewhat more earnestness. Robarts's pinched finances and dusty moral problems are to him so terrible that, as Ford Madox Ford says, they 'give you such pure agony of interest and engrossment as you can get out of the financial troubles over a few pounds. . . . I shiver every time that I think of that book.'[23] The tension comes about not so much because Robarts's financial problems are so tremendous, for they are in fact trivial, but because his decisions do seem to pose a real threat to Lady Lufton's world. Trollope deliberately makes Robarts's initiation story that of everyman. He gives him good reason to rebel against Lady Lufton, who has been genuinely tyrannical, choosing Robarts's career, manner of education, and wife for him, and clearly running parochial affairs in his place. As the novel opens, Mark is accepting Lady Lufton's choice for a parish schoolmaster, though he knows that the teacher chosen may be incompetent. 'I know I had only to explain' (1), Lady Lufton purrs. Indeed this is too much, and Mark must undergo

[23] *The English Novel*, p. 120.

what the narrator calls his slow growth to manhood (42) in rebellion against Lady Lufton so that he may return to her, seasoned
and submissive.[24]

When he wanders away he falls at once into the clutches of West
Barsetshire, the lair of the Duke of Omnium and his dangerous
allies. The motif of seduction here is very strong: the 'young flattered fool of a parson' (4) is lured by the promise of wealth, station,
and preferment into a world which, under the surface, is brutal and
cannibalistic. The Duke is omnivorous, and his empire is built
purely on deceit, on the new power of money. He gathers about
him, as Lady Lufton says, 'the sort of men who are successful
nowadays' (18), that is to say, intelligent frauds. The connections
among these people are like those that hold together Mr. and Mrs.
Harold Smith: 'it had never occurred to her to love him' (24). The
enemies are no longer the enthusiasts but the cynics. West Barsetshire can take care of its own bores, and as long as Harold Smith is
lecturing on Borneo, there is no apparent danger. The danger lies
in becoming 'accustomed' to such a world; Mark is in peril of having
his instincts and imagination corrupted. Since Lady Lufton's world
is built on delicacy of instinct and the expansion of the imagination,
the threat is very grave. When Mark reflects that Sowerby is 'a
pleasant fellow, and [gives] a man something in return for his money'
(12), he shows just how far gone he is toward corruption.

He is saved, of course, but this same Sowerby is not. The novel's
one victim, Sowerby is sacrificed to make a point. From a very old
family, he is not himself a vicious man, the narrator insists, but he
is so caught by the new world where money has replaced all real
values that he loses his grip on the family estate at Chaldicotes. The
narrator explains precisely just what such a loss means: 'to be the
member of one's family that has ruined that family; to have swallowed up in one's own maw all that should have graced one's children, and one's grandchildren! It seems to me that the misfortunes
of this world can hardly go beyond that!' (27). Sowerby wants to
try again—'If only he could get another chance!' (24)—but for
him there is no grace, no forgiveness, and no new chances. His story
is an ironic counter-image to the general comedy, illustrating that
the danger is potentially quite real.

---

[24] Trollope carefully protects Robarts against a charge of mere toadyism. As Cockshut says, 'It is as if he recognised Lady Lufton as the legitimate keeper of his conscience' (*Anthony Trollope*, p. 69).

But though Sowerby is lost, his estate is not, and the defection of a part of the aristocracy finally goes to support the genuine aristocratic values. For Miss Dunstable brings the money from the Oil of Lebanon fortune, marries Doctor Thorne, buys Chaldicotes, and thwarts both the voracious Duke and 'a ruthless Chancellor of the Exchequer, [who disregards] old associations and rural beauty' (3). Miss Dunstable plays the part Mary Thorne had played earlier, bringing new life and power to the aristocracy. She also echoes the temptation motif of the Mark Robarts plot. Her background and her fortune draw her so deeply into the world of the Duke and of London that she is threatened with the hollow and cynical sophistication of Mrs. Harold Smith. But she recognizes the problem: 'she knew that she was hardly living as she should live—that the wealth which she affected to despise was eating into the soundness of her character' (17). Through this recognition, through the use of protective sarcasm, she manages to hold on to enough integrity to be 'two persons' (38), one sophisticated and one natural. It is, then, up to the doctor to step forward once again for his most important work of healing.

By marrying Miss Dunstable he recruits into the pastoral society new power where there was already very much. The enemy is not only beaten back but forced to yield territory and rights. At the ending there is such a hilarious riot of weddings that the narrator has to introduce every artificial and subversive device he can dream up to keep the form of the novel from snapping shut. The assurances are very nearly absolute.

The Small House at Allington *and* The Last Chronicle of Barset:
The Fall and Rise of the Pastoral

But in *The Small House at Allington* they are altogether gone. At a point that looks like a comic climax, the hero, John Eames, saves the powerful Lord De Guest from a bull and wins the Lord's support and friendship. The Lord is a great believer in pastoral values and in his own shepherding powers: 'Guided by faith in his own teaching the earl had taught himself to look upon his bull as a large, horned, innocent lamb of the flock' (21). The wonderful ability to deny empirical fact is not shaken by this experience at all: 'The gentlest creature alive; he's a lamb generally—just like a lamb. Perhaps he saw my red pocket-handkerchief' (21). Johnny thus seems to be protecting the latest descendant of Mr. Harding, who will now confer pastoral blessings on him. Indeed, that is Lord De Guest's firm intention, and he goes to work with an open hand and a very warm heart to arrange the proper marriages and secure the proper alignments to support the old values. But none of it comes off. Suddenly the magic power is gone, and the major values are unrealized.

As a result, this novel is far and away the darkest of the series, so dark that it has sometimes been dismissed by lovers of Trollope who expected an uninterrupted idyllic series.[25] Adolphus Crosbie is the first really powerful invader from London, and the pastoral world seems to collapse before him. The degeneration of the aristocracy, that is to say, the growth in the power of liberal aristocrats, which had seemed to be checked in *Framley Parsonage*, is now out of control. The De Courcy people here operate like a nineteenth-century version of the Mafia, with equal power and equal terror. They tease Crosbie, whom they snatch hold of very quickly, about 'going about with a crook' at Allington (18), and soon teach him to distrust the comic and pastoral values. And he proceeds nearly to smash that world. It is scarcely redeeming that he is to some extent smashed himself.

Now as never before the pastoral seems a small island of virtue surrounded by conditions which are, in their essence, incapable of resolution. The paradigmatic activity in this new ironic world is Mrs. Roper's. She runs a 'genteel' boarding house for miscellaneous sorts in London: 'Poor woman! Few positions in life could be harder to bear than hers! To be ever tugging at others for money that they could not pay; to desire respectability for its own sake, but to be driven to confess that it was a luxury beyond her means; to put up with disreputable belongings for the sake of lucre, and then not to get the lucre' (51). Her daughter Amelia expresses even more succinctly the dominant and pointless immorality: she says she has been a knave and a fool, and 'both for nothing' (59).

In such a world nothing seems stable or connected. True virtue, therefore, is unsupported and can depend only upon itself. It is thus very likely to appear or to become perverse. It has none of the communal reliance which could make that virtue lie easily, unconsciously with the virtuous man. When, therefore, it is clutched firmly, as it must be, it becomes abstracted and unnaturally firm,

---

[25] Bradford Booth, for example, calls it 'perhaps the weakest link in the chain' (*Anthony Trollope*, p. 52).

removed from the rhythms of change and delicate modification that control comedy. Those, then, who would in a better world be chief actors in a natural comedy are now seen specifically as unnatural. Thus the problem of the novel is finally the problem of Lily Dale and the peculiar, twisted psychological position she finds herself in. At one point the narrator comments that 'it is the view which the mind takes of a thing which creates the sorrow that arises from it' (50). Lily's own view seems so outrageously arbitrary that we often want to shake her. The temptation to attack her is almost irresistible. Trollope himself found it more than he could resist.[26] But he also saw that her brilliantly portrayed suspension from the natural currents of comedy was at the heart of the book and its appeal. There is no easy explanation for Lily's state in psychological terms. That she is attracted to pain is certain, but, as in Squire Dale's case, that attraction is partly based on a certain and generally accurate expectation of pain in any case. Neither Lily nor Trollope is purely masochistic or perverse, or, if we choose to think that they are, a perception of the condition is less important than an understanding of its causes.[27]

Lily is not the only character who is firm unto perversity. Firmness is a characteristic of all those whom we are asked to respect in this novel. 'When did you ever know Christopher Dale change his mind?' asks Mrs. Hearn (9). Or any other Dale, for that matter. The theme of constancy is kept alive by frequent reiteration and by parodies in such people as the Hon. John De Courcy, who declares, 'they'll find no change in me' (17), and in his sister, Amelia Gazebee, who has 'done her duty in her new sphere of life with some constancy and a fixed purpose' (25). The fixed purpose is something close to legal gangsterism, but she is constant to it. In its serious reflections, such constancy represents the last grim stand of pastoral

---

[26] Trollope says that he could hardly share his readers' affection for Lily, 'feeling that she is somewhat of a female prig' (*Autobiography*, p. 178). See also James Pope Hennessy, who claims that Trollope's annoyance with Lily is clear within the novel (*Anthony Trollope*, p. 251), and Robert Polhemus's comments on her arid self-love, her 'self-indulgent sentimentality that debases a human soul' (*The Changing World*, pp. 91–5).

[27] Juliet McMaster presents a serious and accomplished argument that masochism and perversity are principles uniting all the plots (' "The Unfortunate Moth": Unifying Theme in *The Small House at Allington*,' *NCF*, 26, 1971–2, 127–44). Pamela Hansford Johnson says that the cross-grainedness is not so much in the characters as in the author, that it seems merely 'perverse' not to allow a happy ending ('Trollope's Young Women', p. 25).

values. It is the necessary reaction to the fluidity of all bonds. The insistence on a constancy at all costs, then, is the inevitable and very dangerous last assertion of permanence in an unstable world. The Dales and those about them have resisted the movements of the world, but their very resistance creates their vulnerability. The attempt to retain innocence in a fallen world leads finally to a mad fixity that displaces them from the world they sought to inhabit. It renders them unable to join the supple currents of a flexible nature: 'Was she not a Dale? And when did a Dale change his mind?' (8).

Ironically, this is said of Lily's sister Bell, who is one Dale who does, in fact, change, and change radically. She is rewarded for her change by being allowed to participate in the novel's only fully comic action. Other plots move toward comedy, but none is allowed to reach its destination, and Lily's plot is derailed entirely. The basic rhetorical strategy here is to play off the lack of fulfilment and resolution in Lily's life and others' against very powerful currents of natural comedy. The novel makes us see as clearly as we did in *Framley Parsonage* that a comic resolution is demanded, but here one is never presented. Everything in the novel moves toward comedy except the action. The major tension is thus established and the appropriate rhetoric of frustration produced. The formal conflict is arranged mostly through the intricate structural parallels in the four main actions: Bell's rejection of Bernard Dale and final marriage to Dr. Crofts, the movement of Mrs. Dale and the Squire toward greater understanding, the growth of John Eames into manhood, and the story of Lily and Crosbie.

The first plot is by far the least noticeable. Bell rejects the arranged love set up for her with the wooden Bernard, who 'had his feelings well under control' (7), so well that his tenacity in clinging to her seems entirely impersonal, a light parody of the twisted constancy elsewhere. Bell has plenty of firmness of her own: 'If there was anything in the world as to which Isabella Dale was quite certain, it was this—that she was not in love with Dr Crofts' (20). But of course that is what she is—in love with Dr. Crofts. Nature is allowed this one victory over unnatural, self-punishing rigidity. Such a triumph shows us what should, but does not, happen elsewhere.

One level more prominent but also one level more complex is the comic rejuvenation of Squire Christopher Dale. The Squire is one of those Trollope characters who is introduced with a long list

of faults and a very short list of virtues, often even made up of spill-
overs from the vices: an idle man does not, at any rate, commit
violent acts; a wrathful man is not idle. But there is always a quiet
climax to such lists that renders the other traits superficial: 'And,
moreover, our Mr Christopher Dale was a gentleman' (1). We
recognize immediately the signal intended here. Mr. Christopher
Dale is the moral touchstone of the novel; he is a gentleman, and,
moreover, his house, like Ullathorne, has Tudor windows. The
symbolism is quite unmistakable. Dale is concerned with the future
of his estate, the continuity of family, and he therefore becomes
deeply involved in the affairs of young people. All this sounds
just like Squire Gresham or a score of Trollope's other secret
heroes, representatives of the conscience of the county. Here, however, the Squire lives in constant expectation of being thwarted.
No one even pays attention to what he says. He is misunderstood
and alone, cut off both from his fellow squires and from his tenants,
really from the entire world: 'It makes me feel that the world is
changed, and that it is no longer worth a man's while to live in it'
(27). He could stand this feeling—it might even grow into the sort
of happy grievance Trollope's Tories love—but he is not able to
live easily with the hostility of his own family, his sister-in-law and
nieces at the Small House: 'You and the girls have been living here,
close to me, for—how many years is it now?—and during all those
years there has grown up for me no kindly feeling. Do you suppose
that I am a fool and do not know?' (37).

Mrs. Dale understands the full force of his complaint and begins
to understand the full warmth of his heart. In doing so, she begins
to come to life herself. She had vowed to 'bury herself in order
that her daughters might live well above ground' (3), another unnatural resolution virtue is forced to make, one the narrator flatly
says is 'wrong'. Mrs. Dale secretly thinks that it is wrong too, finds
no masochistic pleasure in self-denial, and frets about getting back
into life. The pressure of this romantic comedy is so great that we
are bound to pass over the Squire's protestations: 'What, begin
again at near seventy! No, Mary, there is no more beginning again
for me' (37). But, though he does manage to come more to the
surface, offering Lily money and working actively in the conspiracy
to help her, his rebirth is never complete. He never entails the estate
or arranges a marriage for Bernard and is troubled by his failure to
provide for the property. Correspondingly, his psychological growth

is also suspended and the narrator can only say at the end, 'he was a man for whom we may predicate some gentle sadness and continued despondency to the end of his life's chapter' (58).

But the Squire has a much more hopeful counterpart, the Earl De Guest, who refuses to give up on the pastoral world. When Dale tells him that the time for renewal 'has never come to you and me', his friend vigorously denies it: '"Yes, it has," said the earl, with no slight touch of feeling and even of romance in what he said. "We have retricked our beams in our own ways, and our lives have not been desolate"' (33). The similarity of the earl's life to that of Dale is stressed (33), but the earl lives in a different world altogether. He is purely of the country, living with a cosy disdain for London. He has never abandoned the comic premises his life has, on the whole, affirmed. He was poor, but now he is rich. He has, unlike Dale, solidified the estate and become a part of it: 'He knew every acre of his own estate, and every tree upon it' (12). Because he believes so firmly in innocent and beneficent change, he can himself practise a healthy constancy, not the one that is steadfast to pain but one that is loyal to happy alterations, satisfactory endings. He is, potentially, another Prospero, like Doctor Thorne and Lady Lufton, and when Johnny Eames saves him from the bull—more precisely, saves him from having to readjust his principles—the earl vows to support his young friend with all his comic constancy: 'Now, good-night, my dear fellow, and remember this—when I say a thing I mean it. I think I may boast that I never yet went back from my word' (32).

Johnny is the perfect natural hero: generous, open, and imaginative. He is Lord De Guest in an earlier stage of development, as the earl clearly recognizes. Johnny's faults are purely those which easy, natural education will remedy. He comes straight out of an irresistible tradition that rewards the gentle, the meek, the pure in heart. But here the tradition is resisted, just at the last. Johnny's education is, of course, conducted along the standard lines. He learns the first lesson of a Trollope gentleman, his comparative insignificance: 'I made a fool of myself, and have been a fool all along. I am foolish now to tell you this, but I cannot help it' (21). His insight and his impulsiveness are, according to the tradition, sure signs that in the very process of acknowledging himself to be a fool, saying so because he 'cannot help it', he is actively demonstrating his great wisdom and his very good heart. He can, therefore, survive a rough training period in London. He plunges directly into a hellish world.

There everyone struggles to hold on to connections, to bind people by force to vows that are always being broken. Every motive seems perverse, truly as masochistic as poor Cradell's 'moth-like weakness' for Mrs. Lupex's candle (11). Trollope specifically refers to this period as John's initiation and makes it seem all the more real by making it so very unsentimental. John escapes without cost to himself, but others are made to pay, especially the pathetic Amelia Roper: 'But the world had been hard to her; knocking her about hither and thither unmercifully; threatening, as it now threatened, to take from her what few good things she enjoyed' (51). John tries to slither out of this fluid world of the boarding-house with a few platitudes to Amelia about how it is all for the best, how 'we should never be happy'. But Amelia's startling response brings into focus for a moment the ironic world from which for so many there is no escape: 'I should be happy—very happy indeed' (51). But 'John Eames becomes a man' (59) and manages to 'come out of the fire comparatively unharmed' (59). He has so much on his side: 'You have everybody in your favour—the squire, her mother, and all' (52). The 'all' includes here not only the earl, who is speaking, but the whole tradition of romantic comedy. But though he can thrash the villain and win the heart of Lady Julia De Guest, Johnny cannot win the heart of Lily. The energies of the tradition are thus allowed full rein and are suddenly blocked, to our great dissatisfaction.

Trollope's narrator calls attention to this countering of tradition at the very end of the novel with a mock apology: 'I feel that I have been in fault in giving such prominence to a hobbledehoy, and that I should have told my story better had I brought Mr Crosbie more conspicuously forward on my canvas. He at any rate has gotten to himself a wife—as a hero always should do' (59). Crosbie, who is, the narrator insists, 'not altogether a villain' (18), gets what he perhaps deserves—nothing at all. He is punished somewhat by his marriage, but his wife soon flees, and he is liberated from definite punishment into a more appropriate emptiness. The form properly resists either punishing or rewarding him. Here, as elsewhere, resolution is denied. The novel makes it difficult to respond to Crosbie in any simple way. Though a genuine scoundrel, he really never meant harm. And he is a victim of Courcy Castle, which 'had tended to destroy all that was good and true within him' (23). Ironically, he finds it much easier to break the oath he has made to the constant Lily than that he has made to the slippery Courcy clan. There is

a much subtler sense too in which we recognize that he is running
to the Courcy people to escape another kind of victimization from
Lily. After the engagement, Lily puts a sort of pressure on him
that makes him feel caged and on display: 'And then she exacted
from him the repetition of the promise which he had so often given
her' (12). Surely this is merely Amelia Roper on a more advanced or
just less self-conscious level. She throws herself, as it were, into
Crosbie's arms and then looks up beaming, 'Yes, your own, to take
when you please, and leave untaken while you please; and as much
your own in one way as in the other' (15). He is understandably a bit
uncomfortable with the burden and the sly trap it creates for him.
Lily says she desires to 'do everything for you. I sometimes think
that a very poor man's wife is the happiest, because she does do
everything' (15). There is a desire for power here that exposes how
much of her excessive self-effacement, her exaggerated submission
to Crosbie, is really a cry of triumph. Crosbie hears the bray and
retreats. There is, then, a cutting sarcasm at work when Lily's
sentimental and deliberately cute resolutions to punish herself for
forgetting how much Crosbie is giving up by marrying her are
echoed seriously a page or two later by Crosbie, who comes to believe her. Perhaps he *is* giving up too much.

   But Lily's sentimental, mock desire for punishment becomes, in
her humiliation, genuine perversity. She recognizes that she can
discover no reason for her tenacity. At first she declares, 'I believe,
in my heart, that he still loves me' (30), but her firmness is not
shaken by clear evidence that he does not. Like a parody of Lord
De Guest, she turns away from all evidence and embraces a world
of absolutisms: 'I have made up my mind about it clearly and with
an absolute certainty' (42). Lily is not, then, just a masochist but
a sentimental idealist, one who, unlike her sister, prefers novels
whose capacity to minister to wish-fulfilment is greatest. Her pride
contributes to her firmness, too, but Lily represents the attempt
of the pressured pastoral world to reach out desperately for some
stability. The great comic Earl De Guest says at the end that time
will cure all, that Lily, like 'other girls', will change in accord with
the gentle pressures of love, sex, growth. But the earl is wrong, and
his hope for an innocent comic world where all bulls are really
lambs is never realized.

   There is as little hope for an innocent comic world in *The Last
Chronicle of Barset*, but out of the wreck of innocence this novel does

fashion another sort of comic society,[28] that, if less perfect than a pastoral and idyllic one, is also more open and less in need of protection. The optimistic levelling of *Barchester Towers*, the argument that 'we are all of us men', clergymen, authors, readers alike, is subjected here to searching re-examination. The novel begins by suggesting that the absence of a distinction between the clergy and society means not comic communion but mere anarchy:

'Why should not a clergyman turn thief as well as anybody else? You girls always seem to forget that clergymen are only men after all.'
'Their conduct is likely to be better than that of other men, I think.'
'I deny it utterly,' said John Walker.

From these very dark premisses, a new system must be constituted that will find a new source of spiritual authority.

Trollope felt that *The Last Chronicle* was 'the best novel I have written'; he especially admired the 'true savour of English country life all through the book' (*Autobiography*, pp. 274–5). The idyl of England is here concluded and the confirmation of the pastoral values finally effected. The novel is enormously crowded, bringing together all the other novels in the series, sometimes solving their problems—Bernard Dale now does marry and rescue the estate—sometimes admitting that they cannot be solved: Eleanor Bold is still as stupid, Lily Dale as obstinate. The effect of including so much is to suggest, of course, a finale, but all this variety also leads to what appear to be widely scattered, more or less isolated groups. The novel begins in the state of dissolution described in *The Small House at Allington* and rebuilds in the world of experience the values of innocence. It confronts the same unnatural perversity of virtue and makes it natural: 'The cross-grainedness of men is so great that things will often be forced to go wrong, even when they have the strongest possible natural tendency of their own to go right' (63). The novel explores new means of conquering that 'cross-grainedness' and establishing once again a coalition between human life and 'the strongest possible natural tendency' of comedy.

It does so by removing the boundaries that Trollope had so carefully erected in the previous novels. Slope, in effect, is allowed back in; the major enemy now is not the outsider but the fear

---

[28] William A. West's '*The Last Chronicle of Barset*: Trollope's Comic Techniques' also argues that the novel is comic in form. Though I do not see the comedy as quite so absolutely dominant as to make Crawley 'at fault' (p. 140), I find the arguments presented otherwise convincing, and I am indebted to this essay.

of outsiders, protective isolation. London, therefore, even the world of artifice, is enlisted to bolster the pastoral, and a union is thus created of the city and the country, the simple and sophisticated, nature and art. Trollope takes as the moral centre for this new comedy a new hero: an outsider who surely does not meet Lady Lufton's old tests for membership in the pastoral society. Mr. Crawley is neither 'comfortable', nor 'well-to-do', nor 'quiet'. He is uncomfortable, impoverished, rebellious, and in one way or another makes a good deal of noise, testing the society rigorously and finding, to his astonishment, that society passes the test. He threatens a tragic action but is absorbed by the comic society. It is true that his life is a demonstration of the impossibility of ever again erecting the placid society of pastoral, and he has some fine rebukes to the platitudes of comedy: when Mr. Toogood tells him he should take things easier, that he is 'too touchy', Crawley responds, 'Do you try it, and see whether you will be touchy' (32). Still, his harsh experience, which he imagines will disprove comedy, is simply a valuable stretching of it. It is as if Chaucer's Parson joined hands with the Franklin and agreed to learn from him. Crawley's heroism helps rehabilitate the world about him, but in the end that heroism must be put away: 'It's not natural; and the world wouldn't go on if there were many like that' (74). Only when he is reintegrated with the natural can he take over Mr. Harding's old living and inherit also his role as the spiritual centre of the community. He is a very different man indeed, grumbling and fighting, ill-reconciled and suspicious. But underneath it all he is generous and loving, trustful and pure in heart—in short, a gentleman. In the end, the natural wins, as always.

The natural is defined very differently now, it is true. The natural world is principally that of the irrational, and the irrational now is not simply to be equated with comic disorder. It includes severe emotional pain, madness, perversity, even death. But it also allows for love. The point of the rational action of the novel, the detective plot filled with clues and suspects and motives, is that all ratiocination is without point. Crawley's great opponent in all this is not, as he imagines, society, not even Mrs. Proudie, but his own 'woolgathering', that is, his abstraction, his dislocation from community. And the solution to that problem has nothing to do with reason. As Mr. Toogood says, 'One wants sympathy in such a case as that—not evidence' (42). Crawley's dissociation is caused by the world's irrationality, but his integration comes about through the same means, through the irrational exercise of sympathy.

Because of the importance of 'sympathy', women are now at the very heart of the novel. Their response to Mr. Crawley's presumed theft is the wonderful inversion of the threatening insanity, mad generosity. Miss Prettyman's reaction is most expressive: 'It may do for men of business to think [that he is guilty], lawyers and such like, who are obliged to think in accordance with the evidence, as they call it; but to my mind the idea is monstrous' (7). The world of evidence, as they call it, and of such men as lawyers is more absurd, more 'monstrous' than the simple world of the irrational. Miss Prettyman speaks with the sane madness of the creatures in Wonderland, to whom Alice's calm acceptance of predation and death also seems 'monstrous'. Miss Prettyman assumes that the world is more benign even than Wonderland, which is perhaps not so benign, and the novel, on the whole, is on her side. Mrs. Dale and Lily both understand Crawley's innocence fully, but Mrs. Dale expresses doubts about whether a jury will understand the grounds for such belief. Lily answers, 'A jury of men will not' (31). Lady Lufton, similarly, says, 'It's no use talking of evidence. No evidence would make me believe it' (5). Though the gentlemen of Silverbridge 'believed the man to be guilty, clergyman and gentleman though he was', the ladies, knowing much better, 'were sure of his innocence' (5). The ladies will not give up so easily on the whole range of values and behaviour implied by 'clergyman and gentleman'. Nor will the essentially feminine Mr. Harding, who, as his son-in-law says, is *never* wrong: 'I cannot for a moment suppose that a clergyman and a gentleman such as Mr. Crawley should have stolen money' (42). Mr. Harding can leave the world, secure that his values are finally confirmed, not in the quiet, cloistered way he would have preferred, but confirmed all the same. Clergymen are not thieves; gentlemen still thrive.

The plots in the novel are all co-ordinated to illustrate this growth toward reintegration in a more inclusive and dangerous world. The ironic plot involving Lily Dale is now relegated to a cautionary role, not disrupting but limiting the primary impulse, showing that the expansion of the comic world destroys its absolute perfection. The central action, then, is the final story of the county, of what happens to Barsetshire, as traced through Mr. Crawley, the new moral focus, and his daughter. The other flanking action, the London plot, is most remarkable for establishing through very careful parallels the extension of the old pastoral values and the attempt to carry them into full maturity.

Lily is still as she was, will clearly always be that way. But now she is seen at once as both unfortunate and tiresome. Her original attraction to Crosbie is explained as a more or less stupid failing: he 'had come before her eyes for the first time with all the glories of Pall Mall heroism about him' (70). To lose one's life for any delusory heroism is bad enough in Trollope's unheroic world, but to throw it away for the tawdry Pall Mall imitation! Lily is now simply an enemy of fertility. She is stamped with the absurd tag, O. M., and appears thus almost like one of Fielding's comic pedants or an American teacher who insists on being called 'Doctor'. Old-maidism is her humour. There is still pathos in her alienation, and that alienation still suggests the limits of comic power, but she is now far less important and her condition, therefore, seems almost accidental, an unfortunate example of the risks one takes in being alive. Her psychological position now seems far more arbitrary and inexplicable than in *The Small House at Allington*; Mrs. Thorne, in exasperation, calls it simply 'morbid' (59), which it is. Lily seems bent on protecting the comforts of suffering in silence, resolutely spending her time locking any doors that might conceivably open out of her neurosis. She claims, for example, that she still loves Crosbie but that, even if he were to love her, she would not marry him since then 'he would condemn me because I had forgiven him' (23). When it becomes clear that he would like to begin over, she retreats quickly enough. Johnny Eames might then seem to have a chance, but Lily grasps at the absurd letter from Madalina Demolines and uses it 'to harden her heart' against her lover. She has become wedded to whatever pleasures are available in the special tensions she feels and will take no chances on breaking these tensions. Her response to a bleak world is understandable, but disastrous: 'But don't you feel', she says, 'that there are people whom one knows very intimately, who are really friends . . . but with whom for all that one can have no sympathy?' (16). A character who can excite sympathy but feel little or none is finally not very useful in a comic society.

The climactic scene dramatizing Lily's dilemma takes place in a private gallery. Here, in a peculiarly stylized atmosphere, Crosbie presents himself, she bows, he retreats, and she executes a 'queen-like' exit (59). The entire scene carries with it a sense of very self-conscious art, as if we were watching a minuet performed by a row of clock-work dancers—all set against a background of greater artifice, not only paintings but paintings arranged and exhibited. Such artifice heightens the association of Lily with the unnatural and establishes the connection between the world of London and the world of art.

Oddly, this bustling world distances itself radically from its own nature. 'I fancy that I should best like a world in which there was no eating' (80), says Madalina Demolines. Madalina is described more accurately by her friends, who see in her not so much a dainty aesthete as a filthy 'bird of prey' (75). John Eames turns instinctively from Lily to what he hopes is life, but he finds only grotesque art. 'It's as good as a play' (25), he says, but underneath the fun is a desperate and vicious world of swindlers like Musselboro and of suicide, ruin, and absolute heartlessness. Art in London is seen largely as varnish used to cover a very unattractive article and thus deceive buyers. Madalina, John is convinced, 'rehearsed' (75) scenes ahead of time with her talented mother, who, he feels sure, 'must have passed the early years of her life upon the stage' (80); even their servants are 'wonderful actors' (64). All this acting is repulsive, finally, but not particularly threatening, since it doesn't fool John for a moment. He knows already what is art and what is nature. And art, in one sense, seems entirely immoral. Even Mrs. Dobbs Broughton is infected. Her wild playing at romantic roles—she thinks at one point that 'it would be very nice to break her heart' (51)—seems quite harmless. Her art criticism is certainly functional: neither industry nor genius is required in art, she says; 'the heart of the artist must be thrust with all its gushing tides into the performance' (51). But the narrator's suggestions that she is only out for 'a good time' are misleading. She is, in fact, nothing more than her repertoire of shabby romantic roles. She is innocent, of course, 'no more in love with Conway Dalrymple than she was in love with King Charles on horseback at Charing Cross' (38). She is not in love with anything else either, it turns out; she can only attach herself to such grandiose images. When reality comes crashing in on her with her husband's suicide, she has no response at all beyond a vague search for new roles, new costumes. All of London at one point seems like Sir Raffle Buffle: 'There is something imposing about such a man till you're used to it, and can see through it. Of course it's all padding' (35).

But London is finally not this empty, and the novel reaches out
to embrace even its art. The world of defensive artifice is torn down
by reality so that, in the end, reality may be made into art. Conway
Dalrymple's mythological idealizations of rich city merchants and
their wives seem surely the most wildly artificial acts in all of
artificial London. His blithe choice of the subject of Jael and Sisera
for his great painting seems at first wholly ironic. The unspeakable
violence of the subject suggests the underside of the London world,
just as Conway's bland acceptance of the violence suggests the way
art is being used. Johnny Eames significantly turns away from the Jael
and Sisera image with a shudder: 'I never could quite believe that
story' (25). John is of the natural world, however, and, in any event,
has already been initiated into reality by the gentle hands of Amelia
Roper. But Dalrymple needs something stronger and finds it in the
redemptive reality granted by this painting. Through it he meets
Mrs. Van Siever and her daughter Clara, whom he thinks perfect
as Jael, impassively about to drive a nail through Sisera's skull.
These women both appear very 'savage'; that is, they are nature
tormented and turned vicious. Mrs. Van Siever senses the dominant
role of art in society and expresses a decided preference for the
'ugly'; if she had the power, Clara says, there would be no art and
no artists (24). Clara herself is a person whose beauty is apparent
only by daylight, not candlelight (26), and who therefore is scarcely
seen at all in the London world. The artist begins to see through
his own art, however, and tries to propose to her. She is unimpressed
by his exalted language and is discomposed by a proposal from a
man in painter's costume. He finally becomes perplexed by the
dizzying mixture he is involved in, looking 'upon the young lady
before him both as Jael and as the future Mrs. Conway Dalrymple,
knowing as he did that she was at present simply Clara Van Siever'
(60). So he removes his costume and speaks in 'the plainest possible
language' (60). Such language and especially, the narrator says, 'the
very taking off of his apron' win the complete, almost fierce love
of Clara. At the end, the villain Musselboro is expelled and Mrs.
Van Siever finally gives 'full approval' (84) to the wedding. Even
London is alive and can prosper.

These scenes of London art have not always been appreciated,
I know, but they seem to me to represent Trollope's finest use of
a parallel subplot to explain and reinforce the major action. For
there is plenty of art in Barsetshire too. Much of it is of the order of

Lily's romantic neurosis or John Eames's equally romantic compensation: 'He thought that he could look forward with some satisfaction towards the close of his own career, in having been the hero of such a love-story' (35). But the principal artist is Mr. Crawley, who constructs for himself a grand tragic drama in which he takes the leading part.[29] Circumstances and society conspire, of course, to set up the potential tragedy, but circumstances and society are eager to pull down the stage and get on with living long before Mr. Crawley will relinquish the pleasures of grandeur. At first, Mr. Crawley tries to find release from the cruel world about him in a separate, more orderly world: 'He could be logical with a vengeance,—so logical as to cause infinite trouble to his wife, who, with all her good sense, was not logical' (4). Throughout the novel his wife is his link with society and comedy. Right from the start references to her are used to subvert the purity of Mr. Crawley's tragedy and to create a comic alternative. In the first chapter the narrator says that the terrible pressure on Mr. Crawley made him 'morose, sometimes almost to insanity'; as a result, he spends his life 'very much in the dark, as Mrs. Crawley was in the habit of leaving him' (1). This delicate touch connects this grim plot to the comic theme of female dominance and also quietly suggests alternatives to irrational chaos which are held firmly by the women: irrational trust and irrational love. Mrs. Crawley can sometimes even lose patience with her husband: 'Be a man and bear it. Ask God for strength, instead of seeking it in an over-indulgence of your own sorrow' (12). But the suggestion of hen-peckery is extremely light, used only to qualify the absolutism of Mr. Crawley's pride, not his dignity. He is brought back to life by Mrs. Proudie. She awakens in him the wonderfully comforting feeling of having a real and substantial enemy. He can attack and silence Mrs. Proudie, which is more than he can do with poverty. We begin to see, too, that the Proudies have never been real enemies, that they have brought a mild and good opposition that has, in the end, made everyone's life more pleasant. It gives everyone something to attack. The saddest moment in Trollope is when the Bishop refuses any longer to allow his wife her own fun in attacking. She has nothing to do but die, and

---

[29] Polhemus also terms Crawley a 'would-be tragic martyr-hero' (*The Changing World*, p. 131). According to Polhemus, not comedy but 'a melioristic rational world' (p. 131) overcomes Crawley's tragedy. Crawley is a 'genuine tragic figure' (p. 136) whose failure to find tragic resolution is due mostly to Trollope's anxiety to please his audience.

the genuine pathos of this death[30] exhibits to us how unrealistic Mr. Crawley is in casting her as the antagonist in his tragedy.

It gives him pleasure to reflect on the ways in which his sufferings are more exquisite than those of St. Simeon Stylites (41) and to imagine, not unlike Mrs. Dobbs Broughton, what a 'grand thing' it would be 'if the judge would condemn him to be imprisoned for life' (62). He revolves the tragic formulas in his head: 'Great power reduced to impotence, great glory to misery, by the hand of Fate,— Necessity, as the Greeks called her' (62), and he runs stubbornly and contentedly into a perverse absolutism much like Lily's: he wants justice and right to prevail, and he says, 'in the adjustment of so momentous a matter there should be a consideration of right and wrong, and no consideration of aught beside' (68). Giles Hoggett's famous advice, 'It's dogged as does it', is therefore by no means the moral of the tale but a poison to Crawley's system, causing an unnatural growth in his determination to be King Lear. He cannot finally resist the role and incorporates tragic elevation into his everyday language, which is so oratorical, so directly transplanted from the Old Testament, that his wife has a sensation of his acting as strong as Johnny's wonder at the talents of Madalina and her mother. As a result, 'she could not quite believe that her husband's humility was true humility' (32).

The toughest problem in this comedy is to rescue the tragic hero. In the end nearly everybody volunteers for the job, but the leader is Mr. Toogood, who begins the campaign for his cause at his first meeting with Crawley. Speaking of his family, Toogood says they are 'pretty toll-loll for that. With twelve of 'em, Mr. Crawley, I needn't tell you they are not all going to have castles and parks of their own, unless they can get 'em off their own bats' (32). Crawley is 'disgusted by the attorney's bad taste, shocked by his low morality, and almost insulted by his easy familiarity' (32), but still 'he liked the attorney'. Toogood expresses an impulsive and generous love for Mr. Crawley, an absolute belief in his innocence, that begin to lure the clergyman back from art. Toogood's own work, however, he compares to that of 'theatrical managers' (42), and it is partly a new art that wins Mr. Crawley back to nature, a comic art of sympathy. The resolution unites nature and art just as it unites reason again

---

[30] The scene of Mrs. Proudie's death has inspired admiration and extensive commentary. The best of this is by Trollope in *An Autobiography*, p. 276, and by E. M. Forster, *Aspects of the Novel* (London: Edward Arnold, 1927), p. 52.

with natural impulses. Mr. Crawley was not, as it happens, mad or even wrong. Both his mind and the best feelings of the community are preserved. But he must be changed still. He is, as Toogood says, a great subject for pure art—'somebody ought to write a book about it,—indeed they ought' (77)—but not 'natural' enough for life. Mr. Crawley arrives, though, very quickly; he even drops the language borrowed from the Book of Isaiah and begins to speak as ordinary men, astonishing the Dean with his jocularity: 'It was a narrow squeak—a very narrow squeak' (79). He is almost punished with kindness, forced into a lovely old house, a larger income, and the warm protection of the Thornes of Ullathorne, our old *Barchester Towers* friends. He quickly finds some 'intimacy with the haunts of men' (83) and even is reconciled to the archdeacon, who 'is of the earth, earthy', he thinks (83). And so he is, but then so, in a sense, is Mr. Crawley. And they are both 'gentlemen', as the archdeacon insists, thus reconnecting the world and suggesting a renewal of spiritual leadership, an infusion of vigour, even tragic energy, into the relaxed comfort and certain values that had seemed to pass away with Mr. Harding.

The other half of the alliance, the archdeacon, is tested himself, but it is a comic testing, and we know the outcome from the start. So does he. He vows to block his son's marriage to Grace Crawley and never to see his errant boy again, 'and yet as he said it, he knew that he would not have the strength of character to carry him through a prolonged quarrel with his son' (2). The weak, romantic son wins the loyal and poor girl despite the opposition of the father who, all along, is on the son's side in his heart. Such is the formula for many of Trollope's sweetest and least disturbed comedies. It is as if *Rachel Ray* were running through this dark novel. And so it does, asserting very simply the continued life of pastoral values. Grace Crawley tries to argue with Henry that the circumstances around her are so strong they must repress any love. But Henry, backed by a host of encouraging old ladies, especially the Misses Prettyman and Mrs. Thorne, by a spirit of opposition to his father, by an innate stubbornness of his own, and by a flabby but warm heart, argues that love conquers all. He wins, of course, not because his threats to emigrate or to break up the estate are powerful but because his father's heart is so soft, so essentially young. Mr. Harding says of the proposed marriage that 'if the young people love each other, I think it would be the best thing in the world' (49). Not only is he

never wrong, but he is not so different from his son-in-law. In the
end, all the archdeacon wants is for his son not to 'treat me as
though I were nobody' (73). He loses as little power, finally, as
Lady Lufton, because, like her, he is not really removed from the
tenderness and the enthusiasm of the young. When he comes face
to face with Grace Crawley, he recognizes how cultivated her beauty
is. He had been expecting 'the miller's daughter' (57) but finds
instead a woman whose instincts and values are his own. He nearly
falls in love with her himself: 'His soft heart, which was never very
well under his own control, gave way so far that he was nearly moved
to tell her that, on his son's behalf, he acquitted her of the promise'
(57). Because of this pervasive softness of heart, the principal force
in the novel is the force of romantic comedy, of a special artifice:

'If he loves you, Grace, the service he will require will be your love in
return.'
'That is all very well, mama,—in books; but I do not believe it in
reality. Being in love is very nice, and in poetry they make it out to be
everything. But . . .' (41)

As it happens, and as Grace discovers, life is poetry and, as poetry
makes out, love is everything.

CHAPTER 5

VARIATIONS IN IRONY
(*1867–1875*)

THE MAJOR novels of this period proclaim the principles of comedy much more loudly than the earlier novels. There are many passages that read rather like rules from a textbook on the comedy of manners: 'the usual courtesies of society demand that there shall be civility— almost flattering civility—from host to guest and from guest to host' (*The Vicar of Bullhampton*, 8). But equally characteristic is the remainder of this passage and its sarcastic inversion: 'and yet how often does it occur that in the midst of these courtesies there is something that tells of hatred, of ridicule, or of scorn! How often does it happen that the guest knows that he is disliked, or the host knows that he is a bore!' The happy voice is continually being outshouted by the ironic, but then so is the ironic voice challenged by the comic. Again in *The Vicar of Bullhampton*, for instance, there is an especially important scene when the prostitute Carry Brattle tells the Vicar that nobody loves her, that love simply does not exist in her world. Now the Vicar is throwing all of his training and the whole of his Christian belief into reclaiming Carry, and such a declaration challenges that belief directly and, so it seems, success- fully: 'He thought for a moment that he would tell her that the Lord loved her; but there was something human at his heart, something perhaps too human, which made him feel that were he down low upon the ground, some love that was nearer to him, some love that was more easily intelligible, which had been more palpably felt, would in his fraility and his wickedness be of more immediate avail to him than the love even of the Lord God' (25). The Vicar, un- supported in his cause by God and His love, stands for a moment in an empty world. But his next response fills the world again with a new and human substance: 'I love you, Carry, truly. My wife loves you dearly' (25). The form of this particular novel, and of the other major novels of this period, achieves some similar balance between comedy and irony.

But the full satisfactions of neither are available to us, and we are likely to regard all of these novels as interesting failures. Trollope himself spoke very slightingly of the best novels in this group: *The Vicar of Bullhampton* 'certainly is not very good'; *He Knew He Was Right* is 'nearly altogether bad'; *Ralph the Heir* is 'one of the worst novels I have written'; even *The Way We Live Now* is seriously flawed by its satiric exaggeration and flabby love story.[1] He also defended the weakest novels of this period—*Sir Harry Hotspur of Humblethwaite*, *The Claverings*, and *Lady Anna*[2]—probably because he could see little difference between them and their much more admired cousins. In any event, they all seek the same end: the creation of a desire in the reader for a formal resolution that is, in turn, frustrated. The anticipation of the satisfactions appropriate either to comedy or irony is aroused but never fulfilled. These are the novels in which Trollope explores most fully the use of unconventional moral centres: madmen, prostitutes, swindlers. More often, we get the sense of an uncertain focus, of a shifting focus, or of none at all. We often do not know which is the main plot and which the cautionary or exceptional one, which action establishes the hope of the world depicted and which one sets its limits. Is the quixotic Vicar or the embittered, atheistic Jacob Brattle at the heart of *The Vicar of Bullhampton*? Is Roger Carbury in *The Way We Live Now* a moral guide or a crusty senex? Are we meant to attend more to Trevelyan's madness or to the successful love stories in *He Knew He Was Right*? Funerals and marriages come at the same time, and we hardly know in which we are required to participate. Alternate plots in the same novel suggest absolutely opposite conditions of being. The narrator's comments move us in directions contrary to those we are led by the action to anticipate.

The best place to look for an explanation for this curious formal duplicity or ambiguity is, I think, in the major chronicle being written during this time. As with the novels surrounding and infiltrating the publication of the Barsetshire series, these later novels support the Palliser series by providing an opportunity for experiment. The Palliser series is as much a probing of irony as the Barsetshire series was of comedy. The Barsetshire world is best defined by Mr. Harding, the Palliser world by Mrs. Carbuncle and Lord George

---

[1] See *Autobiography*, pp. 333, 322, 343, 355–6.

[2] See *Autobiography*, pp. 335, 197–8, 347; see also the joke in the letter to Mary Holmes, 6 July 1874: 'Lady Anna is the best novel I ever wrote! Very much!! Quite far away above all others!!!' (*Letters*, p. 321).

de Bruce Carruthers. When the Barsetshire values are pressed hardest, Mr. Crawley is isolated, but he is, we see, never alone; Phineas Finn, however, really is alone in a world that is fallen. Such support as he receives is scattered and sporadic, and those he trusts most and who see most deeply into life explain that they can never be certain that any man would not, under the pressure of circumstances, commit murder. For Crawley, those who see most deeply know that no circumstances could ever make a gentleman turn thief. But the word 'gentleman' hardly has public meaning in the Palliser series. There are gentlemen about, to be sure, right at the heart even, but they no longer form a society around those crucial values which define and support the word 'gentleman'. Mr. Harding's values are established, but the Duke finally stands almost entirely alone. Phineas's rescue, unlike Mr. Crawley's, has no social resonance. He and Madame Max stand against the ignorant armies without any hope of bringing light. The Palliser novels are explorations of processes of accommodation, all more or less unsatisfactory, to the ironic world.

Techniques for achieving this delicate balance are developed and tested outside the series. The first novels, *Linda Tressel*, *Sir Harry Hotspur*, and *The Claverings*, are all rather crude and violent attempts to investigate the effects of directly inverting comedy. *He Knew He Was Right*, *The Vicar of Bullhampton*, *Ralph the Heir*, and *Lady Anna*, however, establish the balance by working mostly with the techniques mentioned before: unconventional or uncertain moral standards, contradictory subplots, and a subversive narrator. *The Way We Live Now* continues these attempts and adds a new element, the satiric narrator. Reaching back to the model in Thackeray's *Vanity Fair*, Trollope plays off the alternating comic and ironic plots against a narrator who attacks both. Its reputation to the contrary, the novel seems to me neither successful nor especially dark. It is, however, extremely illuminating; Trollope always is revealing and almost unfailingly interesting when he tries to extend his range— even when, as here, he decides that the attempt was a mistake, even when he reaches that decision before the novel is over.

Nina Balatka and *Linda Tressel*, those odd books published anonymously, are almost as revealing. What reasons Trollope may have had for these and other excursions into new settings are not clear to me, but such settings, whether in Ireland, Prague, Nuremberg, Australia, or America, seem to suggest to him civilizations with highly unsteady principles and therefore less stability than England. In each, therefore, he could work out problems in a simplified form. Linda and Nina and Sir Harry Hotspur are white rats, electrodes and all, helping to establish conditions that will make possible Lizzie Eustace, the Duke as Prime Minister, and the mature Glencora. The simpler characters also participate in actions that attempt the most direct sort of comic reversal.

These novels stand comedy on its head. *Linda Tressel* and *Sir Harry Hotspur of Humblethwaite* both reverse the results of a traditional comic situation wherein a young and spirited heroine holding to the values of the heart stands against the prudent and restrictive maxims of her elders. The histories of rebellious girls occupying the major novels are here reduced to essentials and pushed to grim extremes. In *Linda Tressel* the heroine's instinctive search for love and joy is tested against the power of a Calvinist aunt to convince her that she, her instincts, and the world at large are 'vile'. The aunt, supported by the gruesome wisdom of the townsfolk, sets about to break Linda's spirit and force her into a marriage that is safe and profitable. But, though Linda's mind and even her imagination are captured, her instincts apparently triumph, and she runs off with her anarchist lover. *Rachel Ray* all over again, it appears. There had been many hints prior to the elopement that such a triumph was in store for romantic readers and a romantic heroine. Linda's curls, for instance, though a cause of the greatest concern to her aunt, who wants them to be 'confined' and invisible, 'would be seen over her shoulders and across her back, tempting the eyes of men sorely' (2). But the attempted elopement flops dismally, and all the hints come to nothing. Almost before the conductor has come around for tickets, the anarchist lover has proved himself to be something of a scoundrel, and Linda is plunged into misery: 'For Linda the worst circumstance of all was this, that she had never as yet brought herself to disbelieve her aunt's religious menaces' (14). Her one rebellious experiment tends to verify her aunt's gloom, and there is no escape anywhere for Linda. She has nothing to do but die. It is a pointless death too: the aunt just begins to see the consequences of her life-denying religion, but as soon as Linda is buried, she regains her bearings and 'the fury of her creed returned' (17).

Sir Harry Hotspur of Humblethwaite, 'written on the same plan as *Nina Balatka* and *Linda Tressel*', Trollope says (*Autobiography*,

p. 335), is slightly more subtle, removing such obvious external enemies as Calvinism and substituting conventional romanticism as the final psychological trap. Comic expectations become the major source of disaster. Here a very good-natured and sorely tried Hotspur is attempting to preserve the integrity of his estate by settling the questions of its inheritor. Characteristically, he has no easy choices: his son is dead, and the natural heir is a villain. So he arranges to leave the money and land to his daughter's husband-to-be, trusting to nature, he says (4), to set things right when she marries. But nature is most untrustworthy, allowing the daughter ironically to fall in love with the villain. She is not only in love with him but sees him as 'godlike', 'divine' (2). As the evidence of her lover's swindling, adultery, lying, and cheating mounts, Emily clings the more tenaciously to her romantic image of him. Poor Sir Harry, trying to extricate everyone sensibly, finds comic doctrines being brought against him by friends: 'young people in such contests could always beat the old people' (13). Such comedy is now clear madness, and Sir Harry is forced to watch Emily die of a broken heart. The villain goes 'from bad to worse' (24), and the estate is left to some immensely wealthy and distant cousin who hardly notices the addition to his land, swallowing the Hotspur estate and the name without so much as a blink.

Trollope generally works out such comic reversals with far less simplicity and finality, however. These novels are characteristically not so much reversals as mixtures of comedy and irony, even when, as in *The Claverings*, the mixtures are somewhat lumpy. Trollope questioned whether 'any one reads *The Claverings*' (*Autobiography*, p. 198), a point now beyond question, but the novel is one of his most interesting if also one of his most imperfect investigations of romantic comedy. It explores a variety of solutions to the problems posed by the conflict between prudence and romance. Until the very end, none of the solutions seems very satisfactory. Throughout the novel nature has been able to help very little, but just as things look hopeless, she steps in with some effective but very unusual comic aid: serious illness and death. The vacillating hero becomes so sick that he can be browbeaten into some kind of resolution, and a couple of scoundrels are happily lost at sea. This last act the narrator desperately wants us to see as kindly: 'Was it not well that two such men should be consigned to the fishes. . . ?' (44). The widow, after all, though she feels a little down at present, will soon find out, he says, that she was 'well quit' of her husband, that 'her period of comfort was in truth only commencing' (44). But despite this cheerleading, it is hard to become enthusiastic on the side of illness and death and hard to see how they satisfactorily settle the issue.

In fact, they do not. Trollope tries to graft on to an ironic story a comic resolution, and it does not take.[3] Comedies may include such dire events, but they can hardly be made to depend on them. Until the very end the novel appears to be an exposition on the paralysing effects of doubt, much like Tennyson's 'Supposed Confessions'. The hero endures 'an agony of doubt' (42) for weeks over whom to marry, while the girl who truly loves him says that she will not die if he leaves her but very well may if he does not decide to do something: 'It is only the doubt that kills one' (40). Images of such deadly stasis abound, resulting in some of the most grisly scenes of emptiness between human beings in all of Trollope: a wife says of her husband's response to a little girl who had lived but a year, 'I think he has forgotten Meeny altogether,—even that she was ever here' (20). The novel seems to be set on demonstrating the impotence of all romance. Of another dead baby it is said, 'Yes; the poor little baby is dead, in spite of the pills and the powders, the daisies and the buttercups' (24), and when a character threatens suicide, she is met with: 'Ah! That is what we call poetry. Poetry is very pretty, and in saying this as you do, you make yourself divine. But to be dashed over the cliffs and broken on the rocks;—in prose it is not so well' (27).

Compounding the problem is the fact that the hero is remarkably unattractive, even by Trollope's standards. The narrator seems reluctant, further, to do much to lessen the distance between him and the reader. There are the usual protestations that the hero is like most men about us, non-heroic and weak and average (see chs. 10 and 28), but there is a conspicuous absence of 'we's'. No real attempt is made to identify us with the hero, and the defences of him usually seem perfunctory. As if recognizing the problem, the narrator becomes sarcastic with the reader—'you say, delicate reader, a true man can love but one woman' (28)—which in fact makes matters worse by increasing our estrangement from this curious novel. When the ending is attached, then, the narrator has nothing with

---

[3] Robert Polhemus says that the novel 'ends in shallow dishonesty' as Trollope tries 'to uphold the love ideal' (*The Changing World*, p. 118). There is a good analysis of *The Claverings*, especially its style, by Hugh Sykes Davies, *Trollope*, pp. 28–31.

which to support the comedy and is forced instead to rely on apologies: 'Few young ladies, I fear, will envy Fanny Clavering her lover: but they will remember that love will still be lord of all' (48). But that is not what we, young ladies or not, are likely to remember. Such abstract satisfactions are not offered to us with much confidence, which is well; for they are not likely to prevail for a moment against the dominant ironic force of the novel.

The far more successful *He Knew He Was Right* also plays off death and marriages against one another at the end. Even though the death is much more explicitly present here, as are the madness and torture preceding it, the novel's attempted balance of comedy and irony tips as far into comedy as *The Claverings* sank into irony. Of the five love stories presented in the novel, the one between Trevelyan and Emily ends tragically, that between Arabella French and the Revd. Mr. Gibson ends in pretty grim irony, but the other three are much more than just successful; they are triumphs of pure romance, ending in marriages that combine wit, spirit, love, and property. It is as if three Elizabeths married three Darcys. With Raskolnikov and Mrs. Willy Loman thrown in, one might justly add. It is not an easy novel to sort out. Even if one sees Trevelyan's madness and Emily's distress as the major subjects of the novel, however, there is no denying the strong comic pressure that builds up against that tragedy.[4]

Such a notion of Trevelyan's centrality is perhaps more vulnerable than it at first appears. It is accurate, in a sense, to think of the treatment of Trevelyan as 'psychological', but we generally mean more by that term than just the extraordinarily acute analysis of motive and conscience we receive from the narrator. Such commentary does not, in itself, distance us, but the relentless social context into which the commentary places Trevelyan makes us think of him more as a case, less as a presence. He is always seen as part of a larger group and never really allowed to be alone. He extends the limits of the comic world, but he cannot leave it. We never, I submit, feel him to be existing solely as a being without context as we do sometimes in the presence of Raskolnikov or Heathcliff or dozens of characters in Dickens, beginning with Fagin and Bill Sikes. He is never presented as is a character in

---

[4] Often it is denied or treated as perfunctory. See Cockshut, *Anthony Trollope*, pp. 169–79. Henry James called the novel a powerful and effective 'tragedy' (*Partial Portraits*, pp. 129–30).

a dramatic monologue, never allowed his 'song'. In fact, the presentation of Trevelyan and even some of the analysis emphasize his repellent and grotesque qualities, the self-conscious staginess that coexists with the pathetic madness: 'As he said this, he dashed his hand upon the table, and looked up with an air that would have been comic with its assumed magnificence had it not been for the true tragedy of the occasion' (69). Trevelyan creates true tragedies, but he is never allowed tragic response or even a tragic attitude. The narrator very often directs our attention to such distracting externals as Trevelyan's posings, distancing us and thus protecting us from the pure force of tragedy. His analyses of Emily and Trevelyan's tragedy are sometimes jocularly sarcastic: 'And so it came to pass that that blessing of a rich marriage, which had as it were fallen upon them at the Mandarins from out of heaven, had become, after an interval of but two short years, anything but an unmixed blessing' (11). He can make Emily sound like Eleanor Bold in her 'baby-worship' (11) and even at the end can break the tie between her and the reader by commenting on her presumably heroic return to her husband, 'There is nothing that a woman will not forgive a man, when he is weaker than she is herself' (93).

Trollope later said that the novel failed dismally to realize his intentions, which were 'to create sympathy for the unfortunate man'. Looking back over the story, he realizes the strength of the comic scenes but can find no sympathy for Trevelyan (*Autobiography*, pp. 321–2). Whatever Trollope's intentions may have been, it is difficult to read the novel now and see in the treatment of Trevelyan any failure. The novel is not, of course, a successful tragedy, but it seems never to make that attempt. Trevelyan, however important in the novel's action, stands finally as a signal of the fierce dangers in the world, but not of the world itself. He severely limits the extent and power of comedy without counteracting it. He plays out a prominent but only cautionary plot to a dominant comedy.

It is not a gentle world to be sure. It can strip away the pretences of romance, as it does with the French sisters, and reveal 'two pigs . . . at the same trough, each striving to take the delicacies of the banquet from the other, and yet enjoying always the warmth of the same dunghill' (44). Nature is not to be trusted to arrange matters; things will not work themselves out naturally. Nor is the world a safe guide. Bozzle, the private detective who most 'knew the world' (38), sees as its 'normal condition' 'things dark and dishonest, fights fought and races run that they might be lost, plants and crosses, women false to their husbands, sons false to their fathers, daughters to their mothers, servants to their masters, affairs always secret, dark, foul, and fraudulent' (28). Trollope's representative of the solid instincts of beloved old Toryism here, Miss Jemima Stanbury, finds it impossible now to locate the values she still trusts: 'I like to see a difference between a gentleman and a house-breaker. For the matter of that I'm told that there is a difference, and that the house-breakers all look like gentlemen now' (12). This is not to say that gentlemen and their standards are not present or even, as her nephew admits, that good may not be more common than evil. But, he adds, it is 'not always easy to tell the one . . . from the other' (44). It is a slippery world, totally without certainty, one which can appear to be simply absurd. Colonel Osborne, who starts all the trouble by pursuing Emily, is himself a symbol of pure nothingness: 'it was generally thought of him that he might have been something considerable, had it not suited him better to be nothing at all' (2). But out of this emptiness comes a furious quarrel also over nothing— 'a trumpery quarrel . . . sheer and simple nonsense' (16). And out of this triviality comes death. Trollope does allow us, even while protecting us, to see both the absurdity and pain caused by Emily and Trevelyan. Emily says, 'I have had to learn that torturing has not gone out of the world;—that is all' (95). Their son Louey, 'cowed and overcome . . . by the terrible melancholy of his whole life' (79), is an effective and unsentimental image of the disastrous shipwreck they have brought on themselves.

There are many casualties, certainly, not only Emily, her husband and son, who attempt an alliance, but those who are frightened off and remain by themselves, like Miss Jemima and Priscilla Stanbury. There is no assured protection from nature, no guarantees that love and good will can make for happiness. The only certain security is the security of nullity. One can choose to avoid risk but only at the cost of becoming nothing: 'How many people there are that don't seem to belong to anybody . . . Because they're just nobodies. They are not anything particular to anybody, and so they go on living till they die' (51). Mrs. Trevelyan tells her sister Nora that one had better 'drown herself than do as I have done' (60). But Nora's lover Hugh has an answer for such cautions. He argues 'that safety was not desirable, that energy, patience, and mutual confidence would be increased by the excitement of risk' (70). 'Nothing', he says, 'could ever be done without some risk' (53). And those who refuse to take risks become exactly that nothing. One can either freeze or leap into the darkness, a fairly grim justification on its own, since the darkness may contain Colonel Osborne, Trevelyan, and Bozzle. But Hugh has another point: 'For myself, I own that life would be tame to me, if there were no dangers to be overcome' (53). These leaps in the dark, then, are not simply last-ditch attempts to avoid being ground into powder; they are also fun in themselves and may possibly result in more fun. Trevelyan's tragic story is countered by others which take the same romantic premisses, the marriage for love alone, and end happily. Three out of four is not bad, however little consolation that may be to the fourth party. To those trembling on the brink, it is meant to be directly encouraging. The narrator says that although he cannot guarantee that a purely romantic decision 'will always be better', 'we do feel sure that that country will be most prosperous in which such leaps in the dark are made with the greatest freedom' (33). The argument is almost Benthamite, but it is the closest approximation to the beneficent nature of the pastoral now available. And the greatest number in this novel are provided with the greatest happiness through some lucky leaps. Nora and Hugh are the prominent example, but Dorothy Stanbury and Brooke Burgess risk Miss Jemima's displeasure by boldly declaring their romance and their refusal to submit to her prejudices. Caroline Waddington and Charles Glascock are deterred at first by the lady's fears: 'It would be a leap in the dark, and all such leaps must needs be dangerous, and therefore should be avoided' (56). But finally she abandons the general position and declares, 'I shouldn't fear the leap for myself, if it wouldn't hurt him' (81). From that point the outcome is certain, since no men are likely to hold back, not because they are more courageous than women but because they risk so little.

Women take most of the risks, the novel says, and are therefore required to be better and more desperate athletes if a nation founded on leaps in the dark is to prosper. Nothing about the novel is more remarkable than its image of men floating through a world half-consciously, protected by the power given them by social convention from taking chances, almost from acting, and certainly from thinking. If the novel is psychological in the sense of imagining the creation of thought under pressure, it is so in its treatment of women, not of men. Even Trevelyan never really thinks but only invents new and fantastic forms of protection for his wounded pride. But the pressures on women force them to see clearly or be swallowed up, often to see clearly *and* be swallowed up.

They offer themselves up as sacrifices to the freedom of the men; men use the language of virtuous self-effacement, but women have to endure the reality: 'It is all very well for a man to talk about his name and his honour; but it is the woman's honour and the woman's name that are, in truth, placed in jeopardy. Let the woman do what she will, the man can, in truth, show his face in the world . . . But the woman may be compelled to veil hers, either by her own fault, or by his' (11). The issue is seldom absent from a page of the novel. Both Emily and Nora are bitterly sensitive to this general degradation long before Trevelyan gives much specific cause: Nora thinks 'the lot of a woman' is to be 'wretched, unfortunate, almost degrading'; the fact that 'there was no path open to her energy, other than that of getting a husband' makes her 'almost sick' (4). When her sister says, 'It is a very poor thing to be a woman', Nora answers, 'It is perhaps better than being a dog' (5). Nora says that all men, 'after all', 'despise women' (25), an insight that throws remarkable light not only on Trevelyan but on the other men in the novel. Priscilla mounts an ironic defence of women on the grounds that men at least cannot 'suckle babies' or 'forget themselves', as women can (25). We are never allowed to lose sight of the point. Even Bozzle is provided with a wife who argues that men simply cannot have absolute and total rights: 'I don't believe a bit of his rights' (59). If the narrator takes us for a walk in the streets, casual conversation that we overhear follows the same course: '"There's a young 'ooman has to do with that ere little game," said the pot-boy. "And it's two to one the young 'ooman has the worst of it", said the barmaid. "They mostly does", said the potboy' (32). Even Caroline Waddington worries about the hardness of a woman's lot.

This last subplot also introduces the American feminist Wallachia Petrie, 'the Republican Browning', whose solutions are ridiculed because they are based on a dangerous 'antagonism to men' (77) and also because they are far too simple. She blandly assures her friend that 'things good in theory . . . will be good also when practised' (77) and imagines that it is up to her to institute the practice. She sees none of the complexities. To her, England is simply 'a game played out' (55), a collection of fading decadents, without connection with the new and vigorous land she imagines America to be. But Caroline sees all the connections and sees that women in America, in England, in all the world have it much the same. She sees further that 'the ways of the world are not to be altered because Wally writes poetry' (55). Feminism is burlesqued here, certainly, but the burlesque is conducted in terms that exactly invert those of the usual attack. Ordinarily we are assured that there is no dilemma after all and that the femininsts are proposing radical solutions for non-problems. Here we are led to believe that the dilemma is far too deeply rooted and basic ever to be touched by the feminists' solutions: they are too easy, too optimistic in that they are solutions at all.

For the novel never really suggests that there are solutions. Hugh Stanbury has the best practical insight into the problem: 'I fancy I shouldn't look after my wife at all . . . It seems to me that women hate to be told about their duties' (19). But this is only a tactical operating plan. Even the issue between Emily and Trevelyan amounts finally only to an isoluble question of 'obedience' (9). The narrator provides lots of jokes early on about how difficult Emily was 'to manage' (9). But the demand for obedience soon becomes a fierce demand for total submission. Trevelyan finally wants an admission of infidelity, but when he receives it he cares nothing for it, precisely because, as Dr. Nevill says, his madness has had nothing to do with any notion of her infidelity 'but arose from an obstinate determination to yield nothing' (98). Time and again, like Chaucer's Clerk, Hamlet, and a good many lesser examples, when pressed he turns on all women with terrible, neurotic rage. He finally is interested only in protecting some primitive sense of male power: 'should he yield to her now,—should he make her any promise,— might not the result be that he would be . . . robbed of what he loved better than his liberty,—his power as a man ?' (79). This 'power as a man' is so mysterious and so fragile that it cannot tolerate the slightest jostling, let alone Emily's spirited independence. The only solution to their problem was for her cheerily to accept annihilation: 'Had she been able always to keep her neck in the dust under his foot, their married life might have passed without outward calamity' (98).

In the end Emily does come round, too late, to an agreement of this sort, vowing never to take another leap in the dark (98) and thus connecting herself to others who recognize the terrible risks women run. And these others, seeing perhaps rightly 'that no woman should trust herself to any man' (28), are allowed only to will their own nothingness. Miss Stanbury muses, 'I am very desolate and solitary here. But I rather think that women who don't get married are intended to be desolate' (66). Dorothy's harsher analysis is even more applicable: 'A man who is a nobody can perhaps make himself somebody,—or, at any rate, he can try; but a woman has no means of trying. She is a nobody, and a nobody she must remain . . . She is just there and that's all' (51). Priscilla Stanbury, who in almost any other romantic comedy would be treated as a funny old maid, is here allowed dignity and also wisdom: 'I wonder why it is that you two should be married, and so grandly married, and that I shall never, never have any one to love' (97). Love still provides the meaning and hope for the world, but it is no longer easily come by, nor is the search for it any longer safe. Those, like Priscilla, who recognize the dangers, are likely to be left stranded by that very recognition. Those who, seeing or not, leap outward may find terror or, more likely, love. But even love itself is now corrupted by the neurotic politics of power and submission.

The Vicar of Bullhampton concerns the treatment of those who have been injured by their leaps in the dark. The comic remedies are only partially effective, just as the comic solutions in *He Knew He Was Right* were only partially applicable. 'It is not easy to set crooked things straight', says the Vicar (22), but he tries anyway, fitting splints here and there with a quixotic energy and a radical charity that are at times effective. There are still some who limp, some who cannot be helped, and some who are worse off for the interfering physician. But the odds are generally favourable still; as in *He Knew He Was Right*, there is something of a statistical argument presented. If one cannot establish a pastoral world exactly, one can still try to maintain pastoral values in a few spots, propped and patched up though they be. Crooked things may sometimes be made straight.

But only by something like miracle-working. The Vicar is certainly Trollope's most explicitly religious figure and this novel his most radical statement on the uses of Christianity.[5] Still, as miracle-workers go, the Vicar is a clumsy and undependable one indeed.

---

[5] William Cadbury has called this 'Trollope's most religious novel'. His excellent analysis, 'The Uses of the Village: Form and Theme in Trollope's *The Vicar of Bullhampton*', has been very useful to me.

He has great success with the stupid old Marquis and the matter of the chapel, fair success with Sam Brattle and with his sister Carry, none at all with old Jacob Brattle, and less than none in arranging the lives of Squire Gilmore and Mary Lowther. He is on the side of the best natural forces, but these forces are neither all-powerful nor necessarily benign. There is even a level on which the Vicar plays the part of a nosy intruder: a drunken landlady tells him, '"People know what is good for them to do, well enough, without being dictated to by a clergyman!" He had repeated the words to himself and to his wife a dozen times, and talked of having them put up in big red letters over the fire-place in his own study' (63). This self-knowledge, along with his fallibility, really establishes his basic humanity and makes his successes all the more paradoxical and important. He is one of Trollope's gentlemanly Christians, anxious to make his parishioners comfortable and quick to protect them against the harshness of the doctrine he preaches. But the Vicar is required to extend charity and grace much further than earlier parsons. As a result, he feels, concurrent with his love for peace, a pleasure in pugnacity; he secretly distrusts 'that doctrine of non-retaliation' (19). In supporting innocence, he senses the great power of the sophisticated and thus, without exactly realizing it, turns to a more primitive and forceful Christianity. The Vicar finally fights not just to heal the meek and wounded but to help them in inheriting the earth.

As a result, he has the great strength of radicalism, never worrying for a moment about the doctrinal difficulties he is encountering in helping Carry escape prostitution. He knows whom he loves, and that is enough. Enough for him, that is, but not quite enough for all situations. The narrator gently comments, 'The crooked places of the world, if they are to be made straight at all, must be made straight after a sterner and juster fashion' (40). The Vicar's love, strong as it is, is nowhere near so pure as he would like to think. It is partly a love for his own past and a consequent desire to protect it; it is partly sexual attraction to Carry's undeniable 'prettiness'; it is partly a love for his own romantic castle-building and 'the sweet smiles of affectionate gratitude with which he himself would be received when he visited her happy hearth' (40) after her restoration. Human he certainly is, but his humanity also contains a mercy and generosity that force him closer and closer to the most startling New Testament Christianity. When a modern female

Pharisee tells him that Biblical times and modern times are two very different things and ought not to be confused, the Vicar reflects that this 'was only what the world had said to her,—the world that knows so much better how to treat an erring sinner than did Our Saviour when on earth' (41). He is nearly turned against the world for a time, becoming 'almost tired of his efforts to set other people straight, so great were the difficulties that came in his way' (46). But he never becomes bitter, only tired, and after a brief rest he is back at it. He manages a reconciliation with the prissy Marquis and the dissenting minister and puts an end to the period in which everyone in the town was 'busy hating and abusing somebody else' (36). The Marquis sees the Vicar, not inaccurately really, as an anarchist, a demagogue of democracy, but he is finally brought round. The novel, like the Vicar, is very gentle with fools.

With Mary and the squire, though, the limitations of the Vicar's romantic notions are clearly exposed. It seems a perfect match, and the Vicar brings them together, confident that nature and his own loving encouragement will do the rest. But it turns out that the squire finds an irresistible pleasure in 'puling and whining love' (38), and Mary is nearly forced into settling for the ugly satisfactions of self-sacrifice. The poor, well-meaning Vicar is almost pressed into the role of the hard-hearted and prudent guardian, unable to keep Mary from escaping and unable to console Gilmore when she does. His interference has nearly wrecked things. When, near the novel's close, Mary leaves (or escapes from) the Vicar's house, she picks up the 'crooked-things-straight' motif and reverses it: 'If you could only know how anxious I have been not to be wrong. But things have been wrong, and I could not put them right' (65). The Vicar can only wish that he had never set eyes on such incorrigibles: 'I wish with all my heart that she had never come to Bullhampton' (65).

These extremes of success and failure suggest the alternatives which come together in the much more complex situation presented by the Brattles. The Vicar's staunch defence of the unjustly accused Sam is effective up to a point, but it hardly reconciles Sam to the beauties of the law or a lawful society: 'But it's done now, and there ain't been much justice in it. As far as I sees, there never ain't much justice' (73). Carry's difficult situation requires more of the Vicar's energy and ingenuity; it tests fully the reaches of his humanity. Anyone can pity a whore, but the Vicar can see how useless pity is, how it can be transformed into punishment. Carry doesn't need pity, but imaginative understanding and love. He can offer her that. God's love is meaningless to her, as he understands, but not his own love and his wife's (25). Even more, Carry's past never distances her from him, and he never thinks of her as a case but as a person like himself or—the acid test—his wife. He can, therefore, understand that Carry's life, brutal and painful as it has been, has also had its pleasures and excitements, and that one cannot in true charity offer 'a mode of life that, in its general attractions, shall be about equal to that of a hermit in the desert' (52). The grand inhumanity of this form of charity is based on a desire to make crooked things remain crooked, to experience the haughty pleasures of contemplating 'a monster of ingratitude': 'If we left the doors of our prisons open, and then expressed disgust because the prisoners walked out, we should hardly be less rational' (52). The moving love the Vicar shows for Carry is a positive contrast to the ordinary sort of charity and would be the perfect evidence of the effectiveness of his Christianity, except that it is only partially effective. He can never really persuade Carry's father to accept either his daughter or the doctrine of love the Vicar is preaching. Jacob Brattle's deep agnosticism, his sense that life is more or less accursed, seems beyond the Vicar's reach. A dark transformation of the traditional jolly miller, old Brattle has become so sensitive to basic injustice that the Vicar's words seem to him superficial and childish. He puts comedy to the final test, and comedy fails.

Up to then, though, comedy has worked well enough to represent a decent and lively operating principle, even if it is unsound philosophically. Though Brattle's test of comedy is far more severe than that offered by Trevelyan, we are still more likely to be moved by the comedy in this novel. It seems more ingrained with the method. The Vicar, in a sense, is the narrator, or nearly akin. They both use the same methods of extension, analogy, and then personal application. The Vicar insults virtually everyone with his constant analogies, insisting that Carry is like us all and shouting, 'Then speak of her as you would of any other sister or brother,—not as a thing that must be always vile because she has fallen once' (17). He asks the Marquis to think of himself as if he were Sam Brattle in jail and stirs up everyone with his very unwelcome comparisons. Best of all, he compares himself to others and can receive quietly analogies others apply to him. When Jacob Brattle suggests that he think of himself as father to a whore (63), the Vicar feels compassion, not outrage. The narrator works in the same way on our imagination, both within the action and without, but most centrally in the Preface, where Carry's 'misery' is identified with 'every misery to which humanity is subject'. The Vicar's wife finally illustrates the point at which all these comparisons are aiming: 'Had she, too, been fair, might not she also have fallen?' (53). The charitable imagination can go no further, but neither can it stop short of this point, according to this novel.

Sharing as they do the dangers of this world, all ranks and classes are levelled, all differences made to seem artificial. *The Vicar of Bullhampton* is far and away Trollope's most democratic statement, but its emphasis is clearly not political at all. 'We are all of us men' no longer means what it did in *Barchester Towers*. Now we are all of us weak, erring, fallen; even the best of us are limited, relatively ineffectual, sometimes even harmful. At the same time there is a very strong sense of common pleasure here: the usual Trollope celebrations of friendship, good digestion, and a healthy grievance, but also the highly unusual celebration of sensuality, sometimes put indirectly—'There must be no more laying of her head upon his shoulder, no more twisting of her fingers through his locks, no more looking into his eyes, no more amorous pressing of her lips against his own' (33)—sometimes as a joke—'When it comes to this, that a pair of lovers are content to sit and rub their features together like two birds, there is not much more need of talking' (18)—but sometimes as the lovely expression of strong desire: 'It was sweet to her to see and to remember the motions of his body. When walking by his side she could hardly forbear to touch him with her shoulder' (20). The pastoral protections are given up now, but the values are still alive and may still, here and there, bloom.

Both *Ralph the Heir* and *Lady Anna* also take on the issue of levelling, the first more metaphysically and the second more socially than *The Vicar of Bullhampton*. Neither is as unified or successful as the previous novel. They are, in fact, likely to strike us as peculiar, so inharmonious is the mixture of comedy and irony. *Ralph the Heir* levels by means of a basic cynicism. It argues, as do the comedies of nature, that things should be left to take their course, not, however, because such courses will be happy ones but because even the best plans lead nowhere anyhow. One might as well, then, relax. The chief relaxer or non-planner is the Ralph of the title, also the hero, a totally unsavoury character who is rewarded for his lassitude, one gathers, certainly not for his moral qualities. Nearly everyone perceives the futility of all effort, good or bad, and a strange emptiness and lack of vitality pervade all action and all talk. Accommodation becomes pretty much a matter of giving up. Those who for one reason or another get out of a narrow track, as does Neefit, lose all dignity. The poor tailor, honest and well-meaning, gets nothing that he wants, mainly because he has wanted something in particular and tried to get it. Acceptance, therefore, means taking what there is because there is nothing else available. Old Griffenbottom, M.P., whose life has been neither exciting, nor important, nor moral, nor pleasant, seems to realize this: 'At any rate, such as was the life, it was his life; and he had no time left to choose another' (25).

The novel works on a principle that is not unusual for ironic comedies: deflating illusions. Everyone is presumably educated. The odd thing here is the chaotic nature of the education, particularly the bizarre graduation exercises. Only the scoundrel hero is fully rewarded; prizes are given out with little regard for merit, sometimes indeed almost sarcastically. Comedies of accommodation always ask us to give up a great deal but in return always give us a system that is, if not coherent, decent, and if not decent, pleasant. But here it is none of the three. Despite all this, the novel tries at the end to leap back into comedy. One of the three plots brings its lovers to an incongruous position of being god and goddess to one another, as if the attack on such wish-fulfilment romance, carried on for hundreds of pages, had somehow not reached the area where they dwell. The narrator, similarly, goes to work apologizing furiously and at enormous length for the hero and trying to do something to make poor Sir Thomas Underwood seem less central and less paralysed. All of this confuses the form, 'opening' it, perhaps, but only by botching it.

The hero is one problem, without doubt. Ralph the heir is made the special charge not only of the plot and nature but, he thinks, of 'divine Providence' (36). Religion has a surprisingly prominent part to play in the novel, often advanced as the only answer to these dilemmas. But no one pays any attention to religion, and the dilemmas are apparently solved anyway. So maybe Ralph the heir *is* the favoured of divinity; such a choice would suit the ironic cosmos implied in the novel. At the end, Ralph achieves a marriage with a war-horse who will give him an average sort of life. Sir Thomas tries to claim that 'he will love his own wife and children', perhaps becoming a 'most respectable country gentleman' (56). If so, this says something severe about love and respectability, not to mention country gentlemen. In truth, though, these interminable apologies for Ralph are simply confused—sometimes sly, sometimes ironic, sometimes asking us to identify with him and think of him as an average specimen, sometimes arguing that his is the dangerous villainy of which we should beware. But he is finally neither exemplary nor a warning; he is, as Trollope said, very dull for such a scoundrel (*Autobiography*, p. 343). His wife-to-be and her mother talk about 'fixing' him. It will be hard to do, but they are resolved to try. Such an act is a parody of rebirth and restoration; it is a job for a garage mechanic, not the goddess of spring.

Sir Thomas is an even more difficult problem. The novel opens on a very powerful image of his extreme loneliness. He has 'warm affections' but no friends, simply because 'he lacked the power that way, rather than the will' (1). He wanders about the Inns of Court at night, gazing at lighted windows and imagining conversations in which he can never engage. He isolates himself from his daughters and exists as a consequence with a conscience which can cause him great pain but never move him to act. He stands for Parliament, wins, but then has to go through a petition hearing in which corruption of opponents is exposed and the borough at last disenfranchised. Victory and morality all in one, and all for nothing. He endlessly plans a book on Bacon, never writing it. He agonizes over the truth of Christianity but can neither reach decisions nor rid himself of the question. 'He thought much, but he thought nothing out, and was consequently at sixty still in doubt about almost everything. . . . He was for ever doubting, for ever intending, and for ever despising himself for his doubts and unaccomplished intentions' (40). He is a parody of Mr. Harding, suggesting the man withdrawn in a world that does not protect withdrawal. His instincts are good ones; he is a gentleman honest and true. But he is a mere nothing. The narrator can hardly even try to rescue Sir Thomas for comedy, but neither can he be ignored. So the embarrassment of a hopeful apology must be lived through: 'Purer air', perhaps, might yet produce . . . it has for others . . . let us hope it will. . . . This sort of thing closes the novel. It is clearly not sardonic; one might wish that it were.

Lady Anna suffers from a similar serious and interesting division, this time between comedy and tragedy, between social classes, and also, as in *Ralph the Heir*, between the pattern of accommodation and a world that resists any very pleasant accommodation. Here the last problem is handled more satisfactorily by having the young lovers escape to Australia at the end. The old society can hardly be stretched far enough to tolerate the union of an earl's daughter with a tailor. But the class issue, important as it is, hides a far more serious imperfection. The tailor tells his new wife that 'hearts will be sore. As the world goes yet awhile, there must be injustice; and sorrow will follow' (48). They must live not so much as outcasts, which has its own comforts, but with sorrow and injustice, which have none. The hope contained in the 'as the world goes yet awhile' phrase is entirely confined to the radical tailor, whose Utopian visions the novel very pointedly does not share. It sees fully the grounds for radicalism, the defects in the present world, but it is far less confident about any improvements. The young people have to take enormous risks. Everyone tells them that they are degrading themselves, and that argument is never really met. It is surely a world in which love has little chance.

The conflict between the impulse of romantic comedy and the bleak assumptions of irony are manifested in an odd blurring of the novel's focus. Though the title makes a faint effort to elevate Lady Anna to that position, she lacks her mother's strength and ambition and becomes first simply a pure victim and then simply a pure heroine. She really generates none of the novel's main energies. These come mostly from the inflexible, tragic countess and the imaginatively comic Sir William Patterson. They divide the novel between them. They meet only once, he with his humane wisdom, she with her grim hope that her daughter will die rather than disgrace herself. When Sir William appeals to her as a mother and a Christian to relax into tolerance, she flashes back with Mr. Crawley's words, 'It is easy to say all that, sir. Wait till you are tried' (37). The clash looks a little like that between Tennyson's Rizpah and the charity worker or that implied between Arnold's Wragg and Mr. Roebuck. Actually, however, Sir William's wisdom finally rules the novel—or most of it anyhow. We are asked to respect both points of view, even though they seem to be, and are, irreconcilable.

The countess is much like the Mr. Crawley whose words she repeats, insisting on playing out a tragedy in the midst of a comic world, clinging to her sense of injustice in the face of all attempts at healing. Her love for her daughter becomes so absolute that she threatens to kill her in order to express that love most perfectly. She actually does shoot the tailor. She is like a Webster or Middleton character wildly careering about in a drawing-room comedy. Becoming so involved with the conflict itself, she draws all her sustenance from it. It becomes necessary to her, and she thus resists any solution whatever (8). One must admit that her prose becomes a little strained and stagey toward the end—'Yes! She would face it all' (43)—but she never loses the power to upset things. Even with the wedding imminent, she almost overwhelms her daughter with remorse. But this nearly demonic figure has been presented carefully from the start in a sympathetic light, thus guaranteeing her disruptive ability. The opening sentence says of her, 'no fiercer cruelty was ever experienced by a woman' (1). Her refusal to accommodate herself in any way haunts the counter plea for easy acceptance and makes it seem at times superficial.

The plea is, however, made eloquently by the narrative itself, with the fine support of Sir William Patterson, the Solicitor-General and clearly Trollope's ideal lawyer.[6] He is ideal because he is scarcely a lawyer at all. He has little regard for legal evidence, but much for what he considers the broad rights of the case as a whole. He depends on imagination, not reason, and he is willing to rest opinions on sympathy alone. He understands the world well enough to see that no absolutes are applicable, and he finds a way to operate without ever having final assurances. Significantly, the novel never discloses the facts of the great case that continues throughout. Sir William, in an astonishingly open appeal, finally asks the other lawyers to forget the case and to consider the 'romance' within them: 'Have not generosity and valour always prevailed over wealth and rank with ladies in story?' (30). He is, as one of his outraged enemies says, really a 'poet' (33), not a lawyer. He is the maker of that part of the novel which is comic, presiding over the wedding at the end with deserved satisfaction. The chapter title proclaims 'Things Arrange Themselves' (47), but 'things' have had a great boost from Sir William. He cannot arrange the inclusion of the countess, of course, or even make terms with her, but this failure provides the major interest, as well as the major problem, of the novel.

---

[6] There is an appreciative analysis of this 'lawyer's lawyer' by Henry S. Drinker, 'The Lawyers of Anthony Trollope', pp. 40–7.

The Way We Live Now, like the other novels in this series, attempts to stretch the comic pattern so as to include the darkest and most unlikely processes. In doing so, ordinary materials are twisted far out of shape. Seers, for example, appear in the unexpected form of the weak-headed pair, Dolly Longstaffe and Lord Nidderdale.[7] Dolly's concluding wisdom, 'Most fellows are bad fellows in one way or another', is carried by Nidderdale to a higher philosophic pitch: 'If one wants to keep one's self straight, one has to work hard at it, one way or the other. I suppose it all comes from the fall of Adam' (96). It is the fallen world we live in now, all right, and a great deal of work of many kinds is required to make anything at all out of it. Trollope returns here to his own past, to *The Struggles of Brown, Jones and Robinson*, that deformed child only he has ever loved, and to his friend Thackeray for yet another experiment with comic and ironic materials. *The Way We Live Now* contains a major comic plot played off against another ironic one, with a satiric narrator undercutting both, precisely the formula of Amelia, Becky, and the puppeteer. The novel is Trollope's rendition of *Vanity Fair* thirty years afterwards.

Like most strong satires, it had for its original audience the obvious power of what we now think of as 'relevance', that is, topicality with a moral bent. The *Times* enthusiastically called it 'neither a caricature nor a photograph; it is a likeness of the face which society wears to-day', and the *Saturday Review* huffily proclaimed that, uncivil Mr. Trollope to the contrary, this was not the way *they* lived, thank you![8] Both responses, fervid and immediate, would have been equally pleasing to a satirist, but Trollope was hardly a whole-hearted satirist. His *Thackeray* is filled with protests against the assumptions and effects of that genre, and he could grant to *The Way We Live Now* only that it was 'as a satire, powerful and good'. To Trollope, that meant that it was only a good sample of an inferior species; the book could not escape 'the fault which is to be attributed to almost all satires', namely, that 'the accusations are exaggerated' (*Autobiography*, p. 355). In truth, the novel is only partly satiric anyway; that is, it is satire only part way through. Satiric absolutisms gradually yield to the modifications

---

[7] Robert Louis Stevenson pointed out that these were two of the only three 'nice' people in the novel: letter to Mr. and Mrs. Thomas Stevenson, 21 Feb. 1878, *The Letters of Robert Louis Stevenson*, ed. Sir Sidney Colvin (New York: Scribners, 1923), i. 261.

[8] The *Times*, 24 Aug. 1875, p. 4; rev., *Saturday Review*, 40 (17 July 1875), 88.

of comedy. A comic structure begins to emerge about mid-way and grows more evident as the book proceeds, finally controlling, though not subduing the darkness.[9] That this is a comedy of the injured and mutilated is true, but the cynics (and satirists) are repudiated, and there is room for some romance in the new world. Nature is never spent—nor is England—so long as there are John Crumbs who can invade the city, make Felix 'one mash of gore' and win back to the pastoral world a dutiful wife. Not everyone is rescued, but what appeared sure to be harsh fates, Georgianna Longstaffe's, for instance, are softened and some characters are rejuvenated. And though Paul Montague, the romantic hero, simply escapes from Melmotte and is in no sense triumphant, by the end of the novel 'all family feuds were at an end' (100). At least one great victory is allowed, the miraculous rebirth of 'the chief character',[10] Lady Carbury.

But *The Way We Live Now* is no *Rachel Ray*. That chief character, Lady Carbury, is so immersed in self-disgust that the only love she can show for most of the novel is a diseased love for her son. The world seems to be divided between those who hate themselves and those who capitalize on that hatred. Character after character reflects on the mysterious and sudden changes in social customs that allow behaviour which would formerly have been thought scandalous, indicating a radical depreciation of the underlying moral values. Lord Nidderdale vaguely ponders 'that now it did not much matter what a man did,—if only he were successful' (53). It is the world Trollope always feared, the one ruled by competitive exams, by results, by the future. Those who now succeed, as Nidderdale says, by any means at hand, are naturally those who 'get things done'. Slow and Bideawhile are displaced by the new man, Squercum, who makes himself 'a character for getting things done after a marvellous and new fashion' (58). Such looking to results, waiting for fulfilments, paradoxically causes a sense of growing insubstantiality. It causes also the ascendancy of people like Melmotte and his near kin, 'the Brother of the Sun', whose power is in direct

---

[9] Many of the best readings seem to me greatly to overemphasize the novel's darkness. See Cockshut, *Anthony Trollope*, pp. 204–18; Sabine Nathan, 'Anthony Trollope's Perception of The Way We Live Now', *ZAA*, 10 (1962), 259–78); and especially Tony Tanner, 'Trollope's *The Way We Live Now*: Its Modern Significance', *CritQ*, 9 (1967), 256–71.

[10] Trollope called her this in his notes, which are reproduced in Sadleir, *Trollope: A Commentary*, p. 426.

proportion to their inscrutable emptiness. Actual deeds have been reduced to appearances, men to shirt-fronts, just as the currency of commerce has degenerated from gold to paper to words. It is a world made only for grief: Lady Carbury's 'happiness, like that of most of us, was ever in the future,—never reached but always coming' (12). Her happiness does in fact come, when she finally gives up on the future. Whether this happens to 'most of us' depends in Trollope's terms on how closely we attend to the novel.

We must especially attend to Augustus Melmotte, welcomed to England, where 'British freedom would alone allow him to enjoy, without persecution, the fruits of his industry' (4). England is the one society vulnerable, stupid, and corrupt enough to admit Melmotte, a point stressed throughout, to the intense discomfort of many who agreed with Arnold's Mr. Roebuck or the *Saturday Review*. As Melmotte advances, however, to being chosen 'the great and honourable type of British Commerce' (58), the symbolism becomes clearly public, as in a way it has always been, like Hawthorne's A, not a secret between author and reader but an overt symbol that all can read. Melmotte is much plainer even than the A, and almost everyone reads the symbol correctly from the start. Not many in England are substantially fooled by Melmotte for very long. They at least are never fooled about his morality: 'The tradesmen had learned enough to be quite free of doubt, and in the City Mr. Melmotte's name was worth any money,—though his character was perhaps worth but little' (4). The distinction here is crucial. While it stands as an indictment of the English that ethics are so absolutely divorced from daily practice, it is paradoxically to their credit that they manage for the most part to maintain the distinction. Morality is trivial to them, but the search for money is never made into the search for God; they never confuse money and religion. In Dickens, Melmotte would have been turned into a grotesque saint, but the separations are maintained here, and there is little religious imagery.[11] People never forget that Melmotte is a scoundrel; they just do not care much. Georgianna Longstaffe sees it all from the inside: 'She could understand it all. Mr. Melmotte was admitted into society, because of some enormous power which was supposed to lie in his hands; but even by those who thus admitted him he was regarded as a thief and a scoundrel' (32). Men grant to Melmotte the reality of a slogan only; he is 'the strong rock, the impregnable tower of

[11] There is some in Chapter 35.

commerce, the very navel of the commercial enterprise of the world' (35). They only mistake that slogan for reality and imagine that scoundrels can win.

Melmotte is not a native growth, the natural product of English degeneracy exactly. He is an outsider, a freak whose freakishness is no longer as repulsive as it should be. England has not itself become diseased but has lost the power to detect disease in others. Julia Monogram expresses this dissociation: 'Going there [to Melmotte's] when the Emperor of China is there, or anything of that kind, is no more than going to the play. Somebody chooses to get all London into his house, and all London chooses to go. But it isn't understood that that means acquaintance' (32). She has a point, but she cannot get off quite this easily, nor can the nation. Melmotte is not England itself, but England cannot escape some responsibility for his success.

Melmotte is not so much a satiric reflection of England, then, as a very serious test of her moral worth. More than that, too, England has not only prepared the field and then blandly awaited the grotesque harvest; she has in a way created the farmer. Melmotte is in this sense England's creation and its victim. He soon finds that he is no longer playing the game but is being played by it (35). Even worse, he is almost led to believe in the reality of his own myth, 'the most remarkable circumstance in the career of this remarkable man', the narrator says (56). Trollope finally complicates the originally simple satire by making us feel a sympathy for this man not unlike that evoked by Mary Shelley for the monster. Melmotte is tracked down not by virtue but by Squercum, who thinks that 'to have hunted down Melmotte would make Squercum as great almost as Melmotte himself' (81). There is little pleasure for us in the great merchant's fall. We are made to share in his misery and to admire a strength even greater than that of Mr. Crawley or the countess in *Lady Anna*. Unlike them, Mr. Melmotte will not be tricked into imagining the satisfactions of tragic martyrdom: 'He told himself over and over again that the fault had been not in circumstances,—not in that which men call Fortune,—but in his own incapacity to bear his position' (81). He has been used by the world to give it a false lustre, a sick, fake life, and we are thus unable to share either in the virtuous reaction against Mr. Melmotte when his crimes are known or in the sentimental counter-reaction, the 'white-washing' (88) that takes place later. He is a pathetic and finally moving image of a person used and cast aside by a society that has let him climb to the top without letting him advance an inch toward the heart. In a way, Julia Monogram is perhaps right after all; there is no essential 'acquaintance'. Melmotte is never a fully satiric weapon, then, since the linkages are never direct: society is nearly as conscious of his meaning as are we. The indictment is strong, but it is not finally achieved primarily through satire.

Even stronger than the charge brought against England by Melmotte is the frightening suggestion that he is not alone. Perhaps he is but an earlier and cruder form of what will become a more polished, insidious evil, just as the Mafia is an advance on the cattle-rustler. Mr. Alf, like Melmotte a tough outsider, waits and watches Melmotte's mistakes, hiding in the shadows and then advancing in the same line but with infinitely more stealth. He is determined never to be made an instrument of and thus masquerades as a reformer, proclaiming the corruption of the world more loudly than anyone else and insisting, 'we must make it different' (11). The symbolism in his position, editor of the *Evening Pulpit*, is not meant to be subtle. He knows how to capitalize on the instability of moral values by writing articles which can, at once, support either, both, or neither side of a question. He is a god of irony: 'next to its omniscience its irony was the strongest weapon belonging to the "Evening Pulpit"' (30). He is the first to denounce Melmotte, and he does it, for once, unironically, not because he is morally sensitive but because he is an early version of the P.R. man, accurately sniffing out the wild shifts in public opinion. His view of the world is precisely attuned to its worst features, and because he has no moral sense he has no guilt. His only standard is competence, getting things done: 'Dishonesty is not the general fault of the critics. . . . It is incapacity' (89). Mr. Alf's values and Mr. Alf's tone forecast with grim accuracy the tone and values of such modern men of competence as the Watergate criminals. Like Alf, they believe that the common alternative to ruthless pragmatism is a boggy sentimentality.

There are, however, other tests of England in which it manages better results; contrary indications are given that the old morality, though shrunken, has not altogether gone. Deep within even Dolly Longstaffe and Lord Nidderdale is a sense that things should be different, and it is the disastrous mistake of people like Felix Carbury to imagine that the neglect of morality is really its death. Felix's tests of the society are just as important as are Melmotte's and really much more basic. Felix is a literalist who thinks that there really are no standards now, that it does not in fact matter what one does. But he is wrong. John Crumb comes from the still-alive land like Kipling's Hodge to assert the continuing vigour of old England. But even the London world is repulsed by Felix on moral grounds. Paul Montague, in a moment of cynical despair, says, 'If Felix had £20,000 a year, everybody would think him the finest fellow in the world' (4). He is corrected immediately by the narrator: 'In saying this, however, Mr. Paul Montague showed himself unfit to gauge the opinion of the world. Whether Sir Felix be rich or poor, the world, evil-hearted as it is, will never think him a fine fellow' (4). Evil-hearted it may be, but the world still has a moral sense, is capable of shedding at least some of its enemies, collecting its resources, and granting happiness.

The novel is not purely satiric for very long. There are plenty of indications early on that satire is intended. The first chapter introduces Mr. Booker, whose virtue has been deeply corrupted by 'the usages of his time'. There are many such nudges about 'the times' in the early part of the novel, and there is a strong and clear morality established to support this topicality. Felix is introduced as one whose 'life had been in every way bad' (2), and Mr. Booker's complex compromises with circumstances are contemptuously dismissed with 'he was quite at liberty to break stone, or to starve honestly' (11). This sort of absolutism is unusual for Trollope, and the satiric emphasis on simple 'truth' quite uncongenial. In the first part of the novel the single-minded satiric charge is that truth is no longer respected. As the truth begins to appear more and more complex, however, the sympathies of the novel switch from the hunters after truth (and after Melmotte) to those compromisers and temporizers, groping darkly for some sort of half-truth if they can find it. Truth is pushed out of the way by complexity and, more strongly, by the comic virtues: understanding, tolerance, love.

As the novel switches genres, a greater emphasis is put on the country scenes involving Ruby Ruggles and her struggle to decide between Felix and John Crumb. Actually there is not much deciding to do, as the forces of virtue, bolstered by such unlikely supporters as Mrs. Hurtle, gang up on her and compel her to do the right thing.

But the coercion is, for once, all to the good. John Crumb suggests the pastoral ideal now reduced to violent action and also to speechlessness. Just like Dickens's Joe Gargery, he preserves his innocence by avoiding altogether the sophistications of language. Crumb's world of nature is rough and therefore real; the world of language, in Alf, Melmotte, and Lady Carbury, is now totally unreal. It is a radical distinction but not by any means a pessimistic one. The ability to make such a distinction allows the novel to support a series of triumphs. Mrs. Hurtle looks on Crumb as a type altogether unknown to her in her previous life: 'The man was to her an extraordinary being,—so constant, so slow, so unexpressive, so unlike her own countrymen,—willing to endure so much, and at the same time so warm in his affections!' (71). He is unlike anything in America, precisely because he is the essential Englishman, steady, open, and honourable: 'He means what he says, and I call that the best of good manners' (94), says Mrs. Pipkin, who is in a position to know good manners when she sees them. Crumb is a very new type for the comedy of manners, but in the world that creates Melmotte we are grateful for anything, including this rough cleansing, this diving back to the raw origins of the gentlemanly code.

Crumb's victory with Ruby parallels that of Hetta with Paul Montague. Hetta is curiously detached and protected from her mother's world precisely because she belongs to the world of John Crumb. She has an instinctive hatred of London, saying of Mr. Broune that he has 'that air of selfishness which is so very common with people in London;—as though what he said were all said out of surface politeness' (31). Like Crumb, she rejects all surface, reaching deep to find the moral values that can reform the comic world. Hetta's romantic innocence, so despised by her mother, is finally confirmed. What is more important, Paul is rescued from London—and from Mrs. Hurtle.

Mrs. Hurtle comes to be one of the most important figures in the novel, especially in her capacity as representative of America. For it is America which can eventually be made into a symbol that will drain off the satire and allow for comedy. America suggests the true hell that England should regard as a warning; it stands in place of satire's cruel mirror and allows the readers to look at a projection of their tendencies, not really at themselves. Hamilton K. Fisker, Mrs. Hurtle's countryman, is drawn over from America because he smells in Melmotte a wonderful example of what Americans in

Martin Chuzzlewit call 'our na-tive raw material': 'We're a bigger people than any of you and have more room', says Fïsker; 'we go after bigger things, and don't stand shilly-shally on the brink as you do. But Melmotte pretty nigh beats the best among us' (9). Fisker wonders if perhaps England is new territory ready for annexation, if not exactly by America, then by the American principle. But he finds that he is wrong, that even Melmotte and certainly all the British are, like the poor nine hundred and ninety-nine out of a thousand he has such contempt for, restrained by scruples too ingrained for them to discard (92). He goes back home, and England is safe, not declared innocent, but at least not quite guilty, of the charge of cohabiting with America.

Mrs. Hurtle is treated with sympathy, but it is of the sort accorded to some tiger struggling fruitlessly to leave its brutal ways. She has a great admiration for Melmotte—'such a man rises above honesty' (26)—and thus establishes a moral link to America that is never forged with England. She is anxious also to make Paul 'a hero' (42), but we see what her ideas of heroism are. She is the creature of extreme action Trollope always treated with respectful fear. The restlessness and desperation she evidences are understood fully and pitied, but not on that account does one propose to open the cage. She is given wonderful reasons for self-justification, it is true. She has shot a man trying to rape her and challenges Paul to dare blame her: 'In this soft civilization of yours you know nothing of such necessity' (47). Exactly, which is just why the civilization must be preserved.

Because she is treated with sympathy as an individual, while the civilization she represents is treated with utter disgust, Mrs. Hurtle would never have been easy to get rid of in any resolution of the novel. But as the novel actually turns to comedy, she presents an even greater problem. Trollope attempts the audacious solution of making the tigress into a fairy godmother, cooing over John Crumb and spending endless hours in the most selfless and tedious work of advancing his love with Ruby. She does all this, we are told, 'from pure charity' (87). Trollope said later that he recognized the fact that she 'is kept too long on the stage', explaining that he used her because she was so much better done than the boring Paul and Hetta.[12] The explanation is endearing but inadequate. What has happened to the fierce rebellion? Why should Mrs. Hurtle, of all

[12] Letter to Mary Holmes, 8 July 1875, *Letters*, p. 342.

people, become the spokeswoman for society and for conventional values? The pastoral forces are bolstered, perhaps, by having such a tough supporter, but the support is so unexpected that it reveals the jagged, ill-disguised seams where comedy has been tacked on to the satire.

Even lumpier and more distracting is the change in the role played by Roger Carbury. At first he is a moral man outcast completely from society because of his morality: 'The old-fashioned idea that the touching of pitch will defile still prevailed with him. He was a gentleman' (8). He is, like Mr. Harding, 'always right' (38). He measures the distance the world has travelled from an approved position, making continual pronouncements of a ringing, Biblical sort. When Hetta says everyone is now going to Melmotte's house, Roger answers, 'Is there not another place to which we are told that a great many are going, simply because the road has become thronged and fashionable?' (8). Such figures as Roger can be honoured prophets or street-corner fanatics, depending entirely on the context. While Roger is never ridiculed, he becomes a little like the malcontent in Jacobean drama who is still ranting after many of the problems have been solved. Finally, his separateness and his doomsday morality are out of place, and it takes some extraordinary sleight-of-hand on Trollope's part to keep Roger from slipping into the position of Malvolio, a crank trying to block the festivity. The shift in his position is marked at just about midpoint, where his grim prophecies are countered by those of another gentleman, the Bishop of Elmham, who also holds by the old values, but whose tolerance and moderation represent a new spirit in the novel.[13] When Roger advocates a strict interpretation of the golden rule, the bishop counters with a position the novel itself finally comes to hold: 'But we must hope that some may be saved even if they have not practised at all times that grand self-denial. Who comes up to that teaching?' (55). Far from seeing this imperfection as cause for dismay, for a belief like Roger's that the world is 'going to the dogs', the bishop argues that things are, on the whole, getting better: 'There is a wider spirit of justice abroad, more of mercy from one to another, a more lively charity, and if less of religious enthusiasm, less also of superstition' (55). Justice, charity, and mercy

---

[13] Ruth apRoberts also notes the importance of the bishop, arguing that he shares the centre with Roger: 'he presents that double perspective Trollope always insists on' (*The Moral Trollope*, p. 173).

replace truth. The narrator begins to attribute Roger's 'melancholy view of things in general' more and more to his failure in love (55) and to suggest that he is, finally, a good-hearted gentleman but an untrustworthy spokesman. He is included in the final comedy at the end only when he 'crushes' his heart (100) and leaves the property outside the family, thus departing from 'the theory of my life' (100). Even Roger can change, but one notices the strain involved in including him.

There is no strain with Lady Carbury, however, whose triumph is the most important evidence of the validity of the comic promise. She is totally immersed in the new world at the novel's opening; she is one of the modern artists who uses art as a saleable commodity. Her unscrupulousness is explained by the narrator in terms of a terrible background which has so battered her that 'she had been made sharp, incredulous, and untrustworthy by the difficulties of her position' (2). The notion that circumstances are so powerful is depressing, but such a notion also implies that human beings are not changed but just twisted and thus available for reclamation. Though Lady Carbury is in some senses most fully trapped by the ironic world, the comic pattern catches her up very quickly too. She is cast as one of those traditional parents opposing their children's love with tired, old prudential values. She even sees herself in this role and thinks of it in terms of comic convention: 'Lady Carbury recalled to her mind her old conviction that a daughter may always succeed in beating a hard-hearted parent in a contention about marriage, if she be well in earnest' (12). But she resists any sort of comedy and treats her daughter harshly, even viciously. She so distrusts and fears romantic tendencies that she can hardly tolerate her daughter: 'If there was anything that she could not forgive in life it was romance' (84). To her, 'everybody is a burden to other people. It is the way of life' (84). It is not the way of life, it is only the way we live now, but Lady Carbury understandably cannot see this. In her tough way, she is trying to save her daughter by means of the wisdom she has acquired. She really believes that Hetta will perish unless she gives up all serious ideas of romance: 'The world at large has to eat dry bread, and cannot get cakes and sweetmeats. A girl, when she thinks of giving herself to a husband, has to remember this' (91).

But from this bitterness she is freed by a wave of romance that rescues not only her daughter but herself. She reaches exactly the point achieved by Thackeray's narrator in *Vanity Fair*: 'It was all "leather or prunello," as she said to herself;—it was all vanity,—and vanity,—and vanity!' (99). But this bleak self-knowledge turns out to be false knowledge, and romantic old Mr. Broune shows her that all is certainly not vanity: 'That morning the world had been a perfect blank to her. There was no single object of interest before her. Now everything was rose-coloured' (99). Perhaps, as the narrator says, they did not live ever after with perfect happiness, since no one ever does. But they make a tolerable, in fact very satisfying, accommodation to the way we live now. They even alter that way a little. The first had at one time seemed terribly difficult, the second impossible.

CHAPTER 6

THE PALLISER SERIES

CHARACTERS IN the Palliser chronicle are as uneasy away from London as characters in the earlier Barsetshire chronicle were uneasy in it. So much is obvious, but it is enough to indicate the very great differences between the two series. One chronicle is comic and pastoral, the other ironic and sophisticated. Noticing, then, that Mrs. Carbuncle is less amusing than Madeline Neroni or that Alice Vavasor is more complex than Lucy Robarts gives us no grounds for making any value judgements. Characters in comedy had surely better be funnier, those in irony more serious. Granting that, though, the Palliser novels still seem to me Trollope's finest achievement.[1] They are more unified, both in theme and method, than the Barsetshire series, which suffers from an uncertain start and a very abrupt shift between *Framley Parsonage* and *The Small House at Allington*. The working out of the dramatized issues is in the political novels much gentler, a quality we would expect, but it is also more controlled and more inclusive. The Palliser series as a whole resolves those issues with which it deals far less satisfactorily than does the earlier series, but it deals with more issues of greater intricacy. The inconclusiveness is simply a characteristic of the ironic form chosen, but the comprehensiveness and subtlety are evidence of the size of Trollope's accomplishment.

Just as the Barsetshire chronicle explores the range of comedy, so does this series exploit varieties of irony. The earlier series describes a comic cycle, tracing the fruition, collapse, and renewal of a comic society. But here such cycles are mocked. Opening with at least surface happiness in *Can You Forgive Her?* and *Phineas Finn*, the series then loses touch even with this surface and is never able to reconstruct even superficial comfort. The original affirmations

[1] James, who confesses he has 'not been able to read them', pronounces them 'distinctly dull' (*Partial Portraits*, p. 131), a judgement rightly dismissed by Max Beerbohm as 'nonsense' (letter to H. A. L. Fisher, 14 Jan. 1928, quoted in B. R. McElderry, Jr., 'Beerbohm on Trollope', *TLS*, 12 Oct. 1967, p. 968). In a recent column in *Radio Times* (24–30 May 1974) Stephen Spender airily said that not only had he not read the novels but that he doubted very much whether anyone in the 'Department of English, University College, London' had done so.

are retested in the central novels, *The Eustace Diamonds* and *Phineas Redux*, and never again have power. The last novels, *The Prime Minister* and *The Duke's Children*, are much quieter, teasing us with hopes of a return to the reconciliations available at the beginning. But it is only teasing; all the novels finally describe the same failure. Reconciliations are attempted, but they are now lonely and pointless acts. The archdeacon is no longer there to welcome the return of Mr. Crawley to social life.

I suggested earlier the contrast between Mr. Crawley's isolation and that of Phineas Finn, but the situations are so important that some further attention may be warranted. Mr. Crawley is never without the unshakable support of a large part of the community and a strong and coherent, if irrational, value system. Mr. Harding's testament to his innocence is typical: 'I cannot for a moment suppose that a clergyman and a gentleman such as Mr. Crawley should have stolen money' (42). Mr. Harding is supporting a system, not just an individual; he puts his complete faith in 'clergymen' and 'gentlemen'. Since Mr. Crawley is both of these, he is clearly innocent. The whole flurry of defence and accusation is, according to Mr. Harding, a bother to the good men on the jury. Since the values of the heart are so clear, the rational dependence upon evidence and logic is absurd. When Phineas Finn is similarly accused and similarly isolated, no such deep-rooted value system springs to his rescue. Most of the loyalty he does encounter comes from a gallant resolve on the part of friends to stick to him *even if* he is guilty. Like his closest political friend Mr. Monk, they can have no 'conviction' of his innocence, despite their confidence in him. Sounding initially very much like Mr. Harding, Monk says, 'I believed you innocent with all my heart.' But the heart is no longer enough; as Monk goes on to explain: 'there was always sufficient possibility of your guilt to prevent a rational man from committing himself to the expression of an absolute conviction' (68). Rational men, caught in an irrational world, paradoxically must distrust the irrational values of the heart. Monk sadly explains that he would have no absolute confidence even in himself, 'because both you and I are human and fallible' (68).

Mr. Harding's world and even Mr. Harding are fallible too, but that fallibility did not erase all assurances, as it does in Phineas's case. In one case it is unthinkable that any gentleman could steal; in the other, it might be that one's most intimate and trusted friend could turn murderer. At its lowest point, the Barsetshire world admits fallibility as a condition of life, but in the political novels it becomes the pervasive, almost the only condition. When all intuitive assurances are gone, we are left, these novels imply, with only the paltry resources of reason. As Phineas's case illustrates, one might almost as well trust to blind chance. Without permanent securities, there are no genuine public connections between people, no real society. As we move from the Barsetshire country into London, we find a world more crowded but without cohesion. The Palliser novels deal with the attempts of human beings to live in a world without community. Even the relationship between husband and wife is usually tense and distant; those who try to establish wider connections fail most completely. Just so, the secret plot of the chronicle is the crushing of the one who tries hardest of all, Lady Glencora.

In the Barsetshire series the main energies of all the novels, even the dark ones, were enlisted in trying to accommodate or bring back into the fold those who were pushed outside.[2] Here the corresponding energies are devoted to submerged, frustrated rebellion. From Alice Vavasor's strong resistance to marriage, through Lady Glencora's witty expressions of dissatisfaction, Phineas's consuming sense of injustice, Lizzie Eustace's vague searchings for Byronic excitement, Lady Laura Kennedy's wild frustrations, to Lady Mabel Grex's open bitterness, the chronicle deals with characters unwilling to accept either the absurd restrictions of society or the unmeasured absurdity to be found outside its restrictions. They find that since there is no effective centre to society, no binding code of values, there is nothing substantial against which to rebel. In Barsetshire, potential rebels were always provided with the ideal therapy of a good, solid opponent. Mrs. Proudie, to take the best example, is wonderfully useful to the archdeacon, Lady Lufton, and Mr. Crawley. But here distinctions are so hard to make that enemies are difficult to locate and keep track of. At one point in *Phineas Redux* Quintus Slide is interestingly called 'Slope' by a character who cannot remember his proper name. It is an instructive error, perhaps reminding us how Mr. Slope's deviousness was so simple in comparison, really all of a piece. There is never a chance that he will

---

[2] This is less true of the first two novels in the series, which are somewhat defensive, but it is a notable energy even in *The Small House at Allington*, where the urge toward accommodation establishes a tension with the obstinacy of the characters.

abandon low-church doctrines and go in for chanting. But what or whom is Quintus Slide supporting? What, for that matter, holds together the coalition government headed by the Duke? In all cases such unions as there are arise from restless, irrational self-interest. Any truces are temporary; the usually secure boundaries are badly blurred. Political enmity is all show, as, in the instructive case of Mr. Bonteen, is political friendship. In private life it is the same: even the duel over Violet Chiltern is an ambiguous, murky affair, fought without much purpose between two friends. Madame Max tells Phineas that he must learn to live in this world of shadows and secrets. He is, she says, being undermined by pretended friends and must 'countermine or . . . be blown up'. He says lamely that he'd 'rather fight above ground', but Madame Max knows that things are never that simple or that clear: 'That's all very well, but your enemies won't stay above ground' (37). Social life is no longer the happy open warfare between high- and low-church parties that provided so much spirit and festivity to both camps. It is now genuine and divisive war carried on with secret weapons against unknown foes on hidden grounds and for an unclear cause.

The problems still are social ones, as they were in the Barsetshire series, but now the dominant perspective is the individual's upon society, not the reverse. In the Barsetshire series, we were urged to identify with a community and its values, seeking to incorporate the strays and the eccentrics; here we are asked to identify with a single character looking for some union somewhere. The relation between public and private lives is an essential motif in both series. The Barsetshire chronicle begins with an image of the powerful Tom Towers and Obadiah Slope, insisting on the absolute and disastrous distinction between public and private. The chronicle then moves to heal the breach. In *Doctor Thorne*, Frank Gresham becomes both a real squire, publicly respected and powerful, and a happily married man, suggesting the intimate connection of the public and private beings. In *Framley Parsonage* nearly every character moves out of isolation into a similar union. Mr. Crawley traces the same pattern in the darker world of *The Last Chronicle* and provides a model for that world. In the Palliser series, however, such a union is never achieved by a major character. In the dominant plot both Plantagenet Palliser and Lady Glencora strive for just such a state. He begins with only a public self, as his hilarious by-the-book flirtation with Griselda Grantly shows; Glencora has only a private self. He moves to develop a corresponding inner life, Glencora a reputation; he wants to feel love, while she wants to be Prime Minister. They pass one another on the way, however, and the Duke at the end has to make the best of his imperfect memories. Glencora has her try at getting herself into memoirs, fails, and dies.

The two controlling and linked images throughout are those of marriage and politics. Women characteristically look at marriage as a public act and therefore a violation of their private selves. They either resist as well as they can or propose a desperate marriage of the 'heart' which is equally futile. There seems to be no choice except that between the bland, public perfection of John Grey, Plantagenet Palliser, and Lord Popplecourt, or the dangerous, totally private romance offered by George Vavasor, Burgo Fitzgerald, and Ferdinand Lopez.[3] Women are pressed either to abandon their selves or to plunge into some kind of private insanity. But men in public life face much the same choice. While political opposition provides all the freedom and all the fun, those who stay perpetually in opposition are, like Mr. Turnbull, seen as egocentric, finally useless. There is nothing substantial about such apparently pure private selves. Turnbull's only public being is defined, then, by slogans and newspapers. An unreal man, he mocks the proposed union of the public and private. On the other hand, holding office can require such a suppression of private opinion that the private self disappears, as the Duke finds out when, as Prime Minister, he is asked to be satisfied with being absolutely nothing, a necessary nothing, of course, but nothing all the same. Phineas discovers the great risks that are entailed by a man in office who tries also to have opinions and a selfhood of his own. There is never any balance allowed. Some recommend the satisfactions of a mixture, an in-and-out-of-power rhythm that alternates between roles and might seem to give some pathetic imitation of balance. It is as if a woman were advised to try a variety of marriages, alternating between wild men and respectable M.P.s. This last course is the one that many do attempt in their way. Lady Glencora marries the respectable M.P. and tries to live essentially with the memory of Burgo Fitzgerald. She finds the oscillation as little satisfying as does her husband when he meets the political version of it.

This public–private division controls the chronicle, as characters seek one way or another to express their own beings in relation to

---

[3] *The Duke's Children* presents some exceptions; I will try to deal with them later.

others. Their repeated failures or at best unsatisfactory compromises suggest that final separation between intention and act. What one is, they feel, is violated by what one does. Everyone is looking for a plot that will explain things to him, but such plots as there are only burlesque coherent explanations.

The series opens on a world controlled by the same dark premises that had touched the Barsetshire chronicle only at its lowest point. *Can You Forgive Her?* depicts the same resistance to the arguments of romantic comedy that controlled the themes and form of *The Small House at Allington*. Instead of the obtrusiveness of Lily Dale's holdout, however, *Can You Forgive Her?* keeps open the form more subtly and denies the comic resolution by stressing secret reservations. Such reservations are even more troubling than Lily's since they are seen as normal, not neurotic or exceptional. *Can You Forgive Her?* focuses mainly on the basic division as seen in the marriage theme, introducing only at the novel's close the parallel political theme[4] which is developed centrally in the next novel, *Phineas Finn*. Both of these novels provide a sort of conclusion, but no actual solution, to the problems they dramatize, and thereby give a sense of, at best, a lucky escape from a very bleak world. This world is revealed fully in *The Eustace Diamonds*, which sets out to define the absurd conditions of existence under which one must operate. It thus exposes the secret darkness of the first two novels and provides a suggestion that any of the hopes for fulfilment that come up in succeeding novels will be crushed. By itself, it is a static novel, almost an essay, but it works forwards and backwards in the series, which it, in one sense, interrupts, almost as if it were the key to the secret code, revealed to us when we are half-way through the message. The next novel, *Phineas Redux*, shows the effects of the new revelation. Phineas' luck has now become all bad, and we begin to see all luck as a symptom of absurdity. *The Prime Minister* is the climax of the series, in that it takes the Duke, always with Glencora at the heart of the chronicle,[5] and allows him to plunge directly into the destructive element. The

---

[4] The best discussion of Trollope's political ideas is by Asa Briggs, 'Trollope, Bagehot and the English Constitution', CJ, 5 (1951–2), 327–38.

[5] The Duke's primary importance is emphasized by Audrey L. Laski, 'Myths of Character: An Aspect of the Novel', NCF, 14 (1959–60), 333–43; she says that the series as a whole is the tale of the modification of the mythic Aristocrat, his 'adjustment to the modern world'. Trollope called the Duke and Glencora the two 'safety-valves by which to deliver my soul' (*Autobiography*, p. 180).

Duke is Trollope's strongest character, according to his own judgement, a 'perfect gentleman' (*Autobiography*, pp. 185, 361), but as
Prime Minister he is miscast as badly as Mr. Harding would have
been as bishop. The few acts the Duke is allowed to perform are
dismissed as 'quixotic' even by his staunchest supporters. Glencora
finds a similar emptiness where she thought she would find the
centre of the world. *The Duke's Children* is Trollope's subtlest
novel and a beautiful conclusion to the series. It suggests that the
Duke, or any other 'perfect gentleman', can in fact adjust by learning
to live alone, converting no one to his standards, making no one
understand. The search for society ends with the image of this great
man drawing back into himself.

The chronicle opens with an equally subtle picture of failure.
The plot of *Can You Forgive Her?* follows a comic pattern, but it
is so deeply shadowed as to lend to the whole the disturbing effect
the narrator attributes to winter light: 'It is the light of the after-
noon, and gives token of the speedy coming of the early twilight. It
tells of the shortness of the day, and contains even in its clearness
a promise of the gloom of night. It is absolute light, but it seems to
contain the darkness which is to follow it' (31). Nothing is exactly
what it appears to be in this novel, nor can anyone give voice to
what he is. Plantagenet Palliser is 'very careful in his language',
labouring after 'accuracy' at all costs, and consequently 'he rather
prided himself on being dull' (24). Such language suggests an accuracy that is lifeless because it is emotionless. It accurately reflects
nothing. On the other hand, poetic characters like Burgo Fitzgerald
or especially George Vavasor employ language as a weapon. George's
electioneering slogan—'Vavasor and the "River Bank" '—like all
his words, asserts a meaning, or seems to assert a meaning, that is
not there. Private and romantic language is therefore so suspect
that public men disdain it altogether. Parliamentary etiquette for
public speech puts eloquence first on the list of faults, ahead of
being 'inaccurate', 'long-winded', and 'ill-tempered' (42). One sort
of meaninglessness is substituted for another. Such a split is a desperate one, and it finally guarantees the uselessness of communica-
tion, even between such honest men as Plantagenet Palliser and
John Grey: 'We all know that neither of them would put the matter
altogether in a true light. Men never can do so in words, let the
light within themselves be ever so clear' (77).

In a way, the only language that is truly expressive is the language of attack, the language of wit.[6] Glencora is the true wit, and her language is both more effective and more hostile than that of anyone else. When her husband stuffily rebukes her for using such vulgar expressions as 'the long and the short of it', she sharply defends herself by claiming that the phrase is 'good English' (49). Glencora is the true conservative here and throughout, imagining that the coherence implied by 'good English' can be maintained. She fights to bring back into being another language, one in which words have a direct connection with reality. For her and for Alice Vavasor, the key word and the key illusion is 'freedom'. The novel is, in fact, very largely an ironic exploration of this term.

Can You Forgive Her? opens on an image of the trapped man, old Mr. Vavasor, whose function in this world, endlessly signing forms he does not read, suggests the futility of all energy. He tries to maintain a grumbling sort of dignity, but he can really express no substance. He truly is nothing and thus defines the essential starting-point for the problems involving the major characters, all of whom are women. Three women, Alice Vavasor, Lady Glencora, and Mrs. Arabella Greenow, are each asked to choose between two lovers, each pair consisting of one prudent and one romantic man. Alice and Glencora reject the poetic choice (George Vavasor and Burgo Fitzgerald) and marry into a public life (with John Grey and Plantagenet Palliser, respectively). The minor plot involving the widow Greenow, however, reverses the major plots on this, as on every other, point. Mrs. Greenow chooses 'the rocks and valley' over the substantial dungheaps.

All three provide answers to the pointed question, 'What should a woman do with her life?' It appears that as soon as such a question is asked, as soon as a woman obtains any self-consciousness about her situation, all the easy answers disappear. Wealth and rank are no protection against nothingness, as the Palliser girls, Iphy and Pheme, illustrate. Jeffrey explains that they are not political, being 'too clever to give themselves up to anything in which they can do nothing. Being women they live a depressed life, devoting them-selves to literature, fine arts, social economy, and the abstract sciences. They write wonderful letters' (23). Not all are content to write wonderful letters, however, and try for something more—for

---

[6] Robert Polhemus, *The Changing World*, p. 106, sees Glencora's wit as 'almost desperate'.

wonderful lives. The novel traces three such attempts, two of which are anything but successful, despite the wit and strength of the women involved. The third attempt, made by the widow Greenow, succeeds with such ridiculous ease as to emphasize the central irony. This is what *should* happen, says this subplot; this is how problems should be swept aside. This subplot has the effect of making the dilemmas of the two major characters more apparent and more tantalizing.

None is more tantalizing than the dilemma of Alice Vavasor. 'What are we to forgive?' asked James. Where is the moral question?[7] Why does she marry in the end, if there was such a major issue at stake? Isn't 'the tragedy but a simple postponement of the wedding-day'?[8] Is it not, finally, 'a maddeningly contradictory novel' with this 'hard-hearted, boring prude' at its centre?[9] Though the book does not appear to have been 'the pioneer of the problem novel', as Escott claimed,[10] since so few have noticed that it was working anywhere close to the frontier, there is certainly a problem presented, a major moral and psychological problem. James, who wrote about the same dilemma exactly in *The Portrait of a Lady*, should have known better. Perhaps he did. In any case, Alice, like Isabel Archer, is out to test the conditions and extent of her freedom: 'People always do seem to think it is so terrible that a girl should have her own way in anything' (3). She resists persuasion for the same reasons a rabbit shuns a trap—'I haven't much of my own way at present; but you see, when I'm married I shan't have it at all' (3). As a result, to the imperious Lady Midlothian she seems 'the most self-willed young woman I ever met in my life' (26). Very likely she is; Alice is, or wants to be, literally self-willed. But the assertion of independence, she feels, is an assertion of isolation. She can find no way out of this dilemma. 'All her troubles and

---

[7] Rev. of *Can You Forgive Her?*, *Nation*, 1 (28 Sept. 1865), 409.

[8] Ibid., p. 410. The *Saturday Review* similarly imagined that there were no real moral issues, that the answer to the dilemma was simply 'fall in love, marry the man', a 'smug and comfortable' theory, they thought (Rev. of *Can You Forgive Her?* 20, 19 Aug. 1865, 241). Michael Sadleir says that Alice 'bows to propriety, marries her paragon and lives happily' (*Trollope: A Commentary*, p. 390). David S. Chamberlain's 'Unity and Irony in Trollope's *Can You Forgive Her?*', *SEL*, 8 (1968), 669–80, cites passages from Trollope's lecture on 'Higher Education of Women' to support his contention that Trollope totally disapproves of Alice's desire for independence. John C. Kleis's treatment of Alice is much more sympathetic, but even he complains about the unconvincing resolution ('Passion vs. Prudence', pp. 1408–9).

[9] Polhemus, *The Changing World*, pp. 110–11. [10] *Anthony Trollope*, p. 209.

sorrows in life', the narrator says, 'had come from an over-fed craving for independence' (43). But in the craving for independence is her only hope. The narrator's characterization of her hope as 'over-fed' marks an embarrassed hesitance that shadows a few of the comments on Alice. It is almost as if the narrator wished now and then to disavow the plain implications of the subject, to turn away from the direction in which the study was obviously tending. At one point, as Alice is wrestling with the 'what-should-a-woman-do-with-her-life?' problem, the narrator breaks in impatiently with a blustering answer: 'fall in love, marry the man, have two children, and live happy ever afterwards. I maintain that answer has as much wisdom in it as any other that can be given;—or perhaps more' (11). Whatever its intent, such a simple-minded comment actually heightens our awareness of the difficulties of the complex plight Alice faces. The narrator's answer is a piece of romantic wisdom that applies only to the widow Greenow, who is miraculously blessed by a comic goddess otherwise impotent.

Alice's notions of what she wants are altogether unclear; she 'had by degrees filled herself with a vague idea that there was a something to be done; a something over and beyond, or perhaps altogether beside that marrying and having two children;—if she only knew what it was' (11). She cannot find 'what it was' because 'it' is nowhere objectified or available in her surroundings. What she feels more sure of is that neither of the two choices offered to her, George and Grey, leads to much of anything, different as they appear to be. She flits between the two, each grasping at her and trying to cage her as she retreats from the other. But she hears the chains clanking on both sides and thus tries to fly free. She originally resists Grey, partly to thwart her smug guardians and persuaders, partly because he is too obviously perfect, but mostly because he assumes total command in every smooth, untroubled gesture. He is as secure as a hunter in a duck preserve: 'He shook his head and still smiled. There was something in the imperturbed security of his manner which almost made her angry with him. It seemed as though he assumed so great a superiority that he felt himself able to treat any resolve of hers as the petulance of a child' (11). Grey is a man of pure surface and public language. He looks, Kate says, 'as though he was always bethinking himself that he wouldn't wear out his clothes' (6), a characterization not altogether unfair in its suggestion of his self-absorbed prudence. But though superficial, he is not weak; the surface is almost overpowering: 'he always spoke and acted as though there could be no question that his manner of life was to be adopted, without a word or thought of doubting, by his wife' (3). His ignorant insensitivity is thus a source of strength. Even Lady Macleod, who has been pushing Alice toward a marriage with Grey with all her might, is no longer surprised at Alice's reluctance after she actually meets Grey and sees what his perfection amounts to (15). The theme of Grey's subtly repulsive, masterful perfection is so brilliantly handled that the narrator pretends not quite to understand it himself: 'I do not know how to explain that it was so; but it was this perfect command of himself at all seasons which had in part made Alice afraid of him' (36). By this means we are made to see how deep and how intuitive are the causes for Alice's revolt against him. Grey himself can comprehend nothing of this, of course, attributing Alice's aversion to him to 'the effects of a mental hallucination', 'a disease' (61). The truth is that Alice regards what the narrator terms Grey's 'immobility' (74) as a kind of death. She tries to explain, telling him that while their marriage would add some minor diversification to his old life, she would have to pass 'through a grave' (10). She needs from him some recognition of her humanity, at least the chance to be overcome by persuasion rather than smug assumptions: 'she could not become unambitious, tranquil, fond of retirement, and philosophic, without an argument on the matter,—without being allowed even the poor grace of owning herself to be convinced. If a man takes a dog with him from the country up to town, the dog must live a town life without knowing the reason why;—must live a town life or die a town death. But a woman should not be treated like a dog' (63).

To demonstrate that she is human, Alice decides to escape on a trip with her cousins Kate and George Vavasor. George had previously been engaged to Alice, had been dismissed for some atrocity, and is thus the most indiscreet of partners, which is one of his two charms: no one approves of him. The other is that he is 'poetic'. 'I'm made up of poetry', he says, defining poetry as a kind of enforced obtuseness: 'in this world things are beautiful only because they are not quite seen, or not perfectly understood' (5). George takes such advantage of this uncertain and fluid state of things, plays so on one's pathetic hope for some relief from emptiness, that the narrator feels called upon to issue a warning against him. George is essentially mysterious, 'but to my thinking mystery is a vice' (12). George, just like Burgo, is 'reckless', perceiving clearly enough the artificiality and instability of rules of conduct to be carless about them. Without the support of any rules, he becomes desperate and finally violent. Alice agrees to marry him, telling her father, 'I am prepared to run risks now' (34), but she has no idea what she is in for, what 'poetry' really is. George becomes threatening, treats her as a 'prisoner' (35), and teaches her what it is to be 'desolate and alone in the world' (34). 'He has treated me as I should have thought no man could have treated a woman' (54), she says, a horrible shock that shows her what 'mystery' has to offer and sends her laden with guilt back to Grey.

It is this guilt which is indicated in the title. Alice's cousin Kate could show her how love can be turned to guilt, which in turn becomes an intense desire for punishment. But Alice does not understand. Kate's devotion to her brother is so unnaturally intense that Alice cannot help but notice: '"And who are you?" said Alice, laughing, "You are not going to be his wife?"' (32). She fails to see, however, that Kate is actively seeking her own retribution, trying to find the nothingness Alice is trying to escape: 'If George ever married', Kate says, 'I should have nothing to do in the world;—literally nothing—nothing—nothing—nothing!' (6). Yet her single activity for most of the novel is the attempt to get George married, to satisfy her guilt by becoming nothing. Ironically, Kate eventually resists her brother's demands and breaks this pattern, just as Alice falls into it.

Why does Alice feel such urgent need for forgiveness and, at the same time, fiercely resist the forgiveness she receives? Why, more especially, does the narrator keep punching at us: 'But can you forgive her, delicate reader?' (37). Alice surely would not desire our forgiveness; she is furious when Lady Midlothian offers hers. Though she cannot exactly stop Grey from forgiving her, she can hang on to her own deep guilt: 'I am not fit to be your wife. I am not good enough' (70). As long as she can maintain her grip on this guilt, she can, of course, elude Grey. But there are, I think, other less rational reasons; her sincerity is almost fierce in these passages of self-abasement. The suggestion is that the guilt derives from a secret 'fault', not her love for George, which in truth she never felt, but the independent exercise of will. Forgiving herself for that fault would mean, in effect, renouncing that independent will. As long as she can hold on to her guilt, she can, ironically,

protect the shreds of her freedom. Masochism, then, for her as for
Isabel Archer, is the last defence of independence, the last pathetic
proof that they were and are free.

Grey perhaps senses just a little of this, seeing that his forgiveness
of her will be worth nothing until he can induce her to forgive herself (73). He tries therefore to obliterate the protection she has in
memory: 'Come to me, dear, and . . . the past shall be only as a
dream' (74). But it is the past that supports her and she tries very
hard to block his attacks on it: 'I am dreaming it always' (74), she
cries. Finally she is crushed: 'she had taken her fling at having her
own will, and she and all her friends had seen what had come of it'
(75). She has tried to unite her private being with a public self and
has made a fool of herself. She therefore gives up, accepts forgiveness and grants it to herself, and accepts marriage as the appropriate
sentence on her. There is little question that Grey will be on the
alert against any further outbreaks of spirit: 'He seldom allowed
outspoken enthusiasm to pass by him without some amount of
hostility' (77). We are asked to participate in a very ironic forgiveness, asked, in other words, to assist in the suppression of her will.

Glencora is more dramatic, more witty, and more intelligent
than Alice, but their situations are so very similar that they are
mutually illuminating. To understand more fully why Glencora
married Plantagenet Palliser in the first place, we can look at Alice's
reaction to similar pressures; to forecast what life would be with
John Grey, we have the guide of Glencora's marriage. The major
difference is that Glencora did not have the vigorous anti-romantic
lesson George Vavasor administered to Alice and can, therefore,
maintain some spirit and some contact with a past she now pas-
sionately idealizes. Burgo Fitzgerald is gentle, naturally sweet,
where George is brutal, but both play the same roles. Both are instinctive rebels, united in their 'recklessness'. Burgo's unconscious
beauty, his inability to reflect, his naïve insistence on freedom, all
conspire to imprison him. He is an idyllic character caught in a
world which has no time for idylls, and his reflexive desperation is
much stronger even than George's more calculated rebellion. Burgo
tries to exist in pure, unselfish romance, in a sort of eternal present
(see ch. 50). But the result of such innocence is that even George is
shocked by Burgo's egocentric morality and warns him that he must
not carry off Glencora now that she is married: 'marriage is marriage', he says (29). The pure Burgo and the vicious George achieve

an essential unity all the same: neither instinctive nor planned re-
bellions have a chance. When last seen at Baden-Baden, where men
go for gambling, for suicide, or for both, Burgo shows that he has
finally been thrust out of his world of innocence and has begun
to reflect: 'It seems to have been ordered that I'm to go to the
devil; but I don't know who gave the orders, and I don't know
why' (76).

Glencora's own search for freedom is not blocked so dramatically,
but it is kept alive only by her resolute and powerful comic wit.
She marries a man who, whatever he later becomes, is here an
enemy of youth and its values. When he first came on the scene,
back in *The Small House at Allington*, Platagenet Palliser had been
introduced as 'a thin-minded, plodding, respectable man, willing
to devote all his youth to work' (23). The disguised model for this
marriage is that of January and May, though here the element of
sexual perversion is of course submerged. Even Palliser's generous
attempts to make his wife more comfortable seem shuffling, oddly
insensitive. For all his generosity and kindness, one has a sense that
even in his greatest moment, when he leaves Glencora alone with
Burgo and snubs Mr. Bott, he is exercising in an impersonal way
the grand old gentlemanly code. Glencora is seen primarily as 'my
wife', whom it behoves one to treat with every delicacy and with
no shade of suspicion. He has almost nothing beyond this public
stance to offer. The first words we hear him speak, again in *The
Small House at Allington*, are, 'I don't see anything to laugh at' (23).
Humourless precisely because he has no rebellious instincts to tap,
no fund of embarrassment, anxiety, or aggression that could be
drained, he is the pure public man. Even his face is remarkable
only for being so entirely unremarkable, so totally without individuality: 'It was a face that you might see and forget, and see
again and forget again' (22).

He exactly inverts the values Glencora holds to so firmly. 'To lose
his influence with his party would be worse to him than to lose his
wife' (24). This is a fierce indictment of him, as is his treatment of
Glencora's emotional confession of her love for Burgo: '"You must
love me now", he had replied with a smile; and then, as regarded
his mind, the thing was over' (24). 'His instincts were dull' (43), the
narrator wryly comments. As a consequence, he unconsciously
taunts his wife with his easy assumption of smooth control. He
treats her as a child who wants 'keepers', nearly forcing her, just

as Grey forces Alice, into the same recklessness as her lover: 'I can fancy a woman being driven to do wrong simply by a desire to show her policeman that she can be too many for him' (48). But Glencora really resents Palliser's tyranny less than his hollowness: 'what hard treatment, even what beating, could be so unendurable as this total want of sympathy, as this deadness in life, which her present lot entailed upon her?' (43). She turns to Alice for love and for help, but all that is a little like Claudius asking Hamlet for counsel. Neither Hamlet nor Alice wants to see the problems, precisely because they are their own problems. Alice does not want to imagine herself in Glencora's impossible position because she does not want to see that she is already there. So the one friend who might help is very cold; Alice has no choice but to act as some lecturing fool or not to act at all. She has before been one of Glencora's policemen, guiding her away from romance, but she is now unhappy with that role. She withdraws, then, and Glencora is left to form 'an assured conviction that on either side there must be misery for her' (58). When Glencora ironically helps put pressure on Alice later to marry Grey, another version of Planty Pall, there may possibly be something of vengeance in her motive. Principally, however, both women join with the world against the rebel because they are unable to see any way out of the dilemma and because they are unable really to face what they themselves have lost.

The question is, though, whether Glencora really loses. One might ask whether it is not true that Platagenet Palliser begins courageously to develop privately, even if it is late to begin. The choice to throw over his great dream of public office at the Exchequer in order to travel with his wife seems to signal a genuine change in his values. Even his relative solidity gives Glencora a target for her wit and a happy grievance; his generosity allows her wit nearly unlimited freedom. All this is true, but beneath the progressive growth and deveopment of Palliser as a human being is a strong resistance movement in Glencora's refusal to put up with a half-formed, public lover. Even his warmest, most affectionate gestures seem to her to amount to very little, much less than she has a right to expect: 'He says that he loves me . . . but he does not know what love means' (59). Though she knows that he has behaved 'with genuine, true nobility' (59), the love seems to her paltry. The great kindness, further, seems to her a trap, and she refers throughout the last part of the novel in very barbed jokes to his generosity as her 'defeat'. He kills her with kindness, she says; 'he found that I wanted looking after, and that Mrs. Marsham and Mr. Bott between them couldn't do it' (62).

Such jokes certainly have their sting. Even the narrator reminds us that Palliser's patient generosity costs him very little since 'he had his own way in everything. Lady Glencora did not behave very well,—contradicting her husband, and not considering, as, perhaps, she ought to have done, the sacrifice he was making on her behalf. But, then, she had her own way in nothing' (68). She sees her pregnancy as the last of the great padlocks. Faced with this imprisonment, she retains her wit as the one reminder of the past: 'I wish I had never told him a word about [the pregnancy]. He would never have found it out himself, till this thing was all over' (73). She says 'the devil prompted me' (80) to tell the Duke she expected the baby to be a girl. This devil keeps her alive, even as she goes to Gatherum Castle for the ceremonial birth of the new heir: 'I was completely in their power and couldn't help their bringing me here' (80). By the time of *The Prime Minister*, it is Glencora who wants to reopen the castle, Palliser who wants only to live with those he loves. But this sad reversal is another story.

The other story within *Can You Forgive Her?* is that of the widow Greenow. Trollope liked this subplot,[11] but he has had very little company in this judgement. While it is true that the humour is broad and a bit repetitive, its broadness, at least, is an asset, contrasting as it does with the delicacy of the main plots. For this subplot is a parody plot. The third woman in the novel has all the freedom she wants. She has no dilemmas, certainly no psychological ones, and she manages not only to arrange her own perfect marriage, but those of others too. She turns even her grief, which is not wholly hypocritical, into useful equipment, but this is always used for festivity. Her own suitors—the wealthy, dull Cheesacre, who shares with Grey a preference for the Eastern wasteland, and the disreputable Captain Bellfield—parody the choices facing Glencora and Alice. Mrs. Greenow does not, however, have to decide between two kinds of 'misery', but between two diverse forms of comfort: 'She was essentially a happy-tempered woman, blessed with a good digestion, who looked back upon her past life with contentment, and forward to her future life with confidence' (47). She can be established so simply because in her world things are terribly simple. There are

---

[11] See *Autobiography*, p. 180.

plenty of parallels with the issues dominating the central plots; Mrs. Greenow, for example, is herself a rebel against the smirking female propriety that demands a belief in the notion that 'little babies [are] found about in the hedges and ditches' (64). But such ties only demonstrate the more important contrasts. Mrs. Greenow's story, as much as the comic subplot in Middleton and Rowley's *The Changeling*, effectively sets the major stories over against the comic and romantic assumptions we would like to see maintained. She is made to burlesque conventional narratives of love in order to expose their unreality and suggest thereby the very stark reality of the main plots. It all has something of the effect of a before and after advertisement. Mrs. Greenow makes us see how far we have travelled from the world of wish-fulfilment and romantic comedy.

Phineas Finn is, by itself, a more hopeful story, a very optimistic record of defeat. Joined with its sequel, *Phineas Redux*, into the 'one novel' Trollope insisted they formed (*Autobiography*, p. 320), the Phineas story is a pessimistic view of triumph. *Phineas Finn* is, on the surface at least, a wonderful success story with a coy, downbeat ending. Phineas withdraws, but we respect his reasons for doing so, and we see that any withdrawal is certainly temporary. *Phineas Redux* is also a story of luck, bad luck this time, and Phineas, now without the support of the good fairy of comedy, without any support at all, struggles through a bitter education to a final accommodation with kindly obscurity. Phineas, like Micawber, seems at the end of *Phineas Finn* to have pulled back for a leap; we leave him crouching. But his leap back into English society is about as successful as Micawber's bouts with commerce. And Micawber, of course, is never serious, whereas Phineas puts all he has into his confident return.

The interval in Ireland seems clearly designed to allow Phineas a chance to regain his strength and his luck. Rather like Frye's model for the comedy of the green world, the pattern here makes use of nature to give renewed sustenance to the sophisticated society. Poor Mary Flood Jones, wed to Phineas at the end of the first novel and slaughtered before the second begins, seemed later to Trollope to be a mistake, a victim of crude plot exigencies (*Autobiography*, p. 318). The marriage is essential, however, signalling as it does Phineas's sincere if temporary dedication to pastoral values. The death is harsh, no doubt,[12] but it serves to start the mythoi going in the second novel and seems to me a trivial fault, if it is one at all. The fuss about it illustrates, I think, one of the defects of plot criticism, Trollope's included.

Besides, a great deal more than Mary Flood Jones ties these novels together. Their unity is both interrupted and, at the same time, explained by *The Eustace Diamonds*, whose publication came between the two Phineas novels. *The Eustace Diamonds* depicts with an unmistakable sharpness the ironic conditions that make possible the terrors of *Phineas Redux*. The intervening novel breaks in with a commentary which in the end goes to establish the un-broken unity of the Phineas novel. It tells us how good luck and bad luck are finally the same. While respecting this unity, then, it is useful to show how it is developed—and explained—sequentially.

Phineas Finn picks up where *Can You Forgive Her?* left off, with the feminist issue, and discovers that the woman's dilemma is also man's. The only slightly disguised feminism is still there in Glen-cora, of course, now reinforced by the more subtly independent Madame Max Goesler. Lady Laura resolves 'that she would use the world as men use it, and not as women do' (39). And even Violet Effingham keeps up a steady stream of subversive jokes on the subject: 'I shall knock under to Mr. Mill, and go in for women's rights, and look forward to stand for some female borough' (51). Here the fight of women to preserve independence and personality is carried on with special reference to the public life, to politics. Lady Laura feels 'that a woman's life is only half a life, as she cannot have a seat in Parliament' (6), and Lady Glencora campaigns vigorously for an amount of political power sufficient for ten men. Like marriage, however, the political life is for women mostly a snare; what's more, its futility is pathetically obvious: 'It was manifestly a meeting of Liberals, semi-social and semi-political;—so arranged that ladies might feel that some interest in politics was allowed to them, and perhaps some influence also' (37).

One might say that these ties between love and politics are very artfully arranged to allow Trollope the chance to indulge himself in politics. 'As I was debarred from expressing my opinions in the House of Commons, I took this method of declaring myself', he

---

[12] Mary is, in fact, presented from the start as a sacrificial object: 'She was one of those girls, so common in Ireland, whom men, with tastes that way given, feel inclined to take up and devour on the spur of the moment' (2).

said, adding that he regarded the political parts of the novels as written principally 'for my own sake', the rest for the readers (*Autobiography*, p. 317). But in fact his own concerns and those allowed to the reader are the same. Politics demands of men the same impossible balance between the public and private selves faced by women in love. Does one follow his party or issues, men or measures, the present or posterity, abstract theory or hard-nosed empiricism? There are never any easy answers; perhaps there are no answers at all. On the broad issue of reform, for instance, the narrator intercedes and pretends to give us some help: the popular pressure for reform is premature nonsense trumped up by the press, but those who oppose reform generally are unconsciously protecting nothing but themselves; even the kindly Duke of St. Bungay is sarcastically said to be naturally averse to 'any change in a state of things that must seem to him to be so salutary' (35). The answer is characteristic of Trollope: no definite 'position' can be safe; only a delicate yet firmly grounded sensitivity to the demands of politics, party, God, the future, and the *People's Banner* is admired. When Phineas frets about the obscurity and instability of opposition and the tiresome hypocrisy of office, Lady Laura pompously says, 'Your career may combine the dignity of the one with the utility of the other' (64). But how? Being sometimes in and sometimes out is not a real 'combination'; it is as if one sought to be a balanced teacher by lecturing in a cap and gown for half the term and then joining nude in a democratic massage party for the other half. Phineas is finally searching for an answer to the same question that had concerned Alice Vavasor and Glencora: what is a person to do with his life? More exactly, how can one live publicly and socially and still retain control of his individuality? Mr. Monk, something of a moral arbiter here, explicitly tells Phineas at one point that his grumbling about the slavery of office is only part of a universal dilemma: 'If you mean that you cannot do joint work with other men altogether after your own fashion the same may be said of all work' (65). Marriage included.

Love and politics are the arenas in which this battle for a satisfactory balance is fought out. Phineas brings with him from Ireland the traditional weapons of heroes from the country: strength, good looks, innocence. But he clearly is not here to learn the trade and retire; neither he nor the novel extends its respect to Ireland or the country or the pastoral to the extent of wanting to abide there.

Everyone's values and hopes are tied up with the sophisticated world; idyllic times, like those in Barsetshire, are remembered only in such jokes as the Duke's garden party, where the 'picturesque effect' of lovers beneath haycocks must be purchased by the hour: 'though of all parties a garden party is the nicest, everybody is always anxious to get out of the garden as quick as may be' (63). There is no use worrying about Lily Dale and the corrupted pastoral. But nature is clearly not unimportant here either; it is used.

This use is not easy to describe, nor is it easy to effect with impunity. Phineas may use Mary Flood Jones, but he too is used by his party and friends. Lady Laura once again has a pathetically impracticable solution to this problem of the balance between innocence and experience, country and city: 'I think that a little of both is good for man and woman' (14). In-and-out-of-town is as far from being a real solution as is in-and-out-of-office. Crude oscillations never work. But there is another answer provided: the careful control and training of nature suggested by Madame Goesler. Understanding herself as well as she understands nature, she artfully turns her surroundings into the prettiest and most pleasing rooms in London. Her gardens 'were as bright and gay as money could make them when brought into competition with London smoke' (72). The terms are unsentimental but not satiric; she uses nature as effectively as is now possible. The room in which she receives 'almost looked as though it were a bower in a garden' (72). The pastoral world is not to be fully recaptured, but it can 'almost' be joined to sophistication by means of the tools of the world of experience, primarily money. Money is spent, however, in order to give pleasure: 'The seats, though they were costly as money could buy, were meant for sitting, and were comfortable as seats' (72). She has mastered 'the art of living', the art of nature nurtured. In the world in which she must live the key values are those neither of sophistication nor innocence alone but of taste, the art of equipoise.

The central narrative pattern appears to describe Phineas's education toward such taste. Madame Max, with a little help from Lady Glencora, is the main tutor and thus the figure whose values we must attend to most closely.[13] She is the most apparently sociable of Trollope's women: 'so great was her fertility in discoursing that all

---

[13] Madame Max is attacked with inexplicable but entertaining fury—'one of the most repulsive characters in fiction . . . the woman is a desert'—by Rebecca West, *The Court and the Castle*, pp. 149–52.

conversational grasses seemed to grow with her spontaneously' (40). The mild satire in the indelicate metaphor is directed not at Madame Max but at the assumptions of pure pastoral. Madame Max is no innocent, but she has the secret of transforming private nature to public function. She speaks, moreover, from the very first meeting with Phineas, with a broad and full understanding of all issues, admitting that her radical desire to 'out-Turnbull Mr. Turnbull' might be indulged (like Phineas's, she implies) in the complete safety of ineffectuality but that she does not really 'want to put down ladies and gentlemen'. She concludes, 'But then, Mr. Finn, there is such a difference between life and theory;—is there not?' (40). Endorsed wisdom here, certainly, but to what does it lead? What answers does it provide? The exceptional thing about Madame Goesler as a moral focus is that she is herself adrift, wondering whether she has any 'definite object' at all, certain only that 'the hours with her were too long and the days too many' (54). Perfect insight provides no solutions, and the education of Phineas is thus given an equivocal final goal right from the start. Even if he learns to see and act as she does, what then can he do?

But he is at the beginning of the novel a long way from Madame Max's balanced life of perfect taste. He must first knock around for a time in the worlds of politics and love. In both spheres alternatives are arranged in rather neat dualisms so that as Phineas bangs back and forth between them we can almost leave it to the laws of physics to locate him finally at some midpoint between the equal but opposite extremes. Phineas begins politics as a murky idealist, supported ironically by a man who is on guard to blight any tiny growth of abstract thought. Barrington Erle is sincerely and simply disgusted with notions of conscience, independence—issues of any kind. When Phineas blushingly tells him, 'I have views of my own', Erle claps him on the back with an assured, 'Of course you have, my dear boy' (1). He plans to take charge of Phineas, but Erle's pure empiricism answers far too few questions, and these too easily. He never has trouble making up his mind; he has no sense of future. Phineas soon learns that though decisions must be made, they must be more difficult than Erle supposes. He recognizes something of Erle's attitude even in Quintus Slide's absolute ignorance as to anything beyond a good fight and his grotesque mutual back-scratching sense of community: 'Damn it, I say; what's the good of a brotherhood if it ain't to be brotherhood?' (33).

Phineas's landlord and suspicious friend, Mr. Bunce, forces him to see that there is something more required from those in government than plenty of oil for the machinery. The promotion of the absolutely indolent Laurence Fitzgibbon purely on grounds of party loyalty convinces Phineas that surely 'there was something wrong' (44). But on the other side of empiricism are people like Mr. Gresham, an accomplished idealist 'with no feelings for the past, void of historical association' (29) and thus void also of the necessary complicating intuitions and memories that should make decisions difficult. Mr. Gresham is 'living altogether for the future which he is anxious to fashion anew out of the vigour of his own brain' (29), but it is an incorporeal future, as abstract, as Mr. Monk damningly says, as are Gresham's justice and his generosity. Just as Slide's opportunism ridicules Erle's empiricism, so Gresham's tendency toward abstraction is parodied by Mr. Turnbull's total absorption of the public life into himself. Turnbull constructs nothing, takes no responsibility (even for the accuracy of his charges), and simply slashes away at existing evils. Monk says explicitly that his great fault lies in his forgetting the difference between private and public life. Even at a private dinner party for friends, Turnbull can descend no lower than speeches. 'I wonder', says Monk, 'what sort of a time Mrs. Turnbull and the little Turnbulls have of it?' (18). If there is an approved model for political life, it is this Mr. Monk, uneasily refusing either extreme position, moving into opposition or into office, supporting men or measures, regarding party or principle, as the requirements of each situation demand. He is uncertain about his own abilities and actions, admired but misunderstood by his colleagues. He is a model but hardly a comforting one. Phineas is asked to mediate between absolutism and empiricism, self and service, but it is far from clear what the terms of that mediation are or whether they can be successfully achieved.

He is taught the same confusing lesson in his private life through the contrasted stories of Lady Laura and Violet Effingham. They indicate the alternate poles of this world, bad luck and good luck. There are various explanations given for Laura's tragic condition and Violet's happy one, but none of the explanations explains very much. Lady Laura doubtless marries with her eye too much on power and position, but that hardly accounts for Kennedy becoming a raving, gun-toting lunatic. Similarly, Chiltern's transformation, though subtler, is no less miraculous and just as little explicable by reference to good qualities in his wife. These affairs simply indicate the boundaries, mark out the range of possibilities in a world ruled by luck. One story holds out the promise of comic fulfilment; the other warns of horrible ironic bondage. They illustrate in a stylized, almost didactic way alternate varieties of absurdity: unexplained joy, unexplained torture. Phineas's own mixed life thus seems to be analyzed for him, as its strands are helpfully isolated.

Taken by itself, the story of Violet and Chiltern would be illustrative of a world ruled by secure comic principles. Like the happy lovers in *He Knew He Was Right*, they take a leap in the dark. Or rather she does: 'The risk would be so great. Suppose that I did not save him, but that he brought me to shipwreck instead?' (10). Chiltern himself is a man who seeks out violence and extreme danger, preferring 'to have something to do on horseback' (19), that is, to find the most perilous mount possible. He insists, against all reason, on proceeding with the absurd duel, clearly hoping for some damage, perhaps mostly to himself. He is an original, 'not like anybody else in the world', and thus inexplicable by conventional standards (59). We can sense in this self-destructive individuality some of the force and integrity of the rebellion attempted first by Alice Vavasor and Glencora and later by nearly all the major characters in this series. Here the rebellion on behalf of the self is perverse as long as it is isolated; it has no form and no goal. It is only when it is joined with another's that it takes public shape, transforms itself from personal rebellion to an ordinary, healthy government. Violet is as rebellious as her lover, seeing through Phineas's conventional softness with almost frightening clarity and strongly resisting Chiltern's instinctive desire to imprison her in the past. 'Be a child still' (19), he urges, but she insists on being an adult, quite consciously isolating herself from what she sardonically calls the 'natural protectors' (46) of women. It is the women who make the decisions here, plunging into and directing the new life. The refusal to disengage herself from risk guarantees her individuality: she admits that she shares Chiltern's attraction to danger: 'A sense of danger does not make me unhappy, though the threatened evil may be fatal' (52). By joining this danger without reservation or illusion, without any of the comforting certainties of comedy, she finds comedy after all. This fully mature balance is so successful that it stands throughout the series as a wistful and lonely symbol of what might be. Their union is too dynamic to be contained within a term like 'perfect', but Violet's obvious relish of her role as free, witty, and powerful wife and Lord Chiltern's teeth-gnashing delight in being Master of the Hounds suggest a union of public and private roles that no one else ever comes close to attaining.

But there are hardly reasons to be found for their success, nor is there a school for studying such a pattern. Violet admits jokingly to Lady Laura that 'real tragedy' is altogether beyond her; 'I shall never go beyond genteel comedy' (10), she says. Her fortuitous discovery of genuine comedy is something of a miracle. Lady Laura herself does find 'real tragedy', or would if there were any intelligible shape to her destiny. It runs straight downhill, but final explanations seem referable only to some distant abstractions like Fortune's wheel. Taken by itself, the Kennedy story might indeed be a tragedy of the sort Chaucer's Monk defines, illustrating the control of malevolence or some other more or less comprehensible spirit. But the juxtaposition with the Violet–Chiltern plot indicates that Lady Laura is less a victim of Fortune than of trivial bad luck.

Her marriage to Kennedy is calculated, to be sure, but not entirely heartless. And who would have thought that this nondescript lord would turn out to be a fanatic for power, turning the force of his religion, his family, most of all his maleness against her in order to make 'her feel that her lord and master was—her lord and master' (23)? He not only makes reading lists for her but expects her to follow them—on schedule. He does all this, we are told, because he senses her intellectual superiority and thus is most anxious to insist on his rights, rights which, when pressed, seem to Laura more absurd and more unjust. As she rebels, he becomes more self-righteous and tyrannical, more and more a man of 'hard, dry, unsympathising, unchanging virtues' (32). When pressed, he demands her entire will, and this is just what she feels she must protect: 'There are moments, Robert, when even a married woman must be herself rather than her husband's wife' (39). As he becomes more grimly conventional, insisting always on her 'duty', she naturally comes to associate marriage itself with imprisonment: 'There is no tyranny to a woman like telling her of her duty. Talk of beating a woman! Beating might often be a mercy' (55).

The opposite side of the absurd world is thus a warning to Phineas, just as the Violet–Chiltern union beckons to him. But both illustrate the same principles. They also tell us something about Phineas himself. Violet's rejection of him suggests that his initiation is not yet complete, that he is not qualified for comedy. Laura's tenacious clinging to him, on the other hand, and his growing resistance to her show how far he is removed from her genuine torment. She helps to show us how very slight his problems actually are. He usually realizes this himself, reflecting several times that, bad as his own condition seems to be, he is not, like Lady Laura, faced with 'no escape, no hope, no prospect of relief, no place of consolation' (56). 'The world', he acknowledges, is always 'much better with him than it was with either of those two wretched married beings' (70). When at the end, in the throes of his disappointment, he echoes Laura's 'I am nobody' with 'I also am going to be a nobody' (75), we can see how wrong he is, how certain will be his return. He is never trapped as Laura is, partly because, as she says, a woman for some cruel reason is bowled out very easily, whereas a man may try again (75). Phineas is saved by his temperament, by luck, by the god of comedy, and also by his sex: he is, fortunately for him, not a woman. This last insistence is perhaps the subplot's strongest and most startling contribution to the novel.

But both subplots also suggest another characteristic of Phineas's education: its superficiality. Because he is denied both the rewards and the punishments, we have a feeling that he is somehow protected from the consequences and the real effects of his education. He is allowed to learn a little, but not much. Mostly he just observes. Like a schoolboy, he is shown the adult world but is not allowed to participate in it, and like a schoolboy he imagines that only pleasures are being withheld. Phineas's lucky story, his miraculous overcoming again and again of those odds which are at best 'twenty to one against him' (3), has about it an air of unreality. Success stories of this sort mean little either to Lady Laura or to Violet: it's like telling Captain Ahab and Falstaff about Horatio Alger heroes and expecting them to be stirred.

Phineas comes on the scene, the child of nature and fortune. All the traditional dilemmas of heroes have been solved for him; he doesn't even have to struggle with his father. Mr. Finn's love and admiration for his son are so great that he really absorbs himself into his son's personality. All problems seem to melt as magically before the young Irishman. 'It was simply his nature to be pleasant' (13), and he seems thus literally to be blessed. He has those fine instincts (and bigotries) of a gentleman that always correct him, even when, as with Quintus Slide, he is led an inch or two astray: 'he would have

liked the Banner better had not Mr. Slide talked about the 'Ouse'
(26). Throughout he is attended by the same magic: rivals con-
veniently die or quarrel with one another, rotten boroughs beckon
to him sweetly. But even at the happy time there is to Phineas
something impersonal and therefore unsatisfactory in this luck:
'"I never heard of a fellow with such a run of luck", said Erle.
"It's just one of those flukes that occur once in a dozen elections.
Any one on earth might have got in without spending a shilling"' (3).

'Any one on earth' is not what Phineas aspires to be, and he senses
himself that mere luck tends to deny and not confirm his individuality. Because he is never really tested, then, he is not educated. Floating through the world, he never experiences humiliations
and torments any more real than those that come upon him when he
speaks, or does not speak, or tries to speak in the House. He is
troubled by mock sufferings followed by unreal lamentations: 'I
have simply been the greatest idiot, the greatest coward . . .' (20).
He talks at one point of blowing out his brains, but Monk smoothly
tells him, 'Do not suppose that you have made an ass of yourself,—
that is, in any special degree' (26). Nothing about him is special; he is
like any other adolescent. He moves toward individuality in his
friendship with Chiltern, perhaps, and possibly even in his romantic
affairs. But his ability to bounce back after being disappointed in
love is so reliable as to be amusing. He tells himself that he is
desolate, but goes to a party anyhow: 'A man must live, even though
his heart be broken, and living he must dine' (53). Broken heart
indeed. His dilemmas never become more serious than that posed
by the offer from Laura of her father's controlled seat at Loughton.
He agonizes comically as to the justice of accepting such a seat in
order to fight against the very system that gave him a voice. His
justifications are as shallow as his doubts, and Trollope finds deflating humour in the old earl's abrupt candour. He tells Phineas
that all of his tenants are very 'obliging', and that none of them has
the slightest desire for a lease: 'They know they're safe. But I do
like the people round me to be of the same way of thinking as myself about politics' (33). So much for liberal politics and the purity
of young idealists. Even Madame Max cannot resist calling him
'Lord Brentford's member' (44). He is fretted by the problem and
he frets his friends with it. Monk finally loses patience and angrily
tells him to go to work and keep his mouth shut. This, of course,
is what the Duke is told later when he becomes Prime Minister,

and it is devastating advice. But the Duke's problems are genuine; Phineas's problems, though they take the same form, are not—as yet.

Because his problems are so slight, there is a growing sense of his insubstantiality. He wonders himself how it is that he can love so often, so variously, at such short intervals, and with such over-lappings, thinking that perhaps he is 'two separate persons' (35). But he is not so much a split personality as an incomplete one. The narrator reminds us that he seems 'beautifully ignorant' (39), de-spite what experience might have taught him with regard to Lady Laura. But it is Violet Effingham who gives the shrewdest analysis throughout. He lacks solidity, she claims, telling Lady Laura that he is not a lover but an apprentice, scurrying around practising for the real thing later (45). 'He is', she says, 'a little too much a friend to everybody', lacking in 'individuality' (71).

This suggests exactly why he must return to Ireland. He must acquire and develop that self and then come back without all the protections. He makes a stand on a question whose point is so insignificant that the narrator says he will not bother even to explain it (75). Phineas must choose somewhere to begin to assert himself, and this is as good a place as any. By so asserting himself he casts off luck and withdraws to gather strength for another try with a world whose conditions he now thinks he understands.

The Eustace Diamonds uses the intervening time to explain to us more precisely the nature of the world Phineas is preparing himself for. This is Trollope's most insistent, least relaxed novel; the narrator chooses every opportunity to generalize and to teach. At one point what must be Trollope's favourite song is quoted:

> It is good to be merry and wise,
> It is good to be honest and true,
> It is good to be off with the old love
> Before you are on with the new. (35)

The narrator cannot resist pouncing on any simplicity, even the playful simplicity of this verse: 'There was never better truth spoken than this, and if all men and women could follow the advice here given there would be very little sorrow in the world. But men and women do not follow it. They are no more able to do so than they are to use a spear, the staff of which is like a weaver's beam, or to

fight with the sword Excalibur' (35). There is no effective romance
now, not the slightest illusion, and we are not in this novel ever
to be left in doubt as to the bleak nature of existence.

For all the emphasis on crime, detection, and punishment, *The
Eustace Diamonds* is essentially static, demonstrating its nature in
recurrence rather than cumulative development. We learn from the
acidic portrait of Lady Linlithgow in the first chapter about all
there is to know about this world; the rest of the novel simply repeats the lesson in more and more startling ways. Trollope doubtless
capitalizes on the popularity of *The Moonstone*, but his novel
parodies Collins's methods and assumptions.[14] Trollope's attack on
plot is never used more organically. There is no forward motion
here, no discovery, no real villainy. No action is genuinely purpose-
ful, and effects do not follow causes. Lord George cruelly taunts
Lizzie over and over with the absolute pointlessness of all her
tricks: 'It's been uncommonly clever, but I don't see the use of it'
(51). Even the wiliest character in the novel, Lady Carbuncle, is
involved in a scheme which will wreck her no matter how it turns
out and leave 'nothing around her but failure and dismay' (70).
Failure and dismay are not hard to find here.[15] The people Lizzie
collects at Portray Castle—Mrs. Carbuncle, Lord George de Bruce
Carruthers, Lucinda Roanoke, Sir Griffin Tewett, and Mr. Emilius—
though not exactly a representative cross-section of the world, describe central tendencies of society much more accurately than
society likes to think. Only slightly extending the unscrupulous and
immoral behaviour dominant everywhere, this group of the wild
and ugly are symptomatic of a world which has lost direction and
control. Mrs. Carbuncle presides as an inverted wisdom figure,
whose bitterness is both repulsive and accurate: 'It's the way of the
world. The lower you fall, the more you're kicked' (40). She understands the way of the world so well that she can insist openly on
regular accountings so as not to be cheated. She is even anxious on
such matters as wedding presents, writing to an acquaintance to

14 A very good treatment of the way Trollope transforms Collins's 'high seriousness'
into 'low comedy', 'thereby consciously satirizing Collins' method' is provided by
Henry J. W. Milley, '*The Eustace Diamonds* and *The Moonstone*', *SP*, 36 (1939), 651–63.
Trollope emphasized as much as he could how unconcerned he was with the plot of the
novel, even saying at one point that the idea of Lady Eustace stealing her own diamonds
'only struck me when I was writing the page in which the theft is described' ('A Walk
in a Wood', p. 595).

15 The darkness of the novel is stressed and explained by A. O. J. Cockshut, *Anthony
Trollope*, pp. 180–96.

remind her that the brooch she has sent to Lucinda is clearly not a match for the £10 she herself spent (so she says) on the friend: 'of course you can deduct the brooch if you please' (65). Lord George, a simple brute who can pass as 'interesting' in this society, is equally vulgar, equally proud of having no illusions: 'When you come to this kind of work, promises don't go for much. I don't know that they ever do. What is a broken promise?' (63). When these two slither away, Mr. Emilius comes gliding in, and he makes the other two look like innocents. In such a world, one either adapts, goes grimly mad like Lucinda, or else, like Lizzie Eustace, is protected by a certain vague innocence. Lizzie wades through this swamp without much caution or sense, but she avoids getting in over her head—usually.

It really does little good to turn away from Mrs. Carbuncle, who is, as Melmotte was not, a kind of essence of society. Everywhere we look we see the same fluidity, the same impotence of the old values, the same crass thought and language triumphant. Characteristic Trollopean figures appear in this novel, but they are now very much altered. The crusty old Tory and his colourful ranting against the degeneracy of the age, for instance, is now reduced to this: 'Girls make monsters of themselves, and I'm told the men like it;—going about with unclean, frowzy structures on their head, enough to make a dog sick' (34). Mr. Harding's nearest descendant is gentle Lord Fawn: 'He was weak, and foolish, and, in many respects, ignorant,—but he was a gentleman' (59). But, even as a gentleman, he is nearly an idiot, cast adrift in this environment. Later in the series (in *Phineas Redux*) he really is driven mad by a world he cannot understand. His mother is equally lost. Talking to her married daughter, she mentions the importance of love. 'Laws, mamma, how antediluvian you are!' says Mrs. Hittaway, who goes on to explain the new order of things. Lady Fawn is terribly shocked but finds that 'she could not disbelieve it all, and throw herself back upon her faith in virtue, constancy, and honesty' (60). Such qualities will no longer support even the righteous; they are nowhere to be found. Certainly not in the hero, Frank Greystock. We might expect some patchiness in any of Trollope's deliberately unheroic heroes, but Greystock is far more than weak, and he does more than touch pitch lightly; he wallows in it. His marriage to the heroine at the end does little to alter the novel's sombre tone. The heroine is almost forgotten, in fact, and Frank, who simply 'intended to get on in the world, and believed that happiness was to be achieved by success' (4), makes the mistake of coming into contact with the world. No sort of balance is possible, clearly, between the public and private self.

The most useful characteristics for survival are, first, strength, and, second, acting ability. Almost all the people in the novel are actors. Mr. Emilius is widely regarded as the best since Mrs. Siddons (36), but the others are not far behind. Those who cannot act are lost. Miss Macnulty is 'strangely deficient' in this talent, unable to leave the narrow limits of truth either in action or speech. As a consequence, Lizzie says, 'she was unfit even for the poor condition of life which she pretended to fill' (79). Lucinda Roanoke similarly is unable 'to smile and be pleasant to people whom she could not like' (39), and is destroyed for this lack of talent.

All the people who can act, however, act constantly, until they build a deliberately illusory world and imagine that they are indeed in yet another sort of fiction. Like the diamonds themselves, their art is an attempt to create value out of nothingness. Art is used as it is in *Our Mutual Friend*: rouge on a death's head. In *The Last Chronicle* art is generally seen also as a disguise, but it covers the benignity of nature. Here, as Lucinda Roanoke says of the play they all attend,[16] 'I daresay the play may be very bad ... but it can hardly be so bad as real life' (52). Art is often established in such desperation. Lizzie reconstructs a letter for Lord Fawn, knowing he probably will not believe the revised date, but then 'she hardly ever expected to be really believed by anybody' (73). Nobody suspends disbelief and the dupers hardly expect to dupe, but it still seems better to keep the bad play going than to admit the reality it tries to camouflage.

Lizzie is, of course, the most accomplished of these unconvincing stage-players. She can even produce effects that are momentarily dazzling to the uninitiated, wringing pity from police officers and magistrates: she gestures so brilliantly at the trial, throwing her clasped hands toward the bench, that 'from that moment the magistrate was altogether on her side,—and so were the public' (74). In acting, the narrator stresses, she was simply 'perfect' (61); not so good in real life, in fact not good at all, giving off a scent of unreality, but then, actual parts are so seldom rewarding. They are also

---

[16] The play is identified as 'The Noble Jilt'; this is Trollope's wry joke on his own deformed, shut-in child.

seldom called for in this novel, and Lizzie has perhaps done well to devote her energies to acquiring thespian abilities. Some think her the wittiest woman in England, and it has taken great effort and even intelligence to achieve that sort of image. The narrator states several times that her intelligence was in its way very strong. She appears so stupid, then, only because the demands of her role are so all-consuming as to leave her no time for reality. She has a few poignant moments where she senses the truth—'I would fain marry some one. To be as I have been for the last two years is not a happy condition' (62)—and one brief day hunting when she dips into reality and finds great pleasure. Generally, however, she sticks to her acting. 'The guiding motive of her conduct', we are told, 'was the desire to make things seem to be other than they were' (19). Rather like Emma Woodhouse, she has the artist's desire to 'make things seem to be other'. Art here is debased from that practised in Highbury, of course, and Emma's venial attempts to improve Harriet Smith by painting her a little taller than she is are, in Lizzie's case, intensified to inelegant lies. Still, the impulse is the same. Sensing the great defects of the real world, Lizzie tries to improve it, make it more alive and more exciting.

For her great energy—'I suppose though that nothing would ever really tire Lady Eustace' (76)—and for her creative zeal she deserves and is granted our respect, the same sort of respect we grant to other morally deficient but artistically active characters: Emma, Mr. Pecksniff, or, more exactly in this case, Becky Sharp.[17] There are moments when Lizzie sounds very much like Becky, when she abuses the virtuous heroine, for instance—'that little wizened thing who gave you the ring—that prim morsel of feminine propriety' (31) —or when she acts her domestic role in front of Lady Fawn: 'Of all things that which I most desire now . . . is to know you and the dear girls,—and to be loved by you all' (9). The echoes of Becky's seduction of Jos—'How I should like to see India!'—cling round the early scenes with Lord Fawn, and we can hear Becky too in Lizzie's fierce expression of her real opinion of the Fawn's family circle: 'nasty, stupid, dull, puritanical drones' (9). She claims that 'it is not my plan to be tame' (15) and decides to continue to battle

[17] Parallels to Becky were emphasized by Trollope: 'the idea constantly presented itself to me that Lizzie Eustace was but a second Becky Sharpe' (*Autobiography*, p. 344). For various comparisons and judgements on this point see the Beerbohm letter quoted by McElderry in *TLS*; Booth, *Anthony Trollope*, p. 91; Polhemus, *The Changing World*, pp. 172–3; and Pope Hennessy, *Anthony Trollope*, p. 300.

for Lord Fawn just because the odiously respectable Fawn ladies oppose her. In thus making war on convention and shallow respectability, Lizzie is sustained by the strong rebellious energy that had fed Becky Sharp. The differences between them, in fact, are most apparent not in the characters but in the worlds they inhabit. Becky Sharp can always, even at the end, count on this rebellious appeal; she always has some satiric opportunity. But Lizzie has none, for the conventional virtue of the Fawns is really not a dominant force and there is finally nothing to satirize. Incoherence is not susceptible to correction. Society in *Vanity Fair* at least maintained the pretence of consistent standards, a pretence that could be attacked, but even that consistency is lost in the general cynicism of this novel. There is no clear enemy for satire, and Lizzie's rebellious instincts are frittered away in the pointless effort to save the diamonds.

Her inner life is made as empty as are her attempts at satiric rebellion in public. Lizzie's progress represents a grotesque trivialization of the search for unity and balance conducted throughout the whole series. Faced with an utterly materialistic world, she conceives 'a grand idea of surrendering herself and all her possessions to a great passion' (5). She is 'alive to the romance of the thing' (5), to the romance of any tawdry scheme she can substitute for the drab and dull viciousness about her. Such substitutes are so disconnected from reality as to be nearly absurd, a form of desperate self-deception. She in truth dislikes music but says *and thinks* that she dotes on it; she even imagines that she has read all of *Queen Mab*. This paltry, thin romance is the best thing she can construct out of the materials at hand. It is a ludicrous compensation, but no one else can do much better. Faced with monotonous and lonely scenery, as Lizzie is, one might as well speak of it as a 'rock-bound shore' (21). Even if the rocks are slimy and uncomfortable, we must grant some admiration, considering the circumstances, to her attempt to strike poetic attitudes there and muse on Shelley's lines: 'Instinct with inexpressible beauty and grace, Each stain of earthliness Had passed away, it reassumed Its native dignity, and stood Immortal amid ruin' (21). The narrator sarcastically suggests that such lines were written expressly for such poor, starved, uncritical spirits as Lizzie's; 'which was instinct with beauty,—the stain or the soul, she did not stop to inquire, and may be excused for not understanding'. She tries hard to be moved. Still, she cannot but see, in a very funny flash of insight, that poetry and life are, in the end, difficult to reconcile: 'She liked the idea of ruin almost as well as that of the immortality, and the stains quite as well as the purity. As immortality must come, and as stains were instinct with grace, why be afraid of ruin? But then, if people go wrong,—at least women,— they are not asked out any where!' (21). Unity is impossible; 'poetry was what her very soul craved;—poetry, together with houses, champagne, jewels, and admiration' (68). Lizzie holds on grimly to her crazy romance, trying hard for some sort of reconciliation. She switches to Byron, finding him more adaptable than Shelley and also 'more intelligible' (26). What she wants, she decides, is a Corsair—with a coach and an assured income. But the outside world refuses to be brought into contact with any kind of romance, and Lizzie's continued attempts to combine the two are unfailingly amusing: she tries to defend her silence to Camperdown by citing Sir Walter Scott's refusal to tell whether he wrote the novels (72) and exclaims to Lord Fawn that 'nobody ever heard of anything so mean, either in novels or in real life' (73). Such incorporations of the power of literature into life are the best she can do. Lord George de Bruce Carruthers is not only no Corsair; he doesn't even have material value. Lizzie's pathetic attempt at creating this impossible union of self and society, romance and fact, means that she is really competent in neither world and thus vulnerable to such a one as Emilius. She sees that he is a liar, but, like the play, lies are better than truth; they are the closest things to poetry she can find. 'She liked lies, thinking them to be more beautiful than truth' (79), and therefore opens her heart to the 'dash of poetry' (73) she thinks she spots in Emilius.

She stays afloat finally by sheer determination. The narrator is quick to demand our respect for that strength and to keep us throughout surprisingly close to Lizzie. Most of the absolute judgements against her come very early, in the first chapter in fact. After that, her strong presence and the dominant focus on her, as well as some artful narration, draw us toward her. Even when detailing her faults, the narrator does so jokingly, defusing the force of the moral commentary: 'She had never sacrificed her beauty to a lover, —she had never sacrificed anything to anybody,—nor did she drink. It would be difficult, perhaps, to say anything else in her favour; and yet Lord Fawn was quite content to marry her' (9). The real point here is Lord Fawn's comic stupidity, not Lizzie's immorality.

The humorous context thus provides a way of seeming to grant moral objections to Lizzie while simultaneously brushing them aside. There are also many reflective passages of the 'who-does-not-know-the-terrible-feeling . . .' sort (ch. 37, for example) which ask us specifically to share Lizzie's position.

For she is indeed the heroine of the novel, connected firmly not only to us but to the world about her. At one point Lizzie expresses to Frank great admiration for 'The Holy Grail'. While Trollope is making some comment on the romantic distance he attributes to Tennyson's subject, he is also using the poem to support his own theme. The *Idylls* also presents a world hopelessly divided between spirit and flesh, meaning and act. Both are worlds so ruined that almost no one even understands what has been lost. Lizzie, like Guinevere, does not understand; she does not even understand Arthur's clear explanation of the misunderstanding, preferring, as Frank points out, to side with the Queen.

This preference is not hers alone: 'Your useful, practical man, who attends vestries, and sits at Boards, and measures out his gifts to others by the ounce, never has any heart' (19). This is not Glencora talking about Mr. Palliser, but it might be. The novel still is, in its way, about Glencora and her struggles. Mrs. Carbuncle ironically uses Glencora and her husband as proof of the emptiness of the world she lives in: 'After all, what does love signify? How much real love do we ever see among married people? Does Lady Glencora Palliser really love her husband, who thinks of nothing in the world but putting taxes on and off?' (67). Lizzie is Glencora reduced to a fish-and-chips level. Glencora senses their kinship in rebellion and energy, rushing over to give her support and countenance to Lady Eustace. Lizzie, in turn, recognizes a sister, calls her ally her 'beau-ideal of what a woman should be', admiring especially her 'dash of romance' (62). Glencora is quick to strip off the idealization, however, telling Lizzie that her own state is not so very different after all:

'You have never been left desolate. You have a husband and friends.'
'A husband that wants to put five farthings into a penny! All is not gold that glistens, Lady Eustace.' (54)

Glencora even claims to be 'envious' (47) of Lizzie's greater freedom to act. But neither need envy the other's freedom, since they are both caught together.

Both women are used finally to feed the world's desire for amusement. They are so harmless they cannot even shock but are valued only as curiosities. Lizzie's adventures, all agree, 'had been a godsend in the way of amusing the duke' (47). But Providence is not so kind to Glencora and Lizzie as to those they entertain. Mr. Dove points out how common is their frustration and their misdirection of energies. Lizzie uses all her wit and spirit in the fruitless chase after a 'bauble', just as the best men, he says, use all their ingenuity and courage pursuing some hollow position like a vacant Lord Chancellorship (72). Lizzie is a judgement on the world; there is no one to pass judgement on her. In a curious last chapter,[18] a party is assembled at Matching Priory to act as a chorus and give the final argument on her career. The ailing Duke, the unscrupulous Mr. Bott, Glencora and her husband united in a hostile truce: all these suggest an absurd, loveless world as effectively as the monsters Lizzie had gathered together in Scotland. They are equally unable to understand her; all the standards are gone. Plantagenet Palliser wants simply to avoid thinking of her; horrors are more safely confined at Madame Tussaud's. Mr. Bonteen's perfunctory comment on the trial—'It was a most unworthy conclusion to such a plot'—is about all that can be said. There is no resolution possible. Lord Chiltern provides a stop without a conclusion, banging his cue-stick on the floor and shouting that he is 'sick' of the subject. This novel is a self-consuming artifact, even a self-condemning one, with a vengeance.

The unresolved world having been thus set before us, we are sent back to the Phineas novel, as the hero gives it one more try, this time in earnest. Phineas's life in Ireland, necessary as it has been, has also seemed 'vapid and flavourless' (6); 'his very soul had sighed for the lost glories of Westminster and Downing Street' (1). Obscurity is not for him, nor can he realize himself in nature, which seems 'painfully inspid' precisely because it is 'safe' (1). Longing to find again his run of luck and to locate for himself a recognizable place in society, he plunges back into the world. He finds that now he must compete for a seat in the horrible rough and tumble of Tankerville: 'Loughton and Loughshane were gone, with so many other comfortable things of old days' (4). Things are changed

---

[18] Beerbohm said it is an 'epilogue' with the 'formal grace and irony' of Mozart or Watteau (letter quoted by McElderry in *TLS*).

indeed. Political life and social life as well are held together, if at all, by schemes, power plays, most of all by chance. The action starts with the news of the Conservatives sponsoring a bill to disestablish the Church, a piece of absurdity that sets the tone for the entire novel.

Phineas Redux is a story of rejuvenation, but the major emphasis is on loss. One gives up so much in trying for an accommodation which, even when it comes, provides so much less than it had promised. Even worse, one arrives at accommodation not through a coherent or necessary process but through a series of accidental batterings, escapes, traps. Recovery seems finally allowed by the general indifference of things, not by their comic disposition. The story is, then, perhaps less one of attaining balance than of creating a self against great odds. Society is now not a recipient of personality, providing a setting in which the self can grow, be recognized, and receive confirmation. It is an enemy, out to destroy. The private life is never adequately co-ordinated with the public life; they meet only in violent and unnatural junction in the pages of the *People's Banner* or in a monstrous public trial.

By leaving behind the safety of the pastoral, Phineas is taking a far greater risk than he imagines. He is shocked by the absence of coherence he finds, not only in his own trial but in the earlier bribery trial of his Tankerville opponent, Mr. Browborough. At this event, 'the only man treated with severity was poor Phineas Finn', who is perfectly innocent, while the manifestly guilty Browborough is made a hero (44). And the trial is conducted by a government controlled by Phineas's own party. Phineas is outraged, but when he turns to Mr. Gresham or even Mr. Monk for sympathy, he finds only tired justification. Lady Laura alone offers him sympathy, and her motives, he realizes, are hardly disinterested (44). The novel is dominated by Phineas's sense of injustice and his baffled fury at finding others so insensitive on the point. Where are his friends? Where is the previous coherence that had recognized his virtue and rewarded him with all that good luck?

He does at first seem to float right back into his old luck. He loses the election but is seated after a scrutiny. 'I never knew a fellow with such luck as yours', says Barrington Erle (13). Phineas appears also to be facing a dilemma on disestablishment as crushing as that on the Irish Land Tenant Bill, but the difficulties melt away when he sees that he can support the measure and still vote against the man. Even being missed by the bullet from Kennedy's gun seems to

Lady Glencora to be yet another instance of the marvellous 'special protection' (25) Phineas is granted. But all this luck is so deceptive as to act finally as a trap. There are no protections now, and he must learn finally to rise above all chance.

The model for such heroic adjustment is Madame Max. In a novel which seems to complicate everything, even her previous adjustments are dissolved, but she stands finally as an indication to Phineas of the only way to live in the world. Her own education is accomplished in much more subtle ways, but she must face revelations as shattering as those that come on Phineas without having any of his compensation in the form of a visible grievance. Like Phineas, she is drawn to the top of the world, in her case not the political but the social world. The old Duke of Omnium takes her to his heart, and though she refuses to marry him, ironically having more social vision than the infatuated Duke, she yields to his great need for her to the extent of becoming his constant companion and nurse. These functions, she says, give her real fulfilment: 'It has done me good to think that I have in some small degree sacrificed myself' (17). But things are not this simple; Madame Goesler is not made for obedient and blind service. She cannot help seeing that the Duke's reputation for great and gracious *appearance* has been all too richly deserved, that he has capitalized on the split between public and private roles to parody genuine nobility. 'He had looked like a duke, and known how to set a high price on his own presence', the narrator says, and he had also done less and consumed more than any other man of his time (24). The Duke's death is very touchingly presented. Even old Lady Hartletop, duck-like waddle and all, demonstrates what looks like real affection, and the Duke himself rises to something like self-awareness.

But the soft emotion is harshly extinguished by Madame Max's ruthlessly unsentimental examination of her own feelings: 'She had persuaded herself that there had existed a warm friendship between them;—but of what nature could have been a friendship with one whom she had not known till he had been in his dotage? What words of the Duke's speaking had she ever heard with pleasure, except certain terms of affection which had been half mawkish and half senile?' (30). She sees that she has been victimized by a ludicrous romance with 'a sick and selfish old man'. She regards the whole affair as half a bribe from the Duchess and is forced to endure the raptures of vicious old Mr. Maule, a darker version of Deportment

Turveydrop: 'A great fortune had been entrusted to him [the Duke],
and he knew that it was his duty to spend it. He did spend it, and
all the world looked up to him. It must have been a great pleasure to
you to know him so well' (30). Her 'sacrifice' thus desentimentalized,
the Lily Dale trap of masochism avoided, Madame Goesler can
establish a life that is truly mature. Her disillusionment is as harsh
and bitter as Phineas's, in fact they are parallel, and the two move
together to a love that lies outside appearances. Or rather, she
moves there and pulls him after her. Experiencing before him the
emptiness at the top, she is willing to penetrate into the filth for
him. By journeying to Prague, bribing and spying for him, she
rescues them both. She had earlier told Phineas when they had
together encountered an annoyance in hunting, 'I've known you
before this to be depressed by circumstances quite as distressing
as these, and to be certain that all hope was over;—but yet you have
recovered' (16). She now repeats this encouragement in harsher and
much less hopeful terms: 'There is nothing, Mr. Finn, that a man
should fear so much as some twist in his convictions arising from
a personal accident to himself' (77). One must find a way to live
beyond all accident, beyond all luck, good and bad. It is a solution
that accepts only a limited reconciliation with the world, agreeing
to live in it but not be of it. It is really a withdrawal from the central
conflict, a personal triumph for Madame Goesler and Phineas Finn,
but not a solution to the problem dominating the chronicle. They
rather suggest that there is no solution.

But Phineas is glad enough even of this. He is thrown into a
world that has with little overstatement been compared with that
envisioned by Kafka.[19] Suddenly his luck inexplicably changes.
Even support he had received from Lady Laura, once a comfort, is
now a curse, the most 'unfortunate' (37) thing in a career which now
begins to look as unlucky as it had once seemed blessed. He is
dogged by the mad Kennedy everywhere, and not just by Kennedy.
Like the man in the science-fiction thriller who alone sees the
monsters, he keeps screaming 'Look!' without any effect. When he
complains about the almost incredible coldness and hostility of his
party toward him, his friends offer the blandest explanations. It all
comes, they say, from his independent stand on the Irish question.
He must simply wait. Take it more quietly, they all say; don't show

---

[19] The parallel is drawn by Polhemus, *The Changing World*, p. 179. His treatment of
the novel (pp. 178–85) makes effective distinctions between it and *Phineas Finn*.

your teeth (37). But the party has adopted within a year his exact position on the Irish issue, and the punishment in any case so far exceeds the crime of independence as to fill him with astonished rage. The unruffled acceptance he sees about him makes him feel freakish, seeing different things than other men see and reacting to them as an alien. He feels cut off from all support and, worse than that, unable to arouse anyone's sympathy for his plight.

The women, it is true, do spring to his aid, and a wonderful comic alliance seems to be forming: Lady Glencora, Marie, Lady Cantrip, the Duchess of St. Bungay. Such hilarious diversity and such wonderful schemes—bribe a judge, 'a carriage and pair of horses to every one of the jurors' wives' (54)—surely cannot fail. Imagining failure to such plans is like imagining an end to the Mad Tea-Party. But Phineas imagines just that, and so does the novel. The comic alliance succeeds in keeping Mr. Bonteen out but does nothing for Phineas. In fact, it is damaging to him, poisoning Bonteen further against the hero and making his chances for promotion much more remote than they were. Trollope uses comic expectations so skilfully here that, right to the end, one can hardly believe that Lady Glencora and her mates will not pronounce the trial nothing but a pack of cards, make some jokes, and invite everyone to Gatherum for two or three months.

The worst part of the trial for Phineas is really that this hopeful, communal perspective fails. Friends on the opposite side of the House murmur sympathetically that 'if Phineas Finn were not the murderer, he had been more ill-used by Fate than had been any man since Fate first began to be unjust' (52). Hardly any one other than Mrs. Bonteen is certain of his guilt; most are like these political opponents, cordially doubting but admitting that 'the evidence is strong . . .' He is simply abandoned. No one quite believes in evidence, since the world is clearly not rational, but no one disbelieves in it either, since reason is as good a false guide as any other to an irrational condition. Phineas is not 'ill-used by Fate', as his kind friends would have it; he is ill-used by his kind friends, or rather by the fact that there is no 'Fate', no principle of coherence. Perceiving this, as he is forced to, with agonizing directness, Phineas cannot understand how a man so apparently good as the Duke of St. Bungay can live in an absurd world calmly, accommodating himself smoothly to its chaos. St. Bungay 'had learned at last that all loyalty must be built on a basis of self-advantage' (5):

Phineas cannot understand why such insight has not been shattering. When Chaffanbrass makes clear to him that the trial has
nothing to do with his innocence or guilt but with 'the truth of
the evidence' (60) and that the accused can never shed much light
on that, Phineas wants to scream. During the actual courtroom
scenes Phineas almost disappears. He is seldom mentioned and we
are told very little of what he feels. His absence is appropriate, of
course, since he is, in terms of the trial, the least important man
there. It is a trial of a coat, a key, and of words. It has as much
reference to justice as Lear's trial of the footstool or, more precisely,
the trial of the knave of hearts.

'Sentence first—verdict afterwards' applies here exactly. Phineas
has already experienced the punishment in his alienation and is
understandably not elated when the jury acquits him with a generous
flourish: '"And we are of the opinion," said the foreman, "that Mr.
Finn should not have been put upon his trial on such evidence as
has been brought before us"' (67). Phineas knows by now that such
comments on the sufficiency of 'evidence' have nothing to do with
him. Nor can the friends who flock to congratulate him help him
much. Mr. Monk's grim explanation of the distinction between the
'confidence' which he felt in his friend and the 'conviction' he
could not hold (68), far from urging Phineas back into the social
world, makes him experience all over again his terrible aloneness.
As a result he is bitter and seeks comfort in the cynicism of the
long view: 'What does it matter who sits in Parliament? The fight
goes on just the same. The same falsehoods are acted. The same
mock truths are spoken. The same wrong reasons are given' (68).

He is still alive, though, and must survive physically, so he 'comes
round', as his election agent says he will (71). He even shakes hands
with the prosecutor and can think well of him for his manliness (74).
But he is saved not so much by comedy as by his insignificance:
'Moons waxed and waned; children were born; marriages were
contracted; and the hopes and fears of the little world around
did not come to an end because Phineas Finn was not to be hung'
(69). He is not so much rejuvenated as crudely resuscitated. He
refuses to re-enter office, holding out for a time against the crass
brutality of these men and their appallingly insensitive generosity.
More important, he is holding out against luck itself, refusing any
longer to be dominated by circumstances. The trial might just as
well have ended one way as another, and he has learned from it. He

sees that the office 'was offered to me, not because I was thought to be fit for it, but because I had become wonderful by being brought near to a violent death!' (74). An acceptance of office would be an acceptance of impersonal luck again. He compares the party's offer to a rocking-horse given to him when a child for falling 'from the top of the house to the bottom without breaking my neck. The rocking-horse was very well then, but I don't care now to have one bestowed upon me for any such reason' (74). Such toys are those 'which look to be so very desirable in the shop-windows, but which give no satisfaction when they are brought home' (79). Phineas moves out of childhood and out of luck to the only life which can give satisfaction. He makes his stand against absurdity. Madame Max was, after all, the only one who really understood. Even his other lady friends wanted only to load the 'evidence'; Marie wanted to clear his name. Only Madame Max has not only understood but lived through Phineas's desolation. After that, agreeing to marry him is, as she says, a trifle: 'I couldn't refuse Mr. Finn a little thing like that' (79).

The strength of this union and the difficulty with which it is achieved are highlighted by Trollope's characteristically brilliant use of subplots. The Kennedy plot is still, as in *Phineas Finn*, cautionary, at least at first, but as the novel moves to a personal solution for Phineas, it develops a distinct impatience for Lady Laura's immersion in her grievances and isolation. Her condition is seen as less extreme, more common, and her continued bitterness thus seems a little like self-indulgence. She never really gets beyond herself, even when visiting Phineas in prison: 'Of all my troubles this,—to see you here,—is the heaviest' (55). Violet Chiltern finally expresses this impatience openly, telling Laura to exercise a little more self-control (51). The Kennedys no longer suggest what *might* occur but what very likely *will*, and Lady Laura's refusal even to try to live with indifference is certainly not admired.

On the other side there is a wonderfully idyllic love story, so undisturbed and essentially static that it seems to take place in another land. Gerard Maule and Adelaide Palliser slide together in a life that seems protected by a benign nature. It really is another world they inhabit, or at least it appears to be, since they ask for so little. Maule says that, unlike Finn, he is not ambitious: 'I've sense enough to know I can't do any good' (7). Much like the romance of Jane and Bingley in *Pride and Prejudice*, the subplot ironically avoids all the problems of the main plot by its very unawareness that such problems exist. Complexity seems to occur only to the complex. Ironic parallels are drawn throughout the novel between Phineas's tortured world and the gentle world of Harrington Hall. Ridiculous Tom Spooner of Spooner Hall, for instance, feels himself to be strongly affected by chance and circumstance: 'It makes one feel that he's marked out, you know' (53). But in this plot, characters are marked out only for easy happiness. Lady Glencora may tell Gerard that 'romance and poetry are for the most part lies' (76), but he, in his innocence, knows better.

The effect is tantalizing, slightly infuriating, not only to the reader, who senses the distance between this idyllic subplot and the major action, but to Lady Glencora herself, who has been pretty fully initiated, or so we would suppose. In the background of the novel but never out of mind are Plantagenet Palliser, now Duke of Omnium, and Glencora. She accuses her husband of living in an unreal, fixed world (31) and vows that she will herself change, 'lay down her mischief, and abandon her eccentricity' (26). Even if her husband does not understand the world, she does—she thinks. But the narrator knows better, ending the novel with the assurance that 'nothing will ever change the Duchess'. He thus prepares the way for the climactic episode of the series: the education of the Duke and Duchess in *The Prime Minister*.

His initiation is more open-ended, hers more decisive; but they are both asked to face the same frustration and the same emptiness. These two people, distinguished and important to begin with, gain even larger importance. They are the highest nobility; he becomes the leader of the world's greatest government, she the most prominent and powerful social figure. They advance to the very core of the world. And, like Phineas Finn, who made the same discovery from a much greater distance, they find nothing there. They become so great that they are forced to see their own insignificance. The novel formally projects a sense of flurried movement without substance, an empty centre. This is, after all, a novel about a prime minister, and it comes as something of a shock that the only issues that matter have to do with cork soles and bed linens.

Trollope's most important novel is also his least appreciated. A few modern critics write well about it,[20] and Tolstoy, reading it

---

[20] The best readings are by Polhemus, *The Changing World*, pp. 197–214, and apRoberts, *The Moral Trollope*, pp. 134–47.

while writing *Anna Karenina*, called it a 'beautiful book'.[21] But for
many it is still only 'a pretty dull book'.[22] Trollope's contemporaries
certainly did not understand it, the *Saturday Review* going so far
as to say it marked the novelist's 'decadence'.[23] Trollope himself
seems to have been puzzled by the lack of appreciation for one of
his finest novels. He insisted that the book was far better than the two
more popular novels which followed, *Is He Popenjoy?* and *The
American Senator* (*Autobiography*, p. 362). But he was pushed hard
enough by the poor response to admit that the Lopez plot was
'bad'.[24] The Lopez plot is anything but bad; Trollope seems clearly
to be granting too much, as he often did, to the public taste he had
no wish to transcend.

Most commentary on the novel is content to attack the view of
politics it contains or to point out and exaggerate structural weak-
nesses. The novel's politics are frequently misread as Trollope's
optimum definition of the function of the literal House of Commons. The failure of this view to distinguish art from life is obvious,
but even more serious is the notion that Trollope or the novel somehow approved of the nullity discernible at the political hub. It is
erroneously supposed that Trollope is advocating a do-nothing
policy as a practical guide for all politicians.[25]

The point about the kinship of the plots, however, is much more
real.[26] The Lopez–Wharton plot runs along with the political plot,
but the narrative ties are not very strong; they seem, in fact, to be
almost accidental. The Duchess's interference in the Silverbridge
election is a crucial episode, but there is no very apparent reason
why Lopez is necessarily involved there. The relations between the
plots are mostly formal and thematic, which may mean that 'unity'
becomes some myth which can be fabricated by any critic willing
to see resemblances and ignore obtrusive differences. Without entirely acquitting Trollope of the charge, however, one can still see
not only the resemblances between the plots but their mutual interplay. Both, in the largest sense, are concerned with injury and

[21] Quoted in Pope Hennessy, *Anthony Trollope*, p. 331.
[22] Pope Hennessy, *Anthony Trollope*, p. 329.
[23] Rev. of *The Prime Minister*, p. 481.
[24] Letter to Mary Holmes, 7 May 1876, *Letters*, p. 353; also see letter of 15 June 1876,
p. 355.
[25] An example of this misreading (and of others) can be found in the Introduction to
the Oxford University Press edition of the novel, now unfortunately reprinted.
[26] For a defence of the structural unity of the novel see Fredman, *Anthony Trollope*,
pp. 23–6.

recuperation. Though one is a love story and the other a political story, the love story is also about politics and the political story about love. In any case, love and politics are, as I have argued before, inseparable throughout the chronicle, presenting to characters exactly the same dilemma. In each plot here there is a stable and conservative figure—Mr. Wharton in one plot, the Duke in the other—trying to understand and control the world with values and assumptions that are old-fashioned, perhaps outdated and invalid. Both plots also have rebels, Mr. Lopez (and Emily to a lesser extent) and Glencora, who push hard against these old standards. And in both plots the established figures and the rebels end up equally lost. If there is a spokesman for the general world of the novel, it is, ironically, Quintus Slide, the voice of the people: 'He went out and wrote another article about the Duchess. If a man was so unable to rule his affairs at home, he was certainly unfit to be Prime Minister' (57). With his customary lucid vulgarity, Slide makes the principle of unity in this novel clear. The question is one of governing, whether it be a nation, a party, a wife, or a daughter. That is the question, but there seem to be no satisfactory answers. As in *Phineas Redux* one is educated here in the fundamentals of incoherence. The dominant image is that of the coalition, a collection of men bound together by common loyalty to do a common task. But there are no bonds, and, even worse, there are no tasks. These, we are told, are the conditions of modern existence, and we must somehow or other accept them. One man, reputed 'to know the club-world very thoroughly', raises the unanswerable rhetorical query with justifiable self-righteousness: 'If you turn out all the blackguards and all the dishonourable men, where will the club be?' (60)—or Parliament, one might say, or a family, or a marriage.

'But who *is* Lopez?' The question reverberates through the action of this plot. Is he or is he not English? wealthy? of good family? a gentleman? No one really knows the answer to the first three questions, but the novel begins by assuring us that, however shadowy his antecedents and his commercial position, 'it was admitted on all sides that Ferdinand Lopez was a "gentleman"' (1). So much for public opinion. We know immediately that the public is wrong; the narrator goes on to say how studiously Lopez works to appear natural. His art is the very opposite of the unconscious naturalness of Trollope's true gentlemen. 'He had not the faintest notion of the feelings of a gentleman' (58), the narrator finally tells us bluntly, in case we had gone on accepting the belief echoed 'on all sides'. Lopez is the new man, rootless and insubstantial, whose mock fortune is produced by goods he never really buys with money he never really has. He has a great belief in advertising (54), for Trollope as for Carlyle the epitome of modern vacuity. Like Slope or Melmotte, Lopez tests the society to see if it can distinguish counterfeit from real. But he is more complex than his predecessors, testing not only the society but also the code he mocks but does sincerely want to adopt. He is struggling to find a way out of his emptiness, to discover a substance, and he thinks he can locate it in the code of the gentleman. All tests are failed—by society, Lopez, and the code.

He loses, ironically, because in his way he sees too clearly and acts on what he sees: 'Men, and women too, have become so dishonest that nobody is safe anywhere' (35). Unlike Slope, he is not trying to impress anything new on the society; he merely wants to discover society's values, adopt them, and receive just rewards for his intelligence and adaptability. He is thus really a kind of innocent, one who 'did not know that he was a villain' (54). Countless narrative explanations of Lopez's motives begin, 'He did not know . . . he did not understand.' When he approaches Lizzie Eustace with the mad idea that she is truly romantic and will fly with him to sunny Guatemala, we see how slight his chances have been, how little he has comprehended the grimness of the world: 'Mr. Lopez', says Lizzie, 'I think you must be a fool' (54). Not that Lizzie is the villain, of course. The only villain is the emptiness. When Lopez becomes literally nothing—'the fragments of his body set identity at defiance' (61)—we see his last attempt to adapt, to become that which he sees about him.

So the senex, old Mr. Wharton, has been right all along. His protective, ugly bigotry, his narrow, pinched-in, joyless life is thrust at us, forced on us as exemplary. He is made to stand against youth and the values of the heart, the basic rhythms of comedy, and it is upsetting to find that we are to applaud rather than hiss. When he announces to Emily, 'You ought to feel that, as I have had a long experience in the world, my judgement about a young man might be trusted' (5), we hear the echoes of the voices of a thousand stage fathers, those enemies of fertility, trying to shelter the young. Mr. Wharton hears them too: 'there was growing on him a feeling that ultimately youth would as usual triumph over age' (9). He is told

that he is now outdated, that he is playing a stupid, feudal role: 'The
stern parent who dooms his daughter to perpetual seclusion because
she won't marry the man he likes, doesn't belong to this age' (13).
We see what comes of this new age of youth and freedom. Wharton
is out of date only because he is substantial, a man who acts and
accomplishes, a gentleman. Gentlemen are as hard to find here, in
public or in private life, as dodos.

Because his values have no currency, Wharton has no power to
save his daughter from blindly liberating herself, diving into
nothingness as if it were comic release. Emily finds out almost at
once from her husband the conditions of her freedom: 'You are
a child, my dear, and must allow me to dictate to you what you
ought to think in such a matter as this' (30). Lopez is a simple
tyrant, desiring not just obedience but grovelling submission. She
soon sees all this, recognizes that Lopez is no gentleman, that the
man picked out for her by her father, one Arthur Fletcher, indeed
was: 'Ah,—that she should ever have been so blind, she who had
given herself credit for seeing so much clearer than they who were
her elders!' (39). She learns that in such a world the old are right if
anyone is. One must not trust any appearance, any pleasant impulse.
But it is not at all clear to her what she can do with this knowledge.
She instinctively rebels, arguing that 'surely she could only think
in accordance with her own experience and her own intelligence!'
(30). Even that rebellion fails, however, to protect her from the consequences of her original rashness. Mrs. Sexty Parker, whose husband is being systematically ruined by Lopez, insists that Emily
answer for her husband: 'I look to you to tell me what me and my
children is to do. He's your husband, Mrs. Lopez' (55). Her husband's pathetic death acts ironically to free him but to make her
feel even more responsible to account for things. Since accounting
is really impossible, she can only glide toward that strong desire for
punishment so common in Trollope's rebellious heroines. She is
rescued from this trap, very roughly indeed, by her brother's harsh
attacks on her for spoiling other people's fun with her drivelling
gloom (72) and finally by Arthur Fletcher's command, delivered
'with much sternness', that she marry him forthwith (79).

She is thus wrenched back into some sort of reconciliation, but
the education has been violent and unaccommodated. Her experience with Lopez must be forgotten, not assimilated, and she
must abandon her search for freedom and settle for protection.

Trollope's positive ending here, therefore, has implications as dark as those attending the release of Phineas Finn. That darkness is particularly emphasized by the Parkers, unusual figures in Trollope in that they are absolute and final victims. Sexty, once rich, will never again be prosperous, and his courageous wife is reduced to anticipating 'the one excitement of her life', her journey to collect the weekly 40s. allowed to her by Mr. Wharton, whom she finally regards as 'a man appointed by Providence' (69). In such a world he is as good a symbol of providence as one can find. Heaven is now in a sadly reduced state, unable to reward, even to protect, able only to manage some first aid.

The victims in the main plot are greater in two senses: they are more important; their sufferings are deeper, less relieved. Natural desires seem to be so unnaturally blocked that at one point Glencora blurts out to her husband that he should have been the woman, she the man. With the quiet tenderness so typical of him now, the Duke does not deny that she is right but simply tries to comfort her (42). There is little real comfort for either of them, in private or in public life. The Duke is driven to expose his fragile, newly developed self in public, driven not only by friends but by what he conceives to be the voice of the people, the newspapers: 'When the newspapers told him that he was the only man for the occasion, how could he be justified in crediting himself in preference to them?' (8). Like Phineas and like Emily he will have to learn just how unreliable this public voice is. The only refuge is in crediting oneself. As Prime Minister, the Duke is, ironically, as much an invention of Mr. Slide as is the new pseudo-gentleman, Ferdinand Lopez. The Duke has spent all his life in politics, but he has steadily kept to those areas where genuine activity can at least be feigned, even if it is only the activity of squeezing five farthings into a penny. Now, however, he is lured into what appears to be real power, another raw innocent like Phineas or Lopez. The coalition he heads seems ideal for him; it rids itself of all absolutists, the Irish Home Rulers, the Philosophical Radicals, and so forth, and pulls together right-thinking gentlemen who have no special causes. But, though escaping destruction from the true believers, the coalition cannot avoid the non-believers. Faction comes not from ideological clash but from blind change, simple fluidity.

The Duke comes face to face with the emptiness encountered by others in this novel and in this series and, like them, finds himself alone and unprotected. It is true that some of his problems are caused by his undeveloped private self, his being 'neither gregarious nor communicative' (27). He cannot effect a coalition of public duty and private sociability. But if he fails, the office itself fails more resoundingly. He is forced to come to grips with a reality of politics he had heard in slogans and even repeated: those governments are best which have no particular thing to do. Madame Max, being agreeable to Erle, says, 'there never really is anything special to be done;—is there, Mr. Erle?' He is delighted at her grasp of the essential point, exclaiming breathlessly, 'You understand it all better than anyone else that I ever knew' (11). Glencora says it is clear to her that a Prime Minister should confine himself to 'generalities about commerce, agriculture, peace, and general philanthropy' (56). Even the Duke himself, when confronted with Sir Orlando's notion of a thing to do, is forced to say, 'Things to be done offer themselves, I suppose, because they are in themselves desirable; not because it is desirable to have something to do' (20). But what *things*? When? It is clearly necessary, especially to the Duke, 'to have something to do', but it is never clear how anything so indefinite as a 'thing' is ever done. Only Sir Orlando, with his four new warships, comes forth with a concrete thing to do, but his plan is too clearly cynical, a 'thing' for its own sake, and thus makes the Duke even more unhappy. No wonder that he turns to Lady Rosina and her cork soles. Cork soles are at least cork soles, and 'when she talked about cork soles she meant cork soles' (27).

Cork soles are about the only solidity occupying his life: 'in truth the hours went heavily with him as he sat alone in his study' (37). He has nothing to do and cannot discover just where he is or what he is doing there. He turns for support to his friends, as does Phineas, and finds there the same bland and aggravating insensitivity. The Duke of St. Bungay is ever ready to justify the void that seems so terrible to the Prime Minister. St. Bungay is even willing to apologize for Quintus Slide, whom he sees as a joke, not as a 'sign of the times' at all. He tries to console the Duke by telling him that a Prime Minister should think of himself not as a leader but as a silent monitor whose main job is to be certain that no one else ruffles the calm by trying to do something. The best man for such a job, he says, is 'cautious but never timid, bold but never venturesome; he should have a good digestion, genial manners, and, above all, a thick skin' (41). These sound like qualifications for a genteel museum guard, and St. Bungay doles out comforts as barbed as those given to Job. He suggests over and over that the Prime Minister smilingly accommodate himself to the emptiness. No one dares tell him, as they do Phineas, not to show his teeth, but the advice is the same. The Duke refuses to be guided by such counsel, but he can find little alternative except to fret, which he does constantly. His one attempt to give substance to his position and to himself comes when he grants the garter to Lord Earlybird, who actually deserves it. This bold departure from precedent is, however, almost as pathetic as Sir Orlando's warships; others look on it as merely eccentric. St. Bungay even argues that such attention to the merits of the case might, if continued, pose a serious threat to the whole British theory of government.

Constitutionally a man who must act, the Duke is frustrated because he is not only denied the opportunity to act but is shown that all action is meaningless. Still, even though he senses the futility of power, he refuses to give it up until he is forced to do so, not, appropriately, by a decisive defeat but by an inadequate, teasing majority. Nothing about his tenure has been decisive or even clear. But after his resignation he seems almost to vanish: 'There could be nothing for him now', he thinks, 'till the insipidity of life should gradually fade away into the grave' (72). Even the memory of having been Prime Minister is 'nothing to him' (73). Still, though deeply wounded, he evades full knowledge and is able, in the novel's last words, 'to look forward to a time when I may again perhaps be of some humble use' (80). He retains some illusions; he can always go back to jamming five farthings into a penny.

But Glencora comes out of her education with no such occupation awaiting her and with no illusions. Her last words in the novel are the last words we hear from her ever: 'I did like it in a way, and it makes me sad to think that the feeling can never come again . . . It is done and gone, and can never come back again' (80). She has seen more than her husband and cannot avoid the consequences of that knowledge. It simply crushes her. Her initial enthusiastic hope had been exactly that of her husband: to confirm her identity through positive and real action. She promises full support to him 'if you are going to do anything,—to really do anything' (6). But her fight really runs parallel to his without quite joining it. They undergo similar but separate educations. 'She was essentially one of those women who are not contented to be known simply as the

wives of their husbands' (6), and is therefore out to establish her
own identity, not his. She sees politics every bit as cynically as
Erle as regards 'policy' and 'issues', but she is not cynical about
power. She images that she can even correct her husband's 'simple
patriotism': 'The patriotism may remain, my dear, but not the
simplicity' (6). But her sophistication is all make-believe. She strives
eagerly, almost pathetically, for solidity, for definite position, asking
even to be Mistress of the Robes. 'She, too, wished to be written
of in memoirs, and to make a niche for herself in history' (28), but
she finds that there is now no firm substance into which to carve
niches. Phineas tells her sadly that 'the time has gone by for what
one may call drawing-room influences', and she is forced to reply
with an assertion she knows full well to be false: 'The spirit of the
world never changes' (28). This presumably sophisticated person
is shown to be an innocent, imagining a compassion and coherence
in the world that are nowhere present. As quixotic as her husband,
like him and like Mr. Wharton she tries to assert the values and
beliefs of an old stable world. When she recognizes that 'all the
good times are going' (29), she senses too that her hopes will never
be fulfilled. Like the Duke, she cannot even achieve anything as
definite as failure. She never becomes the 'institution of granite'
she had imagined, only, at best, a 'good sort of fellow', supported 'in
a dull, phlegmatic way' by those 'who ate the ices and drank the
champagne' (37).

In her private life the misunderstandings are equally great and
the reconciliations as unfulfilling. She tries over and over to explain
to her husband that she needs an independent life. When he says
that he recognizes her pure self-sacrifice, her one desire 'of seeing
your husband a great man', her honesty forces her to reply, 'And
myself a great man's wife' (18). His answer indicates the gap between them: 'It is the same thing.' But of course it is not at all the
same thing to Glencora. She must resist this sort of absorption, and
in her resistance she causes her husband to fear that she, 'his wife
the Duchess . . . was Prime Minister rather than he himself' (18).
Her efforts at individuality strike him as rivalry; his inevitable failure
in office seems to her a personal affront, and his grand old chivalric
protection appears a guise for dominance (see ch. 51). With the best
will in the world and with by now a love for one another as convincingly portrayed as any in the English novel, they can manage only
a very imperfect union. Ironically, the similarity of their experiences

in nothingness drives them further apart. The Duke comes to understand very well what her sarcastic wit really means, and she comes to express herself more and more sharply. In the climactic quarrel over her interference in the Silverbridge election, she finally says that her rebellion is 'human nature, and you've got to put up with it' (32). The Duke smiles, kisses her, and goes his way, here as elsewhere, 'by no means satisfied' (32).

When her entertainments are cut off, 'it seemed to her that she was to be reduced to nothing' (42). She sees, even worse, that she had struggled for nothing, had never felt any triumph or sense of accomplishment. She had, she thinks, a more solid social place even as Lady Glencora than as 'Duchess of Omnium and the wife of the Prime Minister of England' (76). Nothing has come of nothing, and she cannot recover. 'As far at least as the outward show went', she seems to rebound, but 'one or two who knew her, especially Mrs. Finn' know that she still carries about with her her grievances and her wounds (80). She does so until they kill her.

The final novel of the series, *The Duke's Children*, shows the Duke's attempts to understand her death and to live with its consequences. The chronicle ends with one last initiation story, the mellowest and most complex in the series. The Duke struggles to retrace Glencora's education and still find the strength to resist its terrible consequences. The immediate problem he has is announced in the novel's first sentence: 'No one, probably, ever felt himself to be more alone in the world than our old friend, the Duke of Omnium, when the Duchess died.' Glencora, 'who had been essentially human, had been a link between him and the world' (1). He must, in struggling to be less alone, forge some sort of new link with those about him. It is the old problem of balance, of reconciliation between self and community, ego and service, dealt with throughout the chronicle. Here, however, the problem is both more extreme and more internalized than anywhere else. The Duke must try to regain contact with the world through what he can still recognize of Glencora around him in his wilful and spirited children. But through them he also comes in contact with all his old fears and conflicts. He must, as John Hagan points out in an admirable study,[27] relive the past through his children, trying to make

---

[27] '*The Duke's Children*: Trollope's Psychological Masterpiece', *NCF*, 13 (1958–9), 1–21. Some support for this reading is given in Polhemus, *The Changing World*, pp. 219–31.

his peace with a wife he could never quite understand when she was alive. In the process, he will presumably be able to make peace with himself. He tries, then, to arrange his children's future around a model of his own past, but in doing so simply reactivates conflicts without at all solving them. Hagan complains that the novel only dramatizes the problem without resolving it,[28] but such, it seems to me, is exactly Trollope's intention. The Duke must find some way to live without the solidity of either future plans or past history; the uncertain, fluid present is finally all there is. He must learn to live uncomfortably with the dark implications of the fact that 'nothing will ever be quite what it used to be' (35). The series thus concludes without a conclusion; the form is deliberately suspended. The Duke is forced to accept loss and isolation, a cold and comfortless accommodation.

Though the novel's primary emphasis is psychological, the Duke's struggle has important social and ethical dimensions. It is true that he has resigned from public life, leaving that emptiness for the time to Sir Timothy Beeswax, who is perfectly suited to lead, understanding as he does that the most successful statesman 'is he who does nothing' (21). Still, the Duke's attempt to bring the past and future into harmony with a set of values he holds dear is, in miniature, the basic social fight portrayed in all Trollope's novels. The Duke is out to see how many true gentlemen there are. He repeats over and over the great precepts of the aristocratic, chivalric code, but no one, including his children, seems to hear. His striving for continuity, therefore, is not merely personal; it is yet another test of the world's coherence. If the Duke cannot instruct his own children, cannot even make them understand what it is he is talking about, all hope for reconciliation is gone.

The major action of the novel is at once comic and ironic, 'happy' yet 'depressing', said the *Spectator*.[29] The movement toward accommodation, the working out of difficulties, represent the victory of one sort of union and, to the Duke at least, the defeat of another. He learns to live in the new world as best he can, but with it, as with the rebellious Glencora, he is 'by no means satisfied'. *The Duke's Children* has many apparent resemblances to *Framley Parsonage*:

---

[28] 'Trollope's Psychological Masterpiece', pp. 18–20.

[29] Rev. of *The Duke's Children*, *Spectator*, 53 (12 June 1880), 755. There is a good reading of the novel, strongly emphasizing its darkness, by Blair Gates Kenney, 'The Two Isabels: A Study in Distortion', *VNL*, No. 25 (1964), pp. 15–17.

the heroine in both novels awaits the approval of the hero's parent, thus confirming the power of that dominant figure and managing to include new life in the society without the necessity of displacing anyone. At least Lady Lufton is not displaced, but the Duke, for all the love and respect he receives, cannot help feeling abandoned. He never is any more fully integrated with this new world than he was with the government of England or his marriage. Renewal and disillusionment are mixed at the end, mirroring in formal irresolution the Duke's frustration in trying for full union.

The conflict is developed most intricately in a battle between different kinds of language. A search for appropriate speech is conducted, but, like everything else in this novel, it is not successfully concluded, though it may perhaps be fruitfully begun. There are scores of passages in which the pervasive battle between the old values and the new is mirrored in wildly contrasting forms of speech. Sir Timothy Beeswax at one point tells Silverbridge, then temporarily in the Conservative camp, that he, Beeswax, looks to 'the young conservative thoughtfulness and the truly British spirit of our springing aristocracy . . . for that reaction which I am sure will at last carry us safely over the rocks and shoals of communistic propensities' (70). Silverbridge's answer, in full, is, 'I shouldn't wonder if it did.' Political fustian, no doubt, but Sir Timothy's language is only a slight exaggeration of the mode of speech adopted habitually by the Duke himself. Though he is never dismissed contemptuously by his sons, his language comes from a world with which they have little contact. The contrast between his abstract vocabulary and long, beautiful periods and their colloquial and concrete speech is pointed and often very funny:

'Do you ever think what money is?'
The Duke paused so long, collecting his own thoughts and thinking of his own words, that Gerald found himself obliged to answer. 'Cheques, and sovereigns, and bank-notes,' he replied with much hesitation.
'Money is the reward of labour,' said the Duke. (65)

When he tries to lecture Silverbridge about the moral dangers inherent in club life, a similar disastrous pause gives his eager son a chance to agree, 'You always see the same fellows' (26). The Duke makes memoranda on his sons' use of slang and vulgar expressions in letters; he tries everything to pass on to them the equipment for complex expressions of thought. They try with the best intentions

imaginable to please him, but their direct, experiential language has
no way of connecting with his. The Duke's language is not so much
useful for experience itself as for subtle and involved explanations of
experience. 'You do not quite understand me, I fear' (25), he says
in pitiable desperation. Their failure to understand seems to him
a failure to comprehend *any* explanations, a mere unprotected immersion in chaos. His speech assumes a solid coherence that does
not exist for them.

But there is perhaps a new form of language beginning, one
initiated by Isabel Boncassen. Though she speaks with the same
forthrightness and simplicity as Silverbridge, she has the capacity to
make generalizations. These are rudimentary, it is true, but they
are solid and assured. She knows that Dolly Longstaff is 'obtuse'
(32), and says so. She sees also that most problems and even most
falseness spring from linguistic confusion: men 'never mean what
they say, because they don't understand the use of words' (33). Her
new language suggests the opening of a new system of moral classification, one that abandons the instinctual basis so dear to the
comedy of manners. The complex set of values and guides for behaviour which had grown up are sadly set aside, but in their place
we can see a new code being formulated. All subtlety and in a way
all delicacy are for the moment ignored in favour of the qualities
necessary for all successful inaugurations: general honesty and
absolute lucidity.

Even here, though, there are some concessions to the old system.
The honesty, unlike the lucidity, is not absolute; the new language
is not simply one of blunt truth-telling. Civilization is still
respected, and those, like Major Tifto, who speak without restraint
are severely criticized. Lady Mabel Grex's language is most
instructive here. It is always 'true', but it is so scalding that it
cannot be finally admitted. Late in the novel she sets Silverbridge
up for blistering verbal punishment by getting him to assert that
he will never tell a courteous lie and then forcing him into one. Once
she traps him, she can fire away: 'Time is but a poor consoler for
a young woman who has to be married . . . In truth, Silverbridge, I
have never loved you' (73). She sees restraint and courtesy in language as mere pious 'hypocrisy' (77). Given her situation, such a
response is understandable, but it is also dangerous. And it indicates
to us that the new speech, begun in bluntness, may move toward
the complex indirectness it had once maintained: '"I want to marry

your daughter", said Silverbridge. Isabel had told him that he was downright, and in such a matter he had hardly as yet learned how to express himself with those paraphrases in which the world delights' (53). Not an unambiguous sentence, certainly, but it does suggest that the Duke's language is not altogether lost, that he is perhaps less alone than he thinks.

But as he sees it himself, his attempts to find links to the world through his children are pretty generally unsuccessful. And no wonder: he is asking them to re-enact and yet correct his own past. He wants them to carry on what he is, but, in another sense, he wants them to supply the romance and the integrated, rich life he has never found. Though his outward life was lived happily only 'among figures and official details', 'romance . . . was always present to [his] imagination' (11). He wants submission and rebellion, and he can hardly expect both. His own lifelong failure to connect his public and private selves is simply confirmed. The diversification he finds should perhaps satisfy him, but of course it does not. In the end, the break with Glencora, the gap between the outward life of duty and the inward life of romance, cannot be healed by anything the children do. Nor can his values ever again apply in the same way. Both psychologically and socially the Duke must come to grips with the new times—and somehow with the old times, his past, as well.

His battles with and through his children are complex and confused. But in all of the battles he is concerned both with the way his sons replay his own past and with the way their future tends to confirm or repudiate his values. The first concern, with the past, is more psychological, tortured, and ambiguous; the second, with the future, is just as intense but a little simpler. Any associations with the past call up for the Duke problems that are insoluble and depressing; with the future, however, the children can, at least in part, be for him or against him. They either understand their duties or they do not, or so he thinks.

Lady Mary's love for Frank Tregear asks the Duke to recast his own past life and thus presents the most purely psychological of his dilemmas. Though agonizing, the problem is hardly submerged in his own mind at all. He sees Lady Mary quite clearly as Glencora (see ch. 2), Tregear as Burgo (3), and their love as 'a repetition of that romantic folly by which she [Glencora] had so nearly brought herself to shipwreck in her own early life' (5). The one fact he cannot admit, however, is that the Duchess has encouraged the young people's love. It is very difficult for him to realize that Glencora has also wanted to replay and rearrange her own past. Therefore, he simply denies that she has ever had anything to do with Mary and Tregear and transfers his fear and anger to the innocent Marie: 'He struggled gallantly to acquit the memory of his wife. He could best do that by leaning with the full weight of his mind on the presumed iniquity of Mrs. Finn' (7). Meanwhile, he creates a triangle, introducing his own counterpart in the present drama, Lord Popplecourt, a man 'quite as insignificant in appearance' (24) and in every other quality as he had been. Popplecourt is a kind of old young man whose good looks are 'of that sort which recommend themselves to pastors and masters, to elders and betters' (34). He is an almost deliberate parody of the Duke, introduced perhaps through some unconscious wish to complete the desertion Glencora had threatened. But on another and contradictory level, he wishes to use Popplecourt to justify his own past, forcing Glencora (Mary) this time to make an even harder decision in favour of duty. If Mary will choose even the lifeless Popplecourt, the Duke will be in some measure reassured. But he is forced in the end to drink wine with the victorious Tregear. He manages this most difficult adjustment, but it provides unshakable evidence of his aloneness.

With his sons, especially with the eldest, Lord Silverbridge, the outcome is more hopeful and the psychology somewhat less strained. This time the Duke wants—or thinks he wants—a duplicate of himself. Though his own conflict between the romantic and the dutiful denies the possibility of a satisfactory duplicate and though he does not fully want one, he can hardly fail to find some echoes and then, along with his disappointments, at least some small satisfaction. The key problem with his sons is one of values. In all of their conversations the Duke feels unable to touch his boys and therefore believes that he is being abandoned. The sons sense his feeling, admiring and loving their father loyally, but inevitably from afar. 'I shall never be like my father' (16), Silverbridge says, but that is finally not so certain. As Gerald, the younger brother, says to an impertinent huntsman who asks if he's shot much, 'Not what you call very much. I'm not so old as you are, you know. Everything must have a beginning' (38). Gerald, as it happens, is an expert shot. Not much training is really required, even perhaps for the courteous and responsible life the Duke advocates. Just so, Silverbridge is clearly educated in the course of the novel: 'All these little troubles, his experience in the "House," the necessity of snubbing Tifto, the choice of a wife, and his battle with Reginald Dobbes, were giving him by degrees age and flavour' (42). As he mellows and matures he moves closer to the position held by the Duke, though it may be that the Duke never fully sees this. Silver-bridge has all along been protected from extremes by his fine gentlemanly instincts, especially by his natural modesty, his capacity for self-doubt. After the wildly enthusiastic reception of his inane speech in support of Tregear—'My friend Frank Tregear . . . is a very good fellow, and I hope you'll elect him' (55)—he goes home to bed thinking, 'perhaps, after all, I did make a fool of myself' (55). Very gently, it is hinted that with Silverbridge this last chronicle bends backward toward the beginning of the first one with the emergence of a new Mr. Harding.

Silverbridge's education in politics is, like the rest of his training, a process of returning to his sources. He imagines that he has de-veloped into a sound and confirmed Conservative: 'What the deuce is a fellow to do? If a man has got political convictions of his own, of course, he must stick to them' (4). 'You see, sir,' he tells his father, 'a man's political opinion is a kind of thing he can't get rid of.' He listens with great attention to his father's patient counter-arguments, admits that 'there was a great deal in what his father had said', but still insists, 'I could not call myself a Liberal.' 'Why not?' asks the Duke. 'Because I am a Conservative.' That almost stops even the former Prime Minister, but he returns to the attack, finally driving Silverbridge to the comic admission that he is probably a Conserva-tive because 'I know that I am a fool' (7). That does stop the Duke. Silverbridge is sorry to hurt his father, but he claims, 'when a man does take up an opinion I don't see how he can help himself' (14). Regarding convictions a little like a mysterious disease, Silverbridge guesses that the source of their misunderstanding might lie in a general sort of transformation: 'times are changed a little perhaps' (14). This is just what the Duke fears, that times are so changed that his sons are disloyal through a kind of unconscious moral idiocy.

But Silverbridge is saved by his fine instincts—'Sir Timothy is such a beast' (55)—and rightly drops convictions altogether. He amazes his father by the sensitivity he displays in understanding that Sir Timothy is using him only to annoy the Duke. The Duke has thought so too, but 'it certainly had not occurred to him that Silverbridge would be astute enough to perceive the same thing' (67). His insight developed to this point, Silverbridge finds it easy to switch parties: 'After all it is not very important' (76). His vision and stability in this case have surpassed his father's. He has demonstrated an open and unembarrassed love, responding in this political reversal with a simple integration of private affection and public action that astounds his father. The Duke has been as loving, but only in secret: 'The father looked round the room furtively, and seeing that the door was shut, and that they were assuredly alone, he put out his hand and gently stroked the young man's hair. It was almost a caress' (26).

Silverbridge's education in love is much tougher, less integrated, than is his political training. His contact with Lady Mabel is harsh, and he only just manages to escape. But she does not. Remarkably, the novel makes us recognize the victims even of such a good-natured hero as Silverbridge. Lady Mabel sees more clearly than any other figure in Trollope just what a woman's lot is,[30] and she is shut out more cruelly—perhaps for that very reason. It is as difficult for the novel to accommodate her unsentimental view of a woman's role as it is for Silverbridge to imagine himself married to one who 'would be his superior, and in some degree his master' (19). She is 'wiser', 'more powerful' than he (19), and he therefore instinctively retreats. Lady Mabel thinks very pointedly about Sisyphus (53), but in the end she denies herself even that heroism: 'A girl unless she marries becomes nothing, as I have become nothing now' (77). Another Charlotte Lucas sacrificed, this time not because she is, like Charlotte, plain and mediocre but because she is superior.

Though we are never protected from Lady Mabel's bitter attacks on all sentimental, romantic assumptions, we are allowed to glimpse, in Isabel Boncassen, the saving idea that all superiority is not sacrificed. Isabel seems, like Mary Thorne, to be the new blood transfused into the old aristocracy, but she plays a part more complex than that. She looks at first to be almost dangerously free; she 'hardly seemed to be under control from the father' (31), going anywhere and doing what she liked. She even expresses the notion that rank is nonsense, that she can 'make a position for myself' (32). But

[30] Perhaps more clearly than any figure in the period. At least Pamela Hansford Johnson believes it to be the subtlest study of a woman in nineteenth-century English literature ('Trollope's Young Women', p. 21).

the last threatening anarchic slogans are uttered to the 'obtuse' Dolly Longstaff and are clearly sarcastic. Everyone expects her to be like Mrs. Hurtle, but everyone is wrong. Even Silverbridge, hoping to make himself agreeable, asks her if she does not believe that all those conventional rules about men and women are 'absurd' (39). Her answer softly rebukes him and suggests her genuine, even conservative, solidity: 'As a progressive American, of course I am bound to think all conventional rules are an abomination' (39). It turns out that she is not really foreign at all. She alone seems to sense fully and exactly what it is the Duke is talking about. She therefore tests the social order, represented by the Duke, not by asking it to expand or change but by asking if it can recognize its own. The Duke tells Silverbridge that in marrying Isabel he is exercising an unlicensed, ignorant freedom, but Silverbridge understands something of how traditional and uneccentric his choice is, justifying it in the grand old terms: 'honour', 'duty', and 'nobility' (61). Isabel kindly asks Silverbridge to 'teach' her the full cultural richness supported by the Duke (72), but we see clearly enough who will be doing the teaching. She is the most pleasantly ironic American import in Trollope, and she demonstrates that the feelings that guided and supported the old gentlemanly code are, after all, not so moribund.

But the Duke is never fully reconciled. Because of the contradictory demands he is forced to make, any marriage, any failure to marry, would leave him equally stranded. He gives his consent to his children but cannot help lamenting openly, 'My opinion is to go for nothing,—in anything!' (71). But he summons courage to live with his children's futures. Though his 'hilarity' at the wedding is forced, he must 'remind himself' as he stands at the altar-steps 'of all that he had suffered' (80). No cure is possible, but he does escape nothingness. He even plans at the end to return to office in Mr. Monk's ministry. He has learned to endure uncomfortably.

As the wedding party walks to the church at the novel's close, they pass by Matching's old Priory ruins, a gentle reminder to us of an earlier scene of half-decisive, ill-reconciled unfulfilment. In the first novel of the chronicle Glencora had walked here thinking of her own past, her present unhappiness, and her unsatisfied passion for Burgo Fitzgerald. In the last novel the Duke now suffers the same frustrating pain, right in the middle of a world that is going so well.

CHAPTER 7

THE LATE EXPERIMENTAL NOVELS

JUDGING ON the basis of the continuity observed within Trollope's two major chronicles and the controlled testing conducted in the early novels written outside these chronicles, one would never have expected the last part of his career to be spent on novels as widely diverse as *Cousin Henry, The Fixed Period*, and *Ayala's Angel*. Though many of Trollope's novels are experimental in the sense that they test formal or generic limits, these late novels seem at first glance to be the random experiments of some mad scientist. Actually, the new range suggests the freedom Trollope found in certainty. The tendency is not so much to expand as to exercise his mastery of craft in new and surprising ways. The novels beginning with *The American Senator* (1877) offer not only new combinations in narrative patterns of comedy, irony, and tragedy, but also a new generic range from anatomy to satire to romance. There are unexpected major effects derived from the grotesque and from the dramatic monologue. Trollope doesn't mind now and then borrowing a technique or a moral point even from Dickens.

Not only do these novels fail to betray an over-all pattern, they seem strongly to resist the imposition of one, springing apart from one another like opposite magnetic poles. The groupings proposed here are meant only to indicate this sense of freedom, the range of the accomplishment; they are neither rigorous nor inclusive, and other schemes would doubtless do as well. However, Trollope's anatomy, *The American Senator*, seems to me distinguishable from those deceptive novels, *Is He Popenjoy?, John Caldigate*, and *An Eye for An Eye*, which seek to establish comedy and then subvert it. Both of these groups are, in turn, distinguishable from those novels with a radically unconventional moral focus established by means borrowed from the dramatic monologue: *Cousin Henry, Dr. Wortle's School, The Fixed Period*, and *Mr. Scarborough's Family*. Standing alone is Trollope's unequivocal romance, *Ayala's Angel*.

The American Senator opens with a description not of the Senator or indeed of any character but of the village of Dillsborough, a place so important that the narrator suggests at the end that the novel 'might perhaps have been better called "The Chronicle of a Winter at Dillsborough"' (80). A 'chronicle' it is, much like *Middlemarch* an anatomy of a country town, a sort of rural *The Way We Live Now*. But the mode is even more generalized than in *Middlemarch*; it is more purely that of the intellectualized anatomy. The characters here, including the Senator, are more typical than in any other Trollope novel: they stand for ideas, outlooks, classes. The tendency throughout is to generalize in order to provide the kind of descriptive classification we associate with anatomy.

It does not take us long, however, to see that the Senator is not a reliable instructor in this classification system. About the time he begins asking why the hunters do not bring along a fox in a bag so that they will be certain to have something to chase (9), we begin searching for some other guide. But it is difficult to find one. The narrator all but disappears after the first few chapters, and certainly no other character seems to be really major. At the end it is suggested that a disappointed lover in one of the subplots, Larry Twentyman, 'has in truth been our hero' (80), but the role could as easily have been assigned to four or five others. In truth, there are no heroes, not for the usual reason that the novel is too ironic but for the reason that it is too impersonal. The impersonal anatomy here is developed by allowing us a variety of perspectives on the same subject.[1] There is no dependable source to guide us in weighing and judging the relative value of these perspectives, and in that sense the novel is ambiguous.[2] But there is no ambiguity concerning the common reality described by each of these views. All try in different ways to come to grips with the irrational. There is some slight convergence toward a cluster of approved values: traditional morality, a love of pleasure, a reliance on the class system. Traditional morality has no necessary or widespread support, however, and the class system, that great 'question of gentlemen and ladies, and of non-gentlemen and non-ladies' (27), seems, like pleasure,

---

[1] This is one of the novels that does fit apRoberts's prescription very well, and she does an excellent job with it (*The Moral Trollope*, pp. 173–88).

[2] John Hagan says, 'The problem to be solved is to which side ... Trollope gives his allegiance' (p. 13). He treats the ambiguity at some length ('The Divided Mind of Anthony Trollope', pp. 11–18), concluding that the case is simply confusing, the problem as to Trollope's own belief not soluble. See also Clement Greenberg, *Art and Culture*, pp. 245–51.

appropriate to this world only because it is, like the world, essentially absurd.

The novel is arranged so that each of its plots offers one of three possible views of irrationality. The Gotobed plot is satiric, the Arabella Trefoil plot ironic, the Mary Masters plot comic. The first plot is corrective, wanting to improve conditions; the next two suggest that the Senator's rationality is insane and that no correction is possible. Arabella's plot shows how the irrational can imprison; Mary's plot demonstrates how it can liberate. Throughout, the dominant symbol is fox-hunting: undemocratic, cruel, and absurd, yet also unifying and in a sense necessary, as it provides the pleasure men must have. The resolution of the comic plot is marked by the decision of the hero, Reginald Morton, to take up hunting; in the ironic plot the hero, Lord Rufford, withdraws from hunting; the Senator remains to the end baffled by the sport.

It is this story of the Senator's clarity and confusion which, though the least prominent of the three main strands, is the most interesting and also the most revealing.[3] He defines the irrational from the elevated position of Pure Reason. He grandly refuses to accept the absurd or the unjust and points them out loudly whenever he sees them. He is nearly always accurate in spotting them, but very seldom right in the terms of his denunciations, though he would be if it were a rational world. 'Is it not the case', he demands, 'that livings in the Church of England can be bought and sold?' (42). And why, he asks, does Lord Rufford's 'model farm' lose money and still hold its unchallenged position as a model? 'If you want to teach a man any other business, you don't specially select an example in which the proprietors are spending all their capital without any return' (68). Here as elsewhere he makes staunch Englishmen mutter into their port, not only because his bluntness is irritating but because he is also, in his way, correct. The natives are propped up by a strong and mysterious inner certainty, but 'they didn't quite see how they were to confute the Senator's logic' (19).

---

[3] Almost all criticism of this novel amounts to little more than a discussion of this character. For a view which regards the Senator and his arguments favourably see David Stryker, 'The Significance of Trollope's "American Senator" ', *NCF*, 5 (1950-1), 141-9. For views as resolutely negative see John H. Wildman, 'Trollope Illustrates the Distinction', *NCF*, 4 (1949-50), 101-10, and Polhemus, *The Changing World*, p. 211. A more balanced, if finally negative, view is given by Greenberg, *Art and Culture*, pp. 245-51. Edgar F. Harden very usefully points out the figure's tie to an earlier tradition of satire and the complex ways in which satire is used in the novel ('The Alien Voice: Trollope's Western Senator', *TSLL*, 8, 1966-7, 219-34).

The Senator has the power of logic, which, although it has the same aberrant quality as the power Don Quixote builds up in his charge at the windmill, is given a kind of wistful respect. Though Gotobed is awkward and often crude, he is not unaffected by the civility and the richness of the established world he sees about him, admitting that the aristocratic life contains a moving 'reality' (29). Nor is he incapable of self-doubt. But he can exercise that doubt only when he is convinced that what he has said is *untrue* (51). He is tied finally to a respected but irrelevant code of rational and coherent truth. It is a code that is no less crazy than any other. If it stupidly denies pleasure to some, it can rescue others from injustice. If it can fail to see that Arabella Trefoil is not 'a good type of the English aristocracy' (68), it can see manifest cruelty. As David Stryker points out, the Senator's crude oratorical American mannerisms tend to disappear as we proceed in the novel.[4] He appears less and less a caricature; even the abstract mode of the novel gives some implicit support to the Senator's abstractions.

At the centre is his testimony on fox-hunting. He can see nothing in it beyond a relic of medieval barbarism or, at best, an exercise in futility. The fact that so many people love it means nothing to him since he firmly believes that effects must follow causes. There is surely no possible cause for pleasure, he thinks, in chasing after dogs or, more likely, only hoping to chase after dogs. The sole evidence he admits is that from the rational world, which in this novel has the same sort of existence as Ruskin's cat. Even so, the Senator's championship of Goarly makes some startling, almost ruthless points about aristocratic pleasure and the system of justice currently depended upon. Why should a poor man's field be invaded? Why should the invader value the damages? Why should the poor man have no redress? Why should the poor man's 'rascality', even if granted, be an issue? The last point is really the crucial one. The Senator himself, though touched by Goarly's poverty, senses that he has climbed into a boat with a bunch of scoundrels. Still, the popular argument across the county to the effect that 'if Goarly could be detected in some offence, that would confute the Senator' (19) seems to him vicious and repugnant. Another American, Louis Auchincloss, has sarcastically commented on village justice from the Senator's perspective: 'What, basically, is the use of principle in crime detection when the good old nostrils of

4 'The Significance of Trollope's "American Senator" ', pp. 141–9.

prejudice can pick out the guilty man nine times out of ten ?'[5] To the Senator, Goarly and his kind are not, as they are to many, 'vermin which ought to be hunted down' but 'men', innocent under the law (69). He wonders if Goarly is not really a general social case, a man whose 'evil condition . . . was due to the evil institutions among which he had been reared' (68). Though the Senator's position—'Who Valued the Geese'? (19)—is still too literalistic and quantitative, he suggests that the grand old instincts create their victims and have their not so pleasant anomalies. He offers no solution to this, only a point of view that has its own sort of limited validity.

There are victims even more serious than Goarly. Arabella Trefoil and her mother, Lady Augustus, are badly battered, and they see things with a cynical bitterness, the validity of which, though partial, is undeniable. Such ladies as these 'can never afford to tell the truth' (31), and who is to say but that they are closer to things as they are than the truth-telling Senator? Trollope said, 'I have been, and still am very much afraid of Arabella Trefoil', but claimed that she has her own virtues and will be rewarded with a 'third class heaven in which she will always be getting third class husbands'.[6] Like the Senator, she is given a sort of fascinated respect without approval. She has throughout a haunting and admirable self-consciousness. Though wading through filth with her mother, trying either to pull herself out or to drag someone else in with her, she none the less never fools herself about where she is. She shifts warily from John Morton to Lord Rufford, smelling richer game, but she does so with no pleasure and with very little confidence. And amazingly she finds in Rufford an empty neutrality far more vicious than her own craftiness. She is really out of her depth. Rufford glides along blandly in an aristocratic current that conceals dangers so terrible as to far outdistance any criticisms of the Senator's. Rufford shows the aristocracy without their vaunted substantial instincts; now there is only the genial surface. Major Caneback's fatal injury while hunting at Rufford's poses a dilemma that threatens to ruffle the surface: how can they proceed with the ball while he is dying? 'Nobody in that house really cared much for Caneback . . . nevertheless, it is a bore when a gentleman dies in your house' (23). Such trying times it is the duty of the aristocracy to master, how-

---

[5] 'Americans in Trollope', *Reflections of a Jacobite* (Boston: Houghton Mifflin, 1961), p. 117.
[6] Letter to [?Anna C. Steele], 17 Feb. 1877, *Letters*, pp. 363-4.

ever, and Rufford's sound feelings and good training are equal to the challenge. Caneback is placed at the end of the hall where he 'won't hear a sound of the music'. After all, 'though the man were to die, why shouldn't the people dance?' (23).

Arabella's nerve in facing this world is greatly admired, and she is given a good deal of unexpected support in her battle with the established aristocracy—or with this faded section of it. Lord Rufford is well padded; 'he had everything to protect him, and she had nothing, absolutely nothing, to help her!' (25). Arabella is even forced to break with her one grimy ally, her mother: 'There are so many people won't have you' (25). This mother, like her daughter, has suffered a life of continual battle, all 'struggle and misery, contumely and contempt' (55), and all for nothing: 'I can see wherever she goes everybody hates her' (60). But though Arabella can afford no pity for Lady Augustus, she is not without heart. The death of Caneback shakes her deeply; 'the sound of that horse's foot as it struck the skull of the unfortunate fallen rider' (55) haunts her imagination. As a result she is 'for a time brought . . . back to humanity' and is 'honest just for once' with poor dying John Morton (55). The narrator makes it clear that her nature 'was not altered' (55) by this shock, nor does her final marriage to a Patagonia-bound clerk promise a great deal (76). In irony there are no violent changes, except of the sort felt by Lady Augustus after the wedding: 'As soon as the carriage was gone, she went to her own room and wept bitterly. It was all done now. Everything was over. Though she had quarrelled daily with her daughter for the last twelve years . . . her life had had its occupation . . . Now it was all over. The link by which she had been bound to the world was broken' (76).

The comic plot suggests to the contrary that this same irrational life and this irrational class system are the source not only of pleasure but of freedom. Though certainly not one of Trollope's best romantic comedies, the story of Mary Masters's love for Reginald Morton makes its point. And that point is the confirmation of the instinctual gentlemanly life and a refutation of all democratic and merely sensible tendencies. Mary's stepmother is sensible, and she is wrong. She bitterly resents the influence of Mary's friend Lady Ushant and the highfalutin doctrines with which she fills the girl. Larry Twentyman, slightly vulgar but sweet, loving, and prosperous, is her candidate for Mary. But Mary is in love with the somewhat crusty recluse, Reginald Morton, and holds out firmly against her stepmother's rationality. The narrator never leaves us in doubt as to who is right in this contest between aristocratic romance and bourgeois actuality: 'It never occurred to Mrs. Masters that perhaps the very qualities that had made poor Larry so vehemently in love with Mary had come from her intercourse with Lady Ushant' (18). The aristocratic system that is pilloried in Arabella's story is in this plot given almost magical powers. Larry is 'our old friend', but we recognize that he hasn't a chance, and we sense also the reasons for his exclusion. This is a gentle, established world in this plot, and Larry, though kind-hearted . . . well, after all! The values are never explained because they are inexplicable, resting on deep and irrational assumptions. These are the very assumptions which are vulnerable to the Senator's attacks and which appear so hollow and dangerous in Arabella's story. But here the same irrationality is a source of strength. The values cannot be explained because they are too fully consonant with the currents of life to yield themselves up to the superficiality of language. Reginald is recognized through all his disguises by us and by Mary, and this somewhat mysterious affirmation of his virtues brings him back to life. His original absorption in studies, particularly to the exclusion of the principal activity of the gentry, hunting, causes widespread comic lamentation: 'When I hear of a country gentleman sticking to books and all that, I feel that the glory is departing from the land. Where are the sinews of war to come from? That's what I want to know' (64). But England and her war sinews are not really in danger. Reginald becomes a vigorous defender of the sport against the weak-headed philanimalists. The real climax of this story is not his declaration of love but 'I think I shall take to hunting' (73).

In the end we recognize *The American Senator* as the chronicle of Anywhere, England. 'The town', says the narrator, 'has no attractions, and never had any' (1). The word 'attractions' is carefully chosen. There is little to delight the eye of such a one as the Senator, but the delights are there for those who know how to look and are lucky enough to find them. So are the perils. The only certainty is that all is beyond reason, beyond certainty. Whether one can or should learn to live comfortably with that fact is an open question.

Is He Popenjoy? has few resemblances to *The American Senator* beyond the curious disappearance after a few chapters of the chatty narrator. Here he withdraws not to bolster ambiguity but to deceive, leaving us at the mercy of a duplicitous shift away from the comedy of manners we had thought we were reading. The plot of the novel is the primary weapon used in deceiving us. There are apparent climaxes that merely collapse, and the energies of the major characters are involved in a detection plot that reveals nothing. The title itself is a fake. Trollope habitually made fun of legalisms and often allowed complex questions of this sort to remain unanswered, but he usually did so in order to demonstrate the triviality of such drivelling rationalism in the face of a kind nature. Nature, not the law, should be allowed to take its course. In this novel, nature takes its course, all right, but problems are solved not by comic miracles but by death. The title is ironic, but not in the gentle way we would like. 'What a rumpus there has been about a rickety brat who was bound to die!' (53) says the little boy's father. That tone and that attitude condemn all the relaxed comic assumptions we have been encouraged to embrace.

Critics often have complained about the novel's cynical tone,[7] but such complaints only reflect the uneasiness we feel at having been so artfully tricked. We suddenly realize that there are two levels to the action, two generic patterns, and that the one to which we have been attending is superficial. Nothing here, we find, is quite what it seems. At the centre of the novel is the display of the new dance, the Kappa Kappa, but is it an innocent expression of joy or the occasion for dark sexual intrigue? Whatever it is, it gives no one any joy. We are certain only that everyone misunderstands it and reacts to it blindly or hysterically. Innocence, like one of the pretty ladies mentioned, seems always about to become one 'mass of whipped cream turned sour' (35). The only answer seems to be to pretend not to notice the taste or smell. Decent life must somehow go on, we are told, even if people are not decent. The dominant motif, then, is reticence: countless virtuous characters solve moral dilemmas, or evade them, by vowing to keep their mouths shut. Those who go about insisting on comic openness and trust are not only stupid but destructive: 'When grown people play at being children, it is apt to be dangerous' (38).

---

[7] The *Saturday Review*, 45 (1 June 1878), 695–6, complained of the novel's harshness and lack of reticence. Polhemus similarly dislikes the novel's 'cynicism', its lack of 'compassion', and its rough 'moral outrage' (*The Changing World*, p. 209). It is interesting in this regard that Charles Dickens the Younger bowdlerized the novel when serializing it in *All the Year Round* (see T. C. D., 'Victorian Editors and Victorian Delicacy', *N&Q* 187, 2 Dec. 1944, 251–3).

Comedy is not just subverted, it is attacked—after we have become attached to it. No wonder the tone seems bitter. The story
at first appears to be very simple; the only real problem, we think,
is in overcoming unnatural resistance to pleasure. Dean Lovelace
has urged his daughter to marry 'gaunt' and 'sombre' Lord George
Germain, but he has no intention of seeing her sacrificed to repressive stuffiness. Like some god of the festivity, he sets out to protect
his daughter from her husband's reading lists. He insists as part of
the marriage bargain that Mary be provided with a house in London
so that she might have fun. The wordly cleric thus pushes his
daughter toward a bright, gay life, urging her to resist her husband
and her dour sisters-in-law. The introduction of the Baroness Ban-
mann, Dr. Olivia Q. Fleabody, and the rest of the menagerie at the
Female Disabilities only adds to the hilarity. The marital strife that
results from Mary attending a Disabilities meeting is surely, we feel,
a mock battle carried on only for the pleasure of celebrating its cessa-
tion. Meanwhile, the Dean is carrying on his own battle with the
Bishop's comic chaplain, Mr. Groschut. Groschut, an even more
obvious outsider than Mr. Slope, is otherwise like him, carrying
his predecessor's low-church nonsense to the point of actually in-
citing public clamour over the Dean's hunting. *Is He Popenjoy?*
looks at first very much like another Barsetshire chronicle.

But the mock enemies, the repressed and the stupid, are replaced
by genuine viciousness. The conflict between pleasure and restrictive prudence starts to melt away about midpoint, and even Lord
George's sisters are seen as sympathetic and compassionate (31).
With the entrance of the Marquis everything changes. The Marquis
observes no rules of conduct, recognizes the necessity of no civility,
freely lying and freely calling honest men liars. But were they so
honest after all? Lord George's flirtation with Mrs. Houghton, for
instance, seems at first comic. Mrs. Houghton even seems a little
like Miss Dunstable; despite her raciness and her vulgarity, she
offers to Mary some 'relief to the endless gloom' (9). There are,
however, worse things than gloom. The Marquis brings with him
something much more frightening; he casts a cynical light on all
actions and forces everyone, reader included, to see all past events
in a new and far less agreeable way. Lord George's flirtation is not
innocent, nor is Mrs. Houghton anything like Miss Dunstable.
Mary's own attachment to Jack De Baron, though innocent in its
way, is almost criminally thoughtless. And the Dean's hustling pur-

suit of pleasure begins to look like stupidity or, worse, gross and selfish vulgarity. He blithely pushes his daughter along into the city and hurries in after her, never thinking that there are any dangers at the fair.

It is through the Dean that one can perhaps best understand Trollope's technique here. Lovelace is introduced as 'urbanity itself' (1), a man much like Archdeacon Grantly but without his snobbery or intellectual limitations. He seems more generous, anxious not only to provide joy to his daughter but to everyone around. He does not wish to counteract Lord George; he wants to convert him to the life of pleasure. 'It is', he tells his daughter, 'your duty to assist in freeing him' (11). The Dean is warm and manly, a lover of an open fight. Though there is a touch of coarseness about his pugnacity—'progress', he claims, can come only if men and women 'look after their own interests' (16)—he sounds sufficiently like Dr. Thorne to pass as one of Trollope's perfect-imperfect clergymen. Even his defects of delicacy and sensitivity are at first disguised by the deceptive comic theme and by the fact that it is the stiff Lord George who notes these faults. Lord George's haughty objections—'the Dean had laughed loud, more like the son of a stable-keeper than a dean' (19)—are at first given very little weight indeed. They really act to make us ignore such things as the Dean's curious absence of dignity in London, his adoption of the role of 'some schoolboy out on a holiday' (19).

But children in an adult world cause harm, the novel insists, and it is the Dean's daughter who first sees the problem. By forcing her into London society, he is forcing her also into contact with Captain De Baron, thus exacerbating her husband's jealousy. 'But of such dangers and of such fears her father saw nothing' (28). He simply tells her not to give in, to 'have her own way' (28). Even here it is possible for us to see the Dean's ignorance as innocence, but his moral stupidity is finally exposed clearly. When the Marquis arrives with the sick, dark child he claims is the heir, the Dean's vigour soon begins to look like callousness or something worse. Anxious to prove the child's illegitimacy and thus secure the title and wealth for Lord George and his daughter, the Dean launches an inquiry with so much energy and so little taste that Lord George, who stands most to benefit, is sickened. The Dean does not scruple to hope that if the legal inquiries fail a kind Providence will help them by slaughtering the little boy. He does not hesitate to say so openly, even though it shocks his daughter. 'Everybody', he claims loudly, 'must feel that it would be better for the family that he should be out of the way' (40). When he hears the news of the child's death, 'he could not control the triumph of his voice as he told the news'. 'Yes, he's out of the way', he brays, repeating the ugly euphemism. 'There was', the narrator says, 'an air about him as though he had already won the great stake for which he had been playing' (54). The game metaphor catches exactly the Dean's dangerous childishness. Even Mary is repulsed by his behaviour: 'I don't think that people should long for things like this [the boy's death]. If they can't keep from wishing them, they should keep their wishes to themselves' (55). If there is no degree of difference between amiable deans and vicious old marquises, they should at least be still and not expose their kinship. But the Dean is never still and licks his chops greedily when the Marquis also dies: 'All that I have wished has come about.' Mary 'shuddered as she heard these words, remembering that two deaths had been necessary for this fruition of his desires' (61).

From this 'pagan exaltation' (61) it is a long way to the comic clerical battles that had occupied the Dean earlier. But at its close the novel sarcastically returns us to Mr. Groschut, reminding us of how we were drawn into a comedy of manners world and then suddenly shown our mistake. The very last words are, 'Of Mr. Groschut it is only necessary to say that he is still at Pugsty, vexing the souls of his parishioners by Sabbatical denunciations' (64). Even this reminder brings up another instance of the Dean's horrible gloating. When Groschut is sent to Pugsty, the Dean expresses his jubilation; Pugsty 'isn't very nice', being too close to the potteries and the poor, where 'the population is heavy'. An innocent old lady then asks what it has never occurred to the Dean to ponder, 'What is to become of the poor people?' (57). The Dean has been far too occupied with fun in a world where no pleasures are any longer innocent or harmless.

John Caldigate, one of Trollope's finest but least-known novels, pushes this generic flip-flopping one step further. The comedy dissolves into bleak irony which at last is made to yield again to comedy. As in the last novel, however, we are made to see each of these stages as final and are purposefully shocked by the changes. The novel appears to reach its first conclusion about one-third of the way through. Young John Caldigate, quarrelling with his unsociable, 'hard, unsympathetic' father (1) over some trivial college debts, actually sells his inheritance, thus, as the tenants see it, undermining 'the stability of this world' and 'bringing misfortune, not only on himself, but on the whole parishes of Utterden and Netherden' (3). The comic problems come flocking round, some serious and some amusing. He is hopelessly in love with one girl but pursued relentlessly by two others, one a cousin who looks upon a kiss in a closet as a binding promise, and another who banks on the mysterious bond created when she slips a copy of Thomson's 'The Seasons' (a mistaken choice, as it turns out) into the luggage Caldigate is taking to Australia. Running to the gold mines down under, he becomes entangled with yet another woman and with some very unsavoury characters besides. But his letters back home are warm and gentlemanly, and they begin to melt his father, who is, in truth, soft-hearted. Before we know it, then, the problems seem to have disappeared. Caldigate is home with lots of money and a new confidence. He escapes from the two pursuing girls and goes to work with a will on the third: 'After that Caldigate did not allow the grass to grow under his feet, and before the end of November the two young people were engaged' (20). A rather perfunctory account of his success, but good things are coming to him so fast that we hardly notice. With almost breathtaking speed he is married. His father, fully reconciled, reinherits him, an heir is born in decent time, and the prospect of a perfect line of descent fills the whole county 'with almost superstitious satisfaction' (23).

But all this solidity crumbles just as quickly as it was established, making for an effect very unusual in Trollope: the grotesque. All the soft sentiment of the first section is juxtaposed against the unrelieved harshness of the central part. Caldigate's Australian past catches up with him, and his success story is inverted. He is put on trial and his wife is imprisoned for a time by her own mother. The grotesquerie of their night-long vigil, where both Hester and Mrs. Bolton refuse to yield and go to bed, is emphasized by the narrative comment: 'Macbeth and Sancho have been equally eloquent in the praise of sleep' (36). Deliberately minimizing the solemnity of the occasion, such remarks make us see the essential absurdity of the fate which has caught Caldigate and his wife. Macbeth and Sancho are as incompatible a mixture as the seriousness and triviality that mark these situations. 'The thing was so full of real tragedy' (30), but nothing like tragic dignity is ever allowed.

Or, thankfully, tragic consequences. For into all this misery is introduced the most un-Trollopean of characters, Samuel Bagwax. Bagwax is discussed often in the novel around and through the narrator's complaints about the unfairness of the attacks on the Civil Service in *Little Dorrit*. It is almost as if Trollope were using these indirect means to alert us to the Dickensian origins of Bagwax, a character he admitted he drew with 'a touch of downright love . . . Was I not a Bagwax myself?'[8] Although Caldigate is in jail, Bagwax, with true romantic zeal, goes to work on the evidence hidden in some cancelled postage stamps: 'Every moment that I pass with that envelope before my eyes I see the innocent husband in jail, and the poor afflicted wife weeping in her solitude' (52). Bagwax's grumpy partner in post office affairs, Mr. Curlydown, complains, 'You'll be going on to the stage, Bagwax, before this is done' (52), but Bagwax is no actor. He is the real thing, like Toddles, or Sloppy, or Tom Pinch, or Mr. Pickwick 'all heart'. He manages even to stir the affection of lawyers. Sir John Joram fully realizes Bagwax's ridiculousness, but he still is 'half disposed to rise from his seat to embrace the man, and hail him as his brother' (48). Trollope is not Dickens, and Sir John keeps his seat, but the impulse is still remarkable, as is the extent of Bagwax's success. By one means and another, Caldigate is released and things rearrange themselves after all. Bagwax, as the narrator finally admits, must be reckoned the hero (64). He has arranged the comedy, after all. He is perhaps Trollope's one traditional hero: simple, noble, and with true romantic energy. He manages the final generic switch, which is, like the first, most unexpected, but, unlike the first, most welcome.

Finally, we can observe a switch less artful but more extreme in *An Eye for an Eye*, where Trollope takes one more of his weak, well-meaning young men and this time unexpectedly sacrifices him. Young Fred Neville is willing to accept his duty as heir to the Earl of Scroope but asks for just a little time to exercise his romantic sense of freedom. But such a harmless oats-sowing turns out to be a disaster. Not only is freedom an illusion, so even are small holidays. Fred takes off for Ireland; he is certain 'that there was much more of real life to be found on the cliffs of Moher than in the gloomy chambers of Scroope Manor' (i. 9). Escaping his aunt's dull sermons, he finds at first at least a fair release from tedium, as does his sweetheart, Kate. One of the many harrowing points suggested

---

[8] Letter to John Blackwood, 6 Feb. 1879, *Letters*, p. 412.

here is that Kate and Fred seize on one another simply as an alternative to boredom. They are willing to settle even for some cheap, conventionalized romance; the wild and rocky cliffs come to seem to Fred like stage machinery from a melodrama. He is fighting against sterility, she against a repressive mother who wants to protect her from a world of 'wolves'. But in the end boredom or a cloister are preferable to what happens.

When Kate becomes pregnant, Ireland, 'the land of freedom and potatoes' (ii. 1), takes on a new aspect, appearing to contain a lot more grubby potatoes than freedom. The original comedy is suddenly blown apart. Fred, however, can adjust to no other world. True to his training in romantic novels, he imagines that he can continue true to freedom *and* duty, that some sort of grand sacrifice or other should carry them through nobly. He even imagines that all these difficulties are secret benefits, insuring a more glorious final triumph: 'There were', he tells himself, 'always difficulties in the way of any man who chose to leave the common grooves of life and to make a separate way for himself. There were always difficulties in the way of adventures' (i. 10). He thinks about tropical islands or a floating yacht, some life of pure love outside such things as marriage and other conventions. He will simply hand over the title to his brother and let him manage that end of things. Impossible as his wild plans are, no one can give him advice that is much more practical: 'It is very hard to say yes, or no' (ii. 6). He must betray the title or the girl, chooses neither, exactly, and is murdered for his wavering by a mother who goes mad as a result. Even worse, the daughter chooses to cling to her illusions, hating not Fred but the mother who has tried so hard to protect her. This turn of events is a fine illustration of what George Eliot called 'ordinary tragedy'. No point is made, no higher causality is served. Catastrophes come about inexorably but with consequences far too severe to be covered by any possible causes. Moralistic explanations—Fred is punished for his looseness, Kate's mother for being either too wary or too unwary—seem absurdly reductive.

In fact, Fred's adventures and his adventurous spirit have throughout been made to seem not grand but timid, even piddling. He has stepped barely an inch out of the common rut, but he has been crushed all the same. Such slight adventures as he has are made conventional so as to forge a very unwelcome link with the reader: 'When young men are anxious to indulge the spirit of adventure, they generally do so by falling in love with young women of whom their fathers and mothers would not approve. In these days a spirit of adventure hardly goes further than this, unless it take a young man to a German gambling table' (i. 2). Noble tragedy isolates and magnifies the hero, but this low-mimetic, 'ordinary' tragedy trivializes him and makes him common. We are connected to Fred much as we are connected to Paul Montague or Johnny Eames, who similarly become 'entangled', as Lady Mary Quin puts it here. But in this novel the paltry, common entanglement is fatal, and our initial involvement with romantic comedy is twisted into an unwilling participation in a stark drama of pointless waste. Trollope's inversions seem to me far more effective when, as in the two previous novels, they are more intricately developed, but *An Eye for an Eye* has an undeniable, if raw, power.

This sort of absorbing power seems to have fascinated Trollope in his later writing. The various experiments with techniques borrowed from the dramatic monologue bear this out. Using morally unconventional subjects and then placing them with a very intense focus, a less and less adequate context for judgement, Trollope produces some of the same effects Browning and Tennyson achieved from their murderous Dukes and mad saints. Judgements become less easy to fix and are more and more held in tension with the demanding force of the speaker's presence, what Robert Langbaum calls his 'song'.[9] Something of this tendency is apparent in *Dr. Wortle's School*, where the community and its values seem shadowy and unsubstantial. The novel gives us no means of placing the Doctor and the issue of bigamy and then judging them. In *Cousin Henry* a despicable hero is given great play against a particularly vicious and self-righteous society. But it is in *The Fixed Period* that Trollope conducts his most bizarre experiment with this form.

This novel, like many dramatic monologues, sets out to 'prove' the impossible case. It is written in the first person with, we are ingenuously told, a clear didactic purpose. The author means to convince, to spread the gospel of the fixed period. This fixed period is a euphemism for euthanasia, a plan for 'depositing' all old men

---

[9] *The Poetry of Experience: The Dramatic Monologue in Modern Literary Tradition* (New York: Random House, 1957). I have argued further about the problems of sympathy and judgement in an article, 'Rhetorical Irony, the Dramatic Monologue, and Tennyson's *Poems* (1842)', *PQ*, 53 (1974), 220–36.

of a certain age for a year, then killing and cremating them. Trollope is reported to have exclaimed, 'It's all true—I *mean* every word of it',[10] apparently suggesting that he supported the scheme. Not everyone has given much weight to that report, however,[11] and Trollope's actual belief is in any case less important than the fact that our initial repulsion toward President Neverbend and his monstrous idea is gradually replaced by a fascination with his character, a growing sympathy for him and even for his plan. Trollope arranges things so that Neverbend's wife is given all the best humane arguments against the President and his scheme and then demonstrates her own inhumanity by deserting him in a crisis. Even more important than this *ad hominem* argument is the fact that Neverbend has not only anticipated all the arguments against the system but actually holds these contrary views himself. He feels all the 'natural' objections to the fixed period very strongly, yet he still believes in the system. The degradation and pain of old age are horrible to him, and he is deeply sensitive to the grim parody of natural life cycles men now create with war, poverty, and murder. As a result he envisions a state where death can be made more fully legitimate. There is no capital punishment, no war, no use of death as a weapon. Death, he says, is not naturally a punishment and can be, if we are strong and rational enough, a controlled and understandable finish to life. Terror, thus, is at least diminished and dignity is allowed.

It is true, of course, that the scheme is also satirized, but all the satire comes early in the novel, as if to drain it out of our system. We are allowed to exercise ridicule, but only so that we will expose and in a way understand the inadequacy of such a response. Neverbend at first mixes in with some good points arguments for the fixed period that are absurdly utilitarian, talking about how costly it is to feed old people, for instance. The cost is great with young people too, for that matter, but 'children . . . are clearly necessary' (1). Lucky for them, we feel, or they might be down in this Benthamite slaughterer's books. He likewise is a defender of euphemism, remembering with fury the time his opponents brought up the annoying word 'murder' (1). He seems a rational monster, irritated that people should object to the depositing of the first subject, Mr.

10 See [Lucas Collins], 'Autobiography of Anthony Trollope', p. 594.

11 Cockshut says that the narrator 'has nothing in common with the author' (*Anthony Trollope*, p. 91), and David Skilton ('*The Fixed Period*: Anthony Trollope's Novel of 1980', *Studies in the Literary Imagination*, 6, 1973, 41) says the novel marks 'Trollope's longest exercise of the use of an unreliable narrator'.

Crasweller, all such objections being illogical and therefore invalid:
'it angered me to think that men should be so little reasonable as to
draw deductions as to an entire system from a single instance' (2).
The novel does seem to be conducting an attack on some half-blind
monster, an attack made accidentally more ominous for modern
readers by such touches as the huge crematorium ovens. Neverbend's wife seems to have the final word: 'It's all very well for the
Assembly; but when you come to killing poor Mr. Crasweller in
real life, it is quite out of the question' (4).

But then the change begins. The dark eloquence of the system
begins gradually to emerge, and we sense that it is the scheme of
a man who is intensely sensitive, not brutal. Neverbend is gradually
humanized, by his love for his son, his humour, and his self-doubt.
And when the English gunboats arrive to capture the President and
enforce humanitarian values with some terrible doomsday weapon,
the switch is completed. The President is captured and told he is to
be shipped off, an act which makes his family 'not very unhappy'
(10). But, alone as he is, he refuses to quit fighting. He has one
more chance, and this a brilliant one, to make his case against the
English idiots. His captors stupidly allow a kind of public debate,
which gives Neverbend a chance to demolish his opponent's views
and assert his own higher humanism. He easily blocks every argument. The Englishman speaks about leaving death to the Almighty,
but Neverbend replies with great power on how the English have in
fact followed that doctrine, with their armies and executioners. His
point throughout is that the Almighty, left to his own devices, does
not do very well with death. One might as well make no attempt to
control fire as abandon death to God.

Neverbend, however, is taken aboard the gunboat and shipped
back to England, a place where he knows that he will have little
chance against their hardened acceptance of death in every grotesque
form. England's culture is built on death, and Neverbend knows he
will make no converts there. He exclaims at the end that his position
is the most piteous and hopeless in the world and then turns and,
in the last words of the novel, 'went down to complete my manuscript'. He understands finally that no one will on any account be
taught, but he proceeds with the textbook anyhow. It is a fine
irrational ending for the dramatic monologue. Like Childe Roland,
he realizes he is going nowhere but tramps along with great determination all the same.

The finest of all these novels held open by thematic ambiguity is *Mr. Scarborough's Family*. The action is carefully structured, with two constrasting plots and a connecting link. Both plots concern money, wills, threatened disinheritance. The link is provided by the lawyer charged with managing all these complex matters. He is also charged with representing the old gentlemanly code of truth and honour in a world that has passed by such trifles as morality. The only other real alternative presented is the radical morality of old Mr. Scarborough. Liar and law-breaker that he is, Mr. Scarborough is a moral man by his lights—and perhaps by ours. It is a question of giving to him not so much moral as imaginative approval. We must participate in his witty and creative search for a new and adequate set of principles. That the search is a futile one is fitting to this ironic fable, as are the terrible conditions under which Mr. Scarborough works: through 'surgical tortures and operations, and, in fact, slowly dying during the whole period that he had been thus busy' (58).

But there is a comic plot too, as the narrator says: 'While some men die others are marrying' (59). This sounds very much like the line in *The Winter's Tale* that announces the transition to comedy: 'Thou mettest with things dying, I with things newborn' (III. iii). But here comedy never really surfaces. It develops only in a shadow plot, which is used to highlight the major action by the curious parodying device used so often in the early drama Trollope so admired. Mr. Scarborough's genuine anguish is mocked by the fake anguish of Peter Prosper: ' "It's the last drawing-room carpet I shall ever buy", he said to himself, with true melancholy, as he walked back home across the park' (64). The happy marriage at the end of this minor plot comes about, the heroine says simply, because she has realized that 'one has to risk dangers in the world, but one makes the risk as little as possible' (64). In the real world one risks everything whether one likes it or not; there are no guarantees and no easy acceptances. The Peter Prosper plot, however, gives those mocking reminders of certainties, the comic protections against any mistakes. Like Scarborough, Prosper is mistreated by his heir and withdraws with his hurt feelings and his foolishness into a kind of sulking isolation, communicating freely only to his contemptuous butler. Continuing the parody of the Scarborough plot, he then threatens his heir, appropriately with the comic weapon of marriage. He will get himself a new heir on his own, he says. But he meets in

Miss Thoroughbung, whom he at first believes suitable for the
honour of giving him a son, a good deal more than his match.
He cannot even use his celebrated letters effectively and is completely humiliated. He feels for a time genuinely alone, believing
that everyone wants him dead (51). For just a moment he seems to
be demanding the sort of attention and sympathy we give to Mr.
Scarborough. Even his illness appears to be real enough. Only when
Peter hops from his bed to be reconciled with the heir, blesses
everyone, and tells them all to come and live with him for six months
each year do we recognize his low spirits as a parody of Mr. Scarborough's slow battle with death. Everything in this minor plot is,
as the heroine says, 'in the common way' (14).

But the main plot emphasizes 'singularity' as its dominant motif.
Mr. Scarborough is able to accommodate himself to nothing and
has therefore to exercise his craft as quietly and shrewdly as he can.
He has married his wife in two separate ceremonies, keeping the
first one a secret in order to have some control over the just distribu-
tion of his estate. By such devices he seeks to subvert the law, which
he sees as unjust, inequitable, positively illegal. Trollope sets this
person before us with a myriad of small distinctions: Mr. Scarborough is, for instance, 'anxious above all things for [his children's]
welfare, or rather happiness' (1). Such distinctions do not so much
explain the major character as present him from a hundred different
perspectives so that by the end of the novel we can feel him as a
presence and therefore 'know' him. We necessarily feel his distrust
of social stability and his sense that genuine life must be sought
outside convention. His fight to provide such a life for his children
may be mistaken, but there is never any question that it is generous
and courageous. It is, simply, heroic, and this subtle establishment
of Mr. Scarborough at the centre of the novel is one of the best
examples of Trollope's mature art.[12]

Now and then there are direct statements of support for this
character: he is called 'upright and honourable' even though he is
certainly not 'respectable' (1). But generally the means for enlisting
our sympathy are more indirect: his enemies are quietly discredited,
and the damage he does is trivialized. He cheats the money-lenders,
but we are encouraged to think that they deserve it. They seem to

---

[12] The best treatment of Mr. Scarborough, by Cockshut, seems to me spoiled by the
assertion, based on a misreading, that Scarborough 'is a maniac' (*Anthony Trollope*,
p. 234).

think so themselves, entering good-naturedly into the fun and becoming 'extremely jocose' over the chance to play the ironic role of
'the honest, injured party': 'Thief! scoundrel! 'orrid old man! It
ain't for myself that I'm speaking now. . . . It's for humanity at
large. This kind of thing wiolates one's best feelings' (36). Mr.
Scarborough is justified finally, however, not by his victims so much
as by the world in which he lives. It is a world in which all conventional pleasure has gone sour, where even fox-hunting turns into
undignified rows. People presumably amusing themselves 'fight on
the road for the maintenance of a trifling right of sport' (29). The
image of Monte Carlo is evoked throughout as particularly ex-
planatory. There pleasure is made possible by death; the free con-
certs and lush surroundings are very nice, 'but by whom—out of
whose pocket are all these good things provided? . . . He has given
his all for the purpose, and has then—blown his brains out. It is
one of the disagreeable incidents to which the otherwise extremely
pleasant money-making operations of the establishment are liable.'
The narrator says sarcastically that he feels 'somewhat shabby' for
having taken advantage of the pleasantness without putting himself
'in the way of having to cut my throat' (11). Commerce, exploita-
tion, murder are inextricably mixed and together now replace the
old pleasures. It is significant that Monte Carlo is so popular with
the English, who look upon it as a kind of Eden (11).

In such a world Mr. Scarborough's efforts 'to do justice to my
own child' can be effective only if he proceeds by 'rectifying the
gross injustice of the world' (8). A kind of moral-philosophical
Robin Hood, then, he has a special sort of *duty* quite distinct from
the old aristocratic notions of responsibility: 'I do not care two
straws about doing my duty, young man . . . Or rather, in seeking
my duty, I look beyond the conventionalities of the world' (56). He
is eager to explain that he has broken the law in order to obey
a higher law (21). Using such arguments, he aligns himself with
a form of justice we customarily associate with radical reformers,
martyrs, and saints. It would seem to be a kind of vigilante justice, of
course, but for the fact that Mr. Scarborough is so heroically
isolated. He wants no mob to support him.

Despite his isolation, his secretiveness, and his unconventional
ethics, he brings nearly everyone who comes to know him into his
sphere. Trollope makes a very effective use of moral reflectors here
to influence us toward Mr. Scarborough. Especially prominent is

Mr. Merton, a conventionally honourable man serving as Mr. Scarborough's physician-secretary. Precisely because Scarborough's honour exists outside standard forms, Merton is at first puzzled by his patient's life and finds himself unable 'to make up his mind whether he most admired his patron's philosophy or condemned his general lack of principle' (38). Finally, however, he cannot resist: 'I think that he has within him a capacity for love, and an unselfishness, which almost atones for his dishonesty' (53). He sees that a defence of Mr. Scarborough is a corresponding attack on the morality he has lived by, but he is drawn against his will toward that position: 'One cannot make an apology for him without being ready to throw all truth and all morality to the dogs. But if you can imagine for yourself a state of things in which neither truth nor morality shall be thought essential, then old Mr. Scarborough would be your hero' (58). Conventional truth and conventional morality are indeed both inessential and irrelevant, and Mr. Scarborough is therefore certainly our hero, one of the very few absolute heroes in Trollope. The long narrative analysis of this character in Chapter 58 depends upon a range of diction Trollope usually avoided. It is both emotional and abstract, supporting this genuinely larger-than-life hero.

Hero that he is, he is able to accomplish nothing. He has gleefully seen his situation as 'a complication of romances' (7) entirely of his own making and under his power, and he has boasted that in such arrangements 'I have allowed no outward circumstances to control me' (21). Proud of his defiance of great physical suffering as a sign of his control over all of life, he repeats at the moment of his death a belief in his superiority to 'actual circumstances' (56). But he finally has as little control over circumstances as he has over the inevitable course of his illness. He can only retard but not alter their grim workings. Life goes on pretty much as if he had not lived. One of his sons, Augustus, inherits his father's thirst for the unconventional without his morality and vanishes ominously into the City at the end. The other son, Captain Mountjoy, has great promise, but it comes to nothing. His father learns to love him and to recognize the virtues that are implicit within his elder boy. Mountjoy grows in everyone else's estimation too. When he is granted the estate, the action teases us into hoping for a comic resolution. But 'though it seemed to his father and to the people around him at Tretton that he had everything a man could want, he had in fact nothing,—nothing that could satisfy him' (41). He is denied the only thing he wants: the love of Florence, the heroine of the other plot. The artistic satisfactions available to his father in fabricating a new morality do not interest him, and he is, therefore, caught in the immoral world. In a crucial scene, he passes through London, with all problems apparently ready to melt before him. But he cannot resist a ruinous gambling expedition. When the kindly lawyer Mr. Grey tells him that he has been victimized by scoundrels, Mountjoy honestly denies it: 'I am one of them' (49). Mr. Scarborough's alternate morality, for all its apparent force, is finally dissipated miserably.

But the conventional morality is equally impotent. Such traditional distinctions as Grey tries to make between the scoundrels and the innocent victims are now absurdly out of date. A man who insists on maintaining them has no place in this world. Mr. Grey tells old Scarborough that he has himself always 'encouraged an obedience to the laws of my country' (19), but Scarborough sees that the law-abiding man can no longer be the truly moral man. Grey tries to hold law and morality in balance and thus appears to Scarborough to be 'an ass' (21). Grey, correspondingly, thinks Scarborough 'the wickedest man the world ever produced' (17). Still, they love one another (see chs. 21 and 39) with a warmth particularly inexplicable to Grey. Each cannot but recognize instinctively the basic decency in the other, even though they are driven so far apart by the incoherence of things as they are.

Grey clings to legality and cannot tolerate Mr. Scarborough's trespasses against that law. 'It is', he says, 'impossible that I should forgive him,' not only because he has through his tricks 'destroyed my character as a lawyer' (55) but because his eccentric morality attacks the very foundations of Grey's life and beliefs. Ironically, Grey finds it necessary to declare his separation from Scarborough at precisely the point at which the world, understanding nothing, begins to admire the old man's rascality. The best men around are thus divided by the absurd stupidity now rampant: 'Everyone concerned in the matter seemed to admire Mr. Scarborough; except Mr. Grey, whose anger either with himself or with his client, became the stronger, the louder grew the admiration of the world' (58). Grey's anger is strong partly because it is so confused. He blames both Scarborough and himself, since there is no other real villain except 'the world'. Failing to understand either Scarborough's radical morality or Grey's traditional morality, the world none the less sweeps past them, leaving them both in meaningless isolation. Grey's partner, Mr. Barry, understands the world much better and sees that the law can adapt itself very well to the new condition of things if only one recognizes the 'folly' of principle and truth-telling (58). Barry makes Grey realize how anachronistic he has become: '"Old times are changed," he said to himself; "old manners gone"' (58). He sees that more really than manners has gone, and he becomes very bitter. 'As things go now,' he says, 'a man has to be accounted a fool if he attempts to run straight'. He sees that by this new and alien 'system' he is one of those fools. 'It may be that I am a fool, and that my idea of honesty is a mistake', he thinks, but he will not ever abandon that folly: 'When I find that clever rascals are respectable, I think it is time that I should give up work altogether' (62). We say good-bye to the honest lawyer in a chapter entitled 'The Last of Mr. Grey'. He and his values are extinguished even before he dies.

The fight is carried on only by his daughter. Her continuing attachment to the old ways is now so bizarre that she appears freakish. There is no visible support for these values except in her father, so she clings to him with a tenacity and fierceness that are deliberately made to appear perverse. She is called the 'conscience' of the law and thus can hardly have a place in the firm ruled by Mr. Barry. When that partner proposes marriage, hoping no doubt to incorporate even the old 'conscience' of the law into his new system, she says, 'Solitude I could bear,—and death; but not such a marriage' (52). The terms seem excessive and melodramatic, but she has, in fact, outlined accurately her alternatives. When her father asks her whom she *would* choose as a husband, she can only answer helplessly, 'You' (33). Trollope's most open excursion into twisted sexuality marks an appropriate symbol for a world that so distorts all the values which count.

The values which count are all there in a rush in *Ayala's Angel*. The novel is Trollope's one true romance, a pattern which forces mundane experience to elevate itself to the ideal, not the reverse. Ayala need not compromise her dream; she simply must realize it. For much of its length, the novel looks a little as if it might depend upon mild and happy disillusionment, but the illusions instead are made substantial. It is above all a novel about art, an art of free pleasure and delicate beauty. Though submerged for a time, art is kept alive in the minds of all the characters and is, in the end, given strong, even gross concrete support. The reintegration of art and life, the ethereal with the material, is the purpose and dynamic of the novel. Art is rigorously conventionalized. All eccentric posings are dismissed as immature and really unnecessary since there is finally no conflict between the artist and the world. Art is realized *in* life, not in opposition to it, not even in opposition to commercial life.

Even the villains are not very threatening. They are mostly the mild and funny enemies of art, the vulgarians. Septimus Traffick is the major offender, never quite realizing Sir Thomas's desperate desire to get rid of this leeching son-in-law who will not leave his house. Traffick absorbs Sir Thomas's most ingenious rudeness like a jellyfish: 'He does become very rough sometimes, but I know that at bottom he has a thorough respect for me. It is only that induces me to bear it' (30). His major crime is that he is a bore; it is he who 'writes all those letters in the Times about supply and demand' (5). But when Ayala dismisses him as a man of business rather than a man of art, the narrator even here jokingly corrects her and denies the distinction: 'Mr. Traffick no doubt would have enjoyed [waterfalls and sylvan forests] very well if he could have spared the time' (5). The harmony is so pervasive that no one is excluded.

The values are, however, truly extraordinary. We are repeatedly encouraged by a gentle sarcasm to side with the pretty, not the virtuous: 'There was much pity felt for Ayala among the folk at Stalham. The sympathies of them all should have been with Mrs. Dosett. They ought to have felt that the poor aunt was simply performing an unpleasant duty, and that the girl was impracticable if not disobedient. But Ayala was known to be very pretty, and Mrs. Dosett was supposed to be plain. Ayala was interesting, while Mrs. Dosett, from the nature of her circumstances, was most uninteresting' (22). Poor Mrs. Dosett says, 'If there is anything I do hate it is romance, while bread and meat, and coals, and washing, are so dear' (39). But even her husband has some aesthetic sense hidden away, and Mrs. Dosett's anti-romanticism, even her poor, mean, struggling life are granted no respect and as little sympathy. Our sympathies are all with Ayala, who is corrected but in the pleasantest and most happily surprising way imaginable.

She feels that she has been cast among the Philistines: 'Sir Thomas had a way,—a merit shall we call it or a fault?—of pouring

out his wealth upon the family as though it were water running in
perpetuity from a mountain tarn. Ayala the romantic, Ayala the
poetic, found very soon that she did not like it' (5). The phrasing
is wonderfully satiric, but it attacks not so much Ayala's romanticism as her mistaken notion that others are not as romantic as she.
When young Tom proposes to her, 'it was the outrage to her taste
rather than to her conduct which afflicted her' (8). She does not
see how similar to her he is, despite his hobbledehoy mooniness and
all those gorgeous rings. She creates for herself a false isolation,
believing her father's self-aggrandizing nonsense about the necessary embattled alienation of the artist. As a result, she fails for a
time to see the art all around her.

More specifically, she fails to recognize the angelic in the hideously
ugly Colonel Stubbs. He is, for one thing, entirely without the
gloomy sublimity of tragedy, and the Angel of Light she carries
around in her mind as an ideal 'must have something tragic in his
composition,—must verge, at any rate, on tragedy' (16). So she
refuses him. Lady Albury says her refusal 'is what I call romance.
. . . Romance can never make you happy' (26). Wrong on both
counts. The true romance comes in accepting him; what's more,
romance will always make you happy. Stubbs sees all this, vowing
'to soar till I can approach your dreams' (25). Ayala clings for a long
time to the insubstantiality of her ideal, the notion that her angel
must be 'altogether unalloyed by the grossness of the earth . . . of
the heaven, celestial' (45). Such tenacity suggests neither an asinine
fantasy nor a neurosis, as we would expect. Ayala for a time almost
believes herself that her dream has been immature nonsense, but
the narrator explains it all to us clearly: 'That the dreams had
been all idle she declared to herself,—not aware that the Ayala
whom her lover had loved would not have been an Ayala to be loved
by him, but for the dreams' (51). She never does have to give up
her dreams, finding that Stubbs 'was in truth the very "Angel of
Light"' (55). In a sense, we recognize the inevitability of this
romantic outcome right from the start. Anyone with a name like
Ayala walking by a man with such an unpromising name as Jonathan
Stubbs in, of all places, Gobblegoose wood is sure to find the bear
to be really a handsome prince, the wood his palace.

Ayala's sister Lucy finds an equally successful but somewhat more
prosaic romance with her artist lover, Isadore Hamel. Lucy is cast
into a world 'altogether without adornment', with nothing but 'the

harsh voice and the odious common sense of her Aunt Dosett' (2). It is the harshness of the unpleasing voice that is hardest to bear. Nor does Sir Thomas's well-meaning munificence at first make matters easier. He suggests to the somewhat Wildean Hamel that he have a public auction of his mythological sculptures to see if he could not unload some of them into merchants' gardens. Hamel blinks in disbelief and then sniffs loudly. The narrator, anxious to hold back nothing in this surprisingly undeceptive story, sets it all straight for us: Hamel believes that 'to create something beautiful was almost divine. To manipulate millions till they should breed other millions was the meanest occupation for a life's energy. It was thus, I fear, that Mr. Hamel looked at the business carried on in Lombard Street, being as yet very young in the world and seeing many things with distorted eyes' (33). Hamel is patiently educated, finally coming to see that 'Sir Thomas was right' (63), that art must be incorporated into the basic fabric of life—even the life of Mr. Jones the wool-merchant. Sir Thomas effectively presides over both plots, granting his commercial, and thus artistic, blessings everywhere.

Many on the outskirts are lured into the blessed world. The originally cynical Frank Houston experiences as much of a reformation as Trollope will ever allow and, encouraged by a wildly romantic old aunt, casts his lot in with his painting and a penniless sweetheart. 'I, speaking for myself, have hopes of Frank Houston' (64), says the romantic narrator, and he is not alone. The romance spreads out like a magic spell. One Lord John Battledore, a by-word for crass worldliness, maintains that he is 'horrified,—nay, disgusted' by Houston's mad imprudence; 'nevertheless, before the end of the year, he was engaged to marry a very pretty girl as devoid of fortune as our Ayala' (63).

Even poor Tom Tringle, wildly in love with Ayala, is not left long in disappointment. He acts his part in the romance very well, as his mother points out: 'He is just for all the world like those young men we read of who do all manner of horrible things for love,—smothering themselves and their young women with charcoal, or throwing them into the Regent's Canal' (40). He is saved from charcoal and the canal, however, so it is certainly no more than we would expect when he is granted new life. He is sent on a recuperative tour, a therapy which, for once, works wonderfully, taking effect perhaps even before the boat docks: 'I have no doubt that

Tom was cured, if not before he reached New York, at any rate before he left that interesting city' (61). He is 'our hero', and the narrator urges, 'Let us, who have soft hearts, now throw our old shoes after him' (61). Trollope does not quite become Mr. Popular Sentiment, but the appeal to us soft-hearts can, just the same, hardly fail to work.

With all this behind us, it is perhaps safest and wisest to mumble a few words about diversity and then rush off to an appendix or a bibliography. I plan to do little more. But one point should be stressed. Throughout Trollope's career, from the simplest short stories to the great achievement of the two chronicles, he strove to diversify and thus rescue the world of instinctive, sensitive morality. Even in the very toughest novels, the agonies come from the apparent absence of those values that would affirm a solid basis on which honourable men could act. Trollope never quite believed, as Orwell says Dickens did, that if only men would behave decently the world would be decent. He saw that decent behaviour required a substantial support from language itself and from a sense of coherent order reflected in language. Decent men, then, like the Duke of Omnium or Mr. Scarborough, cannot depend on their own behaviour as a reflex of other men's belief. Behaviour, as they discover, may be a reflex of nothing. Still, in the end the only values that seem sane or worthy of support are those which can no longer be maintained, the simple and beautiful values basic to the comedy of manners: men are as they act. Despite the exercise of as much ingenuity and as much subtlety as nineteenth-century English literature has to offer, Trollope was unable to bring these assumptions back into being for very long. But he never gave up trying.

BIBLIOGRAPHY OF
ANTHONY TROLLOPE

Like all lists of Trollope's works, this one is heavily indebted to Michael Sadleir's *Trollope: A Bibliography* (London: Constable, 1928).

The Macdermots of Ballycloran: A Novel. 3 vols. London: T. C. Newby, 1847.

The Kellys and the O'Kellys. 3 vols. London: Henry Colburn, 1848.

La Vendée. 3 vols. London: Henry Colburn, 1850.

The Warden. 1 vol. London: Longman, Brown, Green, and Longmans, 1855 [Dec. 1854].

Barchester Towers. 3 vols. London: Longman, Brown, Green, Longmans, and Roberts, 1857.

The Three Clerks: A Novel. 3 vols. London: Richard Bentley, 1858 [Nov. 1857].

Doctor Thorne: A Novel. 3 vols. London: Chapman and Hall, 1858.

The Bertrams: A Novel. 3 vols. London: Chapman and Hall, 1859.

The West Indies and the Spanish Main. 1 vol. London: Chapman and Hall, 1859.

Castle Richmond: A Novel. 3 vols. London: Chapman and Hall, 1860.

Framley Parsonage. 3 vols. London: Smith, Elder, 1861. Serialized in *Cornhill Magazine*, Jan. 1860–Apr. 1861.

Tales of All Countries [First Series]. 1 vol. London: Chapman and Hall, 1861. Serialized in *Harper's New Monthly Magazine* and *Cassell's Illustrated Family Paper*, May–Oct. 1860.

Orley Farm. 2 vols. London: Chapman and Hall, 1862. Published in twenty, shilling, monthly parts from Mar. 1861 to Oct. 1862 by Chapman and Hall.

North America. 2 vols. London: Chapman and Hall, 1862.

The Struggles of Brown, Jones and Robinson: by One of the Firm. 1 vol. New York: Harper and Brothers, 1862. First English edition in 1870 by Smith, Elder and Co. Serialized in *Cornhill Magazine*, Aug. 1861–Mar. 1862.

Tales of All Countries: Second Series. 1 vol. London: Chapman and Hall, 1863. Serialized in *Public Opinion, London Review*, and *The Illustrated London News*, Jan.–Dec. 1861.

Rachel Ray: A Novel. 2 vols. London: Chapman and Hall, 1863 [Oct. 1862].

The Small House at Allington. 2 vols. London: Smith, Elder, 1864. Serialized in *Cornhill Magazine*, Sept. 1862–Apr. 1864.

Can You Forgive Her? 2 vols. London: Chapman and Hall, 1864. Published in twenty, shilling, monthly parts from Jan. 1864 to Aug. 1865 by Chapman and Hall.

Miss Mackenzie. 2 vols. London: Chapman and Hall, 1865.

Hunting Sketches. 1 vol. London: Chapman and Hall, 1865. First published in *Pall Mall Gazette*, Feb. 1865–Mar. 1865.

The Belton Estate. 3 vols. London: Chapman and Hall, 1866 [Dec. 1865]. Serialized in the *Fortnightly Review*, May 1865–Jan. 1866.

Travelling Sketches. 1 vol. London: Chapman and Hall, 1866. First published in *Pall Mall Gazette*, Aug.–Sept. 1865.

Clergymen of the Church of England. 1 vol. London: Chapman and Hall, 1866. First published in *Pall Mall Gazette*, Nov. 1865–Jan. 1866.

Nina Balatka. 2 vols. Edinburgh and London: William Blackwood, 1867. Serialized in *Blackwood's Magazine*, July 1866–Jan. 1867.

The Last Chronicle of Barset. 2 vols. London: Smith, Elder, 1867. Published in thirty-two, sixpenny parts from Dec. 1866 to July 1867 by Smith, Elder.

The Claverings. 2 vols. London: Smith, Elder, 1867. Serialized in *Cornhill Magazine*, Feb. 1866–May 1867.

Lotta Schmidt: and Other Stories. 1 vol. London: Alexander Strahan, 1867. First published in four different magazines from 1861 to 1867.

Linda Tressel. 2 vols. Edinburgh and London: William Blackwood, 1868. Serialized in *Blackwood's Magazine*, Oct. 1867–May 1868.

Phineas Finn: The Irish Member. 2 vols. London: Virtue, 1869. Serialized in *Saint Paul's Magazine*, Oct. 1867–May 1869.

He Knew He Was Right. 2 vols. London: Strahan, 1869. Published in thirty-two, weekly, sixpenny parts from Oct. 1868 to May 1869 by Virtue, the last three numbers being issued in parallel by Strahan.

Did He Steal It? A Comedy in Three Acts. London, 1869.

The Vicar of Bullhampton. 1 vol. London: Bradbury, Evans, 1870. Published in monthly parts from July 1869 to May 1870 by Bradbury, Evans.

An Editor's Tales. 1 vol. London: Strahan, 1870. First published in *Saint Paul's Magazine*, Oct. 1869–May 1870.

The Commentaries of Caesar. 1 vol. Edinburgh and London: William Blackwood, 1870.

Sir Harry Hotspur of Humblethwaite. 1 vol. London: Hurst and Blackett, 1871 [Nov. 1870]. Serialized in *Macmillan's Magazine*, May 1870–Dec. 1870.

Ralph the Heir. 3 vols. London: Hurst and Blackett, 1871. Published in nineteen, sixpenny, monthly parts from Jan. 1870 to July 1871 by Strahan and simultaneously as a supplement to *Saint Paul's Magazine.*

The Golden Lion of Granpère. 1 vol. London: Tinsley, 1872. Serialized in *Good Words*, Jan. 1872–Aug. 1872.

The Eustace Diamonds. 3 vols. London: Chapman and Hall, 1873 [Dec. 1872]. Serialized in the *Fortnightly Review*, July 1871–Feb. 1873.

Australia and New Zealand. 2 vols. London: Chapman and Hall, 1873.

Phineas Redux. 2 vols. London: Chapman and Hall, 1874 [Dec. 1873]. Serialized in *The Graphic*, July 1873–Jan. 1874.

Lady Anna. 2 vols. London: Chapman and Hall, 1874. Serialized in the *Fortnightly Review*, Apr. 1873–Apr. 1874.

Harry Heathcote of Gangoil: A Tale of Australian Bush Life. 1 vol. London: Sampson Low, 1874. First published as the Christmas number in *The Graphic*, Dec. 1873.

The Way We Live Now. 2 vols. London: Chapman and Hall, 1875. Published in twenty, monthly, shilling parts, Feb. 1874–Sept. 1875 by Chapman and Hall.

The Prime Minister. 4 vols. London: Chapman and Hall, 1876. Published in eight, monthly, five-shilling parts from Nov. 1875 to June 1876 by Chapman and Hall.

The American Senator. 3 vols. London: Chapman and Hall, 1877. Serialized in *Temple Bar*, May 1876–July 1877.

South Africa. 2 vols. London: Chapman and Hall, 1878.

Is He Popenjoy?: A Novel. 3 vols. London: Chapman and Hall, 1878. Serialized in *All the Year Round*, Oct. 1877–July 1878.

How the 'Mastiffs' Went to Iceland. 1 vol. London: Virtue, 1878.

An Eye for an Eye. 2 vols. London: Chapman and Hall, 1879. Serialized in *Whitehall Review*, Aug. 1878–Feb. 1879.

Thackeray. 1 vol. London: Macmillan, 1879.

John Caldigate. 3 vols. London: Chapman and Hall, 1879. Serialized in *Blackwood's Magazine*, Apr. 1878–June 1879.

Cousin Henry: A Novel. 2 vols. London: Chapman and Hall, 1879. Serialized simultaneously in the *Manchester Weekly Times* and the *North British Weekly Mail* from 8 Mar. 1879 to 24 May 1879.

The Duke's Children: A Novel. 3 vols. London: Chapman and Hall, 1880. Serialized in *All the Year Round*, Oct. 1879–July 1880.

The Life of Cicero. 2 vols. London: Chapman and Hall, 1880.

Dr. Wortle's School: A Novel. 2 vols. London: Chapman and Hall, 1881. Serialized in *Blackwood's Magazine*, May 1880–Dec. 1880.

Ayala's Angel. 3 vols. London: Chapman and Hall, 1881.

Why Frau Frohmann Raised Her Prices: And Other Stories. 1 vol. London: William Isbister, 1882. First published in four magazines between 1876 and 1878.

Lord Palmerston ('English Political Leaders'). 1 vol. London: William Isbister, 1882.

Marion Fay: A Novel. 3 vols. London: Chapman and Hall, 1882. Serialized in *The Graphic*, Dec. 1881–June 1882.

Kept in the Dark: A Novel. 2 vols. London: Chatto and Windus, 1882. Serialized in *Good Words*, May 1882–Dec. 1882.

The Fixed Period: A Novel. 2 vols. Edinburgh and London: William Blackwood, 1882. Serialized in *Blackwood's Magazine*, Oct. 1881–Mar. 1882.

Mr. Scarborough's Family. 3 vols. London: Chatto and Windus, 1883. Serialized in *All the Year Round*, May 1882–June 1883.

The Landleaguers. 3 vols. London: Chatto and Windus, 1883. Serialized in *Life*, Nov. 1882–Oct. 1883.

An Autobiography. 2 vols. Edinburgh and London: William Blackwood, 1883.

An Old Man's Love. 2 vols. Edinburgh and London: William Blackwood, 1884.

The Noble Jilt. 1 vol. London: Constable, 1923.

London Tradesmen. 1 vol. London: Mathews and Marrot, 1927. First published in the *Pall Mall Gazette*, July 1880–Sept. 1880.

Four Lectures. Ed. by Morris L. Parrish. London: Constable, 1938.

Letters. 1 vol. Ed. by Bradford Allen Booth. London: Oxford Univ. Press, 1951.

The Two Heroines of Plumplington. New York: Oxford Univ. Press, 1954. Originally published as the Christmas Number of *Good Words*, 25 Dec. 1882.

The New Zealander. Ed. by N. John Hall. London: Oxford Univ. Press, 1972.

LIST OF EDITIONS USED

The American Senator. The World's Classics, 391. London: Oxford Univ. Press, 1931.

Australia and New Zealand. 2nd ed. The Colonial History Series, ed. by D. H. Simpson. 2 vols. London: Dawsons, 1968.

An Autobiography. Intro. and notes by Michael Sadleir. Pref. by Henry M. Trollope. The World's Classics, 239. London: Oxford Univ. Press, 1923.

Ayala's Angel. The World's Classics, 342. London: Oxford Univ. Press, 1929.

Barchester Towers. Everyman's Library, ed. by Ernest Rhys. London: J. M. Dent; New York: E. P. Dutton, 1906.

The Belton Estate. The World's Classics, 251. London: Oxford Univ. Press, 1923.

The Bertrams. New York: Harper and Brothers, 1859.

Can You Forgive Her? Intro. by Michael Sadleir. Pref. by Edward Marsh. The Oxford Trollope Crown Edition, ed. by Michael Sadleir and Frederick Page. 2 vols. London: Oxford Univ. Press, 1948.

Castle Richmond. London: Chapman and Hall, 1877.

The Claverings. The World's Classics, 152. London: Oxford Univ. Press, 1924.

Clergymen of the Church of England. London: Chapman and Hall, 1866.

The Commentaries of Caesar. Ancient Classics for English Readers, ed. by the Rev. W. L. Collins. Philadelphia: J. B. Lippincott, 1872.

Cousin Henry. The World's Classics, 343. London: Oxford Univ. Press, 1929.

Did He Steal It? A Comedy in Three Acts. London, 1869.

Doctor Thorne. Intro. by Elizabeth Bowen. Boston: Houghton Mifflin, 1959.

Dr. Wortle's School. The World's Classics, 337. London: Oxford Univ. Press, 1928.

The Duke's Children. Pref. by Chauncey B. Tinker. 1954; rpt. London: Oxford Univ. Press, 1973.

An Editor's Tales. London: Strahan, 1870.

The Eustace Diamonds. Pref. by Michael Sadleir. The Oxford Trollope Crown Edition, ed. by Michael Sadleir and Frederick Page. 2 vols. 1950; rpt. London: Oxford Univ. Press, 1973.

An Eye for an Eye. Intro. by Simon Raven. The Doughty Library, no. 1, ed. by Herbert van Thal. London: Anthony Blond, 1966.

The Fixed Period. 2 vols. Edinburgh and London: William Blackwood, 1882.

Four Lectures. Ed. by Morris L. Parrish. London: Constable, 1938.

Framley Parsonage. London: The Zodiac Press, 1962.

The Golden Lion of Granpère. The World's Classics, 504. London: Oxford Univ. Press, 1946.

Harry Heathcote of Gangoil: A Tale of Australian Bush Life. Intro. by Marcie Muir. Melbourne: Landsdowne Press, 1963.

He Knew He Was Right. The World's Classics, 507. London: Oxford Univ. Press, 1948.

How the 'Mastiffs' Went to Iceland. London: Virtue, 1878.

Hunting Sketches. New York: Arno Press, 1967.

Is He Popenjoy? The World's Classics, 492. 2 vols. London: Oxford Univ. Press, 1944.

John Caldigate. The World's Classics, 502. London: Oxford Univ. Press, 1946.

The Kellys and the O'Kellys. Intro. by Shane Leslie. New York: Random House, 1937.

Kept in the Dark: A Novel. 2 vols. London: Chatto and Windus, 1882.

La Vendée. London: Ward, Lock, [1878].

Lady Anna. The World's Classics, 443. London: Oxford Univ. Press, 1936.

The Landleaguers. 3 vols. London: Chatto and Windus, 1883.

The Last Chronicle of Barset. Ed. with intro. and notes by Arthur Mizener. Boston: Houghton Mifflin, 1964.

Letters. Ed. by Bradford Allen Booth. London: Oxford Univ. Press, 1951.

The Life of Cicero. 2 vols. London: Chapman and Hall, 1880.

Linda Tressel. The World's Classics. London: Oxford Univ. Press, 1946.

London Tradesmen. Forward by Michael Sadleir. London: Mathews and Marrot; New York: Charles Scribner's Sons, 1927.

Lord Palmerston. London: William Isbister, 1882.

Lotta Schmidt: And Other Stories. London: Strahan, 1867.

The Macdermots of Ballycloran. New York: F. M. Lupton, n.d.

Marion Fay. Leipzig: Tauchnitz, 1882.

Miss Mackenzie. The World's Classics, 278. London: Oxford Univ. Press, 1924.

Mr. Scarborough's Family. The World's Classics, 503. London: Oxford Univ. Press, 1946.

The New Zealander. Ed. with intro. by N. John Hall. London: Oxford Univ. Press, 1972.

Nina Balatka. The World's Classics, 505. London: Oxford Univ. Press, 1946.

The Noble Jilt: A Comedy. Ed. with a pref. by Michael Sadleir. London: Constable, 1923.

North America. Ed. by Donald Smalley and Bradford Allen Booth. New York: Alfred A. Knopf, 1951.

An Old Man's Love. The World's Classics, 444. London: Oxford Univ. Press, 1936.

Orley Farm. The World's Classics, 423. London: Oxford Univ. Press, 1951.

Phineas Finn. Pref. by Sir Shane Leslie. The Oxford Trollope Crown Edition, ed. by Michael Sadleir and Frederick Page. 2 vols. 1949; rpt. London: Oxford Univ. Press, 1973.

Phineas Redux. Pref. by R. W. Chapman. 1951; rpt. London: Oxford Univ. Press, 1973.

The Prime Minister. Pref. by the Rt. Hon. L. S. Amery. The Oxford Trollope Crown Edition, ed. by Michael Sadleir and Frederick Page. 2 vols. 1952; rpt. London: Oxford Univ. Press, 1973.

Rachel Ray. Intro. by Ben Ray Redman. New York: Alfred A. Knopf, 1952.

Ralph the Heir. The World's Classics, 475. 2 vols. London: Oxford Univ. Press, 1939.

Sir Harry Hotspur of Humblethwaite. The World's Classics, 336. London: Oxford Univ. Press, 1928.

South Africa. The Colonial History Series, ed. by D. H. Simpson. 2 vols. 1868; rpt. London: Dawsons, 1968.

The Small House at Allington. 1948; rpt. London: The Zodiac Press, 1963.

The Struggles of Brown, Jones and Robinson: By One of the Firm. London: Smith, Elder, 1870.

Tales of All Countries [First Series]. London: Chapman and Hall, 1861.

Tales of All Countries: Second Series. London: Chapman and Hall, 1863.

Thackeray. English Men of Letters, ed. by John Morley. New York: Harper and Brothers, 1879.

The Three Clerks. Intro. by W. Teignmouth Shore. The World's Classics, 140. London: Oxford Univ. Press, 1907.

Travelling Sketches. London: Chapman and Hall, 1866.

The Two Heroines of Plumplington. Intro. by John Hampden. New York: Oxford Univ. Press, 1954.

The Vicar of Bullhampton. The World's Classics, 272. London: Oxford Univ. Press, 1924.

The Warden. Intro. by Ronald Knox. The Oxford Trollope Crown Edition, ed. by Michael Sadleir and Frederick Page. London: Oxford Univ. Press, 1952.

The Way We Live Now. Ed. with intro. by Robert Tracy. Indianapolis: Bobbs-Merrill, 1974.

The West Indies and the Spanish Main. New York: Harper and Brothers, 1860.

Why Frau Frohmann Raised Her Prices: And Other Stories. Leipzig: Tauchnitz, 1883.

BIBLIOGRAPHY

THIS IS primarily a list of twentieth-century commentary on Trollope that has been especially useful to me in this study. Only a few references to Victorian reviews and criticism are included, because anything like a full accounting would swell the section enormously and also because both David Skilton, in *Trollope and His Contemporaries: A Study in the Theory and Conventions of Mid-Victorian Fiction* (London: Longman, 1972), and Donald A. Smalley, in *Trollope: The Critical Heritage* (London: Routledge and Kegan Paul; New York: Barnes and Noble, 1969), have made analyses, selections, and listings of this material readily available.

The bibliography here is divided into four sections: the first, 'General Works on Trollope', includes full-length studies and important chapters or articles which consider more than a single novel, as well as a few crucial primary sources: letters, addresses, and some reprinted notes and essays. The second, 'Studies of Individual Novels', consists of articles, chapters, and reviews which concern themselves wholly or nearly so with one novel. The third, 'Works with Important References to Trollope', lists some of the short but useful comments which are found in letters or in works devoted primarily to subjects other than Trollope. The last, 'General Materials on the Novel and Its Aesthetics', indicates some of the more important works which have been cited or which lend some direct support to the critical methods employed throughout.

GENERAL WORKS ON TROLLOPE

AITKEN, DAVID. '"A Kind of Felicity": Some Notes About Trollope's Style.' *NCF*, 20 (1965–6), 337–53.

ALLEN, WALTER. *The English Novel: A Short Critical History*. London: Phoenix House, 1954, pp. 190–8.

ANON. 'Mr. Trollope's Last Novel.' *Nation*, 31 (19 Aug. 1880), 138–9.

—— 'Mr. Trollope's Novels.' *North British Review*, 40 (May 1864), 369–401.

—— Review of *An Autobiography*. *Saturday Review*, 56 (20 Oct. 1883), 505–6.

—— 'Trollope in the West Indies.' *Listener*, 67 (15 Mar. 1962), 461.

APROBERTS, RUTH. 'Anthony Trollope, or the Man with No Style at All.' *VNL*, No. 35 (1969), pp. 10–13.

—— *The Moral Trollope*. Athens, Ohio: Ohio Univ. Press, 1971.

APROBERTS, RUTH. 'Trollope Empiricus.' *VNL*, No. 34 (1968), pp. 1–7.

—— 'Trollope's Casuistry.' *Novel*, 3 (1969–70), 17–27.

ATLEE, CLEMENT R. 'The Pleasure of Books.' *National and English Review*, 142 (Jan. 1954), 17–21.

AUCHINCLOSS, LOUIS. 'Americans in Trollope.' *Reflections of a Jacobite*. Boston: Houghton Mifflin, 1961, pp. 113–25.

BAKER, ERNEST A. 'Trollope.' *From the Brontes to Meredith: Romanticism in the English Novel. The History of the English Novel*. London: H. F. and G. Witherby, 1937. viii. 112–60.

BAKER, JOSEPH ELLIS. *The Novel and the Oxford Movement*. Princeton Studies in English, No. 8. Princeton: Princeton Univ. Press, 1932.

—— 'Trollope's Third Dimension.' *CE* 16 (1954–5), 222–5, 232.

BANKS, J. A. 'The Way They Lived Then: Anthony Trollope and the 1870's.' *VS*, 12 (1968–69), 177–200.

BELLOC, H. 'Anthony Trollope.' *London Mercury*, 27 (1932–3), 150–7.

BETSKY, SEYMOUR. 'Society in Thackeray and Trollope.' *From Dickens to Hardy. A Guide to English Literature*. Ed. Boris Ford. London: Cassell, 1963. vi. 144–68.

BLAIR, FREDERICK G. 'Trollope on Education: An Unpublished Address.' *Trollopian*, 1, No. 4 (Mar. 1947), 1–9.

BOLL, ERNEST. 'The Infusion of Dickens in Trollope.' *Trollopian*, 1, No. 3 (Sept. 1946), 11–24.

BOOTH, BRADFORD A. *Anthony Trollope: Aspects of His Life and Art*. Bloomington, Ind.: Indiana Univ. Press, 1958.

—— 'Anthony Trollope.' *VNL*, No. 13 (1958), pp. 24–5 [a guide to research materials].

—— 'The Parrish Trollope Collection.' *Trollopian*, 1, No. 1 (Summer 1945), 11–19.

—— 'Trollope and "Little Dorrit".' *Trollopian*, 2 (1947–8), 237–40.

—— 'Trollope and the "Pall Mall Gazette".' *NCF*, 4 (1949–50), 51–69, 137–58.

—— 'Trollope and the Royal Literary Fund.' *NCF*, 7 (1952–3), 208–16.

—— 'Trollope in California.' *HLQ*, 3 (1939–40), 117–24.

—— 'Trollope on "Emma"; An Unpublished Note.' *NCF*, 4 (1949–50), 245–7.

—— 'Trollope on Froude's "Caesar".' *Trollopian*, 1, No. 2 (Mar. 1946), 33–47.

—— 'Trollope on the Novel.' *Essays Critical and Historical Dedicated to Lily B. Campbell*. Univ. of Cal. Publications: English Studies, No. 1. Berkeley and Los Angeles: Univ. of Cal. Press, 1950, pp. 219–31.

BOOTH, BRADFORD A. 'Trollope on Scott: Some Unpublished Notes.' *NCF*, 5 (1950–1), 223–30.

—— ed. 'Author to Publisher: Anthony Trollope and William Isbister.' *Princeton University Library Chronicle*, 24 (1962–3), 51–67.

—— ed. *The Letters of Anthony Trollope*. London: Oxford Univ. Press, 1951.

—— ed. *The Tireless Traveler: Twenty Letters to the Liverpool Mercury by Anthony Trollope, 1875*. Berkeley and Los Angeles: Univ. of Cal. Press, 1941.

BOWEN, ELIZABETH. *Anthony Trollope: A New Judgement*. New York and London: Oxford Univ. Press, 1946.

BRACE, GERALD WARNER. 'The World of Anthony Trollope.' *Texas Quarterly*, 4, No. 3 (1961), 180–9.

BRIGGS, ASA. 'Trollope, Bagehot and the English Constitution.' *CJ*, 5 (1951–2), 327–38.

BROWN, BEATRICE CURTIS. *Anthony Trollope*. 2nd ed. London: Arthur Barker, 1967.

BURN, W. L. 'Anthony Trollope's Politics.' *Nineteenth Century and After*, 143 (1948), 161–71.

BURTON, RICHARD. *Masters of the English Novel: A Study of Principles and Personalities*. New York: Holt, 1909, pp. 252–8.

CADBURY, WILLIAM. 'Shape and Theme: Determinants of Trollope's Forms.' *PMLA*, 78 (1963), 326–32.

CECIL, DAVID. 'Anthony Trollope.' *Early Victorian Novelists: Essays in Revaluation*. London: Constable, 1934; rpt. *Victorian Novelists: Essays in Revaluation*. Chicago: Univ. of Chicago Press, 1958, pp. 245–79.

CHAPMAN, RAYMOND. 'Trollope.' *The Victorian Debate: English Literature and Society 1832–1901*. London: Weidenfeld and Nicolson, 1968, pp. 181–93.

CHURCH, RICHARD. *The Growth of the English Novel*. London: Methuen, 1951, pp. 168–74.

COCKSHUT, A. O. J. *Anthony Trollope: A Critical Study*. London: Collins, 1955; rpt. New York: New York Univ. Press, 1968.

[COLLINS, LUCAS.] 'Autobiography of Anthony Trollope.' *Blackwood's*, 134 (Nov. 1883), 577–96.

COOPER, HAROLD. 'Trollope and Henry James in 1868.' *MLN*, 58 (1943), 558.

COYLE, WILLIAM. 'Trollope and the Bi-columned Shakespeare.' *NCF*, 6 (1951–2), 33–46.

—— 'Trollope as Social Anthropologist.' *CE* 17 (1955–6), 392–7.

CROSS, WILBUR L. 'Anthony Trollope.' *The Development of the English Novel.* New York: Macmillan, 1924, pp. 215–24.

DALLAS, E. S. 'Anthony Trollope.' *The Times,* 23 May 1859, p. 12.

DAVIDSON, J. H. 'Anthony Trollope and the Colonies.' *VS,* 12 (1968–9), 305–30.

DAVIES, HUGH SYKES. *Trollope.* Writers and Their Work, No. 118. London: Longmans, Green, 1960.

—— 'Trollope and His Style.' *REL,* 1, No. 4 (Oct. 1960), 73–85.

DUSTIN, JOHN E. 'Thematic Alternation in Trollope.' *PMLA,* 77 (1962), 280–8.

EDWARDS, P. D. *Anthony Trollope.* Profiles in Literature Series. London: Routledge and Kegan Paul, 1969.

—— 'Trollope and the Reviewers: Three Notes.' *N&Q,* 213 (1968), 418–20.

ESCOTT, T. H. S. *Anthony Trollope: His Work, Associates and Literary Originals.* London: John Lane, 1913.

FRASER, RUSSELL A. 'Anthony Trollope's Younger Characters.' *NCF,* 6 (1951–2), 96–106.

—— 'Shooting Niagara in the Novels of Thackeray and Trollope.' *MLQ,* 19 (1958), 141–6.

FREDMAN, ALICE GREEN. *Anthony Trollope.* Columbia Essays on Modern Writers, No. 56. New York: Columbia Univ. Press, 1971.

GEROULD, WINIFRED GREGORY, and GEROULD, JAMES THAYER. *A Guide to Trollope.* Princeton: Princeton Univ. Press, 1948.

GINDIN, JAMES. 'Trollope.' *Harvest of a Quiet Eye: The Novel of Compassion.* Bloomington, Ind.: Indiana Univ. Press, 1971, pp. 28–56.

GRAGG, WILSON B. 'Trollope and Carlyle.' *NCF,* 13 (1958–9), 266–70.

GREEN, GLADYS. 'Trollope on Sidney's "Arcadia" and Lytton's "The Wanderer".' *Trollopian,* 1, No. 3 (Sept. 1946), 45–54.

HAGAN, JOHN. 'The Divided Mind of Anthony Trollope.' *NCF,* 14 (1959–60), 1–26.

HARRISON, FREDERIC. 'Anthony Trollope's Place in Literature.' *Forum,* 19 (May 1895), 324–37.

HELLING, RAFAEL. 'A Century of Trollope Criticism.' *Commentationes Humanarum Litterarum,* 22, No. 2 (1957), 1–203.

HUTTON, R. H. 'From Miss Austen to Mr. Trollope.' *Spectator,* 55 (16 Dec. 1882), 1609–11.

IRWIN, MARY LESLIE. *Anthony Trollope: A Bibliography.* New York: H. W. Wilson, 1926.

JAMES, HENRY. 'Anthony Trollope.' *Partial Portraits*. London: Macmillan, 1888, pp. 97–133.

JILLSON, FREDERICK F. 'The "Professional" Clergyman in Some Novels by Anthony Trollope.' *Hartford Studies in Literature*, 1 (1969–70), 185–97.

JOHNSON, PAMELA HANSFORD. 'Anthony Trollope, an Odd Fish.' *NYTBR*, 25 Apr. 1965, p. 2.

—— 'Trollope's Young Women.' *On the Novel: A Present for Walter Allen on His 60th Birthday from His Friends and Colleagues*. Ed. B. S. Benedikz. London: J. M. Dent, 1971, pp. 17–33.

JONES, FRANK PIERCE. 'Anthony Trollope and the Classics.' *Classical Weekly*, 37 (1943–4), 227–31.

JONES, IVA G. 'Trollope, Carlyle, and Mill on the Negro: An Episode in the History of Ideas.' *Journal of Negro History*, 52 (1967), 185–99.

KENNEY, MRS. DAVID J. 'Anthony Trollope's Theology.' *AN&Q*, 9 (1970–1), 51–4.

KING, HELEN GARLINGHOUSE, ed. 'Trollope's Letters to the *Examiner*.' *Princeton University Library Chronicle*, 26 (1964–5), 71–101.

KOSKIMIES, RAFAEL. 'Novelists' Thoughts about Their Art.' *Neuphilologische Mitteilungen*, 57 (1956), 148–59.

LEE, JAMES W. 'Trollope's Clerical Concerns: The Low Church Clergymen.' *Hartford Studies in Literature*, 1 (1969–70), 198–208.

MORE, PAUL ELMER. 'My Debt to Trollope.' *Demon of the Absolute*. New Shelburne Essays, Vol. I. Princeton: Princeton Univ. Press, 1928, pp. 89–125.

NEWBOLT, SIR FRANCIS. *Out of Court*. London: Philip Allan, 1925.

NICHOLS, SPENCER VAN BOKKELEN. *The Significance of Anthony Trollope*. New York: D. C. McMurtrie, 1925.

O'CONNOR, FRANK. 'Trollope the Realist.' *The Mirror in the Roadway: A Study of the Modern Novel*. New York: Knopf, 1956, pp. 165–83.

[OLIPHANT, MRS. MARGARET]. Review of *The Claverings* and *The Last Chronicle of Barset*. *Blackwood's*, 102 (Sept. 1867), 275–8.

PARK, CLARA CLAIBORNE. 'Trollope and the Modern Reader.' *Massachusetts Review*, 3 (1961–2), 577–91.

PARKS, EDD WINFIELD. 'Trollope and the Defense of Exegesis.' *NCF*, 7 (1952–3), 265–71.

PARRISH, MORRIS L., ed. *Anthony Trollope: Four Lectures*. London: Constable, 1938.

POLHEMUS, ROBERT M. *The Changing World of Anthony Trollope*. Berkeley and Los Angeles: Univ. of Cal. Press, 1968.

POLLARD, ARTHUR. 'Thackeray and Trollope.' *The Victorians*. Ed. Arthur Pollard. *History of Literature in the English Language*. London: Barrie and Jenkins, 1970. vi. 107–39.

POPE HENNESSY, JAMES. *Anthony Trollope*. Boston: Little, Brown, 1971.

PRAZ, MARIO. 'Anthony Trollope.' *The Hero in Eclipse in Victorian Fiction*. Trans. Angus Davidson. London: Oxford Univ. Press, 1956, pp. 261–318.

PRITCHETT, V. S. 'Trollope Was Right.' *The Working Novelist*. London: Chatto and Windus, 1965, pp. 109–20.

RAY, GORDON N. *Bibliographical Resources for the Study of Nineteenth Century English Fiction*. Los Angeles: Univ. of Cal. School of Lib. Service, 1964.

—— 'Trollope at Full Length.' *HLQ*, 31 (1967–8), 313–40.

ROBINSON, CLEMENT FRANKLIN. 'Trollope's Jury Trials.' *NCF*, 6 (1951–2), 247–68.

SADLEIR, MICHAEL. 'Anthony Trollope.' *Things Past*. London: Constable, 1944, pp. 16–53.

—— *Trollope: A Bibliography*. London: Constable, 1928; rpt. London: Dawsons, 1964.

—— *Trollope: A Commentary*. 3rd ed. London: Oxford Univ. Press, 1961.

—— 'Trollope and Bacon's Essays.' *Trollopian*, 1, No. 1 (Summer 1945), 21–34.

SAINTSBURY, GEORGE. *A History of Nineteenth Century Literature (1780–1900)*. London: Macmillan, 1919.

—— 'Trollope Revisited.' *Essays and Studies By Members of the English Association*. Oxford: Clarendon Press, 1920. vi. 41–66.

SHUMAKER, WAYNE. *English Autobiography: Its Emergence, Materials, and Form*. Univ. of Cal. Publications: English Studies, No. 8. Berkeley and Los Angeles: Univ. of Cal. Press, 1954.

SKILTON, DAVID. *Anthony Trollope and His Contemporaries: A Study in the Theory and Conventions of Mid-Victorian Fiction*. London: Longman, 1972.

SMALLEY, DONALD. 'Anthony Trollope.' *Victorian Fiction: A Guide to Research*. Ed. Lionel Stevenson. Cambridge, Mass.: Harvard Univ. Press, 1964, pp. 188–213.

—— ed. *Trollope: The Critical Heritage*. London: Routledge and Kegan Paul; New York: Barnes and Noble, 1969.

SMITH, SHEILA M. 'Anthony Trollope: The Novelist as Moralist.' *Renaissance and Modern Essays Presented to Vivian de Sola Pinto in*

Celebration of His Seventieth Birthday. Ed. G. R. Hibbard. New York: Barnes and Noble, 1966, pp. 129–36.

SNOW, C. P. 'Trollope: The Psychological Stream.' *On the Novel: A Present for Walter Allen on His 60th Birthday from His Friends and Colleagues.* Ed. B. S. Benedikz. London: J. M. Dent, 1971, pp. 3–16.

STEBBINS, LUCY, and RICHARD POATE. *The Trollopes: The Chronicle of a Writing Family.* New York: Columbia Univ. Press, 1945.

STEBBINS, RICHARD POATE. 'Trollope at Harrow School.' *Trollopian*, 1, No. 1 (Summer 1945), 35–44.

STEPHEN, LESLIE. 'Anthony Trollope.' *National Review*, 38 (1901–2), 68–84.

STEVENSON, LIONEL. *The English Novel: A Panorama.* London: Constable, 1960, pp. 318–24.

—— 'Trollope as a Recorder of Verbal Usage.' *Trollopian*, 3 (1948–9), 119–25.

TAYLOR, ROBERT H. 'Letters to Trollope.' *Trollopian*, 1, No. 3 (Sept. 1946), 5–9.

—— 'Trollope on "The Monk".' *NCF*, 4 (1949–50), 167.

—— 'The Trollopes Write to Bentley.' *Trollopian*, 3 (1948–9), 83–98, 201–14.

THALE, JEROME. 'The Problem of Structure in Trollope.' *NCF*, 15 (1960–1), 147–57.

THORP, WILLARD, and DRINKER, HENRY S. *Two Addresses Delivered to Members of the Grolier Club: I Trollope's America by Willard Thorp, II The Lawyers of Anthony Trollope by Henry S. Drinker.* New York: The Grolier Club, 1950.

TILLOTSON, GEOFFREY. 'Trollope's Style.' *Ball State Teachers College Forum*, 2, No. 2 (Winter 1961–2), 3–6; rpt. *Mid-Victorian Studies*, by Geoffrey and Kathleen Tillotson. London: Athlone Press, 1965, pp. 56–61.

TILLOTSON, KATHLEEN. *Novels of the Eighteen-Forties.* Oxford: Clarendon Press, 1954.

TINGAY, LANCE O. 'Trollope and the Beverley Election.' *NCF*, 5 (1950–1), 23–37.

—— 'Trollope's Popularity: A Statistical Approach.' *NCF*, 11 (1956–7), 223–9.

TINKER, CHAUNCEY BREWSTER. 'Trollope.' *Yale Review*, 36 N.S. (1946–7), 424–34.

TROLLOPE, MURIEL R. 'What I Was Told.' *Trollopian*, 2 (1947–8), 223–35.

TROLLOPE, THOMAS ADOLPHUS. *What I Remember.* 2nd ed. 2 vols. London: Richard Bentley, 1887.

VINCENT, C. J. 'Trollope: A Victorian Augustan.' *Queen's Quarterly*, 52 (1945–6), 415–28.

WALPOLE, HUGH. *Anthony Trollope.* New York: Macmillan, 1928.

WELSBY, PAUL A. 'Anthony Trollope and the Church of England.' *Church Quarterly Review*, 163 (1962), 210–20.

WEST, REBECCA. 'A Nineteenth-Century Bureaucrat.' *The Court and the Castle: Some Treatments of a Recurrent Theme.* New Haven: Yale Univ. Press, 1957, pp. 133–64.

WILDMAN, John H. 'Anthony Trollope Today.' *CE*, 7 (1945–6), 397–9.

—— *Anthony Trollope's England.* Brown Univ. Studies, vol. v. Providence: Brown Univ. Press, 1940.

STUDIES OF INDIVIDUAL NOVELS

The American Senator

APROBERTS, RUTH. 'Trollope's One World.' *SAQ*, 68 (1969), 463–77.

GREENBERG, CLEMENT. 'A Victorian Novel.' *PR*, 11 (1944), 234–38.

HARDEN, EDGAR F. 'The Alien Voice: Trollope's Western Senator.' *TSLL*, 8 (1966–7), 219–34.

STRYKER, DAVID. 'The Significance of Trollope's "American Senator".' *NCF*, 5 (1950–1), 141–9.

TAYLOR, ROBERT H. 'The Manuscript of Trollope's *The American Senator*. Collated with the First Edition.' *PBSA*, 41 (1947), 123–39.

WILDMAN, JOHN H. 'Trollope Illustrates the Distinction.' *NCF*, 4 (1949–50), 101–10.

Ayala's Angel

ANON. Review. *Athenaeum*, No. 2795 (21 May 1881), p. 686.

MILLER, J. HILLIS. *The Form of Victorian Fiction: Thackeray, Dickens, Trollope, George Eliot, Meredith, and Hardy.* Notre Dame, Ind.: Univ. of Notre Dame Press, 1968, pp. 124–39.

Barchester Towers

BANKERT, M. S. 'Newman in the Shadow of *Barchester Towers*.' *Renascence*, 20 (1967–8), 153–61.

CADBURY, WILLIAM. 'Character and the Mock Heroic in *Barchester Towers*.' *TSLL*, 5 (1963–4), 509–19.

KINCAID, JAMES R. '*Barchester Towers* and the Nature of Conservative Comedy.' *ELH*, 37 (1970), 595–612.

KNOEPFLMACHER, U. C. 'Introduction: Entering a Victorian Novel—*Barchester Towers*'; '*Barchester Towers*: The Comedy of Change.'

Laughter and Despair: Readings in Ten Novels of the Victorian Era.
Berkeley and Los Angeles: Univ. of Cal. Press, 1971, pp. 3–49.

KRONENBERGER, LOUIS. 'Barchester Towers.' *The Polished Surface: Essays in the Literature of Worldliness.* New York: Knopf, 1969, pp. 217–32.

[MEREDITH, GEORGE.] Review. *Westminster Review*, 68 (Oct. 1857), 594–6.

SHAW, W. DAVID. 'Moral Drama in *Barchester Towers*.' *NCF*, 19 (1964–5), 45–54.

TAYLOR, ROBERT H. 'On Rereading *Barchester Towers*.' *Princeton University Library Chronicle*, 15 (1953–4), 10–15.

The Barsetshire Chronicle

BORINSKI, LUDWIG. 'Trollopes Barsetshire Novels.' *Die Neueren Sprachen*, N.S. (Dec. 1962), pp. 533–53.

HENNEDY, HUGH L. *Unity in Barsetshire*. The Hague: Mouton, 1971.

KNOX, RONALD A. 'The Barsetshire Novels.' *Literary Distractions*. London: Sheed and Ward, 1958, pp. 134–44.

QUILLER-COUCH, SIR ARTHUR. 'Anthony Trollope: The Barsetshire Novels.' *Charles Dickens and Other Victorians*. Cambridge: Cambridge Univ. Press, 1925, pp. 219–34.

SHERMAN, THEODORE A. 'The Financial Motif in the Barchester Novels.' *CE*, 9 (1947–8), 413–19.

The Belton Estate

JAMES, HENRY. Review. *Nation*, 2 (4 Jan. 1866), 21–2.

The Bertrams

ANON. Review. *Saturday Review*, 7 (26 Mar. 1859), 368–9.

Can You Forgive Her?

ANON. Review. *Saturday Review*, 20 (19 Aug. 1865), 240–2.

CHAMBERLAIN, DAVID S. 'Unity and Irony in Trollope's *Can You Forgive Her?*' *SEL*, 8 (1968), 669–80.

HOYT, NORRIS D. '"Can You Forgive Her?": A Commentary.' *Trollopian*, 2 (1947–8), 57–70.

JAMES, HENRY. Review. *Nation*, 1 (28 Sept. 1865), 409–10.

Castle Richmond

ANON. Review. *Saturday Review*, 9 (19 May 1860), 643–4.

Cousin Henry

APROBERTS, RUTH. '*Cousin Henry*: Trollope's Note from Antiquity.' *NCF*, 24 (1969–70), 93–8.

POLHEMUS, ROBERT M. '*Cousin Henry*: Trollope's Note from Underground.' *NCF*, 20 (1965–6), 385–9.

Doctor Thorne

ANON. Review. *Harper's*, 17 (Sept. 1858), 693.
—— Review. *Saturday Review*, 5 (12 June 1858), 618–19.
DIXON, SIR OWEN. 'Sir Roger Scatcherd's Will, in Anthony Trollope's *Doctor Thorne.' Jesting Pilate, and Other Papers and Addresses.* Sydney: Law Book Co., 1965, pp. 71–81.
MELADA, IVAN. '*Dr. Thorne.' The Captains of Industry in English Fiction, 1821–1871.* Albuquerque: Univ. of New Mexico Press, 1970, pp. 166–71.

Dr. Wortle's School

MAXWELL, J. C. 'Cockshut on "Dr. Wortle's School".' *NCF*, 13 (1958–9), 153–9.

The Duke's Children

ANON. Review. *Spectator*, 53 (12 June 1880), 754–5.
HAGAN, JOHN H. '*The Duke's Children*: Trollope's Psychological Masterpiece.' *NCF*, 13 (1958–9), 1–21.
KENNEY, BLAIR GATES. 'The Two Isabels: A Study in Distortion.' *VNL*, No. 25 (1964), pp. 15–17.

The Eustace Diamonds

MILLEY, HENRY J. W. '*The Eustace Diamonds* and *The Moonstone.' SP*, 36 (1939), 651–63.

The Fixed Period

SKILTON, DAVID. '*The Fixed Period*: Anthony Trollope's Novel of 1980.' *Studies in the Literary Imagination*, 6 (1973), 39–50.

Framley Parsonage

BIĆANIĆ, SONIA. 'Some New Facts about the Beginning of Trollope's *Framley Parsonage.' Studia Romanica Et Anglica Zagrabiensia.* Nos. 9–10 (Dec. 1960), pp. 171–6.

He Knew He Was Right

ANON. Review. *Spectator*, 42 (12 June 1869), 706–8.

Is He Popenjoy?

ANON. Review. *Saturday Review*, 45 (1 June 1878), 695–6.
D., T. C. 'Victorian Editions and Victorian Delicacy.' *N&Q*, 187 (2 Dec. 1944), 251–53.

La Vendée

FLEISHMAN, AVROM. *The English Historical Novel: Walter Scott to Virginia Woolf.* Baltimore: Johns Hopkins, 1971.

The Last Chronicle of Barset

HAMER, NANCY. 'Working Diary for *The Last Chronicle of Barset*.' *TLS*, 24 Dec. 1971, p. 1606.

WEST, WILLIAM A. '*The Last Chronicle of Barset*: Trollope's Comic Techniques.' *The Classic British Novel*. Ed. Howard M. Harper, Jr. and Charles Edge. Athens: Univ. of Georgia Press, 1972, pp. 121–42.

The Macdermots of Ballycloran

DONOVAN, ROBERT A. 'Trollope's Prentice Work.' *MP*, 53 (1955–6), 179–86.

TINGAY, LANCE O. 'The Publication of Trollope's First Novel.' *TLS*, 30 Mar. 1956, p. 200.

—— 'The Reception of Trollope's First Novel.' *NCF*, 6 (1951–2), 195–200.

—— 'Trollope's First Novel.' *N&Q*, 195 (1950), 563–4.

Miss Mackenzie

ANON. Review. *Saturday Review*, 19 (4 Mar. 1865), 263–5.

JAMES, HENRY. Review. *Nation*, 1 (13 July 1865), 51–2.

Orley Farm

ADAMS, ROBERT M. '"Orley Farm" and Real Fiction.' *NCF*, 8 (1953–4), 27–41.

BOOTH, BRADFORD A. 'Trollope's *Orley Farm*: Artistry *Manqué*.' *From Jane Austen to Joseph Conrad: Essays Collected in Memory of James T. Hillhouse*. Ed. Robert C. Rathburn and Martin Steinmann, Jr. Minneapolis: Univ. of Minn. Press, 1958, pp. 146–59.

The Palliser Chronicle

BORINSKI, LUDWIG. 'Trollopes Palliser Novels.' *Die Neueren Sprachen*, N.S. (Sept. 1963), pp. 389–407.

CHAPMAN, R. W. 'Personal Names in Trollope's Political Novels.' *Essays Mainly on the Nineteenth Century: Presented to Sir Humphry Milford*. London: Oxford Univ. Press, 1948, pp. 72–81.

DINWIDDY, J. R. 'Who's Who in Trollope's Political Novels.' *NCF*, 22 (1967–8), 31–46.

MIZENER, ARTHUR. 'Anthony Trollope: The Palliser Novels.' *From Jane Austen to Joseph Conrad: Essays Collected in Memory of James T. Hillhouse*. Ed. Robert C. Rathburn and Martin Steinmann, Jr. Minneapolis: Univ. of Minn. Press, 1958, pp. 160–76.

MOHAN, RAMESH. 'Trollope's Political Novels (Chronicles of Parliamentary Life).' *Indian Journal of English Studies*, 1 (1960), 57–69.

LASKI, AUDREY L. 'Myths of Character: An Aspect of the Novel.' *NCF*, 14 (1959–60), 333–43.

KENNEY, BLAIR G. 'Trollope's Ideal Statesmen: Plantagenet Palliser and Lord John Russell.' *NCF*, 20 (1965–6), 281–5.

KLEIS, JOHN CHRISTOPHER. 'Passion vs. Prudence: Theme and Technique in Trollope's Palliser Novels.' *TSLL*, 11 (1969–70), 1405–14.

Phineas Finn

ANON. Review. *Saturday Review*, 27 (27 Mar. 1869), 431–2.

BLOOMFIELD, MORTON W. 'Trollope's Use of Canadian History in "Phineas Finn" (1867–1869).' *NCF*, 5 (1950–1), 67–74.

Phineas Redux

ANON. Review. *Saturday Review*, 37 (7 Feb. 1874), 186–7.

The Prime Minister

ANON. Review. *Saturday Review*, 42 (14 Oct. 1876), 481–2.

Rachel Ray

ANON. 'New Novels.' *The Times*, 25 Dec. 1863, p. 4.

Ralph the Heir

BOOTH, BRADFORD A. 'Trollope, Reade, and "Shilly-Shally".' *Trollopian*, 1, No. 4 (Mar. 1947), 45–54; 2, No. 1 (June 1947), 43–51.

Sir Harry Hotspur of Humblethwaite

ANON. Review. *Spectator*, 43 (26 Nov. 1870), 1415–16.

The Small House at Allington

ANON. Review. *North American Review*, 99 (July 1864), 292–8.

—— Review. *Saturday Review*, 17 (14 May 1864), 595–6.

MCMASTER, JULIET. '"The Unfortunate Moth": Unifying Theme in *The Small House at Allington*.' *NCF*, 26 (1971–2), 127–44.

The Vicar of Bullhampton

CADBURY, WILLIAM. 'The Uses of the Village: Form and Theme in Trollope's *The Vicar of Bullhampton*.' *NCF*, 18 (1963–4), 151–63.

The Warden

ANON. Review. *Athenaeum*, No. 1422 (27 Jan. 1855), 107–8.

BEST, G. F. A. 'The Road to Hiram's Hospital: A Byway of Early Victorian History.' *VS*, 5 (1961–2), 135–50.

GANZEL, CAROL H. '*The Times* Correspondent and *The Warden*.' *NCF*, 21 (1966–7), 325–36.

GOLDBERG, M. A. 'Trollope's *The Warden*: A Commentary on the "Age of Equipoise".' *NCF*, 17 (1962–3), 381–90.

HAWKINS, SHERMAN. 'Mr. Harding's Church Music.' *ELH*, 29 (1962), 202–23.

HOUSTON, MAUDE. 'Structure and Plot in *The Warden.*' *Univ. of Texas Studies in English*, 34 (1955), 107–13.

KNOX, RONALD. 'Introduction to the Barsetshire Novels.' *The Warden.* London: Oxford Univ. Press, 1952, pp. vii–xix.

MARSHALL, WILLIAM H. *The World of the Victorian Novel.* South Brunswick, N.J. and New York: A. S. Barnes, 1967, pp. 322–36.

SHARP, R. L. 'Trollope's Mathematics in *The Warden.*' *NCF*, 17 (1962–3), 288–9.

STEVENSON, LIONEL. 'Dickens and the Origin of "The Warden".' *Trollopian*, 2 (1947–8), 83–9.

The Way We Live Now

ANON. Review. *Saturday Review*, 40 (17 July 1875), 88–9.

—— Review. *The Times*, 24 Aug. 1875, p. 4.

EDWARDS, P. D. 'The Chronology of "The Way We Live Now".' *N&Q*, 214 (1969), 214–16.

—— 'Trollope Changes His Mind: The Death of Melmotte in *The Way We Live Now.*' *NCF*, 18 (1963–4), 89–91.

HORNBACK, BERT G. 'Anthony Trollope and the Calendar of 1872: The Chronology of "The Way We Live Now".' *N&Q*, 208 (1963), 454–7.

NATHAN, SABINE. 'Anthony Trollope's Perception of The Way We Live Now.' *ZAA* (East Berlin), 10 (1962), 259–78.

SLAKEY, ROGER L. 'Melmotte's Death: A Prism of Meaning in *The Way We Live Now.*' *ELH*, 34 (1967), 248–59.

TANNER, TONY. 'Trollope's *The Way We Live Now*: Its Modern Significance.' *CritQ*, 9 (1967), 256–71.

WORKS WITH IMPORTANT REFERENCES TO TROLLOPE

ALLOTT, MIRIAM. *Novelists on the Novel.* London: Routledge and Kegan Paul, 1959.

BENNETT, ARNOLD. *Books and Persons: Being Comments on a Past Epoch, 1908–1911.* New York: George H. Doran, 1917, pp. 134–5, 149.

BLISS, TRUDY, ed. *Thomas Carlyle: Letters to His Wife.* London: Gollancz, 1953, p. 381.

BOWEN, ELIZABETH. *English Novelists.* London: William Collins, 1942, pp. 32–3.

BRADFORD, GAMALIEL. 'Gustave Flaubert.' *Bare Souls.* New York and London: Harper and Brothers, 1924; rpt. New York: Kraus Reprint Co., 1968, pp. 241–76.

CHAPPLE, J. A. V., and ARTHUR POLLARD, eds. *The Letters of Mrs. Gaskell.* Cambridge, Mass.: Harvard Univ. Press, 1967, p. 602.

CHESTERTON, G. K. *The Victorian Age in Literature.* London: Williams and Norgate, [1913], pp. 134–6.

CLINE, C. L., ed. *The Letters of George Meredith.* Oxford: Clarendon Press, 1970. i. 593.

COLVIN, SIR SIDNEY, ed. *The Letters of Robert Louis Stevenson.* New York: Scribners, 1923. i. 261.

FABER, RICHARD. *Proper Stations: Class in Victorian Fiction.* London: Faber and Faber, 1971, pp. 111–24.

FORD, FORD MADOX. *The English Novel: From the Earliest Days to the Death of Joseph Conrad.* Philadelphia and London: Lippincott, 1929, pp. 119–20.

FORSTER, E. M. *Aspects of the Novel.* London: Edward Arnold, 1927.

GISSING, GEORGE. *The Private Papers of Henry Ryecroft.* London: Constable, 1903, p. 213.

HAIGHT, GORDON S. 'George Meredith and the "Westminster Review".' *MLR*, 53 (1958), 1–16.

—— ed. *The George Eliot Letters.* New Haven: Yale Univ. Press, 1955. iv. 110.

HAWTHORNE, JULIAN. 'The Maker of Many Books.' *Confessions and Criticisms.* Boston: Ticknor, 1887, pp. 140–62.

HOWELLS, WILLIAM DEAN. *My Literary Passions: Criticism and Fiction.* New York: Harper and Brothers, 1895; rpt. New York: Kraus Reprint Co., 1968, pp. 179–82.

—— 'Novel-Writing and Novel-Reading: An Impersonal Explanation.' Ed. William M. Gibson. *BNYPL*, 62 (1958), 15–34.

LANDIS, PAUL, and FREEMAN, RONALD E., eds. *Letters of the Brownings to George Barrett.* Urbana: Univ. of Ill. Press, 1958.

LEAVIS, F. R. *The Great Tradition.* London: Chatto and Windus, 1948.

LEAVIS, Q. D. *Fiction and the Reading Public.* London: Chatto and Windus, 1932, p. 252.

LEVIN, HARRY. *Refractions: Essays in Comparative Literature.* New York: Oxford Univ. Press, 1966, p. 318.

McELDERRY, B. R., Jr. 'Beerbohm on Trollope.' *TLS*, 12 Oct. 1967, p. 968.

MYERS, WILLIAM. 'George Eliot: Politics and Personality.' *Literature and Politics in the Nineteenth Century.* Ed John Lucas. London: Methuen, 1971, pp. 105–29.

SCHUELLER, HERBERT M., and PETERS, ROBERT L., eds. *The Letters of John Addington Symonds, 1844–1868.* Detroit: Wayne State Univ. Press, 1967. i. 451.

SCUDDER, VIDA D. *Introduction to the Study of English Literature.* New York and Chicago: Globe School Book Co., 1901.

THOMSON, PATRICIA. *The Victorian Heroine: A Changing Ideal, 1837–1873.* London: Oxford Univ. Press, 1956.

WHARTON, EDITH. *The Writing of Fiction.* New York: Scribners, 1925, p. 63.

WILLIAMS, RAYMOND. *The English Novel: From Dickens to Lawrence.* New York: Oxford Univ. Press, 1970, pp. 84–6.

WOOLF, VIRGINIA. 'The Novels of George Meredith.' *The Second Common Reader.* New York: Harcourt, Brace, 1932, pp. 245–56.

—— 'Phases of Fiction.' *Collected Essays.* London: Chatto and Windus, 1966; New York: Harcourt, Brace, and World, 1967. ii. 56–102.

GENERAL MATERIALS ON THE NOVEL AND ITS AESTHETICS

ADAMS, ROBERT M. *Strains of Discord: Studies in Literary Openness.* Ithaca: Cornell Univ. Press, 1958.

BOOTH, WAYNE C. *The Rhetoric of Fiction.* Chicago: Univ. of Chicago Press, 1961.

COLLINGWOOD, R. G. *Principles of Art.* Oxford: Clarendon Press, 1938.

COOK, ALBERT. *The Meaning of Fiction.* Detroit: Wayne State Univ. Press, 1960.

FRIEDMAN, ALAN. *The Turn of the Novel.* New York: Oxford Univ. Press, 1966.

FRYE, NORTHROP. *Anatomy of Criticism: Four Essays.* Princeton, N.J.: Princeton Univ. Press, 1957.

GLICKSBERG, CHARLES I. *The Ironic Vision in Modern Literature.* The Hague: Martinus Nijhoff, 1969.

GOLDKNOPF, DAVID. 'What Plot Means in the Novel.' *Antioch Review,* 29 (1969–70), 483–96.

GREENBERG, CLEMENT. *Art and Culture: Critical Essays.* Boston: Beacon Press, 1961.

HARDY, BARBARA. 'Towards a Poetics of Fiction: An Approach Through Narrative.' *Novel,* 2 (1968–9), 5–14.

HARVEY, W. J. *Character and the Novel.* Ithaca: Cornell Univ. Press, 1965.

HOFFMANN, FREDERICK J. 'Searching for Reasons: The 19th-Century Novel and 20th-Century Literature.' *Journal of General Education,* 15 (1963–4), 221–9.

HYDE, WILLIAM J. 'George Eliot and the Climate of Realism.' *PMLA,* 72 (1957), 147–64.

LANGBAUM, ROBERT. *The Poetry of Experience: The Dramatic Monologue in Modern Literary Tradition.* New York: Random House, 1957.

LEVINE, GEORGE. 'Realism, or, in Praise of Lying: Some Nineteenth Century Novels.' *CE*, 31 (1969–70), 355–65.

MENDILOW, A. A. *Time and the Novel.* London and New York: P. Nevill, 1952; rpt. New York: Humanities Press, 1965.

MILLER, J. HILLIS. *The Disappearance of God: Five Nineteenth-Century Writers.* Cambridge, Mass.: Harvard Univ. Press, 1963.

—— *The Form of Victorian Fiction: Thackeray, Dickens, Trollope, George Eliot, Meredith, and Hardy.* Notre Dame, Ind.: Univ. of Notre Dame Press, 1968.

MUECKE, D. C. *The Compass of Irony.* London: Methuen, 1969.

SACKS, SHELDON. *Fiction and the Shape of Belief.* Berkeley and Los Angeles: Univ. of Cal. Press, 1964.

—— 'The Psychological Implications of Generic Distinctions.' *Genre*, 1 (1968), 106–15.

SCHOLES, ROBERT, and KELLOGG, ROBERT. *The Nature of Narrative.* New York: Oxford Univ. Press, 1966.

SCHOLES, ROBERT. 'On Realism and Genre.' *Novel*, 2 (1968–9), 269–71.

—— 'Towards a Poetics of Fiction: An Approach Through Genre.' *Novel*, 2 (1968–9), 101–11.

STANG, RICHARD. *The Theory of the Novel in England 1850–1870.* London: Routledge and Kegan Paul; New York: Columbia Univ. Press, 1959.

INDEX

Extended discussions of a topic are indicated by italicized figures. The following abbreviations, borrowed from the Geroulds' *A Guide to Trollope*, will be used throughout the Index.